A FORGE OF
FREEDOM BOOK

The Thirteen Colonies
~ 1763 ~

THE DELAWARE COLONY

by
H. Clay Reed

CROWELL-COLLIER PRESS
Collier-Macmillan Limited, London

Library of Congress Catalog Card Number: 77–95297

The Macmillan Company
866 Third Avenue
New York, New York 10022

Collier-Macmillan Canada Ltd., Toronto, Ontario

Printed in the United States of America

FIRST PRINTING

PICTURE CREDITS

American Swedish Historical Foundation, 94; The
Bettmann Archive, 77; Culver Pictures, Inc., 8–9, 59, 72, 85;
Delaware State Archives, 51; Historical Pictures Service—
Chicago, 4, 102; Historical Society of Delaware, 96;
University of Delaware, 2, 14, 26, 33, 40, 54, 69, 91, 111, 118;
C. A. Weslager (*A Brief Account of the Indians of
Delaware*), 18; Henry Francis du Pont Winterthur
Museum, 108, 114.

JACKET ILLUSTRATION: *Caesar Rodney's ride.*

To my wife

CONTENTS

THE
DELAWARE
COLONY

Chapter 1

Sweden Founds a Colony

Delaware is unique among the Thirteen Colonies in being the only one founded by Sweden. The Swedes are proud of the part they played in the colonization of North America. Swedish school children learn about the first landing of the Swedes in 1638 at "The Rocks," near the mouth of the Christina River, just as American children read about the landing of the Pilgrims at Plymouth Rock. Many Swedish visitors to the United States make it a point to visit The Rocks, which are now enclosed by a little park maintained by the state of Delaware, next door to Old Swedes Church.

At the 300th anniversary celebration of the founding of New Sweden, in 1938, the Swedish government sent over a whole shipload of Swedish dignitaries, headed by the Crown Prince, now King Gustav VI Adolph, and other members of the royal family. A flooding rain, the worst in years, prevented many people from getting to hear the wel-

Postage stamps commemorating the 300th anniversary of New Sweden

coming address at The Rocks by President Franklin D. Roosevelt, and the Crown Prince was too sick to leave the ship. It was jokingly suggested that the Swedes were having more trouble in getting to Wilmington in 1938 than they had in 1638. The United States Post Office Department and the governments of Sweden and Finland issued stamps in memory of the anniversary.

In the 17th century Sweden was one of the great powers of Europe. Its new line of kings of the Vasa family gave it a strong and effective government. Its greatest monarch, Gustavus Adolphus, was not only an able ruler but a military genius as well, and for a time the Swedish army was the most famous in Europe. He and his successors pursued a policy of territorial expansion. Finland was already under Swedish rule and lands along the eastern and southern Baltic shores were added, which later were taken over by Russia and Prussia. Sweden's ambition, it was said, was to turn the Baltic Sea into a Swedish lake.

But Sweden lacked certain things which were necessary for success in overseas ventures, either for commerce or for colonization. It was thinly populated—hardly a million people in Sweden and Finland together. There was no surplus population of poor people who would jump at the chance of improving their condition by seeking homes in the New World.

Sweden is not rich in natural resources. Good farming land is not plentiful, and, because the country lies so far north, the growing season for crops is short. The principal wealth of the nation was its forests and its iron and copper mines. But Sweden was not a manufacturing nation, and its foreign trade was largely in the hands of foreigners. It lacked both the "know-how" and the money to develop its industries and commerce.

Fortunately for the Swedes, these two important elements were available from the Low Countries, from which a number of enterprising individuals came to the aid of the Swedes. One of them was Louis de Geer, who, with the help of skilled workmen from his homeland, improved methods of iron and copper production, and was able to manufacture weapons of great importance to a warlike monarchy like Sweden.

Another was Willem Usselinx, who is credited with getting King Gustavus Adolphus interested in overseas colonization. For a century Spain and Portugal had enjoyed a monopoly of such activities. By the Treaty of Tordesillas (1494) these two countries had divided the whole non-Christian world between them by drawing a line down through the middle of the Atlantic Ocean. East of this imaginary line, everything was to belong to Portugal—Africa, Asia, and the eastern tip of South America, later known as Brazil. West of the line, which included all of North America and most of South America, was Spain's private preserve. Intruders were kept out by force.

By the close of the 16th century, other nations were ready to challenge the Spanish-Portuguese monopoly, especially the Dutch, the English, and the French. The Dutch

East India Company, chartered by the government in 1602, soon broke the power of the Portuguese in India. Dutch vessels were exploring American waters too, looking for opportunities for profitable trade. In 1621 their efforts were united in the Dutch West India Company, which was given the sole right of Dutch trade and colonization in the New World.

Usselinx played an important part in the founding of this company, but he was dissatisfied with its policies and its lack of appreciation of his services. So he left the Netherlands, apparently with the hope of selling his ideas about colonization to some more sympathetic monarch. He found one in the Swedish King Gustavus Adolphus, who in 1624 authorized Usselinx to go ahead and promote a Swedish company for trade with Asia, Africa, and America. But after five years of unsuccessful efforts to raise the necessary capital among the money-less Swedes, Usselinx gave up and went back to Holland.

Gustavus Adolphus,
Sweden's greatest monarch,
encouraged colonization
in the New World

While Willem Usselinx's project met with failure, it had one important result: it aroused Swedish interest in overseas ventures. The king unfortunately was killed in battle in Germany in 1632, but Chancellor Axel Oxenstierna and other influential men did not allow the matter to drop. At this time the Swedish government was especially anxious to increase its exports of copper, and it was natural for it to look to the experienced and wealthy Dutch for help and advice. The Swedes found their man in Samuel Blommaert, a prominent merchant of Amsterdam. Although a stockholder and a director of the Dutch West India Company, Blommaert, it was said, was "disgusted" with the policies of that company. As it turned out, he was willing to help the Swedes, not only with advice but with money too.

Blommaert's first recommendation to the Swedes was to develop trade with the coast of Guinea, where copper was in demand by the African natives, who could pay for it with gold. Had his suggestion been followed, this history could never have been written. New Sweden, had it existed at all, would have been located on the hot shores of West Africa instead of the pleasant banks of the Delaware River in temperate North America. But while the African proposal was under consideration, still another Dutchman came on the scene. He turned Blommaert's and Chancellor Oxenstierna's attention to America, in fact to the very place where the Swedes were soon to settle.

The newcomer was Peter Minuit. After serving for five years as director of the Dutch West India Company's colony of New Netherland, he was dismissed by the company in 1631 and went back to Holland. He was looking for a job and no doubt feeling resentful toward his former employer when he learned of Sweden's interest in overseas trade. Minuit offered his services to Blommaert and proposed that a company be established under the Swedish flag to trade with America in competition with the Dutch West

India Company. "The English, French, and Dutch," said Minuit, "have occupied large tracts of land in the New World. Sweden ought no longer to abstain from making her name known in foreign countries." He was willing to help start such an undertaking, which, though small at the beginning, would grow into great magnitude. His plan was to make a voyage to certain places well known to him, in the neighborhood of Virginia and New Netherland, which were to be occupied and called New Sweden.

Minuit was a man of energy and ability, and played a key role, first in drawing up the plan which the Swedish officials finally accepted and then in carrying it out. It was agreed to form a company for trade and colonization on the east coast of North America. The first expedition was to be a small one, to be sent to the Delaware region, an area with which, of course, Minuit was familiar because of his previous residence in New Netherland. Minuit was to be in charge of the expedition, and the cost was to be shared by the Dutch and the Swedes.

On the part of the Dutch at least, the money was put up with the idea of making a profit, hopefully a big profit, by men who had money to spare—"risk capital," as it would be called today. Merchant-speculators were harder to find in Sweden, and its share was subscribed by leading men in the government, such as Oxenstierna and Admiral Klas Fleming. While they too hoped to make a profit, no doubt, their motives were mainly patriotic or nationalistic. Cash was less plentiful in poor Sweden than in the rich Netherlands, and the Swedes usually found it difficult to raise the full amount they had subscribed.

The charter setting up the New Sweden Company is now lost, but it probably gave the company exclusive rights to trade with the projected colony for a period of twenty years. A profitable trade was expected in furs and tobacco. The Dutch on Manhattan Island were already buying furs from the Indians along the Hudson and Delaware rivers, and by establishing a post on the Delaware the Swedes would be in a favorable position to get this trade for themselves. The use of tobacco, a plant native to America, was spreading in Europe. Although some people, such as Willem Usselinx, disapproved of it as harmful to health, it was becoming popular in Sweden as elsewhere; for example, as early as 1629 students were using tobacco at the University of Uppsala. Tobacco planting was a booming industry in the neighboring English colony of Virginia, from which the Swedes could easily obtain a supply to send to Sweden. Minuit even suggested that the first expedition take some tobacco seed with it to plant!

Active preparations for the voyage to America began early in 1637. Two vessels were provided by the Swedish government, the *Kalmar Nyckel* (*Key of Kalmar*) and the *Grip* (*Griffin*). Blommaert purchased goods in Holland for the Indian trade and sent them to Sweden—several thousand yards of duffels and other cloth, several hundred axes, hatchets, adzes, and knives, and quantities of mirrors, combs, gilded chains, earrings, and other ornaments. Spades, hoes, and other implements were loaded onto the ships, as well as provisions, including several hogsheads of distilled liquors. Seed wheat, barley, and perhaps other grains were taken for planting in the new settlement. Good sailors were not always easy to hire in Sweden, and probably half the crew was Dutch. The soldiers, however, were Swedes.

It was not until late in October that the two ships were ready to leave Gothenburg. Even then misfortune delayed them. They encountered a bad storm in the North Sea which forced them to put in at Texel in Holland for repairs. These were made, and then there was a further wait for favorable winds. Under the command of Minuit, they finally headed west across the Atlantic on the last day of the year, December 31, 1637. (Blommaert had expected

The Key of Kalmar *docking at the "Rocks,"*

them to leave in August.) We know nothing of the voyage but it could not have been a pleasant one, in the dead of winter and lasting for two and a half months. But they arrived safely in Delaware Bay about March 15, 1638.

Minuit sailed up the bay and river as far as what is now

next to the site of Fort Christina in 1638

the Christina River. Here he landed, firing cannon to call the Indians together, and on March 29 he made an agreement with the Indians to buy all the land along the Delaware from the Christina south to Duck Creek and north to the Schuylkill, paying for it in trading goods. About two miles up the Christina from its mouth a fort was built of palisades and earth. On the river side it faced a convenient "wharf of stone" ("The Rocks") and landward was almost surrounded by marshes, providing good protection against possible Indian attacks. Crops were planted, and about two dozen men were left behind to hold the country and carry on the Indian trade when Minuit departed in June in the *Kalmar Nyckel* for Sweden, taking with him the furs he had collected.

Little did Minuit realize that this was the last he would ever see of the little colony he had left in the American wilderness. His voyage back was made by way of the West Indies, to get tobacco for the return cargo. While anchored off the island of Saint Christopher, Minuit accepted an invitation to dine on board a Dutch ship in the harbor. A sudden storm drove it out to sea and it was never heard of again. After waiting for several days, the *Kalmar Nyckel* set sail for Europe without its leader, arriving in October. The *Grip* had been cruising in the West Indies when the other vessel left New Sweden. After returning to Fort Christina it too departed for Europe in April 1639, arriving in Gothenburg in June.

The furs and tobacco brought by the two ships fell far short of meeting the cost of the expedition, let alone making a profit, and the Dutch investors were unwilling to put any more money into the enterprise. The loss of Minuit was an ill omen for New Sweden's future. But in spite of these setbacks, one fact stood out: Sweden now had a colony. In addition to New Spain, New France, New England, and New Netherland, there was now a New Sweden in America.

Chapter 2

Forests and Indians

Early voyagers sailing along the eastern coast of North America were impressed by the trees. "The forest primeval" stretched westward, a sea of green, as far as the eye and the imagination could reach. A pioneer settler often built his cabin in a clearing surrounded on all sides by dense forest. Travelers told of riding on horseback for miles along paths lined with huge trees towering above them, so thick that the sun could not shine through, in a world of silent twilight.

To the early settler the forest was more a hindrance than a help. He had come to America, where land was plentiful, to get himself a farm and raise crops on it. Of course he needed wood for fuel and for building and would have a wood lot on his farm. But his first need was cleared land, and he got rid of the trees as quickly as he could. He might kill them by girdling and plant his first crops of wheat or corn between the leafless trunks. Later he could cut down or burn the tree trunks and pull out the stumps or let them rot.

The forest was slow in yielding to the attacks of the immigrants. In the 1750's, over a century after the first coming of the Swedes, one of their clergymen said that most of the farms were "newly cleared." Well into the 19th century we find references in the records to persons who lived in "the forest" of Kent County or Sussex.

The American wilderness was teeming with wildlife. An inquisitive English sea captain who sailed up Delaware Bay in 1634 has left a glowing description. He tells of the woods and "stately timber" which covered the earth except in places where the Indians planted their corn, and of the "low grounds, excellent for meadows and full of beaver and otter." There were many deer and elk—and wolves too, though he does not mention them. There was an "infinite number" of wild pigeons, turkeys, and other birds. Plenty of fish were in the rivers and creeks, which in the winter were covered with wild geese, ducks, and other waterfowl. Such a description would appeal to the people of Europe, where the poor often did not get enough to eat.

The engineer Peter Lindeström, who was a resident of New Sweden during the last years of Swedish rule, called it "a land flowing with milk and honey, such a fertile country that the pen is too weak to describe, praise, and extol it" sufficiently. In short, in the eyes of European observers, the Delaware valley was a vacant Garden of Eden, waiting for them to go in and take possession.

When Columbus made his memorable voyage of discovery in 1492, he landed first on some islands which he took to be the fabled Indies of the Far East. Therefore he called the inhabitants Indians. This name not only stuck but was extended to all the natives of the western hemisphere.

It was natural for early European settlers to wonder about the origin of their Indian neighbors, and various theories were advanced. A favorite one was that they were descendants of the lost tribes of Israel. William Penn, for example, thought so, and he guessed shrewdly that they might have come "from the easter-most parts of Asia to the wester-most of America." That is in fact what happened, though it was not the lost tribes of Israel who made the crossing. It is now agreed by students of Indian history that the first human inhabitants of this hemisphere came from Siberia by way of the Bering Strait many thousands of years ago. From this frigid gateway they spread southward, and long before the Europeans came were to be found all over North and South America.

In recent times scientists have been studying Indian remains in detail, adding greatly to our knowledge of Indian cultures. In Delaware archaeological societies are digging up Indian remains, some of which seem to be much older than those of the Indians whom the Swedes found on their arrival there. A large Indian burial ground has been discovered at South Bowers Beach. A section of it has been partially uncovered and roofed over to protect it from the weather. Inside one can still see the skeletons in the earth, where they had lain undisturbed for hundreds of years.

There were less than a million Indians living in what is now the continental United States at the time of the European settlement, but the same territory now supports 200 million people and produces a surplus of food which we sell or give to other countries.

The reason for this difference is that the Indians were still living in a primitive "stone age," through which the Europeans had passed many centuries before. By "stone age" we mean that the people living in it used tools and weapons made of stone, as well as shell, bone, and wood, but not of metal. The people of Europe had learned long ago how to produce bronze and then iron and steel.

The tools they made from these metals were much bet-

The Indian Burial Ground at South Bowers Beach, where over eighty skeletons have been found

ter than the old ones of stone and bone. For example, the Indians could cut down a big tree with a stone ax and hollow it out to make a log canoe or "dugout." But it was a tedious job, even when they helped it along by building little fires at the base of the tree and on the top of the log, to char the wood and make it easier to chip away with their stone tools. As the Indian saw at once, the white man's steel ax served the purpose much better. Likewise the Indian's stone war hatchet could not compare with one made of metal. And so white merchants had steel tomahawks made for the Indian trade, which the Indians used impartially on each other and on the white man too.

The Indians had no domesticated animals except the dog. Without horses, oxen, or other draft animals or beasts of burden, they would have no use for wheeled carts or wagons. For traveling on foot all they needed was a path through the woods. The white settlers, in Delaware as elsewhere, often used these Indian paths and widened them to cart roads. Some of the roads which we use today started as Indian trails.

The Indians traveled by water whenever they could, just as the white settlers did later. Sometimes they would paddle up one stream to the point nearest another stream flowing in the opposite direction. Here they would walk overland with their baggage (including their canoe) to the other stream, down which they would continue their journey by water. Such a land crossover was called a "portage."

The Indians' lack of animals was a handicap not only in transportation and travel but also in their farming. Without draft animals they had no use for plows, and so the cultivation of their fields did not go beyond scratching the earth with a pointed stick or a stone-bladed hoe. Hence, by modern standards, the amount of land which the Indians had under cultivation would be considered very small. The Finnish naturalist Peter Kalm in 1750 estimated that the fields of even a large Indian village amounted to only four to six acres. It may be mentioned here also that our seaboard Indians did not weave cloth. This was because they had neither sheep's wool nor cotton nor flax for linen from which to weave it.

Without domesticated animals the Indians had to depend for their meat supply on the wildlife of the woodlands and marshes—and of course they had no milk, butter, and cheese. They ate deer and bear meat, wild turkeys (the ancestors of the turkeys we find on our Thanksgiving tables), and many smaller animals and birds, whose skin and feathers were used for clothing and decoration. Fish were caught in the rivers, and the Indians who lived near the sea ate large quantities of oysters and mussels, as we know from the mounds of shells they left on the beaches.

At certain seasons of the year, when their farming activities permitted, the whole village would go hunting, living in temporary camps in the woods until they returned to their permanent villages. This is why the Indians needed so much land which to the European settlers seemed to be unoccupied. The Indians' hunting grounds might indeed be used only occasionally, but they nevertheless provided a necessary part of the Indians' food supply. In the earliest sales of lands by the Indians, they thought they were selling only hunting and fishing rights on their land—not the right to cut down all the forest and make farm land of it. The natives soon discovered their mistake but went on selling, tempted by the valuable goods they received in exchange from the white man. Realizing that he was doomed to lose his lands anyway, the Indian decided he might as well get what he could for them.

When the white settlers came, the Atlantic seaboard was inhabited by various tribes of Indians of the Algonkian language family. They were generally peaceful Indians who made their living by farming, fishing, hunting, and collecting wild fruits and nuts. The Indians whom the Swedes found here were of the Lenni Lenape tribe (later called Delawares) who were spread over what is now northern Delaware, eastern Pennsylvania, and New Jersey. Although they claimed ownership of northern Delaware, they seem to have spent comparatively little time there, and their permanent villages were farther north, near the Schuylkill River in Pennsylvania.

Their villages were surrounded by cleared fields in which they raised corn (properly called Indian corn or maize), beans, and squash or pumpkins. They planted the corn in hills, with beans whose vines ran up the cornstalks, while their squash vines spread over the ground in every direction. Maize, or simply "corn," as Americans call it, was grown everywhere in Indian America, and in colonial America too, as soon as the Indians showed the white settlers how to raise it. Corn today is grown all over the world, and the United States at present produces more of it than of all other cereal crops put together.

Had these agricultural Indians been able to keep their lands instead of being driven back by the rising tide of white settlers, they could easily have adapted themselves to the new farming methods and products which the whites brought with them. The Indians realized quickly that many of the white man's things were better than theirs. They were eager to replace their heavy pottery and stone vessels with kettles of brass or iron, their bone fishhooks and awls, their stone knives and axes, with similar articles made of steel. There was a steady demand for European woolen blankets and "match coats," short wool coats like our "car coats," which the Indians preferred to their heavy animal skins. It was unlawful to sell firearms to the Indians but they managed to get them anyway, and powder and lead

(1) Cooking vessel made of soapstone (2) typical clay pottery vessel used in Delaware (3) log mortar with stone pestle for crushing corn (4) gourd water bottle with a corn cob stopper (5) flat stone mortar with a stone grinder for crushing grain or nuts

were necessary items in the Indian trader's stock of goods. After a century of contact with Europeans the Indians of the Delaware valley, according to Peter Kalm, were using metal tools entirely, instead of the old stone ones, and the Indians had even forgotten how to make cooking pots of clay.

Savages though they were, the Indians were not stupid, and it would not have been too difficult to teach them the European way of life, had the white invaders really wished to do so. But for the most part they did not. The Swedes and the Dutch came to Delaware to trade with the Indians, not to civilize them, and the English came later to make homes for themselves on the Indians' lands. The Swedish minister John Campanius, hoping to convert "these ferocious pagans" to Christianity, learned their language and translated the Lutheran Catechism into their tongue; but he went back to Sweden in 1648 and his translation was not printed until nearly fifty years later. Swedish Governor Johan Printz got along peaceably with the Indians through necessity rather than choice. He did not trust them, and wished he could have two hundred more soldiers, with which, he said, he could "break the necks of every Indian in the river."

The Lenape, like other primitive peoples, had their own religious beliefs. They worshiped a "great spirit" called Manito, who made and ruled the world. They thought of the earth as being the back of a large turtle, which rose from the surrounding waters and became the dry land. A tree grew up on the turtle's back and sent out a sprout which grew into a man. Then another sprout appeared which became a woman. There were twelve other gods who assisted the great Manito, and a number of lesser ones, representing the sun, the moon, thunder, and other natural forces. The Lenape believed that the great Manito loved them and made the world for the use of all living creatures. The Lenape's most important religious ceremony took place each year at harvest time and lasted for twelve days. By the time it was over, the Indians felt that they had worshiped everything in the world and their prayers would help everyone on earth.

The white man unintentionally brought with him two evils against which the Indians had no defense. The first was his diseases, especially smallpox, which was bad enough for whites who had not had it, and fatal to the Indians. Disease spread quickly among the natives, often to villages which had no contact with the whites. About all the latter could say in excuse was that they were not doing these things purposely. In 1654 a shipload of colonists arrived in New Sweden with many sick or dying passengers aboard. When their sickness began to spread among the natives, the Swedes pointed out that they were dying too, and reminded the Indians that "sickness had formerly often been among them, through which whole tribes had died out, when none of our ships had come here."

The white man's alcohol was almost as harmful to the Indians as his diseases. Europeans had been accustomed to the use of alcoholic beverages since prehistoric times. The people who settled America drank beer or wine as we would drink tea and coffee, and it was natural for them to continue the habit here. During the 17th century stronger liquors, especially rum from the Caribbean islands, became more plentiful and cheap enough to be used in large quantities in the Indian trade.

But the Indians had had no experience with alcohol. When they drank rum they became violent and quarrelsome, sometimes even falling into their own fires or lying outside to freeze in their drunken condition. While the Swedes ruled New Sweden they seem to have given the Indians liquor only on special occasions. At a conference in 1654, after receiving the usual gifts, the assembled Lenape chiefs were treated to food and some strong drinks, which, said Peter Lindeström, "they love exceedingly." Later, under English rule, there were laws against selling strong liquor to the Indians. But it was impossible to enforce these laws strictly, because the Indians wanted the liquor and there were always some white settlers who were willing to sell it to them.

The Swedish settlements extended from Fort Christina (now Wilmington) north to present-day Philadelphia, and the Swedes had little to do with the territory to the south along Delaware River and Bay. The land was flat and marshy and apparently had few Indian inhabitants. When the English moved in later and bought the land from the Indians, some, at least, of the chiefs who sold it to them were apparently not living on it themselves but on the New Jersey side of the bay. These coastal Indians seem to have been of the Lenape group.

Farther inland to the west was a tribe called the Nanticokes, who lived along the river of that name and its branches. The Nanticoke River rises in what is now southwestern Sussex County, Delaware, but was then claimed by Maryland, and it flows through Maryland into Chesapeake Bay; so the dealings of these Indians were with the government of Maryland rather than Delaware. They need not concern us further, except to say that under the pressure of white settlement, more and more of them began to move west, as did the Lenni Lenape farther north.

The Iroquoian tribes of the interior were aware of the plight of the shore Indians and hospitably offered to make a home for them out of reach of the white man. Many accepted this invitation, leaving the lands of their forefathers to move into the interior of Pennsylvania. But they were not safe there for very long, and as the land-hungry whites advanced, the Indians retreated before them, though fighting all the way. Today descendants of the Nanticokes and the Delawares can be found on Indian reservations as far north as Canada and as far west as Oklahoma.

By the end of the colonial period few Indians were left in Delaware, and today the only Indian blood which remains in the state is in two communities of what students of Indian history call "mixed bloods." One of these, the Moors, is in the small town of Cheswold in Kent County, and the other, the Nanticokes, is on Indian River in Sussex County. From their varied facial types, hair, eyes, and skin color, they appear to be a mixture of Indian, European, and African peoples. But they, especially the Nanticokes insist that they are Indians, and it is their Indian ancestry which has kept them apart from other people, white and black. They live in the same kind of houses and follow the same kind of occupations as their neighbors; but for a long time they had their own schools and churches. The Moors' and Nanticokes' old beliefs and customs and their handicrafts such as the weaving of baskets and mats from corn husks have almost disappeared.

People now are more sympathetic toward the Indian than our colonial forefathers, who would likely have agreed with what later became a saying on our western frontier, that "the only good Indian is a dead Indian." Lindeström said that the Indians were people of "various qualities," but "more inclined towards bad than good."

But "good" and "bad" have different meanings to different people at different times. What we can be sure of is that the Indians were *different* from Europeans, in their customs and their attitude toward many things. As an example, here is a story told to Peter Kalm in 1749 by an old Swedish settler. He said that when old Indians became a burden they were taken into the forest and left to die of hunger. He remembered, as a child, an old, white-haired Indian who had been taken into the forest. Two colonists happened to find him there and wanted to take him home with them and feed him. But the old man could not be persuaded to go. He said that since he had been taken there to die he could not and would not change matters. And the colonists had to leave him there as he wished.

Chapter 3

Swanendael

The little band of Swedes who landed near the mouth of the Christina River were taken there by Dutchmen who seemed to know exactly where they were going, like people who had been there before. As a matter of fact, the Dutch *had* been there before. And so we shall have to backtrack a bit to find out what previous experience the Dutch had had with the Delaware region, or, as they called it, the South River.

The Dutch at this time were the leading commercial nation of Europe. They were ahead in trade within Europe itself and their ships were sailing all over the world, seeking profits in trade with peoples of faraway places. Dutch contact with the part of North America where Delaware is located began in 1609 with the voyage of an English explorer named Henry Hudson, who was then in the employ of the Dutch East India Company. Sailing up the Atlantic coast, he dropped anchor at the mouth of Delaware Bay but did not enter because of shoal waters. Continuing north-ward along the coast, Hudson soon reached the river which now bears his name. He sailed up this river far enough to be sure that it did not connect with the Pacific Ocean. His voyage was a failure because he was looking for a passage through to the Far East and did not find one. (He tried again in Hudson Bay, where he lost his life.) In reporting to his employer, however, Hudson commented on the abundance of fur-bearing animals, and from that time on Dutch vessels prowled about the Hudson-Delaware area, exploring and trading with the Indians for furs. In 1614 some Dutch merchants formed the New Netherland Com-pany which was granted the right to make four voyages dur-ing the next three years to any places discovered by them between 40 and 45 degrees north latitude.

Individual voyaging came to an end with the chartering of the Dutch West India Company by the government in 1621. This huge stock company, as we have seen, was given the sole right of trade and colonization in America, both North and South. It was also authorized to capture Spanish vessels and attack Spanish colonies, indicating that the basic purpose of the whole scheme was to weaken Spain's hold in the New World which she had enjoyed for a century. This was no idle threat, for on at least one occasion Dutch armed vessels captured most of the Spanish fleet carrying the year's production of gold, silver, and other valuable cargo from her colonies back to Spain. That year the com-pany gave its stockholders an extra dividend!

In the midst of these grand designs the West India Com-pany did not overlook New Netherland, and in 1624 it sent over a ship carrying 30 families, to plant a colony there. It was first planned to settle in both the Delaware and the Hudson valleys and to have the director's headquarters on an island in the Delaware River, which has recently been identified by two Delaware historian-detectives as Burlington (New Jersey) Island. But the Hudson was found to be more suitable, and, as good New Yorkers know, the island of Manhattan became the capital of New Netherland instead of Burlington Island. After Peter Minuit became director, the population was concentrated at Manhattan for reasons of economy as well as safety. But for trading purposes a fortified post was built on the South River where Gloucester, New Jersey, now stands, for use when the Indians came with their furs.

Meanwhile, back in Amsterdam, a sharp division of opinion had arisen among the directors and stockholders of the West India Company over further colonization. Some wanted to establish colonies in New Netherland at their own personal expense. Others wished to limit the company's activities entirely to trading, and some even opposed letting individuals start colonies because they might in time interfere with the company's fur trade, which was its chief source of income from the colony. As practical businessmen the conservative members may have been right. But for the moment they were outvoted, and in 1629 the company issued a "Charter of Freedoms and Exemptions" setting up the so-called "patroon" (patron) system of colonization. Under it the patroon was to receive a grant of land extending four leagues along the coast or one side of a navigable river or two leagues along both sides of a river, and as far inland as "the situation of the occupants will permit." He was required first to buy the land from its Indian owners, and then to settle it with 50 colonists within four years at his own expense. The patroon had the powers of government over his colonists but judgments of his court over 50 guilders could be appealed to the company's commander and council.

Of six patroonships applied for in New Netherland only one was carried through to success. Its patroon was Kiliaen van Rensselaer, a rich diamond merchant of Amsterdam.

It was on the Hudson River where Albany now stands and does not concern us further in this history of Delaware. Only one patroonship was located within the bounds of the present state of Delaware. Its patroon was Samuel Godyn, a prominent merchant of Amsterdam. Associated with him were eight or nine others, including van Rensselaer, Samuel Blommaert, who, as we have seen, was later to play an important part in the founding of New Sweden, and a seagoing businessman, just back from the East Indies, named

David de Vries and his followers landed in Delaware to establish the first Dutch settlement at Swanendael

David de Vries, who has left us an account of this ill-fated colony of Swanendael, as the patroonship was called, and his connection with it. He writes:

> *Anno* 1630 . . . We took steps to establish this patroonship and we made a contract with one another, whereby we were all placed on the same footing. We then equipped a ship with a yacht for the voyage, as well to carry on the whale fishery in that region, as to plant a colony for the cultivation of all sorts of grain, for which the country is very well adapted, and of tobacco. This ship with the yacht sailed the 12th of December, with a number of people and animals, to settle our colony upon the South River and to conduct the whale fishery there. As Godyn had been informed that many whales kept before the bay, and the oil was worth 60 guilders a hogshead, they thought that they might realize a good profit thereon and at the same time cultivate that fine country . . .

De Vries goes on to say that the yacht (the smaller of the two ships) was captured by the French on the second day out, but that the larger vessel, which was appropriately named *De Walvis* (*The Whale*), crossed the Atlantic Ocean alone, and after stopping at the island of Tortuga in the West Indies reached the South River safely.

Van Rensselaer has also left a brief account of the Swanendael venture, in which he tells how the patroons equipped the ship,

> ballasting it with all kinds of materials, such as lime, brick, and tiles, also putting on board four large horses, twelve cows with calf, also several boats for whaling, all kinds of ammunition, provisions, and merchandise, and over 80 persons, costing all together, including the yacht, over 50,000 guilders. . . . With this ship they also in 1631 took possession of the bay of the South River, occupying their colony with 28 persons engaged in whaling and farm-

ing, and made suitable fortifications, so that in July their cows calved and their lands were seeded and covered with a fine crop, until finally by the error of their *commis* [commissioner] all the people and the animals were lamentably killed.

The *Walvis* had returned from Swanendael in September with bad news about the whaling. The colony had arrived there too late in the year, and the only oil the ship brought back was a sample from a dead whale cast on shore. After one losing voyage the patroons were unwilling to put up the money for another. But, says de Vries:

> Samuel Godyn encouraged us to make another attempt. He said the Greenland Company had two bad voyages, and afterwards became a thrifty company. It was therefore again resolved to undertake a voyage for the whale fishery, and that I myself should go as patroon, and as commander of the ship and yacht, and should endeavor to be there in December, in order to conduct the whale fishing during the winter, as the whales come in the winter and remain until March. Before sailing we learned that our little fort had been destroyed by the Indians, the people killed —two and thirty men—who were outside working the land.

The ships sailed in May 1632 and in September reached the West Indies, where they loaded some salt, "in case the whale fishery in New Netherland should fail, as salt brought a good price in the Fatherland." After further adventures in the islands they headed north, and on December 5 sailed into South Bay and immediately saw a whale. "Thought this would be royal work," de Vries wrote, "the whales so numerous, and the land so fine for cultivation."

De Vries found the site of the settlement (on Lewes Creek in Sussex County), and "coming by our house, which was destroyed, found it well beset with palisades, but it was

almost burnt up. Found here and there the skulls and bones
of our people whom they had killed, and the heads of the
horses and cows which they had brought with them." He
made friends with the Indians, giving them presents, and
got from one of them an account of what had happened:

An Indian remained on board of the yacht at night, whom
we asked why they had slain our people, and how it happened. He then showed us the place where our people
had set up a column, to which was fastened a piece of
tin, whereon the arms of Holland were painted. One of
their chiefs took this off for the purpose of making tobacco pipes, not knowing that he was doing amiss. Those
in command at the house made such an ado about it that
the Indians went away and slew the chief who had done
it, and brought a token of the dead to those in command,
who told them that they wished they had not done it, that
they should have brought him to them, as they wished to
have forbidden him to do the like again. They then went
away, and the friends of the murdered chief incited their
friends . . . to set about the work of vengeance. Observ-
ing our people out of the house, each one at his work,
that there was not more than one inside, who was lying
sick, and a large mastiff, who was chained—had he been
loose they would not have dared to approach the house
—and the man who had command, standing near the
house, three of the bravest Indians, who were to do the
deed, bringing a lot of beaver skins with them to exchange,
asked to enter the house. The man in charge went in with
them to make the barter; which being done, he went down
from the loft where the stores lay, and in descending the
stairs one of the Indians seized an ax and cleft the head
of our agent who was in charge so that he fell down dead.
They also relieved the sick man of life; and shot into the
dog, who was chained fast, and whom they most feared,
25 arrows before they could dispatch him. They then proceeded towards the rest of the men, who were at their

work, and going among them with pretensions of friendship, struck them down. Thus was our young colony destroyed.

De Vries was a practical man. This atrocity by the Indians, he says, "we suffered to pass, because we saw no chance of revenging it, as they dwelt in no fixed place. We began to make preparations to send our sloops to sea, to set up a kettle for whale oil [for rendering the blubber], and to erect a lodging-hut of boards." Finding their provisions running low, on New Year's Day of 1633 he started up the river with six men in the yacht to buy maize and beans from the Indians, going as far as little "Fort Nassau," which the West India Company used from time to time as a trading post. De Vries made two such trips in January and February and had to be on his guard every minute against treachery by the Indians and also against being frozen in by the ice which formed during any sudden drop in temperature. On the second trip he found the river Indians fleeing from attacking Minquas who had come down from the interior.

While their commander was foraging, not too successfully, the men at Swanendael were chasing whales, also without much success. They captured a total of seven but ten got away. (They struck their harpoons into the whale's tail, but de Vries learned afterward from some Basques, who were old hands at the whale fishery, that the proper place to aim at was "the fore part of the back.") Thus the yield of whale oil was disappointingly small. As de Vries noted, "this voyage was an expensive one for us," and would have been worse, had he not obtained a good price for the salt he had bought in the islands.

After going to Virginia to lay in a supply of provisions for the voyage home, he returned to Swanendael for the last time, took his men, oil, and equipment on board, and

on April 14 set sail for Manhattan and from there back
to Amsterdam. So far as we can learn from de Vries's account, this second expedition was confined to whale fishing
—no planting of food crops or tobacco as had been done on
the first. After these two losing voyages the partnership
broke up. Samuel Godyn died and the patroonship was
abandoned and sold back to the West India Company.

The Swanendael venture therefore was a total failure.
About the only visible result of it was that the name
"Godyn's Bay" began to appear on Dutch maps of the period, to mark what we now call Delaware Bay. Swanendael
may serve to remind us that colonizing was a very hazardous
business, for the investors who risked their money as well
as the settlers who risked their lives. Along with the colonies
which succeeded and have become part of our history, there
were others which failed and are forgotten. De Vries himself was not discouraged by the misfortune of Swanendael
and went on with other colonizing projects, including a
patroonship on Staten Island which also failed.

Although Dutch traders no doubt continued to buy furs
from the Indians in the Swanendael area, nearly 30 years
went by before another settlement was attempted. By that
time the charming name Swanendael (valley of the swans)
had given way to "Hoerekil" (English Whorekill) .

In 1931 the 300th anniversary of the settlement was observed with appropriate ceremonies and "Zwaanendael
House" was built in Lewes as a memorial by the state of
Delaware. It is an adaptation, on a reduced scale, of part
of the old town hall of Hoorn in Holland, the home town
of Captain de Vries. A statue of him tops the front gable
of the building, which is used as a local historical museum
and library.

Chapter 4

The Rise and Fall of New Sweden

New Sweden's best friend in its early years was Admiral Klas Fleming. Like a human baby, an infant colony needs a great deal of care and protection from the mother country, until it is big and strong enough to look out for itself. Even a trading post had to receive a regular supply of trade goods if it were to prosper, for the Indians tolerated the white man among them only because of the European manufactured goods which they obtained from him. To Fleming, New Sweden was not just a trading post; it was an important extension of Old Sweden into the great New World. Who could say what it might become in the future? With such thoughts in mind, Admiral Fleming gave the colony his active support and encouragement as long as he lived.

Even before the *Kalmar Nyckel* got back from its first voyage to America, Fleming was busy with plans for a second expedition. He wanted to send several ships, with plenty of supplies and many colonists. But there were diffi-

*Admiral Klas Fleming
gave money and support
to the young colony
of New Sweden*

culties in the way. First there was a lack of money, and in
the end only one ship was sent. It was hard to find a capable
man to replace Peter Minuit, and finally it was decided to
put the expedition in charge of Peter Hollender Ridder, a
Dutchman who had been in the service of Sweden for several years, but who had no experience in overseas colonization. The government called in vain for volunteers to go
to New Sweden as soldiers or settlers. To the Swedish common people America was still a mysterious land of unknown
fears and dangers. A Swedish provincial governor then suggested seizing army deserters who had gone back to their
families, and others who had committed some small crime,
and sending them to New Sweden for a year or two as a
punishment. This is what was done, not only for this but
for later expeditions.

The *Kalmar Nyckel* was chosen again for the second
voyage, and set sail from Gothenburg in September 1639
"with people, horses, fodder, and provisions." In the North
Sea the ship sprang a leak and put into a Dutch port for
repairs. After starting again the ship was still leaking and
had to return for further repairs. Again it set forth and for
a third time had to put back. The unfortunate vessel was
finally ready to make a fourth start in December, when a

great storm swept the coast, and it was not until February 7, 1640, that the *Kalmar Nyckel* at last got going. It sailed through the English Channel and probably directly across the ocean, rather than by way of the West Indies. After a rough passage, with much sickness on board, the ship arrived safely in New Sweden on April 17, seventy days from Holland, over five months after leaving Sweden, and two years from the time it first entered Delaware Bay.

This was to be the pattern of Swedish colonial efforts throughout New Sweden's existence. Money was always hard to find, and delays and mishaps of various kinds ran up the costs unnecessarily. The expeditions were small, usually one ship and never more than two. During the 17 years of Swedish rule on the Delaware, a total of only 15 ships were sent from Sweden. Of these, three never reached New Sweden and one arrived after the colony had surrendered to the Dutch. It seemed as if a jinx was following the Swedes at every turn.

New Sweden, we will recall, was founded by a commercial company, some of whose members were Dutchmen. These Dutch stockholders were also stockholders in the Dutch West India Company. Their membership in the Swedish company was becoming uncomfortable for them, since it was competing directly with the Dutch company in the Delaware region. The Dutch government disapproved of their activities, the Swedes considered them a hindrance, they had lost money on the first voyage and were unwilling to risk any more. So the Swedes bought them out in 1641, and from that time on the New Sweden Company was entirely under Swedish control. It became, in fact, an arm of the Swedish government.

In the following year a new governor was appointed for the colony. His name was Johan Printz. Like Ridder whom he replaced, Printz had had no previous experience in overseas colonization. But he was a native-born Swede, 50 years old, the son of a minister, but a military man who had spent most of his life in government service. He was a big man. De Vries, who met him in New Sweden, describes him as "a man of brave size, who weighed over 400 pounds." The Indians called him "the big tub." *

Governor Printz may have been overweight, but that did not interfere with his activity. It was his energy, diplomatic skill, and good judgment that held the colony together for the next ten years. With hostile Indians at his back, and powerful nations—the English and the Dutch—on either side of him, Printz was able to get along peaceably with his neighbors without sacrificing Swedish interests. It was not until he had left that New Sweden fell a victim to its stronger rivals.

Printz moved his headquarters up the Delaware to the mouth of the Schuylkill River. On Tinicum Island, south of what is now the city of Philadelphia, he built himself a "splendid" house (probably of squared logs) and set up a post for trading with the Indians. This was a clever move. Before that time the Indians from the interior to the west had had to cross the Delaware River in order to exchange their furs with the Dutch on the eastern side of the river at Fort Nassau. Now the natives could trade with the Swedes as soon as they reached the Delaware, without having to cross over. They did so, and soon the Dutch governor at New Amsterdam was complaining loudly that the Swedes had ruined his company's trade with the natives, both by getting to them first and by paying them higher prices in trade goods.

Both the Dutch company and the Swedish company commanded their respective governors to get along peaceably with their neighbors, and so the Dutch and Swedes fought

* President Roosevelt, in his speech at the 300th anniversary celebration in 1938, quoted a rhyme then current:

> No Gov. of Del. before or since
> Has weighed as much as Johan Printz.

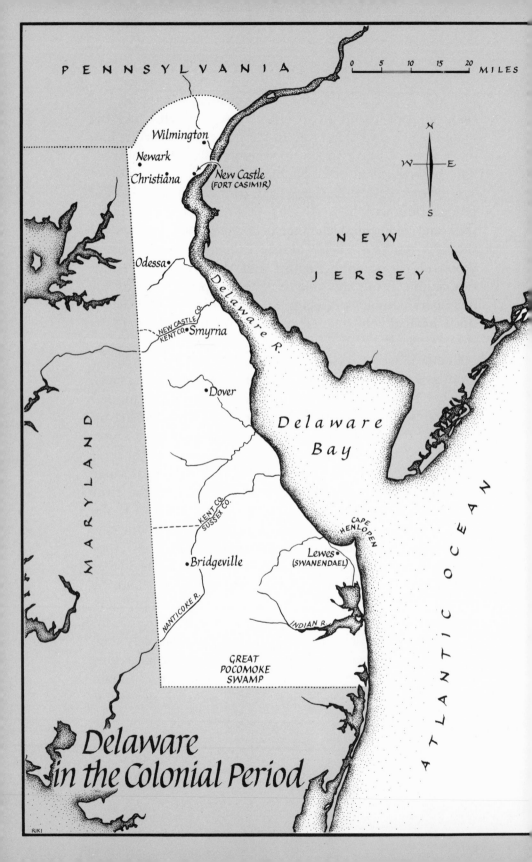

PENNSYLVANIA

0   5   10   15   20   MILES

Wilmington

Newark

Christiana

New Castle
(FORT CASIMIR)

NEW

JERSEY

Odessa

Delaware R.

NEW CASTLE CO.
KENT CO. •Smyrna

•Dover

*Delaware
Bay*

MARYLAND

KENT CO.
SUSSEX CO.

CAPE
HENLOPEN

•Bridgeville

Lewes•
(SWANENDAEL)

A T L A N T I C   O C E A N

NANTICOKE R.

INDIAN R.

GREAT
POCOMOKE
SWAMP

Delaware
in the Colonial Period

RJKI

each other only in battles of words. Claiming the whole Delaware valley by right of discovery, the Dutch told the Swedes that they had no right to be there and ordered them to leave. The Swedes argued that they were the first Europeans to make a permanent settlement on the Delaware and had bought the land from the Indians. Aside from this verbal warfare the Swedes were on friendly terms with the Dutch, bought supplies of all kinds from them, and, when no Swedish ship was available (as was the case most of the time), sent their letters to Europe by way of New Amsterdam. Likewise, the Swedes carried on friendly trade with the English from Virginia and Connecticut, but when the latter sought to make a settlement in Delaware Bay, Governor Printz discouraged them and made some English intruders take an oath of allegiance to Queen Christina of Sweden. In this Printz had the support of the Dutch governor, who realized that his most dangerous rival was not the Swedes but the English. They claimed ownership of the Delaware too. What was more important, they were coming to America by the thousands, compared to hundreds from the Netherlands and mere dozens of Swedes and Finns.

The first reports which Governor Printz sent to Sweden were cheerful and optimistic. "Our freemen," he wrote, "cultivate the land earnestly, not only with rye and barley, but they also plant orchards with splendid fruit trees and they get on mighty well, if only they had servants and a part of them had wives." (One settler complained: "Here one must himself cook and bake and do all the things that women do, which I am not accustomed to, and it is difficult for me.") Most of the settlers, said the governor, "are provided with oxen and all other kinds of cattle which increase and multiply greatly."

During the first five years of Printz's rule, ships came fairly regularly from Sweden, bringing supplies of tools, clothing, and the like for the settlers and trade goods for the Indians, though very few new settlers. The ship *Swan* arrived at the beginning of 1648 with a cargo which included, besides the more common things, a copper brewing kettle weighing 168 pounds, two casks of "dantziger window panes," and a glassblower's outfit. The *Swan* set sail in May with the usual return cargo of furs and tobacco. As the settlers watched the departing vessel fade into the distance, who among them could have foretold that six long years would go by before they saw another ship from the mother country? Yet that is what happened.

When the ships stopped coming the governor's troubles began. In the following year, 1649, the ship *Katt* (Swedish for *Cat*) did indeed start out, with supplies, ammunition, and a considerable number of settlers, including some Finns. But the *Katt* went by way of the West Indies, where, with the bad luck which accompanied so many of the Swedish colonizing efforts, it was wrecked on a small island. The ship never got to New Sweden, and most of its passengers found their graves in the islands.

The failure of the *Katt* expedition was a blow to the colony. Various plans were made to repair the loss, but for one reason or another they all miscarried. Unfortunately for New Sweden its great champion, Admiral Fleming, had been killed in 1644 during Sweden's naval war with Denmark, and no one else of his influence had the colony's interest so much at heart. Printz was left to carry on as best he could, without help from the mother country. Even his letters went unanswered. In 1652 he wrote despairingly that during the past four years, though he had written again and again "about the condition of this country," he had not received "a single letter, messenger, or message from the fatherland." People were telling the Swedes to their faces that they did not belong to any government at all. Some of the soldiers had deserted and others were on the point of doing so. He could not hold them unless aid arrived soon.

Since 1647 New Sweden's Dutch neighbor to the north had been under the control of Peter Stuyvesant, a man who in many ways resembled Printz himself. Like Printz, Stuyvesant was the son of a clergyman but had led a soldier's life. Both men had a physical handicap—in Stuyvesant's case, a wooden leg. Both were aggressive, violent in temper, and tyrannical in their rule, if we may believe the charges made against them. Stuyvesant would have liked nothing better than to take the weak little Swedish colony by force, had his employers, the Dutch West India Company, not prevented him from doing so, saying that they would settle matters with the Swedes by negotiation in Europe. Finally, in 1651, Stuyvesant on his own authority built and garrisoned a little fort on the western side of the Delaware River, several miles below Fort Christina, at a place called the Sandhook (now New Castle). The guns of Fort Casimir, as it was called, could stop any vessel from going past it up or down the river, and the Swedes were therefore bottled up in their own river. Printz could do no more than protest against these highhanded proceedings.

The Swedish governor, finding that letters and even messengers sent by him brought no response from the authorities at home, finally decided to go back and plead the cause of his forgotten colony in person. The danger from the Dutch was increasing and the colony, he feared, was on the point of breaking up if help did not come soon. He had been in America ten years, far longer than had been expected of him when he was appointed to his post. The strain of his position was affecting his health. After careful preparations, Printz, with his wife and four of his daughters, left in October 1653 for New Amsterdam, for the trip (which proved to be a stormy one) across the Atlantic. He left in charge his assistant, Johan Papegoja, who was also his son-in-law; and he promised the people assembled to bid him farewell that within a year "he would either present himself there again in person or send over a ship with a cargo."

Governor Printz's departure, as it turned out, was the darkest hour just before the dawn. His letters were taking effect, particularly the alarming news of the building of the Dutch Fort Casimir on Swedish territory. Even as he was crossing the Atlantic, preparations were going forward for the relief of New Sweden. A letter was sent to him telling him to stay on the job, but it did not reach him in time. The new project was under the direction of Eric Oxenstierna, a son of Axel the chancellor, who was later to become chancellor himself. Eric Oxenstierna, like the late Klas Fleming, was a strong believer in New Sweden and had the ability to get things done.

Two ships were to be sent, the *Orn* (*Eagle*) and the *Gyllene Haj* (*Golden Shark*). The *Orn* was ready first, and it was decided to send her without waiting for the *Haj*,

Fort Casimir was built by Peter Stuyvesant in 1651

which would follow as soon as possible. By this time popular interest in New Sweden had greatly increased. We are told that 350 prospective colonists, including women and children, had been recruited—more than could be taken. We do not know how many actually went. Of those who did go, many died on the way.

Printz had complained of the lack of competent people to help him in running the colony; and so, instead of allowing him to return, several able men were sent over to assist him. Chief among these was Johan Rising, the secretary of the Commercial College, a new government agency which was made responsible for the welfare of New Sweden. Rising was what we would now call an economist, a learned man, who was especially interested in problems of Swedish shipping, trade, and colonies. He was appointed *commissary* and was to be Printz's righthand man in the governing of the colony. Rising was in charge of the expedition going over, and, when it was learned that Printz had left, was appointed governor in his place.

The *Örn* left Gothenburg in February 1654, and after a long, hard voyage entered Delaware Bay on May 18. On Sunday morning, the 21st, as the colonists were on their way to church, they heard the sound of cannon down the river. A ship had come at last! Vice-governor Papegoja found that the immigrants "were now very ill on the ship and the smell was so strong that it was impossible to endure it any longer." They were removed quickly, distributed among the inhabitants, and nursed "with all care," though some of them died. Feeding so many newcomers was a problem too. Nevertheless the coming of the *Örn* brought joy and confidence for the future, banishing the gloom and despair which had hung over the colony for so long. The population was increased fivefold at one stroke, from 70 to over 350 "souls." Needed supplies were now in hand, and more of them as well as more people were on the way.

The new governor announced reforms allowing the inhabitants to trade freely and making it easier for them to acquire land. All in all, the future looked bright.

Among all these good omens, however, an incident occurred which led to New Sweden's downfall in little more than a year. Sailing up the river to Fort Christina, Rising's ship came first to little Fort Casimir, with the Dutch flag flying above it. The Swedish ship fired a salute, to which the fort's commander did not respond because he had no powder for his cannon. Rising landed 20 or 30 musketeers and took possession of the fort without resistance from its garrison of nine soldiers. Its Dutch flag came down and the Swedish flag went up. Fort Casimir was renamed Fort Trefaldighet (Trinity) "because it was taken on Trinity Sunday."

Rising's seizure of Fort Casimir was a mistake, a needless act of aggression which wise old Johan Printz would never have committed. But Rising knew little of the art of war, or, for that matter, of the local situation, which made such an act unwise. As soon as Director Stuyvesant in New Amsterdam heard (probably from the Indians) that a Swedish ship had arrived in the river, he sent a letter to its commander, congratulating the Swedes on their arrival and offering to maintain friendly relations with them. But when Stuyvesant was informed soon afterward about Fort Casimir he was furious, and made up his mind to retaliate at the first opportunity. That opportunity was not long in coming. In September the second ship of the expedition, the *Gyllene Haj,* arrived off the coast. But it missed the entrance to Delaware Bay and sailed into the harbor of New Amsterdam, where Stuyvesant seized it. He not only confiscated ship and cargo but persuaded most of the people on board to stay in New Netherland. Thus New Sweden was deprived of important reinforcements, in men and goods, at a critical moment in its history.

Up to this time Stuyvesant's employers in Holland had kept a tight rein on their impetuous and warlike governor. But the Swedish seizure of Fort Casimir changed all that. The Dutch West India Company directors now ordered him to "do his utmost to revenge this misfortune," not only by regaining the fort "but also by driving the Swedes at the same time from the river." The directors began to collect ships, supplies, and soldiers to send him, and urged him to hurry, before the Swedes received reinforcements from home.

Stuyvesant took his time, however. It was not until August 1655 that he sailed up the Delaware with a fleet of seven ships carrying over 300 soldiers (the Swedes guessed 600 or 700). The defenders of Fort Trefaldighet were overawed by this display of force, and did not fire on the ships as they went by. The Dutch landed unopposed. After some dickering the Swedish garrison surrendered, and Fort Trefaldighet became Fort Casimir again. The officers were well treated by the Dutch governor, who entertained them "at his own table."

Stuyvesant's soldiers then laid siege to Fort Christina, with their cannon aimed at its walls. Within the fort there was only one round of ammunition for their guns. Food was scarce and the garrison was becoming mutinous. Outside, Dutch soldiers were overrunning the countryside, plundering Swedish farmhouses and killing livestock, and some Indians were doing likewise. Stuyvesant had the Swedes at his mercy. But he offered generous terms of surrender. The Swedes were to keep their property. They were to have liberty to leave without hindrance, and if they chose to leave, they were to be transported free of expense to Gothenburg. Those who chose to remain under Dutch rule were free to practice their Lutheran religion. After stalling for several days, Rising and his officers accepted these terms. On September 15, 1655, they signed the articles

of surrender and the little garrison ("about 30 men")
marched out of the fort.

Then, instead of moving his soldiers into the fort, Stuyvesant went to the Swedish governor with an astonishing
proposal. He offered to return Fort Christina to the Swedes
and to leave them in possession of all their lands up the
river, if they would leave the territory south of Christina
to the Dutch. Since the only settlement there was at Fort
Casimir, this was, in effect, a return to the situation which
had existed before Rising captured the Dutch fort. At the
same time Stuyvesant proposed that the Swedes and Dutch
make an "offensive and defensive league," saying that the
country was "large enough for both."

The Swedes would have been less surprised if they had
known that Stuyvesant's council in New Amsterdam was
urging him to return with his soldiers and defend the colony
from a serious Indian uprising which had started during
his absence. This bad news may explain the suddenness
of his proposal, but not the Swedish-Dutch alliance part
of it. That was aimed at the English, and it may have been
on his mind for some time. The Dutch governor had good
reason to fear the English. Only nine years later they conquered New Netherland as easily as he had conquered New
Sweden.

The Swedes considered Stuyvesant's proposal carefully
but decided that they could not accept "such a humiliating
offer," and would abide by the terms of surrender. The
Dutch then took possession of Fort Christina, and Swedish
rule on the Delaware came to an end.

Had Rising and his advisers decided to swallow their
pride and stay on, Sweden might have held its colony for
a long time. England was at war with the Dutch but her
relations with the Swedes were friendly, and they had no
reason to fear an attack from that quarter. New Sweden
was now getting the support from home that had been

lacking in the past. In 1654, as we have seen, the *Orn* had brought at least two hundred settlers, followed by the *Haj* with some of the families who could not find room on the *Orn*. Encouraged by Rising's first report, the Swedish authorities lost no time in fitting out another vessel, the *Mercurius,* which left Sweden in November 1655 with over a hundred emigrants, mostly Finnish families, and had to leave a hundred others behind. More emigrants went to New Sweden in these last two years than in the fifteen previous years of its existence. The directors wrote to Rising saying that they would send more supplies soon, and that steps were being taken in London to settle the boundaries between the English and the Swedish colonies. But it was too late. By that time Rising was on his way back home and a Dutch flag was flying over New Sweden.

Chapter 5 Life in New Sweden

When the Dutch flag was hoisted over Fort Christina in 1655 Swedish rule on the Delaware came to an end, but that was by no means the end of New Sweden. A hundred years later the Swedish language could still be heard on the Delaware.

As we have seen, Governor Stuyvesant offered the Swédes generous terms to remain in the country, and although Rising "admonished" them to go back with him, very few did. In choosing between their *homes* and their *homeland,* they chose their homes. By this time many of the older settlers had become prosperous farmowners and had nothing to gain by returning to Sweden. The new immigrants had equally good reasons for staying. They had sold all their possessions before leaving Sweden and so had nothing to return to. Here they were given land and with hard work could become successful farmers like the earlier settlers. Many of the soldiers, too, under Stuyvesant's urging, chose to remain in America.

The Swedes and Finns were good colonists because they were good farmers. The Dutch were aware of this. When they took over in New Sweden they were pleased to have the Swedes stay and encouraged more to come. The Dutch director in the South River, in asking for more settlers; said that they should be "laborious and skilled in farming." He did not want Hollanders, but people of other nations and especially Swedes and Finns, who, he said, "are good farmers." He added that some were already planning to come because they had heard from their countrymen in New Sweden about "the good opportunity there."

Many of the newcomers found that pioneer life in New Sweden was not much harder than it had been at home. This was especially true of the Finns from the backwoods areas, where they often lived in conical huts (*kota* in Finnish) made of poles stuck into the ground in a circle and coming together at the top, somewhat like an Indian wigwam. The newly arrived Finnish (and perhaps Swedish) settler could easily put up a *kota,* in which he found shelter until he had time to build a house of logs.

Another practice which was common among the backwoods Finns and was found useful in New Sweden was burning over the forest land and then planting crops on it. This technique was common among the American Indians and in fact is found among primitive peoples in all ages. American settlers found that the ashes from the burned tree trunks and branches made excellent fertilizer and would produce good crops of grain for five or six years before the process needed to be repeated. By the 17th century forest-burning (called *svedging* in Swedish) was forbidden by law in Sweden but was still carried on by the Finns in the back country. In the earlier years, when volunteers for New Sweden were hard to obtain, it was suggested that forest-burners be sent over as a punishment, and probably some were. Here they could *svedge* to their heart's content, for it was the accepted way to clear forest land for cultivation. Even quicker than burning, for a first crop, was to "girdle" the trees, thus killing them, and plant Indian corn among the leafless trunks. Later on the trees could be cut down and burned or hauled away.

More than anything else, the early settlers depended for food on Indian corn or maize. It was easy to raise and very productive. Governor Printz was told that "one man's planting would produce enough corn for nine men's yearly food." When bad weather or other misfortune spoiled the Swedes' corn crop, or when extra supplies were needed to feed new immigrants, corn could be bought from the Indians. After a field was cleared of timber and broken to the plow, it could be planted with the small grains which the settlers brought with them from Europe. The Swedes planted chiefly rye for bread and barley which was used for brewing beer. By 1650 they were producing more than they needed, and when the harvest was good they could sell "a few hundred barrels of grain." Oats, peas, and beans were also raised, and the Swedes also had orchards with "splendid fruit trees." Grapes grew wild. Walnuts, chestnuts, and other edible nuts could be gathered in the woods.

At first cattle were scarce and had to be bought from the neighboring colonies. But by 1650 they had increased so greatly that most farmers were well supplied with cows for milk and meat and with oxen for plowing and hauling. Pigs were plentiful and rooted in the woods for their food. Sheep and goats likewise foraged in the open fields. In an early list of the company's servants at Fort Christina we find the names of "the swineherd with his son" and "the boy who herds the cattle." But the freemen who had farms of their own looked after their own animals. Now and then an Indian would cause trouble by appropriating a footloose pig to his own use. Later it became standard practice for each owner to identify his animals by a combination of crops and slits in their ears. His "earmark," as it was called, was entered in the official records of the county in which he lived.

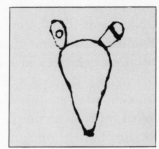

Farmers identified their stock by a combination of crops and slits in the animals' ears

In the early days most work was done by hand, and what we call the "mechanization" of industry still lay far in the future. The Swedish or Finnish farmer harvested his grain and hay with a sickle and hauled it from the field on a sled drawn by oxen or perhaps a horse, if he had one. The grain was thrashed with a flail. Until watermills were built, he ground his grain in a handmill or quern.

In the first few years of settlement the Swedes had to depend on Europe for manufactured articles of all kinds. But as time went on, they made more and more things themselves. Wool from their sheep and linen from their flax were spun and woven into cloth or knit into stockings by the Swedish and Finnish women. Skins of animals were tanned into leather or cured with the hair left on for coats and blankets. Plates, bowls, and spoons were made of wood, as were buckets, barrels, and other containers, as well as household furniture and utensils of all kinds. However, anything made of metal had to be imported and was therefore expensive. Bar iron was imported and was worked up by blacksmiths to repair plows and other implements and to make small articles. The most important implements which the Swedish farmer had to get from abroad were edge tools of steel, such as axes and knives, and guns and ammunition.

Coming as they did from a land of forests, the Swedes and Finns of New Sweden were likely to be experienced woodsmen. They were handy with the ax. An admiring English settler said that a Swede could cut down a dozen two-foot oak trees in a day. He could fell a tree and cut it up sooner than two Englishmen could saw it, and with wooden wedges split it into planks "or what they please." With only these simple tools, and using no iron, the early Swedes built their houses.

The greatest contribution the Swedes made to early American civilization was the log house. The early settlers in America tended to build the kind of houses that they had had in their homelands. The English and most other Europeans put up what we still call a "frame" house—that is, they made a frame of heavy timbers and covered it over with clapboards or shingles nailed on. The Swedes, however, and others from places where timber was plentiful, built their houses of whole logs, round or squared out of the rough, notched at the ends, and laid one upon the other horizontally as high as they wished the walls to be.

The advantages of the Swedish type of house are set forth in the journal of two travelers who started down the Delaware River on a cold November day in 1679. They spent the first night in the house of an English miller at the Falls of Trenton. It was a small frame building covered with the usual long shingles. Better houses of this type were plastered on the inside with clay to keep out the wind; but this one was "new and airy," and though the shivering travelers hugged the fire trying to keep warm, they "passed the night without sleeping much." They had better luck the next night, which they spent in a house built of logs

The log house was the greatest contribution the Swedes made to early American life. This one-room log house was built in New Castle County in the early eighteenth century

"according to the Swedish mode" and quite tight and warm. Spreading deer skins on the floor to lie upon, their journal records, "we were quite well off and could get some rest."

A special kind of log hut or house was the bath house or *bastu* (now often called a sauna) , in common use among the Finns and Swedes. Almost without windows, it had a fireplace in one corner, in which stones were heated and then water poured over them, thus filling the room with steam. In this suffocating atmosphere the bathers sat, perspiring and switching themselves with birch twigs; and then they dashed out to plunge into the river nearby or roll in the snow. An aged Swede told Peter Kalm that in his youth almost every Swede had a bath house. Governor Printz had one built for his and his family's use.

In the 18th century a flood of immigrants poured into the Delaware valley. Landing at New Castle or Philadelphia, many of them headed west to the frontier. On the way they learned how to build houses of logs, and the "log cabin" became the typical dwelling of the western frontiersman for the next hundred years and more.

The Swedes were Lutherans and continued to practice their religion long after Swedish rule was ended. The Dutch and others intermarried freely with the Swedes and became part of the Swedish community, attending the Swedish church services and speaking the Swedish language. By 1693 the last of the Swedish ministers had died. The Delaware Swedes were eager to get others, but had been out of touch with Sweden for so long that they did not know how to go about it. No Swedish ship ever came to the Delaware, and they did not even know the name of the reigning king.

Then a fortunate thing happened. They were visited by a young man named Anders Printz, a nephew of Governor Printz, who had come to Philadelphia on an English ship, and while there got acquainted with the people of his uncle's former colony. Anders Printz was so favorably impressed that he resolved to come back and make his home with the Delaware Swedes. He also promised to help them get the ministers that they needed, and through him the plight of the Delaware Swedes was brought to the attention of King Charles XI.

In the correspondence which followed, the Delaware Swedes were helped by another young man, of Swedish birth and well educated, whose name was Charles Springer. He had got to Delaware in a curious way. A native of Stockholm, he was sent abroad for his higher education. After spending some time in school in London, he was preparing to return home, when he was kidnapped, put on a ship bound for Virginia, and sold there as a bond servant to a tobacco planter. After five years of "unspeakable" hardship, he completed his servitude, and then made his way 400 miles to the Delaware valley, where he had heard there were Swedes living. He was received kindly, married a Swedish girl, and within a few years had two farms of his own. Charles Springer was a lay reader in the Swedish church at the time it was without a minister. A man of honesty and good sense, as well as education, he was of great service to the Swedish community, and was a justice of the county court from 1703 until his death in 1738.

As a result of King Charles' interest, three ministers were sent to New Sweden. Anders Printz was to accompany them as a sort of guide. The voyage was made by way of London, and while they were waiting there for a ship to America, Anders suddenly disappeared without leaving a trace. It was thought at the time that he might have been seized and impressed on an English man-of-war. However that may be, he was never heard of again, and his fate remains a mystery to this day.

The Swedish ministers arrived safely in 1697 and received a warm welcome. "Many cried with joy," said Reverend Erik Björk, "and some would not believe anything until they saw us." Ministers continued to come until the Revolution. But as time went on, more preaching was done in the English language and less in Swedish. Even the church records were kept in English from 1773 on. By that time members of Old Swedes Church, as it came to be called, were no longer Swedes. They were Americans of Swedish descent.

As a result of King Charles's interest, three Swedish ministers were sent to New Sweden in 1697. Old Swedes Church in Wilmington was built in 1698–99, and is still in use

Chapter 6

The Dutch and the English

As we have seen, New Sweden was seized in 1655 by Director Peter Stuyvesant for his employers, the Dutch West India Company. Colonial experts of the company hailed the "South River," as the Dutch called it, as a very valuable acquisition. Its soil was rich, its climate "mild and healthy," and its situation convenient for trade with the English in Maryland as well as with the Indians. All it lacked was people. "In order to maintain the aforesaid acquisition," said the experts, "what is particularly, yea solely required, is that it be properly peopled." But colonizing was expensive, and since the West India Company was hard up financially at this time, it called upon the rich city of Amsterdam for help.

In order to attract colonists, the city was to furnish the emigrants and their families with transportation to the South River and free food and clothing for a year, while they were getting started. They would be given as much land as they could cultivate, which would be tax-free for ten years. They were to be provided with "a proper person for schoolmaster, who shall also read the Holy Scriptures and set the Psalms," and, when their numbers increased, with a regular minister. They were also to have certain rights of self-government (see Chapter 10). It was expected that the new settlers would be able to export grain and other farm products to the mother country as well as masts and timber for ship building, which the Netherlands at that time had to bring in from the Baltic countries.

The Amsterdam city fathers accepted this proposal and arranged to borrow 25,000 guilders to get the project going. The West India Company then ceded the southern half of its South River colony to the city of Amsterdam. Henceforth there was a "colony of the company" comprising the territory up the river from Fort Christina (now called Altena) northward, where the Swedes lived; and a "colony of the city," extending from Christina southward to Cape Henlopen, which was largely unsettled by Europeans except for a small area around Fort Casimir. The first settlement was to be made at Fort Casimir, and a housing development near the fort was named "New Amstel" for a suburb of Amsterdam. It became the capital of the city's colony. The colony was in charge of an able man named Jacob Alrichs.

Alrichs arrived in 1657 with 168 settlers and soldiers with their wives, children, and women servants. During the next two years about 500 more arrived. New Amstel contained 110 houses, in addition to 16 or 17 in the outlying area and 13 or 14 "belonging to the Swedes." As might have been expected, the city of Amsterdam soon wearied of the expense of this subsidized emigration, and for a time threatened to turn the whole project back to the company. But this was not done. Instead, the rest of the South River was made over to Amsterdam, and a new but shorter burst of colonizing activity followed. A hundred new colonists arrived in July

1663, and in December 150 more, including some Swedes and Finns. The tobacco trade with Maryland was increasing and the future looked bright.

But alas, could they have known it, Dutch rule, like that of the Swedes nine years before, was nearing its end on the Delaware. Just as the Dutch had viewed the Swedes as intruders, so the English looked upon the Dutch, whose New Netherland colony drove a wedge between New England on the north and the English tobacco colonies, Maryland and Virginia, to the south. Equally and perhaps more important, New Netherland furnished a convenient base for Dutch trade with the English colonies, which the Dutch were trying to promote, but which England was determined to keep entirely in the hands of her own merchants.

During the wars of the Puritan Revolution in England her colonies had done pretty much as they pleased, so far as foreign trade was concerned. The tobacco planters of the Chesapeake Bay were glad to sell their tobacco to a Dutch skipper at a good price, and to take in return a variety of European manufactures which he offered at lower prices than English merchants charged. "The Dutch trade," said the Maryland Council in 1661, was "the darling of the people of Virginia as well as this province and indeed all other plantations of the English."

However much the English colonists may have liked having the Dutch as neighbors, that was not part of the English government's plan. England had already challenged Dutch supremacy in world trade in a brief commercial war, 1652–54. Ten years later Charles II, restored to the English throne, fought another war with the Dutch, which lasted from 1664 to 1667. This second Anglo-Dutch war began with a surprise attack on New Netherland by the king's brother, James Duke of York, who later became King James II.

In March 1664 King Charles granted to his brother a long

stretch of the North American seacoast which included all the territory between the Connecticut and Delaware rivers. This was of course the Dutch colony of New Netherland, which would have to be taken by force if the duke's grant were to have any meaning. Since the duke was lord high admiral of England and therefore head of the English navy, he was able to prepare his invasion force quietly, without arousing the suspicions of the Dutch. With a gift of £4000 from the king to help pay expenses, the duke outfitted a squadron of four armed vessels which, with 400 soldiers on board, crossed the Atlantic to Boston. From there it sailed down the coast, arriving before New Amsterdam late in August 1664. The commander of the expedition, Colonel Richard Nicolls, immediately called upon Director Stuyvesant to surrender, claiming that all of New Netherland rightfully belonged to the king of England.

Although he had only 150 soldiers on Manhattan Island, Stuyvesant wanted to fight. But nobody else did. The fort, which Stuyvesant once said resembled "a mole hill more than a fortress," was in no condition to withstand a siege. Many of the inhabitants were English or of other nationalities (Stuyvesant told a visitor that there were men of 18 different languages in New Netherland) who had no desire to risk their lives for the Dutch West India Company. The English offered very favorable terms of surrender which were accepted by all concerned except Stuyvesant. He would not sign the surrender, but it is interesting to note that he too stayed on, along with the other inhabitants. He spent the rest of his life under English rule, on his *bouwerie* or farm in New York City, and died in 1672 at the age of 80.

New Amsterdam was conquered without firing a shot, but things did not go so smoothly at New Amstel. As soon as New Amsterdam (now called New York) was safely under his control, Colonel Nicolls sent an expedition to the South River under the command of Sir Robert Carr. On October

Peter Stuyvesant leading his troops in the surrender of New Amsterdam

1 two ships, a frigate of 40 guns and an armed merchant vessel, with over 100 soldiers, appeared before Fort New Amstel. In command of the fort with its garrison of 30 men was Alexander d'Hinoyossa, governor of the South River colony since the death of Jacob Alrichs.

D'Hinoyossa took too long in deciding to surrender, and the English stormed the fort, killing three Dutchmen. The soldiers and sailors then plundered the fort and the village of New Amstel nearby. Instead of stopping the looters Sir Robert joined them. Unlike Colonel Nicolls, an honest and faithful servant of his master the duke, Carr was out to get all he could for himself, acting on the principle that "to the victors belong the spoils." He confiscated everything belonging to the city of Amsterdam, including goods, sheep, horses, cattle, and Negro slaves. Likewise he took the personal belongings of the Dutch officials and granted their lands to his English officers or kept them for himself. All this was done without any authority from Colonel Nicolls.

Aside from the hardships suffered by the New Amstel people, the terms of surrender offered to the South River inhabitants were all they could have expected—as generous as those which the Dutch had extended to the conquered Swedes nine years before. Anyone who wished to depart could do so "with his goods." All who submitted to English authority would be "protected in their estates real and personal." Their present magistrates were to be continued in office for the present. Upon taking the oath of allegiance, an inhabitant would become a "free denizen" of the now-English colony, with "privileges of trading into any of his majesty's dominions as freely as any Englishman." The present freedom of religion was to continue.

And so the mass of the inhabitants accepted these terms and stayed where they were. The Swedes and Dutch were now subjects of the king of England, but they went on cultivating their farms and trading with the Indians as they had done before. The people of New Amstel (now renamed New Castle) were probably glad to be rid of Governor d'Hinoyossa, who had tyrannized over them at the same time that he was cheating the city of Amsterdam in the trade which he was supposed to carry on for the city's benefit. Life under English rule would be as good and in some ways better than it had been under the Dutch.

The Delaware had to endure another conquest before it settled down permanently under English rule. During the third Anglo-Dutch war, 1672–74, after defeating the combined naval forces of the English and French in European waters, the Dutch sent a large fleet to America to capture or destroy as much English shipping as it could find. In August 1673 some 27 Dutch vessels appeared suddenly in New York harbor, fired 2000 rounds at the English fortifications on Manhattan Island, and landed troops to storm the fort. In the face of overwhelming odds the English commander surrendered, and New York became New Netherland again.

Soon afterward the colony on the Delaware River likewise surrendered to the Dutch. The Dutch inhabitants were glad to have their countrymen back, but their joy was short lived. The Treaty of Westminster, which ended this brief war, provided for the return of New Netherland to England; and so, in October 1674, after only a year of Dutch rule, the people of the Hudson and the Delaware valleys became English subjects again. By this time, no doubt, they were able to change their allegiance without batting an eyelash.

While these conquests by foreign powers were an annoyance, the settlers on the Delaware actually suffered more at the hands of their neighbor to the west, the English colony of Maryland. Maryland had been granted by King Charles I to Cecil Calvert, Lord Baltimore, in 1632, just after the Dutch had made their unsuccessful attempt to plant a colony at Swanendael. Although the early Maryland settlements were on Chesapeake Bay, the Calverts claimed that their grant extended to the shores of the Delaware. As early as 1659 one Colonel Utie, a member of the Maryland governor's council, appeared in New Amstel and warned the Dutch to get out, since this was Lord Baltimore's territory. The Dutch were alarmed but stood their ground, and a long dispute began between the Calverts and the Dutch, and later the English, over the ownership of the western shore of Delaware River and Bay, a dispute that was not settled for a hundred years.

The Maryland proprietors claimed the whole Delaware shore, but they made a special effort to get control of what was then called the Whorekill, which included the site of the Swanendael settlement and is now part of Sussex County, Delaware. The Dutch set up a trading post there, and in 1663 allowed Peter Plockhoy and 40 of his followers to settle there. They were Mennonites, a religious group who were being persecuted at this time for their beliefs, which resembled those of the Quakers. In the following year Sir

Robert Carr's men took over for the English, and according to a later account, looted the Whorekill settlement including "what belonged to the quaking society of Plockhoy to a very nail."

The fact that the Delaware territory was now in the possession of the duke of York, a fellow Englishman, did not stop the Calverts. The Whorekill area had already been made a county of Maryland. Land was surveyed and granted to Marylanders at the same time that the duke's governor was making grants, sometimes of the same land, to other prospective settlers. In 1672 Governor Charles Calvert appointed military captains to raise troops and proceed against "all enemies" whom they might encounter. It was charged by the duke's governor Lovelace that Captain Jones rode to the Whorekill with a party and "bound the magistrates and inhabitants, despitefully used them, and rifled and plundered them of their goods." Then, as Governor Lovelace was taking steps to defend his colony, it was captured again in 1673 by the Dutch, as we have seen.

Even worse was to follow. In December 1673, while the Whorekill was again under Dutch rule, a certain Captain Howell with 40 horsemen from Maryland "came into the Whorekill town with swords drawn; and threatened and terrified the inhabitants, who being frighted thereby submitted to them." After living off the Whorekill people for two weeks, Howell went back to tell the Maryland governor (as he said) "that the inhabitants were poor and not able to maintain so many soldiers." Upon Howell's return he ordered the people to assemble at the town for a muster, with all their arms and ammunition. After these had been collected Howell told the people that he had orders from Lord Baltimore to burn their houses, and not to "leave one stick standing." This his men proceeded to do, keeping the people from rescuing their possessions from the burning houses. Howell and his men then left, taking all the boats in the creek as well as the guns and ammunition which they had collected.

Thus, on Christmas Eve, 1673, the Whorekill town was destroyed, leaving the inhabitants defenseless, without provisions and 60 miles away from their nearest white friends to the north.

The burning of the Whorekill marked the end, at least temporarily, of Lord Baltimore's war on the duke of York's Delaware colony, and a few years later the duke's rule on the Delaware was replaced by that of the Quaker William Penn. In 1681 King Charles II made a grant to Penn of a large tract of land which by the king's order was to be called "Pensilvania." The bounds of Penn's grant were stated, and in order not to encroach upon the duke's land Penn's southeastern boundary was to be twelve miles distant from the town of New Castle. (This is the origin of the famous "twelve mile circle," the only circular boundary in all of our 50 states.) But Penn soon found that Pennsylvania lay so far up the Delaware River that it was cut off from the ocean—in other words, he was bottled up; and so he asked the duke to give him his (the duke's) Delaware colony too. This the duke obligingly did, out of friendship for the Penn family, in August 1682. Now Penn had control of the whole length of the Delaware, from the upper reaches of the river clear down to Cape Henlopen on the bay.

This was a defeat for Lord Baltimore, but he did not give up easily. He sent his cousin, Colonel George Talbot, to Penn in Philadelphia to demand the surrender of all the Delaware shore south of the 40th parallel of north latitude as belonging to Maryland. Talbot then by the Maryland governor's order built a log fort at Christina Bridge, guarded by four soldiers while he went about offering to sell land in the neighborhood on favorable terms.

Both of the contesting proprietors then sailed for England to lay their case before the king. The committee of trade and plantations of the king's privy council, after considering the evidence on both sides, decided in Penn's favor, recommending that the disputed territory be divided equally. The half bordering on Delaware Bay was to go to Penn and the other half, facing Chesapeake Bay, to Baltimore. The king, who by this time (1685) was James II, the former duke of York, approved of the committee's recommendation and ordered "that the said lands be forthwith divided accordingly." And so Lord Baltimore lost again in his struggle with William Penn.

In spite of the king's "forthwith," over 80 years went by before the boundary lines were finally run. In the meantime new settlers could not be sure that the land they were buying was in the Calvert family's Maryland or the Penn family's Pennsylvania and Delaware. As population increased there was violence and even bloodshed along the "frontier" between the rival colonies. At length, in 1763, both proprietors agreed to hire "two persons, well skilled in astronomy, mathematicks, and surveying," to come from England and complete the running of the boundary lines. Their names were Charles Mason and Jeremiah Dixon.

Mason and Dixon arrived in Philadelphia in December 1763 with their instruments, which included a telescope and a very accurate clock. They stayed over four years, until January 1768. They spent a little time measuring a degree of longitude (the so-called "degree of Pennsylvania") at the request of the Royal Society of England; but the rest was taken up with calculating, running, and checking the various boundary lines.

Since Delaware's southern boundary had already been run by American surveyors, from old Cape Henlopen (Fenwick's Island) westward to the middle of the peninsula, Mason and Dixon started there and ran their line a little west of north up to the twelve-mile circle. After determining the latitude of the east-west boundary between Maryland and Pennsylvania, they ran that line due west across the Allegheny Mountains, as far as they could go, until stopped by the danger of hostile Indians. It is this boundary that is commonly known as the Mason-Dixon line, because it turned out to be the dividing line between the slave states and the free states. Although most people do not know that Mason and Dixon did any other surveying in America, it was in fact the last of a number of Mason-Dixon lines, and the easiest to calculate.

After running their lines Mason and Dixon set up stone markers at intervals along the lines, many with the coats of arms of the Penn and the Calvert families cut on opposite sides. Some of these markers are still in place, though badly worn after two centuries of exposure to the elements—for example, the stone at the "middle point" which marks the southwestern corner of Delaware. A hiking club looking for a project could spend a whole summer following the trail of Mason and Dixon by means of these markers. Books have been published showing where they are.

Having followed Delaware's boundary disputes to their settlement by Mason and Dixon's survey, we must now turn back to the year 1664, when English rule began on the Delaware under the duke of York. For the old inhabitants life went on much as before. This is especially true of the Swedes, who were settled mainly along the river from Christina north to the present Philadelphia. The English were slow in coming among them, and as late as 1676 the justices of the court of Upland were all Swedes.

New Castle was the chief town and the seat of government under the English, as it had been (with the name of New Amstel) under the Dutch. A Quaker traveller who spent a night at New Castle said that "the inhabitants were most of them Dutch and Finns, and addicted to drunkenness." The Dutch magistrates at the Whorekill remained in office under English rule, and for several years the instructions sent them from New York were in the Dutch language. For many years business accounts were kept in Dutch guilders rather than English pounds and shillings. Even court charges were reckoned in Dutch money; for example, in 1679 the court of New Castle imposed a fine of 150 guilders on a defendant.

The English conquest would naturally stimulate English immigration. The newcomers were attracted to the unsettled shore of Delaware Bay between New Castle and the Whorekill, where good land was available at little or no cost. They seem to have come not from England directly but from nearby English colonies, especially Maryland and Virginia, and as individuals or in small groups. We read in the old records that Captain Nathaniel Walker, "formerly from Boston, lately from Virginia, Eastern Shore," was granted land on Rehoboth Bay in 1679. Likewise Richard Perrot, asking for a grant, said that he and "some other gentlemen of Vergeney came over to Delieware and liking the place we made choice of several tracts of lands for our selfs and nabors." By 1680 enough people had come in to set up a new county, called Saint Jones and later Kent, between New Castle to the north and the Whorekill (renamed Deal and later Sussex) to the south. These are the present three counties of Delaware—New Castle, Kent, and Sussex. They all face on Delaware Bay or River, and some people claim that at high tide there are only two.

The coming of the Quakers begins a new era in the history of the Delaware valley. William Penn estimated that in three years (1682–85) over 7,000 immigrants poured into his new colony of Pennsylvania. They settled mostly in the neighborhood of Philadelphia, but overflowed in all directions, with quite a few going to Delaware, especially the northern part.

Not all of these immigrants were Quakers, for Penn welcomed people of all religious beliefs; but most of them were, because the Quakers were being persecuted in England for their religious beliefs, and were looking for a place where they could make a living and practice their religion in peace. Penn advertised his colony as just such a place.

The Quakers were disliked not only by the Church of England, the religion enforced by the government, but also by people of other dissenting faiths, such as the Puritans, who were themselves being persecuted. This was because the Quakers believed that (as William Penn put it) "the Bible is *a* rule, though not *the* rule, of faith and life." The Quakers listened to God speaking to them through their own consciences—their "inward light." When, for example, the Bible said "Thou shall not suffer a witch to live," and the Quakers' inward light told them not to kill witches, the Quakers obeyed their inward light.

The Quakers had other peculiarities which were annoying to many. But they were honest and hard working. They were good businessmen, whether farmers, merchants, or craftsmen. They brought a higher standard of living and of farm production to the Delaware valley. Soon it was exporting not merely furs and tobacco, but large quantities of foodstuffs (meat, grain, flour, bread), barrel staves and lumber, and horses. These had a ready sale in the West Indian islands, where the planters found it profitable to use their land and their labor force (mostly slaves) for raising sugar cane, and buy their food and various other supplies from the colonies on the mainland to the north.

Early in the 18th century a new and larger wave of immigration from the north of Ireland began, which brought many new settlers to Delaware and especially to New Castle County. These people were mostly descendants of Lowland Scots who had been colonized by the English government in northern Ireland. In America they were commonly called Scotch-Irish. They were disliked by the native Irish and oppressed by the English church and government. They were eager to escape from grasping landlords and tax collectors and go to America, where the fruits of their labors would be their own.

The Scotch-Irish landed at various American ports, but by far the greatest number came to the Delaware valley. A Pennsylvania official wrote in 1727: "We have from the North of Ireland great numbers yearly; 8 or 9 ships this last fall discharged at New Castle." Landing there or at Philadelphia, the newcomers quickly took up the available land nearby. Then, as they kept coming, they went farther west, where land was easier to find, but the danger of Indian attacks was greater.

The urge to go to America spread like wildfire, and, like a fire, fed on itself. "The whole north is in a ferment," said the Anglican archbishop of Ireland (1728). "The humor has spread like a contagious disease, and the people will hardly hear anybody that tries to cure them of their madness." Emigration was exceptionally heavy during years of famine in Ireland, and it continued down to and after the American Revolution.

The Scotch-Irish came mostly from the province of Ulster. They were for the most part Presbyterian in religion. In fact the spread of Scotch-Irish settlement can be traced most easily by the Presbyterian churches which they established. At the time of the Revolution over half of the churches in Delaware were Presbyterian churches, and of these over half were in New Castle County.

Looking back over the first century of Delaware's colonial history, we must admit that for nearly 50 years progress was extremely slow. The Swedes and the Dutch got no more than a toe-hold on the vast stretch of country which lay to the west of their tiny settlements. Under the duke of York's rule things were not much better. There were still not enough people in the Delaware valley to withstand an all-

Many Scotch-Irish, most of them Presbyterian, settled in New Castle County. New Castle Presbyterian Church was built in 1707

out Indian attack, had the Indians chosen to make one. Fortunately they did not!

The coming of the Quakers changed all that. First there were some thousands of Quakers themselves, and they were followed by other thousands of Germans, Scotch-Irish, and English-speaking people from Great Britain, by which we mean England, Scotland, and Wales. A great many of them (how many it is impossible to say) were poor people, too poor to buy land or even pay their passage to America. But they got here in spite of their poverty, and they kept coming in such numbers that by the time of the Revolution even little Delaware had a total population close to 40,000.

Chapter 7

The Land

Almost everybody in colonial Delaware was a farmer.

That is a slight exaggeration, but it would not be if we include the people who worked on farms without owning them and who owned farms or farm lands without working on them. The whole economy of Delaware, like that of most of the colonies, was based on agriculture. The wealth and income of Delaware's people came from the various products of its fields and forests.

It is hard for us today to understand what farm life was like, because so few of us live on farms. It takes scarcely a tenth of our nation's labor force now to raise all the farm products we need. The other nine-tenths are engaged in other occupations, most of which have nothing to do with farming. Boys and girls today may grow up without ever setting foot on a farm, or having a closer look at a cow than one gets while speeding along a super-highway. Today, boy and girl scouts and other youth groups spend much of their time in camping, hiking, and such "back to nature" activities. To the average Delaware youth of 200 or even 100 years ago, this would have seemed rather absurd, because nature was right at his back door, and he spent most of his waking hours in the unpolluted outdoor air.

From the beginning, it was land which attracted settlers from Europe to America. The great mass of the European people at this time were peasants, trying to make a scanty living from the few acres which they tilled or worked on for someone else. In a year of crop failure, famine and starvation were not far off. The standard of living was low for most of the people, regardless of their occupation. Only the fortunate few could enjoy the comforts and luxuries of life. To the poor of Europe, America became the promised land, a land, as the Bible says, "flowing with milk and honey."

Although both the Swedish and the Dutch colonizing companies were primarily interested in trade, they encouraged farmers to come as settlers by offering them free land, as much as they could cultivate. In other words, anyone who was willing to work could get a farm for himself and his family. Under the duke of York, grants of land were made by the county courts to all who applied, on condition that they "seat and improve their respective lands within one year." Such grants might be for 100 or 200 acres or more.

Sometimes land was granted for a special purpose, such as building a mill. In 1680 two men got a grant of 10,000 acres from the Kent County court for this purpose. There were no electric motors or diesel engines in those days, and mill wheels were usually turned by water power. In order to provide a fall of water sufficient to turn the wheel, a dam would be built across a stream at a suitable spot. The water backed up behind the dam created a pond which might cover a large area on both sides of the stream. Water from the mill pond was led through a trough or flume to the top of the mill wheel, which was turned by the weight of the

An eighteenth-century mill operated by water power

water falling on it. The mill stones, connected to the water wheel, revolved and ground the grain.

Wherever water power was available, mills were built. Often they could operate only part of the time. When the water in the mill pond was too low, the miller had to shut down and wait until it filled up again. There were many small mills which catered to the needs of their local farming communities. Whenever meal or flour ran short in the farmer's household, he or his boy put a bag of grain on his horse's back, climbed on top, and rode off to mill to have it ground. The miller ran the grain through the mill, took out his toll, and returned the rest to the waiting customer.

In addition to the small custom mills, as they were called, there were larger merchant mills which bought the farmer's wheat for cash and ground it into flour for export. In the 18th century lower Brandywine Creek became the largest flour-milling center in Delaware, and one of the largest in all the colonies. Wheat could be brought up the Christina River by boat to the Brandywine mills, and the finished flour could be shipped out the same way. The wheat grown in northern Delaware and nearby Pennsylvania produced an exceptionally high grade flour which was in demand abroad. A town grew up here, called Willingtown and later Wilmington, which had its own ocean-going vessels. Wilmington today is the largest and in fact the only city of any size in Delaware.

In choosing a site for a farm or plantation, the Delaware farmer tried to keep close to a stream, because his best means of transportation was by water. Downstate Delaware is flat, and its sluggish creeks and rivers run far up into the land. For example, the town of Dover (the present capital of Delaware) is near the middle of Kent County; but it could be reached by vessels from New Castle or Philadelphia, which sailed down Delaware Bay and up Saint Jones Creek to Dover. Freight and often passengers were carried up and down the Delaware in small sailing vessels called shallops, as well as larger craft. At the outbreak of the Revolution Caesar and Thomas Rodney of Dover owned a sloop, a schooner, and a shallop.

The poor roads of colonial times made land transportation slow and uncomfortable. There was an "overseer of the highways" in each hundred (as townships are called in Delaware), and every citizen was required by law to do his share in "clearing and repairing high ways and other roads and making bridges etc." But the roads were mere tracks through the fields and woods, muddy in wet weather and dusty when dry. Roads were often old Indian trails, widened to allow carts and wagons to pass, and they kept to the higher ground to avoid swampy places.

Until bridges could be built, smaller streams were crossed at fords, shallow places where one could wade across. To take travelers over the larger creeks and rivers, persons were authorized to keep a ferry, often just a dugout canoe, where the road crossed a stream. As population increased, more bridges were built, which sometimes gave their name to the locality. The present village of Odessa was originally called Cantwell's Bridge. Christiana is short for its earlier name, Christiana Bridge.

George Washington often went through Delaware on trips from or back to his home at Mount Vernon. He records in his journal that, on his return from the Constitutional Convention at Philadelphia, he "dined at Christiana Bridge and lodged at head of Elk [in Maryland], at the bridge near to which I narrowly escaped an ugly accident to my carriage and horses. The rain which had fallen the preceding evening having swelled the stream considerably, there was no fording it safely. I was reduced to the necessity therefore of remaining on the other side or of attempting to cross on an old rotten and long disused bridge. Being anxious to get on I preferred the latter, and in the attempt one of my horses fell 15 feet at least, the other very near following, which would have taken the carriage with baggage along and destroyed the whole. However by prompt assistance of some people at a mill just by, the first horse was disengaged from his harness, the second prevented from going quite through, and the carriage rescued from hurt."

Suppose the Father of His Country had been dragged in and drowned in these swollen waters. How different the later course of our history would have been!

The growing number of bridges was an encouragement to land travel. Families could ride in carts and wagons along with their freight, while those who could afford it might even have a carriage. But the easiest and fastest way to travel on land was on horseback. People rode horseback as much in colonial days as they do in the "Wild West" programs we see on television. The most famous ride in Delaware's history is the one made by Caesar Rodney to Philadelphia in 1776 to vote for independence. There is a bronze statue of him on horseback in Rodney Square in Wilmington. We assume that he started from his home in Dover, a distance of about 85 miles, and that he rode horseback because that was the quickest way to go. But all that we know for sure about Rodney's memorable ride is in a letter which he wrote from Philadelphia on July 4, in which he says that he "arrived in Congress (tho detained by thunder and rain) time enough to give my voice for independence."

As land travel became more widespread, and swarms of new settlers came in, Delaware changed gradually from a mere fringe of settlements hugging the shores of the Delaware to a more densely populated rural colony. The days of free land, when one could acquire a farm at no more expense than the surveyor's fee, did not last long. When William Penn became proprietor of Delaware, he and after him his sons and grandsons sold such lands as had not already been taken up. And while the cost was not great, a shilling or two per acre, it was more than many penniless immigrants of the later 18th century could afford. They moved west, to the back country of Pennsylvania or Virginia, where they became illegal squatters on unoccupied land, without paying anything to anybody.

Chapter 8

Labor

When land was so plentiful in colonial America, labor was correspondingly scarce. There is always a lot of work to be done about a farm, even in our day of labor-saving machinery. Most of the time the colonial farmer had more work than he could do. There was the never-ending round of planting, cultivating, and harvesting his crops. In the fall he had to salt and smoke meat for winter use or sale. Winter might be a slack season, but the thrifty farmer used that time in the woods cutting timber, some of which could be sold, such as boards of walnut for making fine furniture. Cedar could be split into shingles. Oak was sawed and split into staves for making barrels. Millions of barrel staves were sent every year from the Delaware valley to the West Indies and elsewhere, to be fashioned by coopers into casks and barrels of various sizes, for the shipping of sugar, molasses, rum, tobacco, and many other articles.

The colonial farmer's wife was just as busy as he was.

Among the early Swedes and Finns, women probably worked in the fields when necessary along with the men, as they did in Sweden. But as time went on and they became more prosperous, women's lot became somewhat easier. Reverend Israel Acrelius wrote disapprovingly: "The man-servant takes care of the foddering of the cattle while the housewife and women-folks roast themselves by the kitchen fire, doubting whether any one can do that better than themselves."

Acrelius was a bachelor and perhaps a little unfair to the fair sex. However that may be, a farmer's wife had plenty to do. Besides caring for the children she cooked and baked bread (once a week or oftener) for the household, milked the cows, made butter and perhaps cheese, looked after the vegetable and herb garden, spun wool and flax for the family's clothing, which she also made. When anyone was sick, she was the family doctor. When she sat by the fire in the evening, her hands were busy spinning or knitting or sewing.

A farmer's wife in colonial Delaware was always busy. She made her family's clothing from the wool and flax she spun

Because there were so many things to be done, farmers were glad to have large families of children. Girls learned from their mother how to do the various things which she did, some of them requiring great skill and practice. (If you doubt this, just try operating a spinning wheel, even after you have watched someone do it!) Likewise, boys learned by helping their father with his many tasks. Plowing was done with a pair of oxen or horses. "The plowman holds each handle with one hand," says Acrelius, while the animals "are guided by a little boy either leading or riding on them." Heavy three-cornered harrows, for smoothing the surface of the ground after plowing, could be drawn by a pair of horses with a boy on the back of one to guide them. "When a boy does the work," says Acrelius, "the laborer is spared a great deal of trouble."

And so children worked from an early age in colonial Delaware, as they did in the other colonies. From chores like bringing in firewood and weeding the garden, they went on to more responsible tasks as they grew older. By the time a farm boy was old enough to vote, he had had enough experience to run a farm himself; and a girl was ready to take over from her mother in managing the household, or more likely marry and start one of her own.

As long as land was plentiful, an ambitious father could acquire enough to provide each of his sons with a farm of his own. Thus Charles Springer in 1719 petitioned for 200 acres of land near Red Clay Creek "for the settling of his children, he having several sons and but little land for them." He was granted the land on condition of improving it. Later, after his sons Israel and Andreas died within a week of each other, the father disposed of the land to a neighbor. As late as 1775 James Nixon of Brandywine Hundred (an ancestor of President Richard M. Nixon) was able to leave a 100-acre farm to each of his two sons.

Families in Europe customarily had household servants

if they could afford them. Emigrant families, especially if there were several children, might come with a maid-servant or occasionally a man-servant. Because of the shortage of women in the colonies, the maid-servants did not remain servants very long, but married and started families of their own. Orphans and children whose fathers died, leaving the mothers unable to support the children, were bound out to other families of the neighborhood, by order of the county courts. Boys were bound until the age of 21 and girls till 18 "or until married," as was sometimes specified in the court's order. (Early marriages were the rule, rather than the exception, in colonial America.)

Orphan children as young as five or six were bound out in this way. In their new homes they were expected to work as much as they could, for their keep and without money wages. At the end of their service they received their "freedom dues"—a new suit of clothes and sometimes some tools or a cow, depending on the terms of the contract under which they were bound. We read in the Kent County records of 1702 that Anne Baxter, an orphan girl aged 13, was bound in the usual way by the court to Michael Lober, who immediately sold her services to Tunis Tobias for 46 shillings. The court then ordered Lober to buy a heifer with the money, which, "with her increase, is to be for the use of the said Anne Baxter."

In binding children out the courts were following the laws and customs of the English apprenticeship system, with which they were familiar. The purpose of the courts was to find homes for children who would otherwise have been homeless. This could be done without any cost to the taxpayer, because labor, even the labor of children, was in such great demand. Families could always be found who were willing to go to the trouble and expense of caring for homeless children in return for the work that they could do. These children were under the control of their new masters and mistresses in the same way that they had been under their parents. At the same time, they were also wards of the state, and the court might intervene to protect them from mistreatment when necessary. In 1676 the New Castle court put out a motherless girl for three years, "provided the child have good usage, so that no complaints be made, which if so the maid to be taken from them."

The 18th-century emigration from Europe brought thousands of new settlers to Delaware. Many of them were too poor to pay for their own passage, and came C.O.D., so to speak. When they arrived in America, usually at Philadelphia or New Castle, the ship captain who brought them sold them to anyone who would pay for their passage. Adults usually sold for four or five years' service. The contract which the passenger signed before leaving Europe, permitting his sale by the captain in America, was called an indenture, and hence the servant was called an indentured or indented servant.

It was said of Pennsylvania (1756) that "every kind of business here, as well among the tradesmen and mechanics as the planters and farmers, is chiefly carried on and supported by the labor of indented servants." This was equally true of Delaware and other colonies. There was a constant demand for these servants, and their transportation from Europe became a profitable business for shipowners. Ships would bring a cargo of immigrants from London or Bristol or Rotterdam to America, and then load up with tobacco and other American products for the return voyage.

The trade in servants was well organized. Agents of the shipowners went through the countryside and the cities, telling about the charms of life in the new world to anyone who would listen, and signing up anyone who could be persuaded to go. In the earlier years of the trade, people were actually kidnapped, as in the case of Charles Springer mentioned above. But the English government cracked down on such practices, to prevent unwary persons from being brought to America against their will.

Although many kinds of people came to America c.o.d., they were in general of two sorts. There were many, such as the Scotch-Irish, who found it impossible, no matter how hard they worked, to make a decent living where they were, and were willing and expected to undergo hardships in getting started in a new life on this side of the ocean. These people often came in families, and sometimes were able to pay part of their passage money.

But there were many others who were misfits at home and continued to be in America. Emigrant agents were not particular about the character of the people they enlisted, or the likelihood of their succeeding in the New World. The agents made as much profit from a vagabond picked up in the streets of London as from the most industrious and deserving poor. And as for the poor, even the trustees of the new colony of Georgia, which was founded in 1732 as a refuge for poor debtors, had to admit that "many of the poor who were useless in England were inclined to be useless likewise in Georgia."

Probably the vast majority of indentured servants worked out their terms or died during their service without leaving any trace on the pages of history. But some ran away from their masters and were advertised in the newspapers. If they were captured they were brought before the local court, which added to their time of service, as compensation to their masters for the time they were absent and for the expense of pursuing and bringing them back. In this way a runaway gone only a few weeks might have to serve as much as a year extra for his misconduct.

Many young servants came to America without indentures. In such cases the masters who bought them had to bring them before the county court, which decided how old they were and how long they should serve. All we know about most of them is in these matter-of-fact court minutes; but if we could go behind these brief records, we should find a human interest story in every one of them. One wonders about two boys named Nathaniel Linton and James Martin, whose master brought them before the Kent County court in 1700. The court judged both of them to be 17 years old and ordered each to serve his master a full five years, and at the end of that time to receive "his corn, clothes, and tools according to law."

And that is all we know for sure about these two boys. Why had they come to America? We do not know. Were they buddies in England? Were they poor and unhappy at home? Did they meet some emigrant agent and sign up for America on the spur of the moment? Did their Kent County master treat them harshly or well? How did they get along in Delaware? What happened to them finally? The record is silent on all these questions about Nathaniel and James.

One poor boy who made a name for himself in America was Charles Thomson, secretary of the Continental Congress during the Revolutionary War, who came from Ulster when he was ten years old. After their mother died Charles's father decided to bring his six children to Pennsylvania. The father was sick during the voyage, and as they were nearing the entrance to Delaware Bay he died and was buried at sea. Charles never forgot his father's dying prayer: "God take them up." After stealing their father's money the ship captain set the children ashore at New Castle, penniless and without friends or relations in a strange land.

According to local tradition, Charles lived for a while with the family of a blacksmith in New Castle. When he learned that they were thinking of having him indentured as an apprentice, Charles ran away one night. The next day as he trudged along the road, not knowing where he was going, he was overtaken by a traveling lady of the neighborhood. As they went along, talking together, she asked him what he would like to be in future life. He said that he would like to be a scholar. This interested her so much that she took the boy home with her and arranged to send him to school.

Charles went to Francis Alison's new school at New London. He must have done well in school, for at the age of 21, he became the first tutor in Latin and Greek at the new Academy of Philadelphia. Later he went into business and was very successful. After the Revolution he turned to his classical studies again and worked for 20 years on a new translation of the Bible from the Greek into English. Published in 1808, Thomson's Bible is now a rare work, but can be found in some old libraries.

Chapter 9  Negro
Slavery

In addition to white servants, another important addition to the colonial labor supply was Negro slaves. We think of slavery as belonging only to the south, but it existed in all the colonies until after the Revolution. The advantage of slavery was, as William Penn remarked, that slaves were held for life, instead of only a few years, as in the case of white servants. He might well have said forever, because, according to the code of laws which developed in 17th-century America, the children of slave mothers were also considered slaves. Under these laws the slave had no hope for the future; he and his children and his children's children would always be slaves.

For the farmer the disadvantage of Negro slavery was its cost. He had to pay several times as much for a slave as for a white servant, and only the wealthier farmers could afford this outlay of money. Likewise, only those in the higher income brackets could afford to have slaves as house servants. At first slaves were few in Delaware, but as population and wealth increased in the 18th century the number of Negroes increased, too.

The black man has been in Delaware almost as long as the white man. The first Swedish settlers arrived in the spring of 1638, and the first Negro early in 1639. He was an Angolan purchased in the West Indies during a voyage there by the Swedish ship *Grip*. He is called "Black Anthony" in the company's records. So far as is known, Anthony was the only slave brought in by the Swedes, and he may have become a freeman before the end of Swedish rule.

The first Negro slaves arrived in Delaware in 1639

The Dutch West India Company was actively engaged in the African slave trade, and it brought a considerable number of Negroes into New Netherland to labor for the company. After some years some of them were set free "on account of their long service," although their children remained slaves, according to a critic of the government who claimed that it was "contrary to all public law, that any one born of a free Christian mother should be a slave." After the Dutch took over in New Sweden the company imported slaves there too. They were seized later by the English, along with cattle and other property of the government. Under the duke of York's rule slaves were few in Delaware and the Swedes had none at all. But in the 18th century as slavery spread in Maryland and Virginia, it increased in Delaware, too. By 1790, when the first national census was taken, over one-fifth of Delaware's people were Negroes. About 30 percent of them were free.

As we have seen, the trade in white servants was big business for shipowners; and so was the slave trade. Even before the discovery of America, blacks were kidnaped on the west coast of Africa and sold as slaves in Portugal and Spain. Slaves were taken to the Spanish islands in the Caribbean from the early 16th century on, and for the next three centuries thousands were imported into America each year. At first the English colonies on the mainland bought their slaves in the islands, but later they began to bring Negroes directly from Africa. The Royal African Company was organized in England, with the duke of York as one of the stockholders, to engage in the slave trade.

As in the transportation of white servants, the slave ships were overcrowded. But health conditions were even worse, and many of the unwilling passengers died on the voyage. In the African slave trade the ships took cloth, bar iron, and other trade goods (including rum) to various places along the west coast, where native chiefs had collected large numbers of their fellow Africans, captured in raids on other tribes or villages. These prisoners were exchanged for the slaver's trade goods, and the ships could take on their human cargoes quickly, without going to the trouble of sending raiding parties into the interior.

We know even less about the slaves as individuals than about the white servants. It is true that Negroes were sometimes slaves in the land of their birth, but the kind of household slavery they endured in Africa was less severe than the plantation slavery of America. In Delaware there undoubtedly were cruel masters as well as kind masters, as in the other colonies; but Delaware did not have the large plantations found farther south, which were worked by gangs of slaves managed by a hired overseer whose only object was to get as much work as he could from the Negroes under him.

In the earlier years there was a tendency on the part of some slaveowners to treat their Negroes like any other human beings. An unusual example of this is the case of Sherey and Freegift Wansey, slaves belonging to an Englishman in Maryland named Joseph Sone. In 1674, being about to sail for England, Sone made a will providing that, in case of his death before he should return, his two Negroes should be free, "they and their heirs forever." The will also left to Sherey the 200-acre farm on which Sone was then living, his cattle, and his personal property. All this was to go to Sherey, "unto him and his heirs forever," and he was made executor of his master's will. Apparently Joseph Sone did die, for eight years later Sherey Wansey had the will recorded in Kent County, Delaware, along with a certificate stating that he was a "free man of our County of Dorchester," Maryland.

When an African was sold as a slave in America, there was hardly any chance of his ever getting back to his native land. One of the few exceptions was Job ben Soloman, whose story has a happy ending. Job was the son of the high priest of Bondu, a devout Mohammedan, and well trained in the Arabic language. In 1730 Job's father sent him to sell two slaves to an English sea captain then in the Gambia River, in exchange for paper and other necessaries. But unluckily Job and his companion were captured by an unfriendly African tribe and sold to this same captain, who took them to America with the rest of his slave cargo.

Job was sold to a tobacco planter on Kent Island on the Eastern Shore of Maryland. Unhappy with his situation and still unable to speak much English, Job left his master and made his way through the woods into Kent County, Delaware, where he was picked up as a runaway and held in the county jail in Dover. An Englishman named Thomas Bluett, who happened to be attending court at the time, perceiving that Job was "no common slave," came to his aid. The English philanthropist, James Oglethorpe, had him sent to England. There he was entertained by the English nobility and presented to the king and queen. Bluett wrote a book about Job—which is why we know so much about him. Valuable gifts were showered upon him, and he finally went back to his native country on a ship of the Royal African Company and lived happily ever afterwards.

At first Negroes in Delaware were subject to the same legal regulations as white servants, and the law made no distinction between black and white, even though the courts in their decisions sometimes did. But at the end of the 17th century the Delaware legislature began to enact a long series of laws limiting the Negroes' "civil rights," as we call them today. Some of these repressive laws remained in force until only a few years ago, when they were overthrown by decisions of the United States Supreme Court and by civil rights legislation enacted by Congress. In passing these harsh laws Delaware's legislature was not doing anything new. It was merely imitating the "black codes" of other colonies where slavery had already become a problem.

The first of these Delaware laws was an act for the trial of Negroes, passed in 1700. This law provided that, instead of being tried by a jury in the regular courts, Negroes accused of murder and other "high and heinous offences" were henceforth to be tried by two justices of the peace, together with six of "the most substantial freeholders of the neighborhood." Persons convicted in these special courts were to be executed by the sheriff of the county in which the crime was committed.

This was a quick and cheap way of trying slaves accused of crimes. The law was changed later to apply only to Negro or mulatto *slaves,* and also to pay the owners of slaves who might be executed under its operation, two-thirds of their value, the money to come from the county treasury. The law was thus greatly to the advantage of slaveowners, and it was they no doubt who persuaded the legislature to pass it.

The act of 1700 also prohibited Negroes (later only Negro slaves) from carrying weapons of any kind, and from meeting together in any number above six, "upon no lawful business of their masters or owners." These restrictions were imposed because of the constant fear of slave revolts. So far as is known no slave uprising ever occurred in Delaware, but jittery masters were always afraid that one might.

As the number of slaves grew, the number of free Negroes did also. To the slaveholders the presence of so many free Negroes was a nuisance. A law enacted in 1740 said: "It is found by experience that free Negroes and mulattoes are idle and slothful, and often prove burdensome to the neighborhood wherein they live, and are of evil example to slaves." This law required owners of slaves who wished to set them free, to be responsible for their support in case they became ill or otherwise unable to support themselves. The law also provided that children of free Negroes whose parents could not support them should be bound out to service, whether the parents wished it or not.

It is not until late in the colonial period that we find any Delaware laws for the protection of the colored population, slave or free. The first such law was passed in 1760, and it concerned the illegitimate children of white mothers and Negro or mulatto fathers. By an earlier law such children were to be put out to servitude until they reached the age of 31. The act of 1760 begins thus:

> Whereas the children of white women by Negro or mulatto fathers and their descendants, entitled to their freedom, are frequently held as servants or slaves by people pretending to be their masters or mistresses, and frequently are sold by them to persons who reside in other governments, to prevent their procuring proof of their being entitled to their freedom . . .

The act then imposed a fine of £100 (a large amount in those days) on such masters or mistresses and made it easier for the courts to proceed against them.

By this time the Quakers were beginning to come out strongly against the whole institution of slavery, as did other humane people, and henceforth the Negro was never without a friend at court. Warner Mifflin, a Quaker of Kent County, tells in his memoirs how he became an opponent of slavery. When he was a boy of 14 on his father's farm in Virginia, he was in the field one day with his father's slaves. A young man among them asked Warner if he thought it could be right that they should be toiling to raise him and send him to school, and that by and by their children would have to do the same for his children. This, said Warner, annoyed him at first, but as he thought about it he became convinced that the young slave was right; and Warner resolved "never to be a slave-holder" when he grew up. However, it took him a long time to become reconciled to the loss of so much property. But he finally did, and freed his wife's slaves and then those of his mother and father who had voluntarily come to live with him. Later Mifflin's father freed his slaves too, about a hundred of them.

The early Methodists also preached against slavery and worked to bring religion to Negroes as well as whites. Richard Allen, founder and first bishop of the African Methodist Episcopal Church, grew up as a slave on a farm near Dover. His master (a man named Stokeley), was a humane man, says Allen in his autobiography, "more like a father to his slaves than anything else." They were encouraged to go to the Methodist meetings, and Richard was converted, as were his brother, sister, and mother. When the neighbors predicted that "Stokeley's Negroes would soon ruin him," Richard and his brother resolved to work night and day, if need be, "to get our crops forward, so that it might not be said that religion made us worse servants." The master, though unconverted, allowed Richard to bring Methodist preachers to the house. After being exposed for several months to Methodist prayers and preaching, particularly a sermon by the noted Freeborn Garretson, the Allens' master became convinced that it was wrong to hold slaves.

Richard Allen was the founder and first bishop of the African Methodist Episcopal Church

Since Stokeley was much in debt, and realized that after his death his slaves would probably be sold, he proposed to Richard and his brother that they buy their freedom from him. This they agreed to do, for £60. Richard then started out in the world, working at any job he could find to support himself and pay his debt to his former owner. This was during the Revolutionary War, when salt was in great demand, and he got a regular job hauling salt by wagon up state from Rehoboth in Sussex County. He had, he says, "regular stops and preaching places on the road, and enjoyed many happy seasons in meditation and prayer while in this employment." After the war he located in Wilmington and then went to other nearby states, working for his living and preaching in his spare time. He is remembered as one of the great Methodist preachers of his generation.

The emancipation movement was getting under way in Delaware on the eve of the Revolution, and it was helped by the Declaration of Independence of 1776, which said that "all men are created equal." Slaveholding declined rapidly in the 19th century, until by 1860 less than one-tenth of Delaware's colored people were still slaves, most of them in Sussex County. But slavery was not entirely done away with in Delaware until the Thirteenth Amendment (which Delaware opposed) abolished it throughout the United States.

Chapter 10 Government

The trend in modern times is to call upon the government to do more and more things for us. Providing schools is a good example. A bigger slice of Delaware's tax dollar now goes for education than for anything else, but in the colonial period the government spent nothing at all on schools. People provided their own schools, when they had any. The movement for free, tax-supported schools does not begin in Delaware until after the Revolution.

The colony of New Sweden, as we have seen, was founded and ruled by a trading company. The governor was appointed by the company and was responsible to it, but not to the people under him. According to Governor Printz's instructions he was to rule in the name of the queen and was given full powers. He was to decide disputes "according to Swedish law and custom." He could punish wrongdoers by imprisonment and even by death if deserved—"yet only after a careful hearing of the case, with the foremost and the

Johan Printz, first governor of New Sweden, ruled in the name of the crown and had full powers

most prudent associate judges for assistance and counsel."

Although he was subject to his superiors at home, Printz's authority in the colony was practically absolute, as perhaps it needed to be in a new country, 3000 miles from home, and settled by people whose reason for being there was, in many cases, that they had been law breakers in the mother country. Printz was a man of military habits and violent temper. His rule probably was harsh and tyrannical, as the settlers charged. But he was in a difficult position, and a governor of less force of character might not have been able to bring the colony through, as Printz did.

The period of Swedish rule lasted from 1638 to 1655, and was followed by nine years under Dutch control, 1655–64. New Sweden became part of the Dutch colony of New Netherland, which was the property of the Dutch West India Company and was governed by a "director" appointed by and responsible to the company. Director Peter Stuyvesant appointed a vice director for the Delaware River settlements, who, with a council of two civilians and two military officers, was to keep order and "administer law and justice to citizens as well as soldiers."

Vice Director Jean Paul Jacquet and his council sometimes called upon the inhabitants for help in deciding
matters of general interest. In November 1656 the whole
community was called together at Fort Casimir, where they
nominated four persons, from whom the vice director would
choose two to act as tobacco inspectors for the colony. At
the same time two overseers of fences were nominated. This
is, so far as we know, the first popular election ever held
in Delaware.

Further progress toward popular government came with
the cession of part and later all of the colony to the city of
Amsterdam. In order to attract colonists, the city promised
to set up a government like that which was then in use for
Dutch towns and cities. Government in the city's colony
was to be by a "schout" or "head of justice," to be appointed
by the director at New Amsterdam; three burgomasters, to
be elected by the townspeople from among the "honestest,
fittest, and richest" of the inhabitants; and five or seven
"schepens" or magistrates, to be chosen by the director from
a double number nominated by the people. Such a government was set up in New Amstel in 1657, but little is known
about it because its records have not survived. Further concessions were offered by the city, but they came to naught
with the conquest of all New Netherland by the English in
1664.

Under the duke of York's rule on the Delaware, popular
participation in government ceased. The local magistrates
were continued in office, but by the authority of the duke's
governor in New York, rather than by popular election.
From 1664 to 1682 he appointed the county court justices,
who in turn decided local matters and chose local officials.
Further progress toward self-government was delayed until
William Penn took over.

During most of these first 45 years, therefore, Delaware
was ruled by dictators—by a succession of governors, Swed-

ish, Dutch, and English, who were responsible only to their superiors on the other side of the ocean. The people had no control over them. Their government, however, was less despotic in practice than in theory. In one way or another the people made their wishes known, whether they participated officially in the government or not. In a new country where land was plentiful and settlers were scarce, when governors became too despotic their dissatisfied subjects could easily move into nearby Maryland. Thus in 1660 an angry settler bluntly asked Vice Director William Beeckman "whether he and the other freemen were to be treated forever as boys." They would not always be "ruled by such clowns." Things would have to be different, he said, if he were to stay here any longer.

Representative self-government—that is, government of the people by their elected representatives—was brought to the Delaware valley by the great Quaker liberal, William Penn, when he became proprietor, first of Pennsylvania and then of Delaware too. "You shall be governed by laws of your own making," he assured the people of Pennsylvania in 1681. And when Delaware was added to his original

William Penn was proprietor first of Pennsylvania and then of Delaware

grant, its inhabitants were invited to join in the government he had planned for Pennsylvania. In it he as proprietor would share the power of making laws with an elected assembly having an equal number of representatives from each of the three Delaware counties (New Castle, Kent, and Sussex) and the three counties into which the new province of Pennsylvania was divided.

Delaware accepted Penn's offer, and an assembly was elected representing the combined "Province and Territories" of Pennsylvania. It met regularly from 1682 to 1701, at either Philadelphia or New Castle, and passed laws for both Pennsylvania and Delaware. During this time the membership of the assembly was equally divided between the Pennsylvania and the Delaware counties, and so neither could outvote the other. But the new city of Philadelphia was growing rapidly in population and demanded more members in the assembly. This would have upset the balance in favor of Pennsylvania.

Rather than become a minority, the Delaware counties seceded, and were allowed by Penn to have a legislature of their own, separate from Pennsylvania. This they did, and from 1704 to 1776 Delaware and Pennsylvania each had its own assembly, elected by the people. But they had the same governor, appointed by the proprietor, who had a veto on legislation—that is, it could not become law without his approval. The Delaware counties never seem to have adopted a name. They called themselves "the Government of the Counties of New Castle, Kent, and Sussex upon Delaware," and were commonly referred to as "the Lower Counties."

Because of their veto power the Penn proprietors, through their governors, had as much to say about making the laws as the people did through their elected representatives. Delaware seems to have gotten along quite well with its various governors. The governor usually lived in Philadelphia and came to New Castle when the assembly was in session. It met regularly in October of each year for a week or ten days, sometimes longer. Often there was another session in the spring. The assembly always put off voting the governor his salary until the end of the session. In 1762 the assembly was so pleased with the governor "for his great readiness in passing all such bills as were presented to him" that they gave him an extra £50 in addition to his usual £200 salary. Holding back on the governor's salary was a regular practice in other colonies too, and sometimes, when an assembly was at odds with its governor, it granted him no salary at all and held up other grants of money which he asked for to carry on the government. The assemblies' control of the purse strings thus enabled them to bend the governors to their will.

An important power which Penn reserved to himself was the appointment of certain government officials. The proprietor or his deputy governor appointed and commissioned justices and judges, surveyors, registers and recorders, and other officers in positions of trust or profit. He allowed the voters of each county to nominate a double number of candidates for county sheriff and county coroner each year, from whom he chose one for each office. Such officers naturally tended to support the proprietary interest in the contests which arose from time to time between the proprietors and the popularly elected assembly. We have the same sort of party rivalry in our government today. When a Republican governor displaces a Democratic governor he tends to put Republicans in office instead of Democrats, and vice versa.

The colonial legislative assembly was elected by the people, but not all the people could vote. One had to be 21 or older—a restriction which we still have. More important, the voter had to own at least 50 acres of land, 12 of which must be "cleared and improved," or otherwise to own

property of some kind to the value of £40. This requirement excluded indentured servants and slaves, since they
had little or no property. In the early years, when land was
plentiful, almost any free man of average industry and ability could, with a few years labor, acquire a farm big enough
to qualify him as a voter. But this became more difficult as
time went on and unoccupied land became scarcer.

We do not know how many free Negroes in colonial Delaware had enough property to qualify as voters, and whether
any of them voted at elections. After the Revolution Negroes were barred by law from voting and even from being
near the polling places on election day. The Delaware constitution of 1792 removed the property qualification but at
the same time limited the vote to free white men, thus
excluding both Negroes and women. So far as is known,
women neither voted nor wanted to vote in these early
times. The movement for "women's rights" was still to
come.

People who were entitled to vote but neglected to do so
without good reason were subject to a fine of 20 shillings.
There is no evidence that this law was enforced very strictly,
but it shows our ancestors' attitude toward voting. To them,
the vote was not the right of all citizens, to use or not as they
chose. It was a privilege limited to those who had "a stake
in the country," and it was the duty of all who had this
privilege to exercise it.

We should note also that for most people voting was a
much bigger chore in colonial days than it is now. The
present-day voter can stop at his polling place and vote in a
few minutes, on his way to or from work. But then all voting
was done at the county town of each county. Unless the voter
lived right in New Castle or Dover or Lewes, it might take
him all day to ride or walk five or ten miles or more into
town, cast his vote, and get back home again.

There was a great deal of "politicking" in the annual elections for representatives, sheriffs, and coroners. The highly organized political parties of today were still to come. Candidates aligned themselves with either the "court" party, which represented the aristocracy, or the "country" party, which was (or at least sounded) more democratic; but it was mostly a contest between the "ins" and the "outs."

In addition to the usual political speeches, candidates made an alcoholic appeal to the voters. According to the Anglican clergyman in Dover, writing in 1762, "to ingratiate themselves with the people, the candidates appointed places where they invited the inhabitants to treat them with liquor. These meetings were held once a week for near two months before election day, and he was best liked who gave the most liberal treat." By these means, the minister complained, "the people's morals were entirely debauched." In spite of disapproving frowns from some quarters, such political treats, as they were called, continued for a long time. But they are now a thing of the past, and we even have a law which requires bars and liquor stores to be closed on election day.

The county courts were the first and they remained the most important agency of government in colonial Delaware. They were the part of government with which everybody was familiar. Most people seldom if ever even saw the governor. Few had any reason to attend the brief sessions of the legislative assembly at New Castle. But everybody was interested in what went on at the sessions of their county court, and the quarterly "court day" drew crowds of people. Some of them were plaintiffs or defendants or witnesses in cases. Others were serving on juries or in some other official capacity. Still others were merely spectators who had taken a day off to come to town and see the show. They could greet old friends and acquaintances while watching the county VIP's in action.

The county justices of the peace, acting together, were

the county court. The number of justices varied. Twelve were appointed by the governor on the Kent County commission in 1705. Perhaps half of them, on the average, were in attendance at any one session of court. The county sheriff, who, as we have seen, was elected by popular vote, was the executive officer of the county. He was responsible for getting men to serve on the grand and petty juries and for carrying out various orders of the court. At first he collected the county taxes. Prisoners and others bound over to appear at court were in his custody. He was in charge of the county's jail, when there was one. The counties were slow about building jails and court houses (usually one building) and in the meantime the courts met in some tavern and the sheriff had to do the best he could about the safe keeping of persons for whom he was responsible.

There were also officers called constables, who were appointed annually by the court, one for each hundred. They served writs and summonses and carried out other orders of the court. Being a constable was a thankless job Rarely was a constable willing to serve longer than the year for which he was appointed. Like justices, constables were officers of the peace—that is, they were sworn to keep the king's peace and to proceed against those who violated it

Most of the court's time was spent in the trial of cases. The majority of these were civil suits, in which one person brought an action against another for the payment of a debt, for trespass on his land, for misappropriating his cattle or hogs, and so on. There were also criminal cases, which, because they were considered to be breaches of the king's peace, were prosecuted by the king's attorney. Capital crimes were tried by higher courts (except those by slaves, as mentioned earlier). Lesser offenses came within the view of the county justices. Drunkenness and profanity (which often went together) were punishable by a small fine or being set in the stocks for a couple of hours.

Constables were appointed by the court and were sworn to keep the peace

Petty thievery was usually punished by fine or whipping. Horse stealing was more serious, but as common in those days, probably, as car stealing is today. Horse stealing was a problem which our colonial lawmakers were never able to solve. In 1742 they tried making it a capital offense. But it was found that this harsh penalty did not deter the would-be thief, and made juries less willing to convict him. The result was that guilty persons were sometimes acquitted and thus escaped punishment entirely. During the Revolution the capital penalty was abolished, and instead the horse thief was to be whipped with 39 lashes, to stand in the pillory for one hour, and to have part of one ear cut off.

(This change, it was found, was no more effective in doing away with horse stealing than the previous laws had been.)

In addition to its judicial business the county court had important administrative duties. It appointed overseers of the highways, whose job it was to keep roads and bridges in repair and lay out new ones as required by the court. The overseers called upon the people of the neighborhood to work on the roads as needed, and persons who did not respond to this call of duty were liable to be fined by the court for their neglect.

The court also appointed overseers of the poor. The poor were few in number at first, and were helped as needed. Thus in 1701 the Kent County court ordered that Elizabeth Shurley, "a poor widow, have £8 per annum allowed to her out of the public stock of this county, towards her maintenance for the future." In Sussex County John Johnson, "free Negro aged 80 and poor and past his labor," prayed the court "to take him into the public charity of the county," and the court did so, arranging with a man "to maintain the said John Johnson his lifetime."

As population increased in the 18th century, so did the number of poor who had to be provided for at public expense. Each county tried to prevent persons likely to become public charges from coming into the county to live. Parents and grandparents were required to support children and grandchildren who could not work, and vice versa. Later, recipients of poor relief had to wear a badge with the letter P, calling attention to their poverty.

Each county court levied taxes to meet the cost of running the county government. So far as possible government was made to pay for itself. County officers received no salaries, and were paid by fees collected from the persons involved. Even persons found not guilty of a criminal charge had to pay their fees. Once a year the court held a session with the grand jury and the assessors to calculate the county's expenses and how much tax should be levied for the ensuing year.

Colonial Delaware's county courts were held "by the king's authority and in the proprietary's name." As such, they commanded the respect and obedience of the people under their jurisdiction. The court did not hesitate to crack down on persons who failed to show it the proper respect. When the newly established court of Kent County learned that one Robert Willin had "abused his royal highness's justices of the peace by saying that he did wonder that the Duke of York was such a fool as to make such inconsiderable ———— to be justices," it fined Willin 500 pounds of tobacco and bound him to his good behavior for a year.

About the same time six Kent County men "did in contempt of the court contrary to the obedience and respect due to his majesty's justices in a riotous manner pluck up and bear away the stocks." For this offense the court fined them 500 pounds of tobacco each. The stocks seem to have been a favorite target of attack by persons who wished to express their dissatisfaction with things in general. It was reported to the Sussex County court in 1684 that Robert Johnson boasted that he "had carried away part of the stocks and flung it down the bank, and if he had had his ax there he would have cut down the whipping post too."

Since there was no police force in those days, and no national guard, we may well ask how the orders of the courts were enforced. The answer is that under the English common law sheriffs and constables could call upon anyone in sight for aid in performing their duties, when needed, and such persons were required by law to come to the officer's assistance. The *posse comitatus* ("the power of the county") could be invoked by its officers whenever they needed it. According to tradition, Thomas McKean, one of Delaware's signers of the Declaration of Independence, while holding court one day was disturbed by a noisy mob outside. When he ordered the sheriff to disperse them, the sheriff replied, "I can't do it." "Then summon your *posse*," roared McKean. "I have, and they are useless." "Then, sir, summon me." "I do summon you," said the frightened sheriff. Whereupon the towering McKean rushed out in his judicial robes and seized a couple of rioters by the throat; and the rest of them, overawed by this unexpected addition to the sheriff's *posse*, quickly retired.

Only rarely do we find any reference to a person failing to help the county officers when called upon to do so. An exceptional case was that of William Kanning, who seems to have been something of a wag. When the sheriff called upon him for aid in putting a man in stocks, Kanning refused, "saying if it was to put the sheriff in the stocks, he would help." Kanning's refusal was duly noted in the Sussex County court minutes for 1687; but what, if anything was done about it is not recorded.

Colonial self-government was a success in Delaware, as it was in the other English colonies, for the reasons which have been described. First, the people made their own laws through their elected representatives. Second, the law was administered in each county by its own leading citizens, some of whom were elected by the people themselves. And third, when force was needed to secure obedience to the laws, that force could be provided by the whole body of the county through the *posse comitatus*. In other words, the people not only made but enforced their laws.

Chapter 11

The Coming of the Revolution

The 18th century was a period of steady growth in Delaware. By the outbreak of the Revolution there were about 37,000 people in the three counties. The basic industry was farming. It provided a livelihood not only for the farmer but also for many others in related occupations. There were merchants, large and small, who bought the farmer's products and sold him manufactured goods from England and other articles such as sugar and rum from the West Indian islands. This trade was carried on through the port of Philadelphia and later, to an increasing extent, from the new town of Wilmington.

There were millers everywhere who ground the farmer's grain, but the most important of them were in Wilmington. They built up a big export trade in flour and some of them became quite wealthy. Many of them were Quakers. Since goods were carried by water wherever possible, ships, large and small, were in demand, and shipbuilding flourished in the creeks along the coast, giving employment to ship carpenters and woodsmen who furnished the timber. Young fellows who wanted to see the world could hire out as sailors, and if they stayed in the business might become well-paid captains and mates of ocean-going vessels. For those who stayed on land a profitable occupation was the tanning of leather, which was carried on in places where cattle were plentiful and the bark for tanning was available from nearby forests.

By mid-18th century there were not only more people in Delaware, but more people of wealth and culture—children or grandchildren of the original immigrants. Perhaps the best indication of their increasing prosperity is the houses they built for themselves. In the 17th century the typical dwelling house was made of wood. In the 18th more people, even the Swedes, were building of brick or stone. In 1762 a young Quaker from Philadelphia was shocked to find his uncle living "in a lonesome cottage, a small log house that serves for kitchen, parlor, hall, and bed chamber." Such crude log houses have long since disappeared, but many 18th-century brick houses are still to be seen along country roads. The finest dwelling house in colonial Delaware was built at Odessa by William Corbit, a well-to-do tanner. (It is now a museum.)

By the time of the Revolution Delaware and the other English colonies had come of age, had grown up. Together they contained between two and three million people—an impressive number, considering that the population of England itself at this time was only six or seven millions. The second-largest city in the whole British Empire was Philadelphia; and while it was tiny in comparison with London, it was nevertheless larger than any other English city. Delaware people had close connections with Philadelphia, with

The William Corbit house in Odessa was the finest house in the colony

many family ties and business relationships. There were no newspapers in Delaware until after the Revolution. So Delawareans kept in touch with what was going on, locally and in the rest of the world, by reading the Philadelphia newspapers.

In trying to explain why the Thirteen Colonies broke away from the mother country, we must note first that the English, in common with other peoples, believed that colonies existed primarily for the benefit of the mother country, and only secondarily for their own benefit. The colonies themselves probably never agreed with this theory, but as long as they were small and weak they had to abide by it; and if it were too strictly applied the colonies would not flourish and grow. The English colonies, however, did prosper, and the reason was that the mother country's restrictions on them were not very strictly enforced.

Almost from the beginning England had required her colonies to trade only with her or with each other. Most trade with other countries, Holland, for example, was forbidden. That, as we have seen, was a reason for forcing the Dutch out of North America; it was too easy for the colonies to trade illegally with them where they were. During the 18th century, Britain fought a long series of wars with France, partly because the French in Canada were a menace to the English colonies, threatening them from the north and the interior, into which the French were going by way of the Great Lakes.

In its wars with France the British government called upon the colonies for all the help they could give, in men and supplies. In granting them, the colonies got concessions which would not otherwise have been made. For example, the government was opposed to the colonies issuing paper money. But the various colonies, Delaware included, passed acts authorizing new issues of their paper money, out of which grants were to be made for helping in the current French war. Rather than lose this aid, the British government allowed these paper money bills to go through. The government was scandalized at the way the colonies kept on trading with the French islands when the two countries were at war; but the colonies insisted that without the profits from this trade they could not help with the war. At other times when the navigation laws were too oppressive, the colonists resorted to smuggling. It was said of the Boston merchants that they went to church on Sundays and smuggled the rest of the week.

The land fighting against the French took place on the frontiers of Pennsylvania, far away from Delaware; but on the sea, its whole coast was exposed to attack from French and Spanish warships and privateers. They seldom got very far up the river, but on more than one occasion the town of Lewes on lower Delaware Bay was plundered by enemy vessels. Since Pennsylvania was governed by the Quakers, who were opposed to war, it was left largely to Delaware to protect itself from hostile ships in the bay.

During the War of Jenkins' Ear Delaware raised at least one company, perhaps more, for service against the Spaniards in the West Indies. Militia laws were passed requiring "every freeholder and taxable person" to provide himself with "one well-fixed musket or firelock" with ammunition as a means of defending the colony against foreign attack. In the French and Indian War the legislature appropriated thousands of pounds both for home defense and for taking part in the military expeditions against the French in western Pennsylvania. Part of this cost was later repaid to Delaware by a grant from the British Parliament.

The French and Indian War (or, as it was called in Europe, the Seven Years War) ended in a brilliant victory for the British. By the terms of the Peace of Paris in 1763, France was driven out of North America, ceding to Great Britain all its settlements in Canada and its claims to the interior.

Foreign observers predicted freely that when the French menace was removed, the English colonies in America would cut loose from the mother country, since they no longer needed her protection. That prediction came true, and sooner, perhaps, than most people would have expected.

The long war with France had doubled Britain's national debt. The British farmer's taxes had increased greatly, to pay for a war which had been of little benefit to him. The party in power in Parliament thought that from now on the Americans should help a little, by at least paying part of the cost of governing and protecting them from foreign attack. To that end Parliament passed the Stamp Act, which laid a tax on legal documents of all kinds, on newspapers and pamphlets, and even on playing cards and dice.

The Stamp Act of 1765 raised a storm of protest in the colonies. In October nine of them sent representatives to meet together in New York, to consider what measures to take against this unprecedented attempt to tax them without their consent. Delaware was represented in the Stamp Act Congress by Thomas McKean and Caesar Rodney. Rodney was greatly impressed by the men he met there—"an assembly of the greatest ability I ever yet saw," he called it.

Another Delawarean attended the Stamp Act Congress, John Dickinson, who was serving as a delegate from Pennsylvania. Dickinson is often called "the penman of the Revolution," since he played a leading part in opposing, by his writings, the attempts by Parliament to tax the colonies He drew up the resolutions which were adopted by the Stamp Act Congress. Later he published a series of articles in a Philadelphia newspaper called "Letters from a Farmer in Pennsylvania," opposing the British policy toward the

Thomas McKean was a representative from Delaware at the Stamp Act Congress

colonies. These letters were copied by other newspapers throughout the colonies, and were reprinted in pamphlet form both here and abroad.

John Dickinson is claimed by two states, Pennsylvania and Delaware. He was equally at home in both. (For example, after the Revolution he was elected governor of Delaware, and served in that office until he was chosen governor of Pennsylvania.) Dickinson was born in Maryland but grew up on his father's estate near Dover, Delaware. (The house where he lived has been restored and may be visited by the public.) Dickinson was taught at home by a young Scotch-Irish tutor named William Killen, who later became chief justice of Delaware. Dickinson then studied law, first in Philadelphia and later at the Inns of Court in London, and became a successful lawyer in Philadelphia. His later life was spent in Delaware, and he died and was buried in Wilmington in 1808.

Dickinson's resolutions, as adopted by the Stamp Act Congress in 1765, declared that the king's subjects in the colonies were entitled to all the "rights and liberties" of his subjects in Great Britain; that it is "the undoubted right of Englishmen that no taxes be imposed on them but with their own consent, given personally or by their representatives;" that the colonies "are not, and from their local circumstances cannot be represented" in Parliament; "that the only representatives of the people of these colonies are persons chosen therein by themselves, and that no taxes ever have been or can be constitutionally imposed on them, but by their respective legislatures."

At the next meeting of the Delaware legislature, in May 1766, McKean and Rodney reported on their attendance at the Stamp Act Congress. They were warmly received and were paid handsomely for their "trouble and expense." The assembly adopted some resolutions relating to the "liberties and privileges of the inhabitants of this government" and appointed a committee of correspondence to keep in touch with the other colonies. By this time the odious stamp tax had been repealed by Parliament, and, on McKean's motion, the assembly sent an address of thanks to the king. It was couched in the most flattering terms, and ended with their "prayers to Heaven, long to preserve your sacred person a blessing to all your subjects." The assembly was informed later that "the king was so pleased with it that he read it over twice."

In their joy over the repeal of the Stamp Act, the colonies conveniently ignored the "declaratory act" which accompanied it. This act stated that the colonies are and ought to be "subordinate unto and dependent on the Crown and Parliament of Great Britain" and that Parliament had full power to make laws binding on the colonies "in all cases whatsoever." Most Englishmen believed in the doctrine of "the supremacy of Parliament," as it was called. Even the friends of the colonies thought that Parliament could tax the colonies if it chose, though it would be bad policy to do so.

In the following year, 1767, Parliament made another attempt to tax the colonies, with duties on glass, paper, painter's colors, and tea imported into the colonies. These were an "external" tax, in contrast to the stamp tax to which the colonies had objected, which was an "internal" tax. It was at this time that Dickinson published his Farmer's Letters, objecting to any kind of tax at all. The colonies brought pressure to bear on Parliament by agreeing among themselves not to import their usual goods from English merchants. The merchants then complained to Parliament about their loss of business. So in 1770 the duties were repealed, all except the tax on tea.

Arrangements were then made to sell the tea at a lower

John Dickinson published Letters from a Farmer *in which he objected to all forms of taxation*

price, even with the tax included, than people in England had to pay for it. This was denounced in the colonies as a trick, to get bargain-hunting Americans to submit to taxation by Parliament. But the plan did not work. In Philadelphia a "Committee of Tarring and Feathering" warned the Delaware pilots in advance not to guide the tea ship up the Delaware. When it arrived in December 1773 it followed another vessel up to Philadelphia. There it was turned back by a crowd of 8000 people and the tea was never landed. The people of Boston went even further. On the night of December 16 a band of men disguised as Indians boarded the tea ships and dumped the tea into the Boston harbor.

The Boston Tea Party was an act of vandalism in open defiance of Parliament. The government could not let it pass unchallenged. Parliament therefore ordered the port of Boston to be closed until the tea was paid for, thus throw-

ing many townspeople out of work. It also suspended the
Massachusetts legislature (as it had already done in New
York), prohibited town meetings, and put the colony under
the control of the governor. There were already British
troops stationed in Boston upon whom he could call for help
if needed.

These measures, commonly called "the Intolerable Acts,"
aroused great excitement throughout the colonies. In Delaware money was collected for the relief of the suffering
people of Boston. "We consider each colony on this continent as a part of the same body," said the Delaware committee of correspondence. An attack on one would affect all.
If Boston were forced to submit, the other colonies, one by
one, would suffer the same fate, and "there would be an end
of American freedom for a century at least."

In August 1774 a convention of members of the Delaware assembly elected Caesar Rodney, Thomas McKean,
and George Read as delegates to the First Continental Congress in Philadelphia and gave them a set of resolutions to
present to that body, declaring their allegiance to the king,
but also their "fixed and unalterable resolution" to maintain their liberties. And they urged sending "decent and
becoming" petitions to the king and Parliament for the re-
dress of their grievances.

In the spring of 1775 fighting began at Lexington and
Concord and Bunker Hill. King George would receive no
more petitions from his rebellious subjects. Instead he prepared to send more troops, including hired Hessian soldiers,
to America, and called upon his "obedient and loyal subjects to withstand and suppress such rebellion."

Up to this point the contest between the American colo-
nies and the British government had been a battle of words.
The Americans acknowledged all *due* subordination to the
Crown and Parliament, but they stood on their rights as

George Read, one of the three delegates from Delaware to the First Continental Congress

Englishmen, which included the right not to be taxed without their consent—"no taxation without representation." The British ministry even offered the colonies representation in Parliament, if that was what they wanted. But the colonies did not want it, for they would have been in a minority. Nor, probably, did the home government especially desire it, for, with the rapid growth of the colonies, it was obvious that before long they would have had a majority in Parliament. At any rate, representation in Parliament, which would have been a sensible solution to the problem, was not seriously considered.

In Delaware and the other middle colonies there was much loyalty to England. Thomas Robinson, the most prominent loyalist in Sussex County, seems to have gone along with the early protests against Parliament's attempts to tax the colonies. But later we find him selling tea in his store, contrary to the boycott which had been proclaimed against it. He told people that the Continental Congress which was now running the country was an illegal body. When summoned to appear before the Sussex County committee of safety, he sent word that he could not think of doing so unless he brought 40 or 50 armed men with him. Later he led a crowd of 1500 Sussex Countians who besieged the garrison at Lewes until militiamen were sent from Philadelphia against them. Robinson and others were arrested but were soon pardoned by the assembly, which was then under the influence of moderates such as George Read. Robinson finally took refuge on a British warship and did not return to Delaware until after the Revolution. His property was seized and sold during his absence.

In Kent County also, by 1775, some people were beginning to have second thoughts about opposing "the vast power of the British nation," and stern measures had to be taken against them by the patriots. Dr. Charles Ridgely of Dover was threatened with tar and feathers. A man who wrote to the Philadelphia newspapers saying that nine out of ten Kent Countians would rally to the king's standard if it were raised, was forced to retract. Another who said that he "had as lief be under a tyrannical king as a tyrannical commonwealth, especially if the d——d Presbyterians had the control of it," was likewise required to eat his words. When a Quaker from Duck Creek refused to accept Continental paper money, he was denounced by the Kent County committee of correspondence. Millers would not grind his grain, shallopmen refused to transport it, and the schoolmaster sent his children home.

Although the Scotch-Irish were found everywhere in Delaware, they were most numerous in New Castle County The great majority of Delaware's people were of English descent, and of the Anglican or Church of England religious faith, and their ministers kept praying for the king as long as they could. The Presbyterian ministers, by contrast, were in the forefront of the revolutionary movement. For example, Rev. Matthew Wilson of Lewes not only preached resistance from the pulpit but helped the tea boycott along by publishing a list of substitutes for tea. Presbyterians and

In CONGRESS, July 4, 1776.

The unanimous Declaration of the thirteen united States of America.

Caesar Rodney, George Read and Thomas McKean signed the Declaration of Independence for Delaware at the bottom of the fourth column

Scotch-Irish are prominent in every phase of the Revolution. On the battlefield there were such men as Colonel John Haslet, Captain Robert Kirkwood, and Colonel Allen Mc-Lane. The first president of the independent state of Delaware was Dr. John McKinly. In the legal profession Thomas McKean and William Killen were outstanding. It is hard to see how the revolutionary movement could have succeeded in Delaware without the strong push given to it by the Scotch-Irish.

It may have been true, as John Adams said, that there were "in this little state more Tories [loyalists] in proportion than in any other." But the logic of events was pushing all the colonies, however unwilling, toward independence. They could give up the struggle, lose the rights for which they had contended, and be punished as rebels and traitors in the bargain; or they could keep on, and, hopefully, get help from Britain's old enemy, France. The colonies by 1776 were listening to Thomas Paine, who said that it was absurd for a continent to be ruled by an island. "To know whether it be the interest of this continent to be independent," he wrote, "we need only ask: Is it the interest of a man to be a boy all his life?"

The radicals in the Second Continental Congress worked hard to line up the various colonies in favor of independence, hoping to get a unanimous vote for it. After weeks of maneuvering, the vote was scheduled for July 2. Of the three delegates from Delaware, Caesar Rodney and Thomas McKean were for independence and George Read was against it. But Rodney had gone home to help put down a Tory uprising in Sussex County, and without his vote the Delaware delegation would be evenly divided. So McKean sent an express to Delaware urging Rodney to hurry back to Philadelphia. Rodney did so, in his famous ride, and arrived in time to swing Delaware's vote in favor of independence. The Declaration of Independence was formally adopted on July 4.

Congress had already, in May, recommended to the colonies to change their governments if needed as a preliminary step toward independence. When this news was received in Dover, Caesar Rodney's brother Thomas happened to be walking "down town" with John Dickinson, just arrived from Congress. Rodney "observed to him many advantages that would follow our assuming government," to which Dickinson agreed, saying "it would not prevent but perhaps promote a more speedy reconciliation." Rodney was less hopeful. "Peace and reconciliation," he said, "will henceforth be my ardent wish, but never to mix our government with Britain's any more."

What neither of them could foresee was that seven years of war lay ahead of them before peace and reconciliation could be achieved.

Americans tend to view their Revolution as a local event, of significance mainly to them. But it was more than that. It was also important to the future of the world, because it divided the English-speaking people. In the next century and a half the United States got along very well as an independent nation, and the British got along very well without the United States. Britannia was able to rule the waves without America's help, down to the World War of 1914–18.

The four exhausting years of that war strained British resources to the breaking point. If the English-speaking British and the English-speaking Americans had still been together, there probably would have been no World War I, or at least it would have been a short one. Without World War I there would have been no World War II and no Russian Communist revolution. The 20th century would undoubtedly have its problems, but they would be different from those we face today.

BIBLIOGRAPHY

EBERLEIN, H. D., and C. V. D. HUBBARD, *Historic Houses and Buildings of Delaware*. Dover: Public Archives Commission, 1962.

ECKMAN, JEANNETTE, ed. *Delaware: a Guide to the First State,* rev. ed. New York: Hastings House, 1955.

————. *New Castle on the Delaware,* rev. ed. New Castle: New Castle Historical Society, 1950.

————. *Crane Hook on the Delaware, 1667–1699*. Newark: University of Delaware Press, 1958.

MUNROE, J. A. *Delaware Becomes a State*. Newark: University of Delaware Press, 1953 (pamphlet).

————. *Federalist Delaware, 1775–1815*. New Brunswick: Rutgers University Press, 1954.

POWELL, J. H. *The House on Jones Neck*. [Dover]: Friends of the John Dickinson Mansion, 1954.

TYLER, D. B. *The Bay & River Delaware: a Pictorial History*. Cambridge, Md.: Cornell Maritime Press, 1955.

WESLAGER, C. A. *A Brief Account of the Indians of Delaware*. Newark: University of Delaware Press, 1953 (pamphlet).

————. *Delaware's Buried Past,* rev. ed. New Brunswick: Rutgers University Press, 1968.

————. *Delaware's Forgotten River: the Story of the Christina.* Wilmington: Hambleton Co., 1947.

————. *Dutch Explorers, Traders and Settlers in the Delaware Valley, 1609–1664.* Philadelphia: University of Pennsylvania Press, 1961.

————. *The English on the Delaware, 1610–1682.* New Brunswick: Rutgers University Press, 1967.

————. *The Log Cabin in America.* New Brunswick: Rutgers University Press, 1969.

IMPORTANT DATES

1609—Henry Hudson anchored in Delaware Bay, but did not enter because of shoals.

1610—Samuel Argall named bay for Thomas West, Lord De La Warr, governor of Virginia.

1631—First settlement by Dutch at Swanendael (Lewes); destroyed by Indians 1632.

1638—March. First permanent settlement by the Swedes at "The Rocks" (Wilmington).

1639—First Negro slave brought to Delaware by Swedes.

1651—Dutch built Fort Casimir (New Castle).

1655—New Sweden conquered by Dutch.

1664—Dutch conquered by English duke of York.

1673—Delaware retaken by Dutch; restored to English 1674.

1682—August. Duke of York granted Delaware to William Penn. December. Delaware joined Pennsylvania in representative government under Penn.

1698–99—Old Swedes church built (Wilmington).

1701—Twelve-mile circle boundary surveyed by Isaac Taylor and Thomas Pierson.

1704—Delaware set up legislature separate from Pennsylvania.

1739—Willingtown granted charter as borough, renamed Wilmington.

1743—Alison's school opened at New London; chartered as Academy of Newark 1769.

1761—First printing press in Delaware set up by James Adams at Wilmington.

1764—Delaware's western boundary line run by Mason and Dixon.

1765—Delaware sent delegates to Stamp Act Congress.

1774—Delaware sent delegates to First Continental Congress.

1776—July 2. Delaware voted for independence.

July 4. Declaration of Independence formally adopted.

September 20. Delaware adopted constitution as independent state.

PLACES TO VISIT

Delaware is a small state. You can drive from one end of it to the other in three hours or less, and across it in half an hour more or less. You are never far from some historic place.

Some of these relating to the colonial period are given below.

WILMINGTON. At the foot of Seventh Street near the mouth of the Christina River is Fort Christina Monument, a little park enclosing "The Rocks," the landing place of the first Swedish settlers in 1638. In it are a monument by Carl Milles, given by the people of Sweden on the three hundredth anniversary of the first settlement, and an old log house moved there from Prices Corner. Adjoining is Old Swedes Church, built 1698–99, still in use. Here also is the Hendrickson House, headquarters of the Delaware Swedish Colonial Society.

The Historical Society of Delaware maintains a library and a museum in the Old Town Hall, Sixth and Market Streets.

On the outskirts of Wilmington are two museums of national importance. Winterthur has over one hundred period rooms containing American furnishings of the eighteenth and nineteenth centuries. Hagley is a museum of early American industry.

NEW CASTLE, colonial capital of Delaware. Dominating the Green is the Old Court House, where the colonial legislature met, restored to its eighteenth-century state. Nearby are Immanuel Episcopal Church, the Old Presbyterian Church (1707, restored), the Old Dutch House and the Amstel House (both small museums), and other colonial and later buildings.

ODESSA, in colonial times called Cantwell's Bridge, was a shipping point on Appoquinimink Creek for a fertile grain-growing area. The Corbit House, 1772, completely restored and now a museum, and the Wilson House, 1740, are outstanding.

DOVER, county seat of Kent County and from 1777 the state capital. On the Green in the middle of town are the Old State House and other old buildings.

The Delaware State Museum occupies three buildings on Governors Avenue. The principal one is the Old Presbyterian Church, in whose yard Colonel John Haslet is buried. In another, a one-room log house, early eighteenth century, has been re-erected.

Caesar Rodney is buried in the churchyard of Christ Church (1734) on South State Street.

Five miles southeast of Dover on Jones Neck is the John Dickinson Mansion, built in 1740 by his father and now restored as a museum.

LEWES, colonial county seat of Sussex County, site of the earliest Dutch settlement at Swanendael. Some of the small houses on Pilot Town Road are very old. Zwaanendael Museum, 1931, is a smaller-scale adaptation of part of the old town hall of Hoorn in Holland. It serves as a regional museum for lower Delaware.

New Castle, Dover, and other towns have a certain day each year on which private residences and other buildings are opened to visitors.

INDEX

THE SCREEN IS RED

THE SCREEN IS

HOLLYWOOD, COMMUNISM, AND THE COLD WAR

RED

BERNARD F. DICK

University Press of Mississippi • Jackson

www.upress.state.ms.us

Designed by Peter D. Halverson

The University Press of Mississippi is a member of the Association of American University Presses.

First printing 2016

∞

Library of Congress Cataloging-in-Publication Data

Dick, Bernard F.
The screen is red : Hollywood, communism, and the Cold War / Bernard F. Dick.
   pages cm
Includes bibliographical references and index.
Includes filmography.
ISBN 978-1-4968-0539-3 (cloth : alk. paper) — ISBN 978-1-4968-0540-9 (ebook)
1. Motion pictures—Political aspects—United States—History—20th century.
2. Motion picture industry—Political aspects—United States—History—20th century. 3. Communism and motion pictures—United States—History. 4. Cold War in motion pictures. I. Title.
   PN1995.9.P6D525 2016
   791.43'6581—dc23

                    2015031977

British Library Cataloging-in-Publication Data available

In Memory of My Stepfather, Wallace A. Burns (1902-70)

CONTENTS

ACKNOWLEDGMENTS

MY PROFOUND THANKS TO NED COMSTOCK, BARBARA HALL, KRISTINE Krueger, MaryAnn Sena, Kathy Stein-Smith, and the staff of the Margaret Herrick Library.

I also wish to express my gratitude to Anthony Greco for supplying me with tapes of hard to obtain films; to Grover Crisp, Vice President, Asset Management & Film Restoration, Sony Pictures Entertainment, for DVDs of Columbia Pictures' Cold War movies; to the two readers who provided fine suggestions and gently called attention to my mistakes; and to my wife, Katherine Restaino, who proofreads with an eye for detail that I wish I had.

Lastly, I want to acknowledge those victims of the blacklist I have been privileged to know and from whom I have learned much: Lester Cole, Louis Harris, Ring Lardner Jr., Sadie Ornitz, and Joan Scott. Marsha Hunt may not know this, but when I was writing *The Star-Spangled Screen: The American World War II Film*, I asked Lou Harris if he could see whether Lester Cole would send me his script of *None Shall Escape*, which starred Marsha Hunt and Alexander Knox. Lester sent me Marsha's script. I now want to repay an old debt to an actress who suffered loss of employment owing to her political convictions.

I used to believe in the adage, "He that loves a book will never want for a faithful friend." I now believe that "He or she who writes books will always need faithful friends."

TEANECK, NJ
MARCH 2015

THE SCREEN IS RED

INTRODUCTION

WHEN I WAS IN THE EIGHTH GRADE, A CLASSMATE INFORMED ME IN ALL seriousness that *Reader's Digest* was communist. If this were a line in a drawing room comedy, the rejoinder would be a jaded "Isn't everything these days?" To me, *Reader's Digest* was another piece of reading material on the table in my dentist's office, together with a pile of other two- and three-month-old magazines patients read while waiting for an appointment that always started late. The early 1950s were a strange and scary time. It seemed as if every day some famous person was outed as a communist, including Lena Horne, Judy Holliday, and even Lucille Ball! The "communist conspiracy" was so pervasive that anyone—your pastor, rabbi, kindergarten teacher—could be a member. As a fan of Larry Parks, whose performance as Al Jolson in *The Jolson Story* (1946) ranks high in the pantheon of historical impersonations, I was crestfallen when I learned in 1951 that he had been a communist. But my loyalty to Parks was strong enough to convince me that there were both good and bad communists, and that a good communist is like a good Catholic. A communist was just baptized into a different faith, learned from a different catechism, and, like good Catholics, believed in love of neighbor, the performance of good works, and equality for all. Or so it seemed to an idealistic adolescent.

I grew up in an Eastern European neighborhood, where my mother and I lived in the home of my maternal grandmother, a Lithuanian immigrant. Next door and across the street were our Russian neighbors. No one ever said "Soviet." When I heard about the "godless" communists—always identified as Russians (China was not part of the equation then, and Korea was a few years away)—I could not believe that my neighbors would ever want to replace our form of government with one based on the Soviet model. As a product of the Great Depression, I started reading about America in the 1930s, learning that socialism was very much a part of the political

3

landscape and, in fact, had been proposed as an alternative to capitalism, which seemed the refuge of the affluent. But fascism seemed equally attractive to those who wanted a dictator as a leader, as if the office of president resulted from poor judgment on the part of the framers of the Constitution. I know now that any study of Hollywood's role in the Cold War must begin in the thirties, during which filmmakers—like many other Americans— did not know what path to pursue and instead portrayed what might happen under either system. Communism was harebrained utopianism. Fascism, however, had a powerful appeal—as Hollywood showed, sometimes frighteningly.

No longer an idealist (Who can be after living through World War II, Korea, McCarthyism, the assassinations of Medgar Evers, John and Robert Kennedy, and Dr. Martin Luther King Jr., Vietnam, and 9/11?), I now feel I can tell the story of the culture that formed a generation's political conscience and fueled its suspicion of a technology capable of world annihilation, as science fiction films of the period imply.

There was a time when Hollywood glorified the former Soviet Union as America's World War II ally. It is impossible to discuss the pro-Soviet movies of World War II without looking at the way Hollywood approached communism during the Great Depression. Unlike domestic fascism, as imagined in *Gabriel over the White House* and *This Day and Age*, communism did not loom large as a threat to American democracy. Communists were vapid young women espousing a cause they imperfectly understood (*Red Salute, Public Deb No. 1*), parasites sponging off the idle rich (*My Man Godfrey*), and radical collegians (*Red Salute*), whose revolutionary rhetoric was loud-mouthed demagoguery. All a female commissar needs is a trip to Paris, champagne, fancy lingerie, and a suave lover to convince her to convert to capitalism (*Ninotchka*), and all it takes to convince a Soviet trolley car conductor (Hedy Lamarr) to defect to the United States is Clark Gable (*Comrade X*).

Hollywood exited the satiric mode after Hitler attacked the Soviet Union in 1941, making Russia a worthy if short-lived ally in the war against fascism. Now Mother Russia was mythologized (*Song of Russia*), and collective farms showed no trace of famine (*The North Star*). Not even Lillian Hellman at her Stalinist best could top *Mission to Moscow* in ennobling of the Soviet Union, one of the most shameless travesties of history ever foisted on moviegoers.

After Sir Winston Churchill delivered his "Iron Curtain" speech in 1946, Hollywood knew its myth-making days were over as far as our erstwhile ally was concerned. The Soviet Union's drive for nuclear parity with the United States spawned a cycle of espionage films, in which Soviet agents and their henchmen replaced the Nazi spies and saboteurs of the 1940s. Hollywood was ambivalent about the bomb. Nuclear power was initially a gift from God that humankind would use for good (*The Beginning or the End*), but it was also a means of instilling fear in moviegoers in a spate of science fiction and doomsday films that dramatized the bomb's repercussions. Atomic testing could create mutants that overran communities, even states. A nuclear war could either leave a quintet of survivors (*Five*) or none at all (*On the Beach*). "Manhattan Project" and "Los Alamos" were shorthand for the source of aberrations such as giant insects or sea creatures. The bomb that ended one war triggered another, unwaged but unnerving.

The Cold War, which precipitated twin assaults on the First Amendment—the House Committee on Un-American Activities (HUAC) and the Army-McCarthy hearings—found its mirror image in Korea, where another undeclared war allowed Hollywood to resurrect the combat film, always a perennial. Even in the 1950s, World War II was recyclable (*Force of Arms, Operation Pacific*), as long as there were stars like William Holden, and John Wayne for marquee appeal.

Korean War movies made no attempt to mythologize a grim and visually bleak affair. The best were filmed in black and white, which suited a terrain as uninviting as the war that had intruded upon it. Hollywood made it clear that Korea was a war against communist aggression. It could not do the same with Vietnam. In Oliver Stone's *Platoon* (1986), Chris (Charlie Sheen) reflects in the end that the men who came to Vietnam to fight the enemy discovered that they were the enemy—and that they were fighting themselves. No character in a World War II or Korean War movie would make such a statement. But then, there could never have been a World War II or Korean War movie like *Casualties of War* (1989), in which an army sergeant in Vietnam orders his men to kidnap a Vietnamese girl for some "R & R."

The implosion of the Soviet Union in 1991 did not mean the end of Cold War films. Young filmmakers, used to unprecedented freedom of expression on social media, will continue to wonder how a nation could have remained so passive while First Amendment rights were being violated and careers were being destroyed. The question may seem naïve when one recalls that in 2014 the world went into shock when more than two hundred girls were kidnapped in Nigeria by Boko Haram, then sold into some form of slavery. The question may also seem naïve in light of the beheading of journalists by the self-proclaimed Islamic State. But the answer is simple: Nations protest, authorize air strikes, and go about their business. Then someone makes a movie or a documentary about the tragedy.

Periodically, filmmakers are inspired to return to the Cold War, which is gradually receding into the mists of Brigadoon. There have been some attempts to recreate the era (*The Front, The House on Carroll Street, Guilty by Suspicion, One of the Hollywood Ten*), but one of the most successful reimaginings has come not from Hollywood but from television: FX's *The Americans*, which features a married couple in a Washington, DC, suburb who speak perfect English but who are really Soviet agents. The Cold War may not be a war for all seasons, but it will always find its season—on either the big or the small screen.

Chapter 1

THE ROAD NOT TAKEN

FEW BUSINESSES ARE AS MUCH A VALIDATION OF CAPITALISM AS THE film industry, created largely by Jewish immigrants and their sons. Moviemaking was the pinnacle of the American Dream, realizable with the right Machiavellian combination of initiative (*virtù*) and luck (*fortuna*). But during the Great Depression—especially in the early and mid-1930s—it seemed that capitalism's potential had been exhausted. There were the one per centers and the rest, the victors and the victims: stars like Claudette Colbert, who could command $50,000 a picture, and the masses that had difficulty shelling out a quarter to see the film. William Manchester began his popular history *The Glory and the Dream* with a bleak picture of 1932, "the cruelest year of the Depression," with its failing banks, burgeoning welfare rolls, foreclosure riots, bootleg coal, shoes with pasteboard soles, wedding rings sacrificed for instant cash, pawned furniture, "payless paydays" for teachers, students suffering from malnutrition, and men riding the rails in search of work. People scavenged for food in refuse dumps and garbage cans, even as farmers killed livestock that could not be sold as meat and dumped milk on the ground rather than sell it at two cents a quart when distributors charged eight.

Racist and anti-Semitic paramilitary groups—the Order of Black Shirts; the Silver Shirts, which emulated Hitler's Brown shirts; and the Khaki Shirts or US Fascists—cast a shadow over the land, as if they were waiting in reserve for a crisis to happen. But the crisis would be a crisis of faith in an economic system that seemed to be working—until the crash. Was fascism the answer? Columbia University president and Nobel Prize winner Nicholas Murray Butler stopped short of saying so, although he extolled totalitarian regimes for producing "men of far greater intelligence, far stronger character, and far more courage than the system of elections." The situation was so extreme that Clare Boothe—before she married Henry Luce and became a well-known playwright, journalist, and ambassador—exclaimed in exasperation, "Appoint a dictator," even though she was hardly a fascist sympathizer. "Happy Days Are Here Again" had upbeat lyrics, but these days were nowhere in sight.

Perhaps a dictatorship—at least a benevolent one—was the solution, or "share the wealth" socialism. Maybe even American-style communism, more red than white and blue. Hollywood would endorse neither fascism nor communism, both of which would have subverted the free enterprise system on which the industry was founded. Still, a wavering faith in democracy was not a topic Hollywood could ignore, any more than it could ignore the disillusionment of the veterans of the Great War. A few films of the 1930s (*Wild Boys of the Road, Dead End, Heroes for Sale*, even *King Kong*, in which out-of-work Fay Wray is discovered by a director as she filches an apple) painted a bleak canvas of the period, a striking contrast to the upbeat WPA murals that were sprouting up in public places. In *I Am a Fugitive from a Chain Gang* (1932), James Allen (Paul Muni), a veteran of the Great War, returns to an indifferent America and an uncertain future. An unwitting participant in a robbery, Allen is sentenced to ten years on a chain gang, from which he escapes. Essentially a decent man wrongly accused of a crime he did not commit, Allen evolves into a model citizen, and he is persuaded to return to the chain gang for nine months, after which he supposedly will be released. But the prison commission refuses to act. Allen, realizing the situation is hopeless, breaks out again, this time embarking upon a life of crime. A man who wanted only to build bridges becomes a criminal because of a corrupt system.

I Am a Fugitive from a Chain Gang is not so much an indictment of the punitive system—with its "concentration-camp atmosphere," which did not need an exposé—as it is a critique of a justice system, which is portrayed as a totalitarian bureaucracy where inmates serve as sport for sadistic wardens and guards. *Road Gang* (1936) went even further in its dramatization of prisoner abuse: Inmates are flogged, electrocuted on high-voltage fences, and sent off to the coalmines. In *I Am a Fugitive from a Chain Gang*, prison is an alternative America, an ever-expanding fascist microcosm.

Allen's plight occasions editorials with accusatory headlines: "Where Is Civilization?" and "States Rights? What Has Become of *Them*?" But even a sympathetic press fails to secure his release. His sentence is a fait accompli. Allen must pay for a crime he did not commit. The moral is simple: Don't be in the wrong place at the wrong time, or you'll end up spending a decade on a chain gang—and you'll be lucky if you're not put in a sweat box. Justice is blindfolded, and her scales are imbalanced.

Heroes for Sale (1933) featured another lost soul abandoned by his country. Thomas Holmes (Richard Barthelmess), a World War I vet whose heroism has gone unrecognized, returns to civilian life, where he is befriended by a luncheonette owner. Holmes is on the road to reintegration when he is accused of instigating a workers' demonstration that has turned violent. He is sentenced to five years in prison. Upon his release, he joins the ranks of the homeless. Even after he comes into some money, he hands it over to the luncheonette owner to feed his own kind, preferring to remain a man without a country and a home. In *I Am a Fugitive from a Chain Gang* and *Heroes for Sale*, the protagonists pay the price for serving in the war to end all wars and making the world safe for democracy, which seems to have vanished during their absence. Each is wrongly imprisoned and is never the same afterwards.

In crime movies, prisons are rarely humane, and wardens are rarely benevolent. There are exceptions, of course: the wardens in *The Criminal Code* (1931), *20,000 Years in Sing Sing* (1932), and *Crime School* (1938). But portraying prisons as fascist fiefdoms with commandant wardens and their lackeys and chain gangs as a form of slave labor was not especially controversial. Moviegoers accepted the idea that in a republic that promised liberty and justice for all there was a colony known as the prison system, where liberty was suspended and justice often denied. They had become accustomed to prison-as-purgatory, in which prisoners are either purged of their sins or consumed in the process of purgation. Even in a movie from Poverty Row, PRC's *Lady in the Death House* (1944), an off-screen voice turns grimly epigrammatic: "The state that cannot give life demands the right to take life."

What was unsettling in the 1930s was the prospect of a fascist America, not a republic with a few pockets of fascism. American fascism was a subject the industry would have preferred to ignore, but it had "what if?" possibilities. The trick was to show what *could* happen. There would be an open-ended dénouement allowing some to believe that fascism—or at least benevolent fascism—would be acceptable if it featured a leader charismatic enough to inspire confidence, even if such a system resulted in curtailment or suspension of civil liberties in order to promote the common good. Others would regard the film as a cautionary tale, engrossing but implausible.

Gabriel over the White House (1933) qualified as both. In that film, after an automobile accident caused by reckless driving, President Judson

Hammond (Walter Huston) awakens from a coma a changed man. Determined to solve America's economic problems and rid the country of organized crime, he converts the republic into a dictatorship by dissolving Congress and imposing martial law, justifying his subversion of the Constitution by invoking the law of God as promulgated through him by the angel Gabriel. Apparently, angels were not just in the outfield, but also in the White House. Once the president accomplishes his goals—full employment, the execution of criminals, world disarmament—he peacefully expires, leaving America and the world a supposedly better place. Is the film implying that the president's measures are temporary, remaining in force until order is restored, after which the country will revert to its old democratic self? Or that fascism is the only way of dispelling the miasma of the Great Depression? If so, the dictatorship would be permanent in case the same circumstances that brought it about should recur. The similarity between the president and the new chancellor of Germany, Adolf Hitler, was striking. Just as Hitler dissolved the Reichstag, President Hammond dissolves Congress. Both leaders were also committed to full employment, but was fascism the only way to achieve it? In Germany, *Gabriel over the White House* was regarded as a "*fascist* satire," with a protagonist whose policies validated Hitler's. Reactions were mixed in the United States, with "some calling it a satire [while] others agreed with its agenda." There is another way of interpreting the film, as a utopian fantasy reflecting the desires of the unemployed who would accept a dictatorship—benevolent or otherwise, especially one that had God's imprimatur—if it meant they could be guaranteed jobs. Chicagoans would be thrilled to live in a gangster-free city. Pacifists would have nothing to protest against in a world committed to disarmament. It would be the fulfillment of Isaiah's prophecy (2:1–5), with swords beaten into plowshares, spears into pruning hooks, and nations no longer warring with each other. Eden had returned and taken root in American soil.

The President Vanishes (1934), less ambivalent but nonetheless utopian, arrived with an impressive pedigree: a script based on a Rex Stout novel; a prominent director, William Wellman; and an assistant director, Dorothy Arzner, who was establishing herself as a major filmmaker in her own right. The film was based on another fantasy premise: an isolationist president's discovery that Americans equate isolationism with cowardice and expect him to involve the country in a war that has already started in Europe. Although the world was still five years away from war, *The President Vanishes* posed a real dilemma. Does national honor demand that a country become entangled in a foreign conflict to maintain its status as a super power, refusing to stand by while ignorant armies clash by night? The president, hoping to teach the people a lesson, allows himself to be kidnapped by the Grey Shirts, obviously modeled after William Pelley's Silver Shirts. The president narrowly escapes getting murdered and, once freed, continues preaching the gospel of non-intervention, which was pretty much the status quo in America until the country was awakened from its lethargy on 7 December 1941. *The President Vanishes* is notable for its subtle conjunction of war and munitions manufacturers, who depend on wars to remain in business. At a banquet hosted by a lobbyist for a quintet of warmongers, the lobbyist's wife (Rosalind Russell) compares the group to a flock of birds. When one of them asks what kind, Russell, with her signature disdain, replies, "Eagles." It was a drawing room comedy exit line, delivered by an actress who had few peers when it came to acidic line readings. All *The President Vanishes* could do was jolt the complacent into accepting—or at least understanding—the issues: the folly of believing that war is the only way of validating a country's honor; isolationism as the only way of avoiding a repeat of World War I; and munitions plants as the only defense against war. That each canceled the others out seemed unimportant. America could at least encase itself in the cocoon of isolationism for a few more years.

It was a confused—and confusing—era. The end seemed to justify the means. If a United States president could take the law into his hands, why not the youth of America? In Cecil B. De Mille's *This Day and Age* (1933), a band of civic-minded youths, frustrated by their elders' inability to prosecute a notorious gangster, decide to kidnap him, bring him to a brickyard, and lower him into a rat-infested pit to provoke a confession. The only charge brought against them is car theft (a female accomplice commandeered the automobile to summon the police). But whatever time the young vigilantes might serve will be spent in surroundings considerably more comfortable than those in which Allen and Holmes found themselves. The kids benefited the community by breaking the law, and their offense is treated like a minor infraction. Paul Muni's Allen and Richard Barthelmess's Holmes merely served their country.

In the films of the thirties, communism was pictured more as a nuisance than a threat. When communists weren't spouting the party line, they were mouthing clichés. The parasitic Carlo (Mischa Auer) in *My Man Godfrey* (1936) inveighs against money, "the Frankenstein monster that devours souls," but thinks nothing of sponging off his rich patrons. Two films dating from around the same time, *Our Daily Bread* (1934) and *Red Salute* (1936), addressed communism differently: the former by preaching collectivism; the latter, by lampooning campus radicalism. *Our Daily Bread* steered clear of ideology. There was no dialectic in the story of a husband without prospects and a wife with an uncle who offers the couple a farm in the appropriately named community of Arcadia. The farm swells into a cooperative, whose philosophy, in the vernacular, is "You help me, I help you. We help ourselves by helping others." This attitude, unlike Marx's "From each according to his ability, to each according to his needs," is never expressed ideologically, although it amounts to the same thing. The rationale behind the cooperative harks back to Plato's theory of the origins of society in Book 2 of *The Republic*: No one is self-sufficient, but all are co-dependent, relying on the skills and talents of others. In *Our Daily Bread*, a mason has trouble putting up the frame for a house, while a carpenter is similarly frustrated by his inability to lay a foundation. Once they realize each has a skill the other lacks, they exchange places, and the house gets built. The incident illustrates the principle of division and specialization of labor, the only way in which the farm can grow and thrive. When the husband first questions the men about their abilities, he is more favorably disposed towards farmers, carpenters, masons, plumbers, bricklayers, and tailors than towards the lone violinist, who nonetheless is welcomed into a community from which no one is excluded, including a potential home wrecker (Barbara Pepper at her blowziest).

When the issue of self-determination arises, the members argue about what form of government they should adopt. Someone suggests democracy and is roundly booed: "That kind of talk got us here in the first place." Another proposes socialism, which would make sense in a collective, except that depicting the farm as a socialist enclave would have alienated moviegoers who could accept a community where people helped each other, but not one founded on an "ism" that many considered a diluted form of communism and no less inimical to free enterprise. Politically, the commune will be an anomaly: a democratic collective founded on group effort. A salt-of-the-earth type (the wonderful character actor, John Qualen) admits his ignorance of "isms," but is clear about what is needed: "a big boss"—namely, the husband, "the FDR of Arcadia," as Andrew Bergman dubbed him.

Our Daily Bread glorified collectivism at a time when similar measures enacted by the Soviet government led to famine in Ukraine, implying that the experiment that caused more than seven million people to die of starvation in the Soviet Union could succeed in the United States, where cooperative farming is a choice, not a mandate. The Arcadian farm was not a footnote to President Roosevelt's New Deal; it was a new deal proposed and ratified by the people, not the government, a cooperative venture entered into freely—a distinction that makes all the difference between a social contract and formal legislation. *Our Daily Bread*, however, glossed over the downside of collectivism, the weakening of the competitive spirit. If everyone works for the good of the community, every individual's talents are subsumed into the mass, with a corresponding loss of individuality and recognition. Collectivism—at least in America—is utopianism. Individuals may be willing to suppress the competitive instinct temporarily, but human nature will out. Pure communism, in which the individual subordinates him- or herself to a higher authority, is possible in religious communities where the higher good is divinely sanctioned. But after a time, even fervent believers have been known to defect. The selfless life is for saints who may realize they are superior to some of their peers, but who still choose to lay their talents on a communal altar.

The cooperative efforts are vindicated in the dizzying climax when the men form a pick and shovel brigade to dig an irrigation ditch. Director King Vidor timed their movements to the beat of a metronome: "The picks came down on the counts of one and three, the shovels scooped dirt on count two and tossed it on count four." Vidor was actually following Sergei Eisenstein's theory of rhythmic montage, in which a metrical pattern is imposed on the shots, with each succeeding the other like notes in a musical score. With drought no longer an issue, Arcadia looks as if it were blessed from above. Like the Greek pastoral with its Arcadian setting, *Our Daily Bread* partook of the purity of myth without providing the substance of reality.

Red Salute (1935), on the other hand, was moored in reality—specifically, in the 1930s college scene. The typical 1930s college movie was a musical (*College Humor* [1933], *College Rhythm* [1934], *Collegiate* [1936], *College Swing* [1938]), depicting campus life as a pre-hookup oasis where academics took a back seat to athletics and romance. *Red Salute*, however, portrayed college—in this case, one situated in the nation's capital—as a haven for left-wing activists. Informed audiences would not have been surprised that college students, unable to find a satisfactory explanation for the Great Depression, looked to the Left for answers, which it gladly supplied. Excessive speculation in the stock market on the part of the wealthy was to blame. This scenario, the Left indicated, would not have occurred under socialism, where the means of production are government-owned. Although campus radicalism in the 1930s was not as widespread as it was during the Vietnam War, leftist college organizations did exist, such as the League for Industrial

Democracy (LID), an offshoot of Upton Sinclair's Intercollegiate Socialist Society and the inspiration for the film's Liberty League—International Students. The latter was a clever title, implying that the malcontents were not Americans, but foreigners intent on imposing an alien sociopolitical "ism" on the United States.

However, one need not worry. *Red Salute* was a politicized screwball comedy that opened with a student proclaiming at a campus rally, "The world's sick, and you're going to pay the doctor's bills." Unsurprisingly, the announcement is greeted with laughter. The audience consists of red-blooded Americans, while the demagogue is just a Red—and an exchange student at that. A general's daughter (Barbara Stanwyck), enamored of the firebrand and his "ism," refuses to accept her father's arguments about the good life she has enjoyed under capitalism. The father retaliates by shipping his daughter off to Mexico, where she encounters a brash American soldier (Robert Young). Once they discover each other's politics, he dubs her "Red"; she responds by christening him "Uncle Sam."

To avoid paying a bar bill, Red and Uncle Sam hit the road, like Ellie Andrews and Peter Warne in *It Happened One Night* (1934). In the course of their odyssey, there is a stopover at a cornfield (compare the haystack in *It Happened One Night*) and a genial kidnapping that provides them with a trailer (see the motor court in *It Happened One Night*). The couple arrive in Washington, DC, in time for May Day and the agitator's rabble-rousing speech about the need to replace the old order with an import from abroad (country unspecified). Uncle Sam counters with his own speech, addressing everyone as "comrade." His intentionally provocative offer to tear down the American flag leads to a melee. Capitalism has triumphed, the student radical is deported, and Red and Uncle Sam spend their honeymoon in the trailer, a more intimate space than the motor court to which Ellie and Peter return at the end of *It Happened One Night*.

Soak the Rich (1936) took a more satiric approach to college radicalism, much sharper than *Red Salute*, as one might expect from the screenwriting team of Ben Hecht and Charles MacArthur. *Soak the Rich* anticipated James Thurber and Elliott Nugent's play, *The Male Animal*, filmed in 1942, in which a college professor champions academic freedom at a conservative institution from which instructors suspected of being communists have been fired. In *Soak the Rich*, a professor's endorsement of a "soak the rich" program—inspired by the 1935 Revenue Act known as the "soak the rich" tax, which imposed a higher income tax on anyone making over $5 million—galvanizes a campus. Capitalism is victorious, although the writers' sympathies seemed to lie with the supporters of the tax, depicted as youths finding their way into adulthood. Anyone expecting a tidy resolution was disappointed. Student radicals often grow up to become capitalists, and then all's right with the world—but only in the movies. In 1936, seven million Americans were still out of work. The rich—particularly the "rich rich," as F. Scott Fitzgerald characterized them—experienced a slight drizzle, while dust storms continued to plague Oklahoma, civil war erupted in Spain, and Hitler remilitarized the Rhineland, breaking the Treaty of Versailles. The world was three years away from war, having been given a prevue of coming attractions in Spain, where civil war was being waged. The Loyalists, abetted by the Soviet Union, hoped to establish a republican form of government more socialist than democratic, while the Nationalists, aided by Nazi Germany and fascist Italy, were determined to keep the country under the control of the military and the church, so Spain could become a malleable ally. The Nationalist victory in 1939 did not augur well for the western democracies, particularly after Hitler invaded Poland in September of that year.

For Hollywood, 1939 had a different significance. An industry that had earlier avoided offending Nazi Germany now realized it had nothing to lose. There was no hope of reconciliation with a nation determined to deracinate the stock from which most of the studio founders had come. It was time to address German anti-Semitism, which gave every indication of leading to a pogrom far worse than anything Jews had experienced previously. Hollywood's degree of daring can be seen in two 1939 films, one from Poverty Row, the other from one of the Big Five, Warner Bros. In October 1939, Producers Distributing Corporation (PDC), the forerunner of Producers Releasing Corporation (PRC), planned to release its exploitation film, *Hitler, Beast of Berlin*. But PDC encountered opposition from the Motion Picture Producers and Distributors Association (MPPDA), which declined to give the film a Production Code seal, citing violation of article 10 (national feelings) of the Motion Picture Production Code: "The history, institutions, prominent people and citizenry of other nations shall be represented fairly." Hitler was certainly a prominent person, and Germany was not a belligerent, at least not to the United States at the time. The title was then changed to *Beasts of Berlin* (a.k.a. *Goose Step* and *Hell's Devils*). Despite the opening disclaimer that it was free of "hatred, prejudice or bias to any class," *Beasts of Berlin* did not flinch from showing a concentration camp, where Jews, Catholics, Social Democrats, and communists were interned, brutalized, and humiliated. A Jewish inmate is forced to say "I am swine," and a priest is stripped of his cassock. *Beasts of Berlin* may seem like a curio, but it remains a shocking exposé of the inhumanity of the Third Reich at a time when the German-American Bund under Fritz Kuhn was able to attract an audience of twenty thousand to New York's Madison Square Garden where, in February 1939, Kuhn denounced the New Deal as a "Jew Deal." There were enough anti-Semites in America to cause any studio to wonder about the advisability of releasing an anti-Nazi movie that year.

Since Warner Bros. had been barred from the German market in 1934, the studio's primary concern about *Confessions of a Nazi Spy* (1939) was how American audiences would react. The film's production history has been well documented. Briefly, in June 1938, Warner Bros. bought the rights to a *New York Post* series, "Confessions of a Nazi Spy," which concerned German espionage in the United States. What could have been an explosive revelation was defused by a jittery White House, which had already been infiltrated and preferred that the public not know as much. The studio feared a libel suit if the spies' names were used, even though they had been indicted, and death threats caused producer Robert Lord to arm himself with a revolver. The project also aroused the ire of the German consul, Georg Gyssling, and the German-American Bund. When the smoke cleared, what remained was a rough-edged semi-documentary, nothing as engrossing as Fox's *Boomerang* (1947) and *Call Northside 777* (1948). Although *Confessions of a Nazi Spy* did not generate big box office, it had the distinction of being the first film made by a major studio that alerted Americans to the existence of Hitler Youth-style camps in the United States, where children learned to honor the Führer; to the continual threat of espionage; and to the racist German-American Bund. In 1939, with newsreels, *Beasts of Berlin* (under whatever title one saw it), and *Confessions of a Nazi Spy*, no moviegoer could claim ignorance of a movement that was casting an ever-widening net over Europe and a pall over America.

Neither film, however, was part of that *annus celestis*, 1939, in which more classics were released than ever before: *The Wizard of Oz, Stagecoach, Dark Victory, Mr. Smith Goes to Washington, Goodbye, Mr. Chips, Wuthering Heights, The Hunchback of Notre Dame, Young Mr. Lincoln, Gunga Din*, and of course, *Gone with the Wind*. Plus Ernst Lubitsch's *Ninotchka*.

While communism was eminently suited to satire and screwball comedy, Billy Wilder and Charles Brackett believed it could also work as romantic comedy—deliciously satiric and mildly screwball—without detracting from the basic story line. Ninotchka (Greta Garbo) is transformed from humorless Stalinist to amorous woman, wooed by the playboy Count Leon

(Melvyn Douglas) and seduced by capitalism, Parisian style. Ninotchka first appears as a literal-minded, unsmiling envoy extraordinary, dispatched to Paris to check on the three Bolsheviks who had been sent there to sell a collection of jewels confiscated after the Revolution. Meanwhile, the comrades have discovered that capitalism can supply them with luxuries unheard of in Moscow. After Ninotchka encounters Count Leon, who breaks down her defenses, she grows increasingly feminine, as only Garbo can, becoming the incarnation of the anima, the feminine principle, and imbuing it with a rarefied sensuousness. It was as if her body had departed to another world, leaving behind the essence of the eternal feminine. Leon woos her with images from nature—snails encircling each other, flowers opening their petals—and then delicately presses his lips against hers. Previously, she had accused him of being talkative. After the kiss, Leon asks, "Was that talkative?" to which Ninotchka replies, "No. That was restful. Again." She is now a capitalist in the making. Communists do not kiss like Leon.

Once Ninotchka discovers the transformative power of fashion—from hats to lingerie—and the liberating effects of champagne, she turns girlish, as if she were experiencing first love retroactively. Garbo's characteristic look of yearning suggests that the transformation is nearing completion. She cannot slough off the skin of capitalism even after returning to Moscow. But Leon has a way of extricating her from a way of life in which she no longer believes. As often happens when the male controls the narrative, Leon arranges for Ninotchka's return to Paris, then threatens to embark upon a personal crusade to convert Russians everywhere into capitalists unless she remains in Paris with him. But Ninotchka can play this game, too. Slyly (and Garbo is at her most sphinxlike in the fade-out), she acquiesces—for the good of her country: "No one shall say Ninotchka was a bad Russian."

Brackett and Wilder prick the inflated balloon of communism without causing it to burst. Wit trumped politics. When Ninotchka visits a working class bistro and orders raw carrots and beets, the shocked waiter responds, "This is a restaurant, not a meadow." The team knew how far they could go with "comrade" and "little father" and references to show trials and tractor shortages. The focus is on Ninotchka's capitalist flowering—and with Garbo undergoing the process, the flower emerges in full bloom.

Nonetheless, there is an air of sadness about *Ninotchka*, which premiered a month after World War II erupted in Europe, eventually darkening the city of lights. The opening title suggested as much, asking the audience to recall a time "when a siren was a brunette, and not an alarm—and if a

Frenchman turned off the light, it was not because of an air raid." *Ninotchka* was a temporary farewell to prewar Paris, where discretion was the better part of infidelity, and a boudoir was not always a bedchamber.

Once the Soviet Union and Nazi Germany signed a short-lived nonaggression pact on 23 August 1939, a mere nine days before Hitler invaded Poland, communism was no longer an aberration from which a woman is wooed, but one from which she must be rescued. MGM intended *Comrade X* (1940) to be the companion piece to *Ninotchka*. Like the earlier film, it originated as a story by Walter Reisch, which Ben Hecht and Charles Lederer converted into a screenplay that was more vodka than champagne. Wit, for the most part, was absent. In its place, spiky dialogue—not sharp enough to cut, but only prick—left a droplet of blood. In 1940, only Stalinists would have questioned the film's equation of communism with totalitarianism and its portrayal of the Soviet Union as deceitful and xenophobic.

In the opening scene, an American journalist in Moscow (Eve Arden) grumbles about censorship and duplicity, envisioning a time when the press will be "blindfolded and led around by seeing eye dogs." To her, the Kremlin is a corporation of "stuffed shirts, double crossing the masses," who someday "will take it apart brick by brick." Her prediction came to pass half a century later, when the system, internally corrupt and increasingly dysfunctional, imploded without the need for dismantling.

Comrade X is an uneasy mix of hammer-heavy melodrama, anemic romance (which is surprising with Clark Gable and Hedy Lamarr playing the leads), and a rescue operation with the wackiness of a silent movie car chase—this time with tanks. Anti-Soviet stories by "Comrade X," the nom de plume of newspaper reporter McKinley Thompson (Gable), have so outraged the Kremlin that all members of the foreign press have been forbidden to leave Moscow until "Comrade X" is unmasked. Hecht and Lederer resurrected Gable's scoop-hungry reporter from *It Happened One Night*, changed his name, and dispatched him to Moscow. As Peter Warne, Gable had an easier time; all he had to do in *It Happened One Night* was accompany a runaway heiress from Miami to New York. Here, in addition to romancing Golubka (Lamarr), a communist "motor man" working under the name of Theodore because only males can operate streetcars, Thompson must also bring her and her father, Vanya (Felix Bressart), to America. Thompson commandeers a tank that the versatile Golubka can drive—and which, for plot-resolving reasons, can he, too. The tank sequence is the film's highlight. Thompson's tank had been chosen to spearhead a maneuver with other tanks following in formation, as if playing follow-the-leader.

Ironically, the leader is an American bringing two Russians to freedom. The trio's arrival in Romania climaxes in a jubilant finale consisting of a newspaper headline ("Russia Invades Romania") and a shot of Thompson, Golubka, and Vanya at Ebbets Field, watching the Dodgers play the Red Sox. Golubka roots for the home team, while Vanya despairs of understanding the great American pastime.

Satire and romance were delicately intertwined in *Ninotchka* like strands of gossamer strong enough to keep the film airborne. In *Comrade X*, satire and romance square off like fighters, and conflicting ideologies erupt in a literal battle of the sexes with Thompson and "Theodore" going at each other as if they were in the ring, each obsessed with winning a round for his or her side. Garbo succumbed to Douglas's wooing. Gable does not woo Lamarr; instead, he imposes himself on her. Unfortunately, Hecht and Lederer expected Lamarr to evoke Garbo when Gable's masterful virility gets the better of her. Convinced that her capitalist suitor has a soul, she admits he has a strange effect on her and promptly kisses him. In *Ninotchka*, Douglas planted the kiss, and Garbo demanded an encore. Director King Vidor aimed for an easy "ah" from the audience; Lubitsch preferred a knowing sigh.

So much of the film is taken up with simplistic explanations of communism and its many inconsistencies. Vanya tells Thompson that his daughter's unswerving commitment to the party could lead to her death. Communists are expected to have ideas, he explains, but anyone who has them is eventually killed, since only the government's ideas matter. The most damning criticism of communism is the process of succession through elimination, when a would-be head of the secret police meets with an "unfortunate accident," allowing his rival to succeed him until it is his time for a similar accident. Golubka and her father had great hopes for Commissar Bastakoff, an intellectual far superior to the Kremlin apparatchiks. Yet this poet of the revolution will stop at nothing to stay in power, even killing his own supporters to assert his authority. At least Hecht and Lederer caught the fraudulence within the system, in which "comrade" is a meaningless form of address, and dissent is punishable by imprisonment or death by disappearance.

When Hitler invaded the Soviet Union in June 1941, the scenario changed. Hollywood had to think differently about Russia, particularly after 7 December 1941, when the Soviet Union became an ally. Like the non-aggression pact, the alliance was short-lived, but it lasted long enough for Hollywood to glorify Russia at the same time it was demonizing Germany.

Just as the first movie about Pearl Harbor, Republic's *Remember Pearl Harbor* (1942), was produced by a Poverty Row studio, the first film about our newest ally was PRC's *Miss V from Moscow* (1942). Immediately after the Japanese attack, Republic rushed *Remember Pearl Harbor* into production, so that it was ready for a May 1942 release. Except for the climax, in which a playboy private redeems himself by flying, kamikaze style, into a Japanese machine gun nest—screaming "Remember Pearl Harbor, you yellow rats"—the film had nothing to do with 7 December, but instead concentrated on fifth columnists in the Philippines on the eve of the attack. *Remember Pearl Harbor* has the dubious distinction of introducing the yellow peril dialogue that became characteristic of World War II movies ("If you see any Japs, don't shoot until you see the yellow of their eyes.").

Miss V from Moscow (1942), which reached the screen five months after *Remember Pearl Harbor*, starred a blank-faced Lola Lane in the title role as a Soviet agent who happens to be a ringer for a German spy. Ever loyal to the homeland, Miss V is dispatched to Paris, where she masquerades as the spy, convincing some but not others. The skeptics are destined for plot limbo so Miss V can continue her undercover work, transmitting messages to Moscow about American convoy ships en route to the Soviet Union in danger of being torpedoed by Nazi submarines.

Superficially, *Miss V from Moscow* is pro-Russian, yet apart from the opening scene, in which the heroine agrees to assume the identity of the spy, most of the action takes place in occupied Paris, making it a different kind of anti-Nazi film. Here, a Russian patriot risks her life to aid her country by working with the French Resistance to speed American aid to the Soviet Union. Miss V embodies the true spirit of allied cooperation: She serves Russia, France, and—indirectly—America. She is her own tricolor.

Despite Lane's indifferent performance, there is enough suspense in this sixty-five minute programmer to warrant a look, as Miss V roams around Paris, leaving a two-franc piece as her calling card for members of the Resistance and encoding information on specially treated handkerchiefs. The ending must have generated cheers in some quarters. The execution of a German officer, who had been infatuated with Miss V, is followed by a close-up of Lane wearing a peasant dress and a screen-filling smile on a hay wagon with the American soldier she had saved—although what he is doing on a hayride in the USSR is never explained. If the final shot was meant as a sign of coalescence, Lane was about as Russian as a saloon singer from Brooklyn. But 1942 was not a time to question relations between the US and the USSR. *Miss V from Moscow* is the first of a series of films, epitomized by *Casablanca*, in which the French Resistance was portrayed as having far more members than it actually did. One gets the impression that half of Paris worked for the underground. Since America had barely recovered from Pearl Harbor when *Miss V from Moscow* was released, the myth made the reality easier to bear. It was good for morale and better for the box office.

Chapter 2

THE RED SEXTET

ON 13 OCTOBER 1947, A WEEK BEFORE AYN RAND WAS TO TESTIFY BEFORE the House Un-American Activities Committee (HUAC) in Washington, DC, a special screening of *Song of Russia* (1944) was arranged for her at MGM studios in Culver City. The film, which Rand missed when it came out in early 1944, would inspire a significant part of her testimony about communism in Hollywood. HUAC considered *Song of Russia* a prime example of communist propaganda, seemingly oblivious to the fact that it was MGM's tribute to an ally. *Song of Russia* was only one of several films that HUAC had labeled subversive. But it was important that the Russian-born Rand parse the film for the committee, pointing out pro-communist elements that would have gone undetected by a novice. *The Fountainhead* (1943) had made Rand a best-selling author and celebrity, but she had expressed her antipathy to communism earlier in *We the Living* (1931) and *Anthem* (1933). She converted the former into a play, *Night of January 16th*, which ran for 235 performances on Broadway during the 1935–36 season and was filmed under the same title in 1941, with Robert Preston and Ellen Drew in the leads. Moviegoers who paid attention to credits, particularly screenwriters' names, might have recalled that Rand wrote the scripts for two Hal Wallis productions, *You Came Along* and *Love Letters* (both 1945). In fact, she had been working in film in various capacities ever since she emigrated from Russia in 1926.

On 16 October, Rand and her husband boarded a train for Washington, DC, where she testified before HUAC four days later. Rand had no illusions about publicity-hungry HUAC, for which she had little respect. Her fear of a communist-dominated movie industry was the primary reason for her cooperation with the committee. It was easy to see how *Song of Russia* intensified her fears. This film was a collaborative effort on the part of screenwriters Paul Jarrico and Richard Collins, both communists—although

Collins later recanted and gave HUAC twenty-three names. The screenplay was based on a story by Guy Endore, Viktor Trivas, and Leo Mittler. Endore and Trivas were communists, and Mittler was at least a fellow traveler. At a nightclub, a singer delivers a soulful tribute to his native land, "And Russia Is Her Name," with E. Y. "Yip" Harburg's lyrics set to a Jerome Kern melody. Harburg was often accused of being a communist. He was certainly a left winger, who did not conceal his sympathy with the masses, which was strikingly revealed in the Depression classic, "Brother, Can You Spare A Dime?" and in "When the Idle Poor Become the Idle Rich" and "That Great Come and Get It Day" from the musical *Finian's Rainbow*, whose book he also coauthored. For his part, Victor Navasky, author of *Naming Names* (1980), insists that Harburg "never belonged to the Communist party," although Harburg's support of various leftist and progressive organizations made him suspect. The film's director, Gregory Ratoff, was the exception. Refusing to live under communism, the Russian born actor-director immigrated to America in 1920. Hollywood was a haven for Ratoff, who worked as an actor specializing in ethnic roles (notably the producer, Max Fabian, in *All About Eve*) and displayed his versatility as a director in a variety of genres. He directed musicals (*Rose of Washington Square, Irish Eyes Are Smiling, Carnival in Costa Rica*), melodramas (*Adam Had Four Sons, Moss Rose*), comedies (*The Heat's On, Where Do We Go from Here?*), period pieces (*The Corsican Brothers, Black Magic*), and love stories (*Intermezzo: A Love Story, The Men in Her Life*).

The word "communist" was never uttered in *Song of Russia*, but it was used in one of Ratoff's earlier films, *Public Deb No. 1* (1940), in which an heiress (Brenda Joyce) is introduced to communism by her butler (Mischa Auer, inveighing against capitalism again as he did in *My Man Godfrey*). After attending a communist rally, she is so committed to the cause that she starts lecturing a waiter (George Murphy) in a Russian restaurant, becoming so bothersome that he spanks her in full view of the customers. Inevitably, heiress and waiter, parlor pink and red-blooded American, resolve their differences, and true love surmounts the barriers of class in the best tradition of screwball comedy. The title is a pun on "Public Enemy No. 1," which aptly describes the heiress and her type, who are children of privilege seduced into a movement that, if it ever succeeded, would have converted their mansions into workers' apartments—perhaps including a cubicle for the converts. But what makes *Public Deb No. 1* (released in October 1940) different from *Comrade X* (released two months later), is not the heroine's disillusionment with a revolutionary hero turned murderous dictator

(*Comrade X*), but her disillusionment with communism itself, brought about by Russia's invasion of Finland on 30 November 1939 (*Public Deb No. 1*). The non-aggression pact between the Soviet Union and Nazi Germany, signed three months earlier, only proved that both countries were equally ruthless, determined to divvy up Europe as if they were carving a roast, with Hitler getting the prime cuts. With the invasion of Finland following on the heels of Hitler's Polish blitzkrieg on 1 September 1939, it seemed that the Soviet Union was understudying Nazi Germany. Disenchanted, the heiress returns to the capitalist fold with all its perks—including a prospective mate: the waiter, whom her uncle has made vice president of his soup company. So the classes are not that far apart, after all.

History also intervenes in the last reel of *Song of Russia*, dimming the glow of peasant life in the mythical village of Tschaikowskoye, a neverland unaffected by famine and purges. Although the villagers greet one another as "comrade" like good communists and acknowledge Stalin as their commander-in-chief, they practice their own form of communism: the Russian Orthodox variety, which allows them religious freedom. The cleverly conceived screenplay is deliberately ambivalent; it is both Russian and Soviet. To undiscerning audiences, the film seems to concern the Russia of yesterday on the eve of the Nazi invasion, a Russia where people can get married in a religious ceremony. To the American left—and particularly to party members—*Song of Russia* is about the Russia of 1944, Soviet Russia, the largest of the sixteen republics that once made up the USSR.

Song of Russia has a frame narrative, beginning and ending in Manhattan Hall (think Carnegie Hall), where John Meredith (Robert Taylor) is conducting what seems to be a benefit concert for Russia that is being broadcast. An announcer explains that Meredith had been in Russia earlier on a concert tour and witnessed the devastation caused by Hitler's invasion of the Soviet Union in August 1941, proving that the non-aggression pact was a matter of expediency, with one party waiting for the other to make the first move. Hitler was the prime mover, but Russia put up a valiant defense, giving America time to mobilize after Pearl Harbor.

The bulk of the film, then, consists of a flashback. As Meredith begins the concert with "The Star-Spangled Banner," the scene dissolves from Manhattan Hall to a Moscow airport, with the national anthem serving as a musical bridge until Meredith's arrival. Then the music changes to Tchaikovsky's Fifth Symphony, as the conductor receives a royal welcome from a rapturous crowd. Rand, who had apparently taken notes at the screening, was shocked by the opening: "[The conductor] starts playing the American national anthem [which] dissolves into a Russian mob, with the sickle and hammer on a red flag very prominent above their heads. I am sorry, but that made me sick . . . .It suggests literally and technically that it is quite all right for the American national anthem to dissolve into the Soviet . . . . It really was symbolically intended and worked out that way."

Although it seems unlikely that the dissolve was "symbolically intended"—a dissolve was a common way of fading out of one location and into another—one can understand how a staunch anti-communist like Rand would experience the change of scene as a metaphor for America being folded into the USSR. The average moviegoer, accustomed to flashbacks, would just interpret the dissolve as a change of time and place.

Nadya (the lovely Susan Peters), a budding pianist, persuades Meredith to visit her village of Tschaikowskoye during its music festival. Intrigued by Nadya's innocence (and beauty), Meredith requests a tour of Moscow, only to learn that this is her first visit to the city. Meredith then takes the initiative and shows her the sights, thus introducing a city tour montage, which makes it seem that Moscow in spring 1941 was like Paris before the Nazis marched down the Champs Elysées on 14 June 1940. High-end restaurants provide gourmet food, and nightlife flourishes. Is this the real or the mythic Moscow? In the nightclub sequence, the soulful music and lyrics of "And Russia Is Her Name" underscore the script's deliberate ambivalence. The lyrics can either be a lament for the Russia of yesteryear or a tribute to the Russia of today, and the music either a farewell to the past or a hymn to the present.

But the entire film is ambivalent. Tschaikowskoye seems to be a collective farm that has escaped the dire effects of collectivization, particularly starvation. When Meredith is taken aback by the sight of Nadya doing farm work, she replies that it is "a privilege to drive a tractor," sounding more Soviet than Russian. At sunset, the workers troop back from the fields, in full voice singing the "Song of the Reapers" from Tchaikovsky's *Eugene Onegin*. We could be back in tsarist Russia. The village is postcard quaint, the villagers endearingly joyous and cloyingly sincere. Tschaikowskoye is an Eden that somehow managed to survive the revolution—but not for long.

Religion and politics are treated casually, and one is obliged to parse the dialogue and deconstruct the scenes. When Nadya realizes that she is attracted to Meredith, she hints at "serious differences" between them. The decoding is simple: She is a humanitarian communist, determined to build "a better life" for her country, and he is an American capitalist on a good will mission promoting music as the bridge across an ideological divide.

Meredith succeeds, and the couple is married in an Orthodox ceremony, quite different from the marriage of Clark Gable and Hedy Lamarr in *Comrade X*, in which the couple fills out some forms and is married by a civil servant.

Every Eden has its serpent, and Tschaikowskoye had Hitler. A calendar page, 21 June 1941, is ominously displayed along with a picture of the Führer at a Nazi outpost near the Polish border. The next day saw the invasion of Russia. The villagers mobilize, and Stalin delivers a radio address, using the rhetoric of the radical left—phrases like "war of liberation" and "common struggle" and ordering "collective farmers" to drive off their cattle and burn their wheat so it does not fall into the hands of the invaders. The scorched earth finale is a powerful piece of cinema, uniting pre- and post-Soviet Russia in a cause that neatly coincided with the Allies' goals. Meredith, still on tour, makes his way back to Tschaikowskoye, where he is reunited with Nadya in the familiar "he spots her in the crowd" scene, as he shouts her name and she breaks away, rushing into his arms. Although Meredith is now a committed antifascist, willing to fight alongside his wife, the frame narrative prevents them from becoming comrades in arms. Meredith must return to the States, along with Nadya, so the film can end where it began: at Manhattan Hall, with him conducting Tchaikovsky's First Piano Concerto and Nadya serving as soloist. The message was truly mixed. Within Soviet Russia, there was a Brigadoon, where communism meant camaraderie, and people seemed as free as they would be on a farm in Minnesota. But when the barbarians are at the gates, political and religious differences are suspended for the duration. Tschaikowskoye returns to the Soviet fold until the enemy has been crushed. With peace came another war, the Cold War, undeclared and unwaged, until history decided it was time to bring down the Iron Curtain permanently.

Song of Russia is a triumph of propaganda worked into a bicultural romance, allowing viewers to swoon over a love story with an attractive couple and spiritually join the partisans in their defense of Mother Russia. Moviegoers can either ignore the motherland's Sovietization or proudly embrace it. The film may be great propaganda, but it is faulty history. At best, it requires moviegoers to cross a suspension bridge of disbelief into a world untouched by history. Although the Manhattan Hall framing device is set in late 1941 or early 1942, the main action takes place between spring and early summer 1941, perhaps from early May to the end of June. By the time Meredith arrived in Moscow:

- the second world war had begun in Europe;
- Poland had been partitioned between Germany and Russia;
- Russia had invaded Finland;
- London was being bombed by the Luftwaffe;
- France, the Netherlands, Norway, Denmark, and Greece had fallen to the Nazis; and
- the Baltic states—Lithuania, Estonia, and Latvia—had been absorbed into the Soviet Union in 1940, only to be occupied by the Nazis a year later.

What was an American conductor doing in Russia when Europe was in such turmoil and the Soviet Union was a pariah to the western democracies? Meredith's was not a goodwill tour arranged by the State Department, it was an excuse for a film that would appeal to the left, Russophiles, moviegoers looking for an inspiring love story, and music lovers—who would be rewarded with excerpts from Tchaikovsky's First Piano Concerto, his fifth and sixth symphonies, *Eugene Onegin*, *The Nutcracker*, *Swan Lake*, and the *Romeo and Juliet Overture Fantasy*. There was something for everyone—except Ayn Rand, who was not deceived by the red, white, and blue giftwrapping with a hammer and sickle seal.

In April 1942, Endore, Trivas, and Mittler submitted a treatment to MGM for a film, entitled "Scorched Earth," about Russia on the eve of the Nazi invasion. The treatment was passed on to Paul Jarrico and Richard Collins, who, by July 1943, had completed a draft of a screenplay called "Russia." By October, the screenplay, now known as *Song of Russia*, was ready for the cameras.

In August 1942, while Jarrico and Collins were struggling to make "Scorched Earth" palatable to a mass audience so that it would seem communist to some and Russian to others, Lillian Hellman had also completed a draft of an original screenplay about the invasion. The setting was similar: a collective farm, identified as such (unlike the more evasive *Song of Russia*) in Ukraine called the North Star. *The North Star* was also the name of the film, released in early November 1943, three months before *Song of Russia*. Hellman, who was a prominent figure in left wing Hollywood and New York, was strongly pro-Soviet. Since 1934, she had been under contract to Samuel Goldwyn, for whom she had already co-authored the screenplay of *The Dark Angel* (1935; filmed earlier as a silent), and converted her drama *The Children's Hour* (1934) into *These Three* (1936), divesting the play of its lesbian overtones, except for those would knew the original and sensed a subtext at work. In the film, two women (Merle Oberon and Miriam Hopkins) are both in love with the same man (Joel McCrea); in the play, one woman harbors a secret desire for the other and resents her engagement to a local doctor. Goldwyn was delighted with Hellman's makeover of the play, which was considered so controversial that its name could not be used in the credits, which only indicated that the film was based on an (unnamed) play by Lillian Hellman. Goldwyn was also pleased with her adaptation of Sidney Kingsley's *Dead End* (1937), which went beyond the original in its criticism of a society so economically polarized that a high rise can face a tenement as if asserting its superiority.

Hellman next had a chance to bring to the screen her greatest stage triumph, *The Little Foxes* (1941), which Goldwyn teasingly referred to as "The Three Little Foxes." Her contract originally called for "screen adaptations of five stories, to be furnished and designated by us [Goldwyn]," with a guarantee of $2,500 a week for ten weeks. But by 1942, energized by the antifascism of her fourth play, *Watch on the Rhine* (1941), Hellman had turned her attention to Russia, now engaged in a life and death struggle with Nazi Germany. Still on good terms with Goldwyn, she informed the producer that her next film for him would not be an adaptation like the others, but an original screenplay. Conceived as a documentary, *The North Star* (1943) evolved into a feature film with the tone of a documentary—or so Hellman intended. But that was not how the director, Lewis Milestone, envisioned it.

Hellman was never much of a collaborator, even though film is a more collaborative medium than theater, where she chose to direct *Another Part of the Forest* (1946) and the 1952 revival of *The Children's Hour* herself. Although neither was a box office hit like *The Little Foxes* or *Watch on the Rhine*, Hellman at least had the satisfaction of knowing that each production reflected her vision of the play, not someone else's. The ghost of Ibsen hovered over the revival of *The Children's Hour*, which came off as stark melodrama, leaving the audience devastated but unpurged. *The Children's Hour* may have lost some of its shock value by 1952, but the theme—a child's lie that alters one woman's life and destroys another's—was still relevant at a time when HUAC was doing the same thing to many in Hollywood who marched in the wrong parade, supported the wrong cause, attended the wrong meetings, or subscribed to the wrong publications. The revival lasted for only 183 performances, compared to the original, staged by Herman Shumlin, which ran for 691. *Another Part of the Forest*, the prequel to *The Little Foxes*, made a star out of Patricia Neal as the young Regina in the process of becoming one of the foxes that spoil the vines. The play held on for 182 performances, nowhere near the 410 *The Little Foxes* enjoyed. Hellman's direction may have contributed to these plays' respectable but disappointing runs.

Hellman had been spoiled by working with William Wyler, who directed her screenplays, *These Three, Dead End*, and *The Little Foxes*. Writer and director functioned as a team, sharing the same view of the material and enjoying an artistically satisfying collaboration. But there was no collaborating with Lewis Milestone, artistically or otherwise. Initially, Hellman accepted his suggestions, many of which made improvements, such as an emphasis on Nazi atrocities (children bled to death to supply plasma for wounded Nazi soldiers, a woman punished by having her arm and leg broken) and the introduction of a new character—a Nazi doctor, Von Harden, played dispassionately by Erich von Stroheim. Assuming that she had satisfied Milestone, Hellman was shocked that other changes were made without her consultation. As a Polish Jew, Samuel Goldwyn (né Schmuel Gelbfisz) felt that the film lacked an authentic Eastern European flavor; specifically, it lacked folk music. He got no argument from the Russian-born Lewis Milestone (né Leib Milstein in Moldova), who came to the United States at seventeen. Goldwyn then hired Aaron Copland to compose the score, which would include folk melodies set to lyrics by Ira Gershwin. Copland and Gershwin, the sons of Lithuanian and Russian Jews, respectively, fitted in perfectly with Goldwyn and Milestone's concept of the film. *The North Star* was to be a tribute to Russia that would begin with a quintet of carefree young hikers—Damian (Farley Granger); Marina (Anne Baxter); Damian's brother, Kolya (Dana Andrews); Clavdia (Jane Withers); and her younger brother, Grisha (Eric Roberts)—on their way to Kiev on 21 June 1941, unaware that on the next day the invasion would leave Clavdia dead and Damian blind. Kolya, a bombardier, reports for duty, leaving the eleven-year-old Grisha with Marina, who must—and does—carry on valiantly.

When Hellman saw a rough cut of *The North Star*, she was reduced to tears. Although she did not expect Milestone to treat her screenplay as holy writ, she did not anticipate his tampering with it, and certainly did not expect scenes of collective farmers singing lustily as if they were in a folk opera like Smetana's *The Bartered Bride*, having miraculously been spared the starvation that ravaged Ukraine in the early 1930s. Hellman regarded *The North Star* as *her* script. Milestone wanted Ukrainians to speaks in quaint idioms, the kind that he was familiar with as a child and that would conform to an audience's idea of peasant speech. Hellman's screenplay opened with Karp (Walter Brennan), driving a wagon full of squealing pigs and talking to the one next to him. Milestone preferred a less irritable and more benign Karp in keeping with the film's leisurely beginning and in contrast to the next day's events. In the film, Karp, a likeable eccentric, drives his wagon through the village, greeting passersby—including a school of ducks. The few musical interludes add little to the film. Singing on the open road is a commonplace. The hikers' songs are blandly innocuous ("We're the younger generation / and the future of the nation"; "Sing me not of other towns / of towns that twinkle and shine"), reflecting their innocence and patriotism—the latter put to the test when the bombs start to fall.

As Carl Rollyson has shown, the bulk of Hellman's screenplay—including two powerful speeches—reached the screen. The first speech occurs during a confrontation between two doctors representing different ideologies, Kurin (Walter Huston), the humane Russian, and Von Harden (Erich von Stroheim), the amoral Nazi. When Kurin produces as an example of Nazi inhumanity the body of a boy who had been bled to death, Von Harden replies dryly, "They took too much blood. I am sorry for that." With muted rage, calculated to result in violence, Kurin denounces Von Harden: "To me, *you* are the real filth. Men who do the work of fascists and pretend they are better than those for whom they work. Men who do murder while they laugh at those who order them to do it." In a sense, Kurin has delivered a death sentence, after which he shoots Von Harden and his lackey, Richter.

Then there is Marina's climactic speech: "None of us will be the same. Wars do not leave people as they were. All people will learn that, and come to see that wars do not have to be. We will make this the last war; we will make a free world for all men. The Earth belongs to us, the people, if we fight for it. And we will fight for it!" These sentiments, expressed by Ukrainians loyal to the Soviet Union, were universally shared in both the free world and the enslaved. Of course, the Nazis were filth. Although war changed people, in some cases radically, there is always hope that the last war will be the war to end all wars. Marina's are heartfelt words, falling like grain on rocky ground. "The people," to whom the Earth belongs, have no control over those who rule it.

The North Star is openly socialist. There is never any doubt about the setting, a democratically run collective farm. The socialist anthem, "The Internationale," erupts from the soundtrack as the guerrillas prepare to take on the invaders. Kolya describes himself as a member of the air force of the Union of the Soviet Socialist Republics. The guerillas see themselves as defenders not of their village alone, but of the Soviet Union, swearing that they "will not lay down their arms until the last fascist is driven from the land." "Comrade" is a warm greeting, not a perfunctory form of address. Unlike *Song of Russia*, *The North Star* is completely Soviet.

In his *New York Times* review (5 November 1943), Bosley Crowther, impressed that *The North Star* was deemed important enough to open at two Broadway showcases, the Victoria and the Palace, described the film as "moving and triumphant." He commended Hellman for writing such a powerful indictment of fascism, singling out Kurin's "*you* are the real filth" speech as an example. Although he took issue with the musical interludes, he believed they "may be generally overlooked." The Academy of Motion Picture Arts and Sciences thought so, too. Although *The North Star* did not win a single Oscar, it was nominated in six categories, including best original screenplay, cinematography, and music (Copland's score, exclusive of the songs).

Three months later (17 February 1944), Crowther reviewed *Song of Russia*, declaring it "the best film on Russia yet made in the popular Hollywood idiom," a surprising claim since there were so few. He emphasized the title as the "key" to the film, which he considered a musical—albeit one of a special type. *Song of Russia* was not only "a musical picture," but also "a honey of a musical." Crowther's reaction was not surprising given the sound track, which was Tchaikovsky lite. Jarrico and Collins had done their job well. The musical sugarcoating complemented the mythologizing of Soviet Russia, where there was no dissent. How could there be in a land where everyone—from restaurateurs to collective farmers—seems to have benefited from communism? If *Song of Russia* is a tribute to anything, it is to music's power to sweeten an otherwise bitter brew.

While *Song of Russia* is remembered primarily because of Ayn Rand's HUAC testimony, *The North Star* achieved a different form of notoriety when it was transformed into an indictment of the failed 1956 Hungarian uprising. National Television Associates (NTA) re-edited *The North Star*, cutting thirty minutes from it, retitling it *Armored Attack* (1957), deleting every "comrade," and turning a pro-Soviet movie into an anti-Communist one with a voiceover message delivered in the gravest of tones: "This is the story of people betrayed, who defended their homes and children only to see them destroyed by the arms of a godless invader. It is the story of how they met the attack and how they fought back." But who betrayed whom? In breaking the nonaggression pact, the Nazis betrayed the Russians. But the voiceover made it seem that the Russians were betrayed by their own people. Adding another instance of aggression, NTA incorporated newsreel footage of a Soviet tank in Budapest. In case anyone failed to get the point, the voiceover epilogue spelled it out: "Today, as in all dictatorships, the lie, the double cross, and the sell-out build the communist dream of empire. The Nazi war machine has been replaced by the armor of the Soviets. The gallant struggle of the Hungarian freedom fighters stands as a shining symbol of man's love of freedom. Perhaps some day there will be an end to bloodshed. But until that day, every person and every nation must be aware of the menace of Communism."

With its proselytizing for Soviet Russia, *The North Star* was catechetical compared to *Mission to Moscow* (1943), the gospel according to Joseph E. Davies, President Roosevelt's appointee as ambassador to Russia (1936–38). Roosevelt rewarded Davies, a prominent Democrat, for supporting his 1932 bid for the presidency. That Davies knew little about the Soviet Union was irrelevant. Loyalty was what mattered. Besides, Davies was married to an heiress, which helped.

During his time in Russia, Davies recorded what he saw—or rather what he was allowed to see—in his memoir, *Mission to Moscow* (1941), an immediate best seller that sold seven hundred thousand copies and was translated into thirteen languages. There are two versions of the way *Mission to Moscow* became a Warner Bros. film, one more plausible than the other. The highly ambitious Davies, anxious for his memoir to reach the screen, pitched the idea of a movie version to President Roosevelt. Such behavior was characteristic of the fame-seeking Davies. When Warner Bros. bought the rights to *Mission to Moscow* for $25,000, Davies was given script approval and "proceeded to use it for all it was worth," requesting revisions, adding dialogue, and demanding that in the purge trial scenes the accused be portrayed as Trotskyites, and that under no circumstances should the Winter War (1939–40) be construed as the Soviet Union's invasion of Finland. Having accepted the great lie, Davies was now a confirmed Stalinist, even refusing to aid Americans in Russia who were victims of communist repression. Diplomat and historian George F. Kennan found Davies thoroughly unsuited to the job and despaired of him understanding that the purge trials were Stalin's excuse for ridding himself of real or imagined rivals.

Given his access to President Roosevelt, Davies would logically have been the initiator of the project. In an alternate version, it was the president who proposed the idea during a White House dinner with Davies and either Harry or Jack Warner (more likely the latter), knowing that a movie would reach an even wider audience than would the book. That President

Roosevelt was enthusiastic about the film and conferred several times with Davies about its progress suggests he was anxious for it to succeed, hoping that it would convince those who still harbored doubts that a socialist nation whose official religion was atheism could be a reliable ally. Davies believed that Warner Bros., which produced the first major anti-Nazi film, *Confessions of a Nazi Spy* (1939), should also be the studio to launch the first pro-Soviet film. It would unfold like a historical tapestry woven by diverse hands, including:

- American ambassador Joseph E. Davies (Walter Huston), his wife, Marjorie (Ann Harding), and daughter, Emlen (Eleanor Parker);
- Soviet ambassador Maxim Litvinov (Oscar Homolka), his wife, Ivy (Barbara Everest), and daughter, Tanya (Maria Palmer), a parachutist;
- Premier Vyacheslav Molotov (Gene Lockhart), Litvinov's replacement, and Molotov's wife, Polina (Frieda Inescort, uncredited), head of a cosmetics factory;
- German foreign minister Joachim Von Ribbentrop (Henry Daniell), who negotiated the non-aggression treaty with Molotov, often referred to as the Molotov- Ribbentrop pact;
- Famed ballerina Ulanova (Cyd Charisse, uncredited), Pavlova's successor;
- Prosecutor General Andrey Vyshinsky (Victor Francen), state prosecutor at the purge trials;
- Mikhail Kalinin (Vladimir Sokoloff), nominal head of the Soviet Union;
- Renowned engineer and author Stephen Timoshenko (Kurt Katch, uncredited);
- Japanese ambassador to the Soviet Union Shigemitsu (Peter Goo Chong);
- General Secretary Joseph Stalin (Manart Kippen, uncredited), head of the USSR;
- Winston Churchill (Dudley Field Malone), shortly before becoming prime minister in 1940, and his wife, Clementine (Doris Lloyd, uncredited);
- Emperor Haile Selassie of Ethiopia (Leigh Whipper, uncredited);
- Purge trial victims Krestinsky (Roman Bohnen), Yagoda (Daniel Ocko), Bukharin (Konstantin Shaynek), Radek (David Hoffman), Pyatakov (Alex Melesh), Tukhachevsky (Ivan Triesault)—all uncredited except Bohnen—accused of attempting to overthrow the Soviet government; and
- President Roosevelt, as a presence only, with Captain Jack Young providing the voice that sounds as if it is coming from off screen.

Mission to Moscow was a faux epic with a mammoth cast in which un-billed actors, even in important roles, outnumbered and often eclipsed the billed. The film was not so much history for dummies as dumbed-down history, the kind in which Stalin, cordial but hard-nosed, explains to Davies that the Soviet Union would gladly join the western democracies in oppos-ing Hitler, but had no intention of "pulling other people's chestnuts out of the fire." Davies understood the metaphor. If England and France would not come to the aid of Czechoslovakia, neither would the Soviet Union. Collective security was the answer, although historically it never was. When Hitler added Czechoslovakia to his growing list of conquests, France and Britain were silent, causing the Soviet Union to sign a non-aggression pact with Hitler. The pact's secret protocols divided Eastern Europe into "spheres of influence," with the Soviet sphere consisting of eastern Poland, the Baltic states, and Finland.

Two weeks after Hitler invaded Poland, the Soviet Union claimed the eastern part of the doomed country for itself, despite the 1932 Soviet-Polish non-aggression pact. Such pacts are the equivalent of breakable contracts, leaving the weaker member at the mercy of the stronger. Finland, which signed a similar pact with the Soviet Union in 1932, experienced this truth when it was later invaded. Still, in the film Davies insists that the Molotov-Ribbentrop pact was motivated by the Soviet Union's need for self-protec-tion, implying that it could no longer rely on England and France for sup-port and, in effect, blaming them for driving the Soviet Union into the arms of Nazi Germany.

Davies vouched for the film's authenticity. Appearing in person in the prologue, he presented himself as a truthful recorder of what he had wit-nessed. Professing to have come from pioneer stock, he averred that his "re-ligious convictions" were formed by his "sainted mother, an ordained min-ister of the Gospel." The sole purpose of *Mission to Moscow*, Davies insists, is to clear up misconceptions about the Soviet Union, whose people are "sincerely devoted to world peace." Russia comes off as the land of milk and honey—or at least vodka and honey—over which hovers the bluebird of happiness. The Davieses behave like tourists, awed by everything they see. Mrs. Davies is amazed that Madame Molotov (the stately Frieda Inescort) is commissar of the cosmetics industry—that there even is a cosmetics indus-try in the Soviet Union. Emlen Davies wonders how a skater she assumes is an ordinary Russian could know where the embassy ball is being held. "How did you know?" Emlen asks. "I live there," the young woman replies politely. She happens to be Tanya Litvinov. Although in 1943 film audiences expected Muscovites speaking in English, and not Russian with English subtitles, much is made of the Russians' bilingualism, while the Davieses seem to know but one Russian word, *spasibo* ("Thank you").

Davies's idea of truth can be seen in three crucial sequences: the purge trials, his rationalization of the Soviet Union's invasion of Finland, and his meeting with Stalin. The victims of the purge trials are portrayed as Trotskyites, working covertly with Germany and Japan to seize the Kremlin and establish a military dictatorship. In return, Germany would have access to Ukraine, acquiring more Lebensraum ("living space"), and Japan would be guaranteed oil from Siberia in case of war with America. The trials were a travesty, staged as a spectacle for gullible types like Davies, who believed the accused were traitors and saboteurs, not victims of Stalin's czarist-like paranoia (one thinks of the title character in Mussorgsky's opera, *Boris Godunov*), which drove him to liquidate his opponents—or, in most cases, those whom he perceived as such.

Equally spurious are the explanations that Davies (Walter Huston, speaking with scary conviction) gives to a crowd of isolationists, one of whom asks, "How about poor little Finland?" He answers, "Russia knew she was going to be attacked by Hitler so the Soviet leaders asked Finland's permission to occupy strategic positions to defend herself against German aggression. She offered to give Finland twice as much territory in exchange, but Hitler's friend Mannerheim refused and the Red army moved in."

Davies's version is a half-truth. Relations between Finland and the Soviet Union had been strained since Finland became independent from Russia in 1917. In the fall of 1939, the Soviet Union, emboldened by the secret protocols of the non-aggression pact, had no qualms about demanding that Finland move its border twenty-five kilometers from Leningrad and lease the Hanko peninsula for a Soviet naval base, with an offer of twice as much land in return. Davies neglected to say that the land was wilderness that had originally been part of Finland but now belonged to Russia. The Finnish government—not Mannerheim, then commander-in-chief of the Finnish armed forces—declined, likening the arrangement to exchanging "two pounds of dirt for one pound of gold." The Soviet Union then invaded Finland, precipitating the Winter War, which was relatively brief, lasting little more than three months (30 November 1939–13 March 1940). Although the Finns fought bravely, they were pitifully outnumbered. The war concluded with a peace treaty requiring Finland to cede even more territory to the Soviet Union than had originally been requested. In the end, Mannerheim was not Hitler's "friend." Knowing Hitler's expansionist designs, Mannerheim kept him at arm's length. It was Stalin who branded Mannerheim a fascist, a charge Davies never questioned.

The showstopper comes near the end of the film, when Davies finally meets Stalin on the eve of Davies's departure from Moscow. After agreeing on the need for collective security, Davies praises Stalin as a "great builder." (What Stalin built is never specified, but history has provided the answer: gulags.) Stalin, flattered, does not reply, and after Davies leaves, the Soviet leader enigmatically lights his pipe. The scene is so convincingly acted that one can understand why Stalin was given the sobriquet "Uncle Joe."

Released fourteen months after Pearl Harbor, *Mission to Moscow* took advantage of Hollywood's own war against the Japanese, who now ranked first among screen villains. At an embassy ball, the bespectacled Japanese ambassador, Shigemitsu, eyes widened into spheres of duplicity, approaches Davies, insisting that Japan has no designs on the Philippines and Hawaii, and that China was responsible for the outbreak of hostilities between their two countries. Always the diplomat, Davies listens patiently and then dismisses Shigemitsu's explanation as "pure bunk." Confused, Shigemitsu requests a definition of "bunk" from Bukharin, who simply shrugs. When Shigemitsu learns that Tanya Litvinov is a parachutist in the reserves, he snidely remarks that the young people of Japan prefer other "sports." Tanya, coldly polite, replies that she has seen examples of such "sports," referring most likely to the rape of Nanking.

Davies believed that communism was closer to the spirit of Christianity than Nazism because of its commitment to the brotherhood of man, as if "comrade" were the great equalizer. The film ends with a chorus of heavenly voices, like those at the close of Gounod's *Faust*, singing "You are your brother's keeper now and forever." Edifying, perhaps, but tragically phony. Although *Mission to Moscow*'s historical value is a few degrees above zero, it is mesmerizing cinema, persuasively acted—especially by Walter Huston, who, as Davies, exuded such Lincolnesque sincerity that one had to fight hard against being converted. The only truth in *Mission to Moscow* is the truthfulness of the performances, not the film, which—though enticingly staged—is pure bunk.

Nineteen forty-three was literally a red-letter year, during which Hollywood produced *The North Star* and *Mission to Moscow*. Some would also include *Song of Russia*, although it was not released until early 1944. Two lesser films also appeared that year: *Three Russian Girls* and *The Boy from Stalingrad*. *Three Russian Girls* was an American remake of the Russian film *The Girl from Leningrad* (1941). The title characters in the remake are Red

Cross nurses, one of whom (Anna Sten) falls in love with her patient, an American flyer (Kent Smith), making the film more of a wartime love story than a war movie. Similar to *The North Star* is *The Boy from Stalingrad*, also set at the time of the Nazi invasion, but told from the point of view of the children who witnessed it. Although the children temporarily outwit the Nazis, they are powerless against their aggressors. Any hopes for a happy ending are dashed when some of the children are killed. *The Boy from Stalingrad* is a companion piece to *The North Star*, each depicting the plight of children in war—bled to death in *The North Star*, mercilessly gunned down in *The Boy from Stalingrad*.

Days of Glory (1944) and Counter-Attack (1945) also share a common theme: the bravery of the Russian guerrillas who fought their own war against the Nazis. Casey Robinson both wrote and produced *Days of Glory* for RKO, introducing two new stars to moviegoers: his third wife, the world-famous ballerina Tamara Toumanova, whose art was so exquisite that she was crowned "the black pearl" of ballet, and Hollywood's latest discovery, Gregory Peck. Robinson, who had written the screenplays for some of Bette Davis's best films (*Dark Victory, The Old Maid, All This and Heaven Too, Now, Voyager, The Corn Is Green*), could not do the same for his wife. Peck, on the other hand, achieved greater success that same year in Fox's *The Keys of the Kingdom*, setting him on the first leg of his journey to stardom.

Why Robinson thought *Days of Glory* was the right vehicle for Toumanova is hard to fathom. She plays Nina Ivanova—like Toumanova herself a star of the Russian ballet—who joins a band of Russian partisans headed by Vladimir (Peck). The partisans hide out in the cellar of an abandoned monastery near the city of Tula, an important industrial and rail center under siege by the Nazis. It is a straight acting role, and those unfamiliar with Toumanova's reputation, which was not confirmed on film until *Invitation to the Dance* (1956), would have to take it on faith that "Comrade Stalin" sent her to the front to entertain the troops. At one point, we almost think we'll be treated to a demonstration of the art of the ballet. When Nina learns that the young Mitya (Glenn Vernon) had never been exposed to theater, she tries to recreate the experience—only to be interrupted by the arrival of a Nazi, whom she later kills, earning the respect of the others, who had written her off as useless.

Days of Glory, derived from a story by Melchior Lengyel (who also provided Wilder and Brackett with the template for *Ninotchka*), is the least political of the pro-Soviet movies of the 1940s. Because it is set during the war, there are no pre-invasion scenes of happy Russians on their collective farms, singing and dancing when they are not toiling in the fields. The partisans have organized themselves as a collective, in which everyone is addressed as "comrade," with the educated Semyon (Lowell Gilmore) serving as "comrade professor," assigning each member his or her duties—except Nina, who can neither cook nor sew, but later proves that she can shoot. "Comrade" has no more political significance than "Mr." or "Ms.," but it is used for the sake of authenticity.

Robinson had all he could do to sustain audience interest in a story with limited playing areas, consisting primarily of the cellar and the forest. At one point, Semyon reads Tatiana's letter to Onegin from Pushkin's *Eugene Onegin*, which, like many Russian school children, Nina had memorized. She begins reciting it rapturously, as if it had been imprinted on her soul. At that moment, *Days of Glory* came to life. It was not a war movie with Russians as heroes and Nazis as villains, but a performance, a rendition of one of the best-loved passages in Russian literature.

Robinson also knew that he could not turn the tide of the war, with the partisans defeating the Germans. No one in the film survives. Realizing they are doomed, Nina wants to die a guerrilla and begins taking an oath, which Vladimir administers. She begins, "I, Nina Ivanova, a citizen of the Soviet Socialist Republics, swear . . . ," as a German tank plows into the two of them, bursting into flames, and they perish in a fiery but nonetheless romantic death.

Days of Glory may have been pro-Soviet, but it was not pro-communist. Because Robinson was apolitical, the film is curiously apolitical. Most of the guerrillas would seem to be communists—except Nina, who wears a cross around her neck. Vladimir probably is one. After Yelena (Maria Palmer) has been killed, a funeral service is held in a monk's cell. Nina attends, but Vladimir remains outside, making it seem as if he is the only Stalinist among the partisans. Yelena must have been a Christian; otherwise, there would have been no service. That the partisans have taken refuge in a monastery cellar makes "Comrade" no different from "Father," "Sister," "Mother," or "Brother," the forms of address used in religious communities. Vladimir may die as a communist, but Nina dies as a Christian who swore allegiance to the Soviet Union, which may make her a Christian communist. But then, so are monks. Since *Days of Glory* cost $958,000 and failed to turn a profit, it is doubtful that many moviegoers pondered the characters' religion, or lack thereof, or were aware of Robinson's Christianizing a Soviet enclave, as if he were washing everyone in the blood of the lamb.

The most honest film of the lot is *Counter-Attack* (1945), which John Howard Lawson adapted from a play called *Counterattack* by Janet and Philip Stevenson, which starred Morris Carnovsky and lasted on Broadway for eighty-five performances during the 1942–43 season. In fact, Lawson's screenplay was an adaptation of an adaptation. The Stevensons' play was an adaptation of *Pobyeda*, a Russian drama by Ilya Vershinin and Mikhail Ruderman. In Plato's terms, the movie was three degrees removed from reality. Still, *Counter-Attack* is refreshingly non-ideological. It neither proselytizes for communism nor portrays the Nazis as sadists and buffoons. The film's straightforwardness makes it unique, as does its setting, which is even more constrictive than the monastery cellar in *Days of Glory*.

Lawson was an anomaly. He graduated from Williams College in 1920 with a BA in English and three years later saw his first play, *Roger Bloomer* (1923), produced on Broadway. By 1928 he had written four more plays— heavily expressionistic, alternately surreal and absurd, and revealing an uncanny ability to treat such subjects as strikes (*Processional*), politics (*Loud Speaker*), and revolution (*The International*) both seriously and satirically. Race, war, and big business were presented as vaudeville for those who dote on the outlandish, and as Aristophanic farce for those who could detect the interplay of ideas beneath the comic veneer. Later, with *Success Story* (1933), Lawson showed he had also mastered the art of traditional plot construction in a melodrama about the rise and fall of a heel. But the play that really demonstrated that his radicalism was no longer merely incipient was *Marching Song* (1937), a true "power to the people" drama that is blatantly pro-labor and anti-management, complete with greedy capitalists and villainous strike breakers. Lawson could have become a major playwright, screenwriter, and critic had he not been sidetracked by left-wing radicalism, becoming a Stalinist and Hollywood commissar.

Yet as a screenwriter, Lawson was not didactic. The closest he came to preaching was at the end of the Spanish Civil War movie, *Blockade*, in which Henry Fonda, lamenting the plight of civilians in war, looks straight into the lens and asks, "Where's the conscience of the world?" Lawson knew that to survive in Hollywood his scripts had to be ideology-free, but pro-Soviet sentiments could be inserted surreptitiously, as they were in *Action in the North Atlantic* (1943). Dane Clark, looking up at some Russian planes, cries, "They're ours!" But except for some comrades in the audience who may have nudged each other and nodded approval, few moviegoers would have caught the veiled tribute to a short-lived ally.

Counter-Attack is pro-Soviet only in the sense that Kulkov (Paul Muni), a Russian paratrooper, and Lisa (Marguerite Chapman), a guerrilla fighter, manage to keep seven Nazis at bay in the basement of a bombed out factory building, where they have all taken refuge. The Nazis are not portrayed as evil. They do not bleed children (*The North Star*), shoot them (*The Boy from Stalingrad*), or hang them (*Days of Glory*). Nazis are merely the enemy, and the Russians are patriots resisting their invaders. There is no glorification of Soviet ingenuity. Even the construction of an underwater bridge to allow tanks to cross over without being seen is treated as an act of expediency. Lawson makes no attempt to ennoble Kulkov or any of the Soviets. Kulkov, though enamored of words, is peasant-like in his simplicity. But the close quarters in which everyone is confined transform him into a strategist. In order to survive, he works out a deal with Major von Sturmer, the only officer among the seven Nazis: Kulkov will reveal what he knows about Soviet plans if the major will reciprocate. Unfortunately, Kulkov slips and reveals the presence of the underwater bridge, prompting a disparaging look from Lisa. But the slip is not fatal. Hearing the sound of digging, Von Sturmer assumes that a German rescue party has arrived and rushes toward the opening, whereupon Kulkov shoots him. The only German to come through is Kulkov's German shepherd dog, followed by the Russians.

Counter-Attack is more of a psychological melodrama than a war movie, reminiscent of films like *Blind Alley* (1939), remade ten years later as *The Dark Past*. In this film a psychiatrist plays a cat-and-mouse game with a neurotic murderer. *Counter-Attack* also resembles *The Desperate Hours* (1956), in which a family is held hostage in their own home by two escaped convicts. Lawson could not open up the play much, except to make it less claustrophobic by having Kulkov shed his ingenuousness so that the film's centerpiece would be the truth-telling game between Kulkov and von Sturmer.

Hollywood paid homage to a Russia under siege with a series of films that ran the gamut from a musical romance set in operetta land (*Song of Russia*); to an idealization of Soviet- style collectivism (*The North Star*); to shamefully erroneous propaganda (*Mission to Moscow*); to tributes to the Russian guerrillas who helped defeat Hitler's armies (*Days of Glory, Counter-Attack*). The films appeared at a time when patriotism was rife, when Nazis were archfiends from hell, and when any country under attack was an ally, deserving of our sympathy.

Everything changed when the war ended. When HUAC began its hearings concerning the nature and extent of communism in Hollywood, *Song of Russia* and *Mission to Moscow* were cited as prime examples of party line propaganda. When Louis B. Mayer testified before HUAC on 20 October 1947, he was specifically questioned about *Song of Russia*, which was produced by his studio, MGM. Asked if it had been made at the request of the government, he hesitated, but later he recalled speaking with some government (Office of War Information, or OWI) representatives, who wanted "a pat on Russia's back to keep them fighting." Whether or not the OWI encouraged Mayer to make the film, *Song of Russia* would have been consistent with the department's mission, dissemination of propaganda. The OWI encouraged studios to address the following issues in their films: the war and why it is being fought; the enemy, its objectives and methods; the production of war materiel in defense plants and aircraft factories; the sacrifices made by Americans on the home front; and the various branches of the armed services, including our fighting allies. *Song of Russia* portrayed the enemy as duplicitous and deadly. Nadya taught her students how to make a Molotov cocktail, which qualified as a homemade weapon of defense, and the film itself was an ode to an ally. What more could be expected of a movie set in 1941? The OWI's first question about a film was, "Will this picture help win the war?" No picture could. But since the OWI had been created specifically as an agency of propaganda, *Song of Russia* offered an outstanding example for its reason for being.

Robert Taylor, a friendly witness, appeared before HUAC two days after Mayer. When the question of government involvement in *Song of Russia* came up, Taylor stated correctly that the script was in development before there had been any OWI involvement. A treatment had been submitted on 31 March 1942, and the OWI was created by President Roosevelt on 13 June 1942. Later, Taylor recalled a meeting with OWI's Hollywood liaison, Lowell Mellett, in Mayer's office. Obviously, the OWI was interested in a pro-Russian film from Hollywood's biggest studio. However, MGM would have made the film regardless.

Although Taylor did not name names, he singled out Karen Morley and Howard da Silva for being disruptive at Screen Actors Guild meetings. Since they were later blacklisted, their disorderliness might have been construed as un-American. Questioned about *Song of Russia*, Taylor insisted he "objected strenuously" to appearing in it, but did so because movies were then being made "to more or less strengthen the feeling of the American people toward Russia." He also added, "I don't think it should have been made." As for Hollywood communists, he said, "I would love nothing better than to fire every last one of them and would never let them work in a studio or in Hollywood again."

On 20 October, the same day that Louis B. Mayer testified before HUAC, so did Jack Warner, who was grilled about government involvement with *Mission to Moscow*. Warner's answers ranged from "I can't remember" to outright rambling, much to the annoyance of HUAC counsel and interrogator Robert Stripling. Even a question as simple as whether Warner thought *Mission to Moscow* was pro-Communist "now" (1947) received a "That I would have to think over" answer. His response to the question, "Who asked you to make *Mission to Moscow*?" was phrased in the subjunctive mood: "I would say the former Ambassador Davies." Warner retracted this response, alleging that his brother Harry "made the deal with Mr. Davies."

Warner's vagueness was exasperating enough, but his treatment of Howard Koch, the highly respected writer who wrote the *Mission to Moscow* screenplay, was unconscionable. Friendly witnesses, including Warner, supplied HUAC with a list of "so-called Communists" which included Koch, one of the "Hollywood Nineteen," unfriendly witnesses opposed to the investigation. Koch was certainly a liberal, but not a communist. Yet he was obliged to take out an ad in the *Hollywood Reporter* stating that he was never a party member. Warner later offered a worthless apology, claiming that he got "carried away" and became "very emotional," as if his confused state of mind could justify jeopardizing someone's career. The transcript of Warner's testimony—if one can call it that—is revealing. It seems as if he informed HUAC that he fired Koch, along with some other writers, because of their politics. When Stripling asked if Koch was one of the writers that had been "dismissed," Warner bristled: "Let us get it correct. I never dismissed anyone for any activity. His contract expired and we didn't renew it." Had Koch been employed since then, Stripling inquired. "We didn't make a new deal with him," Warner replied.

After *Mission to Moscow*, Koch wrote three more screenplays for Warner Bros.: *In Our Time* (1944), *Rhapsody in Blue* (1945), and *Three Strangers* (1946), one of his best. After 1946, Koch wrote no more movies for Warner Bros., even though he had been working steadily at the studio since 1940, earning two screenplay credits that year. He went on to earn two in 1941; two in 1942—including one for *Casablanca*, for which he shared a best screenplay Oscar with the Epstein twins, Philip and Julius; and one each in 1943, 1944, 1945, and 1946. Then the music stopped. No "new deal." Politics? What else? Despite his admission in the *Hollywood Reporter* that he never was a communist, Koch found himself blacklisted in 1951, when he moved to London for five years before returning to America.

Unlike Warner, Mayer did not implicate the *Song of Russia* writers, Paul Jarrico and Richard Collins, who he probably knew were communists. *Song of Russia* may have mythologized Russia, but *Mission to Moscow* is a travesty of history. Still, Howard Koch only adhered to Davies's memoir, working from an early draft by Erskine Caldwell and producing a script that Warner called "excellent," an important piece of information that Warner never revealed to HUAC.

With the end of World War II, the noble Russian bear became the seven-headed red dragon of the apocalypse. The 1945 Yalta conferences resulted in another spheres-of-influence arrangement, with the Soviet Union turning Eastern Europe and East Germany into a microcosm of itself. And what Yalta proposed, the Potsdam Conference ratified. A new totalitarian regime had arisen, an even greater threat to democracy than Nazi Germany, whose conquests were puny compared to those of the Soviet Union. The Cold War was officially declared seven months after the end of World War II—and not by the United States Congress.

Chapter 3

CALLING DR. DEATH

ON 5 MARCH 1946, AT WESTMINSTER COLLEGE IN FULTON, MISSOURI, Sir Winston Churchill employed a phrase that immediately entered the international lexicon when he declared, "[A]n iron curtain has descended across the continent," referring specifically to Central and Eastern Europe. "Iron curtain" was not original. The phrase had even been used by Hitler's minister of propaganda, Joseph Goebbels, who committed suicide with his wife, Magda, after arranging for the murder of his six children with a combination of morphine and cyanide. Churchill, on the other hand, was the British messiah, who appealed to the House of Commons on 13 May 1940, demanding "victory at all costs—victory in spite of terrors—victory, however long and hard the road may be, for without victory there is no survival." Five years later, victory was achieved, but survival was problematic. Another threat to world peace had emerged: the Soviet Union, our erstwhile ally, now our mortal enemy.

At first, Americans felt secure. "We had the bomb, they didn't" was the prevalent—if cocky—attitude. But could "they" develop one? Could anyone who had access to uranium and knew the formula? And what about Stalin's boast a year after the war had ended that America would no longer have a monopoly on the bomb? Was that why, in July 1945, Stalin was unfazed when he was informed at the Potsdam Conference that the United States had perfected "a very powerful explosive" that could end the war? Plot lines for screenwriters mushroomed.

The bomb was a plot point even before Hiroshima. Henry Hathaway's *The House on 92nd Street* (1945) was produced by Louis de Rochemont, the great documentary filmmaker who revolutionized the newsreel, with *The March of Time,* raising it to the level of photojournalism. From 1935 to 1951, the series enlightened moviegoers about events omitted, ignored, or encapsulated in the average newsreel. *The House on 92nd Street* seemed like a

March of Time movie, with voiceover narration and a script that replicated the series' occasional inclusion of staged scenes amid newsreel footage. In lieu of reenactments and archival material, *The House on 92nd Street* featured a plot loosely based on an actual spy case, with on-location filming, authenticated by omniscient narration soberly delivered by Reed Hadley. With its interweaving of fact and fiction, *The House on 92nd Street* became one of Fox's first semi-documentaries, followed by *Boomerang* (1947), *Kiss of Death* (1947), *Call Northside 777* (1948), *The Street with No Name* (1948), and *Panic in the Streets* (1950).

The House on 92nd Street dramatized the relentless quest of New York-based Nazi agents for Process 97, "the secret ingredient of the atomic bomb." According to the opening title, the film was "adapted from cases in the espionage files of the Federal Bureau of Investigation" and included information that "could not be made public until the first atom bomb was dropped on Japan." The screenwriters, Barré Lyndon, Charles G. Booth, and John Monks Jr., worked fast. A shooting script was ready by mid-April 1945, with Process 97 remaining unidentified "until release by proper authority can be obtained." When *House* premiered on 10 September 1945, a month after atomic bombs had been dropped on Hiroshima and Nagasaki, Process 97 was still unidentified—but by then it did not matter. Whether named or not, the "secret ingredient" was plutonium, atomic number 94 (the writers came close). The once taboo word was now in the public domain.

If the Nazis had been interested in developing a bomb during the war, what about the Japanese? "Japan Developed Atomic Bomb; Russians Grabbed Scientists" was the dramatic headline of the 3 October 1946 issue of the *Atlanta Constitution*. Dispensing with a lead, reporter David Snell cut to the chase: "Japan successfully tested an atomic bomb three days prior to the end of the war." The site was Konan in what is now North Korea. When Japanese scientists learned that the Russians were advancing toward Konan, they destroyed as many documents as they could so as to keep them out of Russian hands. Actually, Japan had been conducting nuclear research since the 1930s—a fact that was unknown to screenwriters, whose primary concern was developing a post-Hiroshima, one-size-fits-all template. If uranium was needed to produce plutonium, the hunt was on for the talismanic element. Hollywood did not discriminate among the hunters; they could be anyone or any country.

There was no connection between the 3 October *Atlanta Constitution* news story and *Flight to Nowhere* (1946), released two days earlier. Distributed by Screen Guild Productions, the film was deemed too insignificant for a *New York Times* review. Densely plotted, thoroughly implausible, and strangely fascinating, *Flight to Nowhere* envisioned an international cartel hoping to sell the Japanese a map that pinpointed the site of uranium deposits submerged in the shallow waters off an atoll. How occupied Japan would gain access to the uranium is never explained. However, the screenwriter, Arthur V. Jones, who had been working in B pictures since 1936, was probably inspired by the March 1946 evacuation of Bikini Atoll in preparation for nuclear testing there. Thus, the presence of uranium at an atoll (Bikini, obviously) was not that far-fetched—although the plot certainly was.

Nineteen forty-six also saw the release of Alfred Hitchcock's *Notorious*, in which ex-Nazis in Rio De Janeiro stored uranium ore in wine bottles in anticipation of the Fourth Reich. If Jones had written a script about a colony of Japanese scientists working under the radar in an underground laboratory to produce a bomb of their own in retaliation for Hiroshima, it might also have worked—provided it was as plausible as Ben Hecht's screenplay for *Notorious*, in which there were no missing links in the narrative chain. *Notorious* was a masterful concatenation of cause and effect, time and place, performance and direction, sound and silence, and suspense rather than surprise (a Hitchcock trademark). There was also no violation of verisimilitude. Could the Nazis, although defeated, still be considered a threat? *Notorious* argued persuasively that they could; *Flight to Nowhere* evaded the question altogether. There was no time for an answer. The film was rushed into production and shot in about four weeks, between mid-April and mid-May 1946.

Flight to Nowhere opens with a title, "Honolulu," followed by the murder of a Korean courier in possession of a map. A shot of a mushroom cloud follows, intimating that Hiroshima was America's response to Pearl Harbor. The Honolulu-Hiroshima juxtaposition, however, was not what Jones intended; rather, he intended to indicate that the bomb ushered in a new era of espionage—atomic espionage, with secrets for sale. The credits then roll, and the torturous plot begins in Los Angeles, where a pilot (Alan Curtis) is approached by mysterious woman (Micheline Cheriel) offering him $500 to fly her and her party to Death Valley. Everyone but the demure Evelyn Ankers is a trafficker in atomic secrets, eager to find the map and sell it to Japan. The ringleader is Jerome Cowan, the embodiment of the dark side of American capitalism. The cartel is exposed, the map retrieved, and Alan Curtis and Evelyn Ankers go into a clinch. Eventually, Japan rises out of the radioactive ashes to become a world player in electronics, many bearing the brand name Sony, which in 1989 became the owner of Columbia Pictures, now part of Sony Pictures Entertainment. The vanquished had become the victor.

Two years after Hiroshima, MGM decided that it was time for a movie about the bomb, a mélange of fact and fiction that would ease Americans into the nuclear age. *The Beginning or the End* (1947) would be a film about the birth of the bomb, a film about the Manhattan Project. While Hollywood was mythologizing Russia, a group of scientists was working covertly in such unlikely places as Oak Ridge, Tennessee, the University of Chicago, Hanford, Washington, and Los Alamos, New Mexico. Some of these scientists were émigrés, like Leo Szilard and Edward Teller of Hungary, Niels Bohr of Denmark, and Enrico Fermi of Italy. Others were Americans, like J. Robert Oppenheimer, John Wheeler, and Arthur Holly Compton. All were part of Manhattan Project, headed by Major General Leslie R. Groves. The code name "Manhattan Project," which sounded like a New York apartment complex, was intentionally deceptive, designed to obscure the real mission of the enterprise: the extraction of plutonium from uranium, which, if successful, could be used to produce "extremely powerful bombs of a new type," as Albert Einstein wrote in a letter to President Roosevelt in 1939. Einstein later regretted sending this letter.

Groves demanded absolute secrecy. A billboard at the Oak Ridge facility spelled out his policy:

What You See Here
What You Do Here
What You Hear Here
When You Leave Here
Let It Stay Here.

On 16 July 1945 at 5:30 am, a plutonium bomb, code-named the "Gadget"— the forerunner of "Fat Man," the bomb dropped on Nagasaki—was detonated in the Alamogordo Bombing Range (code name Trinity), a desert area 230 miles south of Los Alamos. Less than a month later, a uranium bomb, Little Boy, equivalent to 12,500 tons of TNT, would fall on Hiroshima. After the Gadget was tested at Alamogordo, Oppenheimer recalled a verse from the *Bhagavad-Gita*, which he had read in the original Sanskrit: "Now I am become Death, the destroyer of worlds." Oppenheimer was not the only destroyer.

If *The Beginning or the End* had been a semi-documentary like *The House on 92nd Street*, it might have had greater impact. But the hybrid genre was alien to the "Tiffany of Studios." Instead, what should have been the true story of the Manhattan Project became a conventional drama with a mammoth cast that played a mix of fictional characters and historical figures—the latter portrayed by actors who mostly bore only faint resemblances to their real life counterparts. The exceptions were Godfrey Tearle's uncanny FDR and Ludwig Stossel's wiry Albert Einstein. As for the others, audiences would neither have known nor cared what they looked like. These characters included: Manhattan Project director Leslie R. Groves (Brian Donlevy); his secretary, Jean O'Leary (Audrey Totter); head scientist at Los Alamos, J. Robert Oppenheimer, the so-called "father of the atom bomb" (Hume Cronyn); physicists Enrico Fermi (Joseph Calleia) and Leo Szilard (John Gallaudet); and Harvard president James Conant (Frank Ferguson). To audiences, these figures were characters in a movie. And no one would have confused Art Baker with President Truman in a rare instance of an actor impersonating a president who was not only living but still in office. The film's Truman deliberated over dropping the bomb, but the historical Truman did not. To him, this was a military decision he did not regret. Expediency was all: "[The bomb] seems to be the most terrible thing ever discovered, but it can be made the most useful."

The Beginning or the End was fact-inspired hagiography, designed to tell the world that the end of the war heralded a beginning—but of what? MGM had high hopes for *The Beginning or the End*, a title inspired by President Truman's response to the proposed film, implying the either-or consequences of nuclear power. Press kits attesting to the film's accuracy, with an endorsement from the president himself, were distributed to exhibitors and reviewers. Although press kits are notoriously flawed, this one at least documented the movie's genesis, which began with a fan letter from a star to a scientist.

When MGM contract actress Donna Reed learned that her former high school chemistry teacher, Dr. Edward R. Tompkins, had been part of Manhattan Project, she dashed off a letter on 25 October 1945, thanking him for helping to bring the war to an end. The letter prompted a reply from Tompkins, which included a suggestion for a movie about "the personalized drama of the men and women who bent to their will the forces of the atom bomb"— in short, a movie about the Manhattan Project that would answer critics like William D. Leahy, chairman of the Joint Chiefs of Staff, who likened the bombing of Hiroshima to the carnage wrought by "the barbarians of the Dark Ages." Reed showed Tompkins's letter to her husband, agent-producer Tom Owen, who in turn passed it on to MGM's legendary story editor, Sam Marx, who was so enthusiastic about the idea that he agreed to sign on as producer. But first Owen and Marx needed President Truman's blessing, which they received, along with a title. Tompkins also received a credit as "scientific technical advisor," and Owen received one for his "Cooperation."

Frank Wead, who blended fact and fiction smoothly in *They Were Expendable* (1945), one of the better World War II movies, wrote the script for *The Beginning or the End*, in which the "personalized drama" overshadowed the historical. At the heart of the film is the story of Manhattan Project scientist Matt Cochran (Tom Drake, the eternal boy next door), who died of radiation poisoning. Cochran was modeled after Canadian physicist Louis Slotin, who died of exposure to a lethal dose of radiation at Los Alamos in May 1946. In the film, Cochran dies before Hiroshima, not at Los Alamos, but on Tinian island in the Marianas, where Little Boy was assembled, and from which the Enola Gay took off around 2:45 am on 6 August. Although Cochran was conflicted about the bomb (and Drake's face was made for youthful angst), he resolved his doubts and left a letter for his wife (Beverly Tyler) in which he all but justified his death in the interest of a higher cause: "God has not shown us a way to destroy ourselves. Atomic energy is the hand He has extended to lift us from the ruins of war and lighten the burden of peace . . . . Men will learn to use this new knowledge well. They won't fail. They can't fail. For this is the moment that gives all of us a chance to prove that human beings are indeed made in the image and likeness of God."

Cochran's letter reads like the peroration of a sermon, which may have comforted the congregation, small as it was. In 1947, most moviegoers gravitated to non-atomic MGM films: *Good News* with June Allyson, *This Time for Keeps* with Esther Williams, *It Happened in Brooklyn* with Frank Sinatra, *The Hucksters* with Clark Gable, Ava Gardner, and the studio's new star, Deborah Kerr, and *Green Dolphin Street*—with its spectacular earthquake and tidal wave, along with Lana Turner, who also costarred that year with Spencer Tracy in *Cass Timberlane*.

MGM had not given up on the bomb. Five years later, it released *Above and Beyond* (1952), a biopic about Colonel Paul Tibbets (Robert Taylor), the pilot of the Enola Gay, which dropped Little Boy on Hiroshima. A few moviegoers might have remembered that Barry Nelson played Tibbets in *The Beginning or the End*; if the bombing of Hiroshima looked familiar, it was because it came from the same stock footage used in *The Beginning or the End*.

Above and Beyond opens with a prologue stating that the film could not have been made without the release of classified information. The information was nothing as revealing as the McGuffin in *The House on 92nd Street* that turned out to be plutonium. Instead, it was the toll the oath to absolute secrecy took on Tibbets and his wife (Eleanor Parker). Determined to prevent any leaks about the creation of the bomb that would end the war, Tibbets behaved autocratically, issuing color-coded passes and ordering dismissals for the slightest infraction. He was more haunted than tragic, and his wife was a mater dolorosa who must endure her husband's mood swings and spend her days not knowing when he will come home or, at times, even where he is. If their tension-riddled marriage ended in divorce even before Hiroshima, it would not have come as a surprise. The Tibbets eventually divorced, but did so in 1955, three years after the film's release.

Above and Beyond dramatized the crushing responsibilities the mission imposed on Tibbets, who subordinated everything—wife, family, and friends—to its success. After President Truman "regretfully" authorized the use of the bomb, Tibbets was confronted with a dilemma that only he could resolve: If the bomb could save five hundred thousand American lives and end the war, would it be worth the loss of a hundred thousand Japanese lives? With Pilate-like washing of the hands, Tibbets's superiors leave the decision to him. If anyone's hands were to get bloodied, they would be his. *Above and Beyond* did not canonize Tibbets. When an aggressive reporter asked how he felt about what he had done, Tibbets replied angrily and perhaps out of guilt: "Ask *them* [the Japanese] how they felt about it." The historical Tibbets was totally dispassionate: "It was all impersonal."

Above and Beyond did mediocre box office in a year filled with more memorable MGM fare, such as *Singin' in the Rain* (Gene Kelly, Debbie Reynolds, Donald O'Connor), *Million Dollar Mermaid* (Esther Williams), *Pat and Mike* (Spencer Tracy and Katharine Hepburn), *Because You're Mine* (Mario Lanza), and *The Naked Spur* (James Stewart). Robert Taylor had a better vehicle in the highly profitable *Ivanhoe*, costarring Joan Fontaine and the violet-eyed Elizabeth Taylor. This was the Robert Taylor audiences wanted: the Saxon knight, not the pilot who ushered in the era of fear and trembling.

The Manhattan Project returned to the screen again in *Fat Man and Little Boy* (Paramount, 1989), with Paul Newman as Lieutenant General Leslie R. Groves. Newman dominated the film, unlike Brian Donlevy in *The Beginning or the End*, in which Groves was a supporting role. Although *Fat Man and Little Boy* was overlong, it avoided hagiography in its depiction of the scientists who behaved like ego-driven academics at a faculty meeting, and it did not gloss over the fact that J. Robert Oppenheimer had a leftist for a lover. Still, it is worth seeing for its characterization of Oppenheimer (Dwight Schultz) as a brilliant but arrogant scientist who could barely conceal his contempt for Groves.

The definitive bomb movie derives from a Mickey Spillane novel that does not feature any historical figures, although it is haunted by history. *Kiss Me Deadly* (1955) weaves such a web of entrapment around its characters—pulling in the audience—that all a viewer can do is remain within its strands until they snap. Ironically, "bomb" is never uttered; all we know is that a number of people are involved in the quest for a "whatzit," which is only identified as such in a climactic image. Everything is askew in the film, including the credits that roll backwards. Clues are ellipses: a line from an obscure poem by Christina Rossetti, a swallowed key in a corpse, a locker with a leather box that is literally hot, a bogus roommate who may be a murderess, Schubert's Unfinished Symphony serving as a metaphor for an unfinished woman, and a coolly perverse private eye who breaks a Caruso record in front of a would-be opera singer and closes a desk drawer on a greedy hand.

Adapted from, or perhaps more accurately, inspired by Mickey Spillane's *Kiss Me Deadly* (1952), the screenplay by the sadly ignored A. I. Bezzerides—novelist, short story writer, and Hollywood's unacknowledged littérateur—is virtually an original work. Bezzerides retained Spillane's series detective, Mike Hammer. He even reproduced the novel's opening scene: a woman in a trench coat caught in the headlights of Hammer's car, which almost hits her. Then he goes his own way—from the mean streets of Spillane's New York, to the meaner ones of Los Angeles, where day is eye-squinting glare and night is a skein of shadows. Bezzerides's Hammer is more of a sleazy shamus than a tough-talking gumshoe. His Hammer is also ambivalent about his female factotum, Velda (Maxine Cooper), whom he both loves and manipulates when he needs evidence for a case. Yet when she is kidnapped, he rescues her from a burning beach house as if he were a fire fighter. Best of all, Bezzerides kept Hammer's integrity from reaching zero, even when it seemed about to plummet. "Integrity" is not part of the vocabulary of Spillane's Hammer, who has no qualms about pulling the trigger to settle a score.

Hammer is not one of Raymond Chandler's displaced detective-knights, like Philip Marlowe. Chandler portrayed Marlowe not just as a private eye, but as a knight, whose "code is hopelessly anachronistic in the modern world." When Marlowe enters the Sternwood mansion at the beginning of Chandler's *The Big Sleep*, he notices the stained glass image of a knight trying to untie a damsel from a tree: "I stood there and thought that if I lived in the house, I would sooner or later have to climb up there and help him."

"Thus was born the private eye as knight figure, as rescuer of the weak and defenseless." But Spillane's Hammer has no pretentions about being a grail seeker. Hammer is only a private eye who can make it uncomfortable for uncooperative suspects. His favorite sport seems to be shooting men in the eye. If he wore armor, it would have been tarnished and dented. His signature attire is unpressed suits and shirts with loosely knotted ties and functional cuff links. He can be tender in his hardboiled way, giving Velda a perfunctory kiss before sending her out on a job, but the "whatzit" is all that matters. As played definitively by Ralph Meeker, Hammer is not on a quest for the black bird or the mystery woman, but for the "whatzit" that dares not speak its name—and in fact never does, except through inference. Bezzerides's Hammer steps out of Spillane's pulpy world into the whirlpool of ultra-noir, a black and white limbo with no grey scale.

The villains in Spillane's novel were mafiosi, and the "whatzit" was narcotics. Spillane was influenced by Malcolm "Mike" Johnson's articles about corruption on the New York waterfront, which appeared in the *New York Sun* in 1949. Spillane was also attracted by Senator Estes Kefauver's Senate Crime Investigating Committee, which left "thirty million households . . . with the distinct impression that something was rotten in U.S. cities." When Bezzerides read the novel, he knew he could do better, and he did. The Mafia did not dominate the news in the 1950s; the bomb did. Atomic testing was occurring on a regular basis in Nevada. The Soviet Union, which tried out its first atomic bomb in 1949, exploded two more in October 1952. Klaus Fuchs admitted that when he was at Los Alamos, he passed on classified information to the Soviets, as did David Greenglass, who also implicated his sister, Ethel, wife of Julius Rosenberg. The Rosenbergs were electrocuted in 1954. From the Army-McCarthy hearings, one would get the impression that communists were ubiquitous. Even J. Robert Oppenheimer was denounced as a traitor, who had "worked tirelessly . . . to retard the United States H-bomb program." Worse, he was branded a Soviet spy, denied security clearance, and barred from military installations. Certainly his romantic involvement with the physician-psychiatrist Jean Tatlock, a party member who committed suicide in January 1944, did not enhance his image. It was a case of last year's savior, this year's Satan. America was ripe with paranoia, the feeding ground of film noir. *Kiss Me Deadly* would reap the harvest, radiated though it was.

When Hammer has still not figured out the nature of the "whatzit," his police detective friend, Pat Murphy (Wesley Addy), gives it to him in three short blasts: "Manhattan Project, Los Alamos, Trinity." That is all he needed to know, and Bezzerides assumed the same of the audience—at least a 1955 audience. The villains are atomic thieves; the prize, a radioactive isotope apparently stolen from Los Alamos. The climax is a conflagration like Spillane's, but a high-grade one, a junior-size Hiroshima.

The three-name clue is typical of Bezzerides's allusion-sprinkled script. He changed the name of the woman caught in the headlights from Berga Torn to Christina Bailey, named after the pre-Raphaelite poet Christina Rossetti, whose sonnets she knows intimately—so much so that, before Christina is tortured to death and strung up like a deer carcass, she leaves a two-word note for Hammer: "Remember me." With some help from Velda, Hammer locates the "Remember me" sonnet, finding a clue in the lines: "But if the darkness and corruption leave / A vestige of the thoughts we once did have." Christina, who had known darkness and corruption, left a "vestige," even though she is now a corpse lying in a morgue. Spillane's Hammer could never have engaged in such exegesis. Bezzerides could, and did so through a stand-in played by Ralph Meeker, a Northwestern University alumnus who gave ample evidence that he had been exposed to the New Criticism. The vestige is a key Christina had swallowed which was removed during an autopsy. The key belongs to a locker containing a leather case, which, if opened just a bit, sears the flesh.

The suspense, like that in most noir, is not calibrated, but ratcheted up until it can go no higher, then followed by a dénouement that is often an unmasking. The film is nearing the end and needs to wind up. *Kiss Me Deadly* observes that tradition, redeeming it as well. Bezzerides went beyond Spillane, who ended the novel in a blaze of horror. In Spillane, the bogus Lily Carver opens her terrycloth robe, revealing the effects of a fire that left her "a disgusting mass of twisted, puckered flesh from her knees to her neck." Pressing a gun against Hammer's belt, she demands that he kiss her "deadly" before she pulls the trigger. Hammer obliges by flicking open his lighter and igniting her robe, "turning the white of her hair into black char." Bezzerides devised a different incineration, this time nuclear, at the beach house of Dr. Soberin (Albert Dekker), where the leather box has been taken and where Velda is being held prisoner. Soberin is a smart dresser and a suave sadist with a mistress/moll, Gabrielle (the German-born Gaby Rogers, whose accent suggests an international conspiracy). Gabrielle, who posed as Christina's roommate and may also have murdered her, covets the box, assuming that its contents will provide her with the good life. Soberin, an erudite villain, as versed in mythology as Hammer is in *explication de texte*, cautions Gabrielle against opening the case, warning that doing so would make her another Pandora. The allusion is lost on Gabrielle. Nonplussed, Soberin continues spouting mythology, comparing the contents to the head of Medusa, the snaky-haired gorgon who turned whoever gazed on her to stone. But like Pandora, Gabrielle cannot resist temptation. After shooting Soberin, who likens himself to the three-headed dog Cerberus guarding the entrance to Hades, she opens the box, which contains the radioactive isotope.

What looks like a phosphorescent block of ice turns her incandescent and sets off an explosion, suggesting what might have been in store for Los Angeles. The house detonates in a burst of blinding light that glazes the sand, driving Hammer and Velda into the ocean. A doctored version of the film released shortly after the May 1955 premiere suggests that they did not survive, presumably demonstrating that even the invincible Mike Hammer is not immune to radioactivity. Mickey Spillane fans who saw the other version would have assumed their hero pulled a Houdini and went back to work, eventually moving on to television, where he was portrayed by Stacy Keach in *Mickey Spillane's Mike Hammer* and later in the syndicated *Mike Hammer: Private Eye*. A series detective is killed off by his creator, not an editor who excises some frames. But even if Hammer and Velda perished, the message would have been the same: No one is safe these days, so learn to live on the edge.

Once the Soviet Union successfully detonated an atomic bomb in Kazakhstan on 29 August 1949, America's nuclear monopoly was at an end, as Stalin had predicted—unless it could come up with a super bomb. Enter the hydrogen bomb, tested successfully at Eniwetok atoll in the Marshall Islands in November 1952. The following year, the Soviets detonated their own H-bomb, which was not as powerful as the one tested at Eniwetok, but still a start. A year later, in 1954, the United States tested an even deadlier H-bomb at Bikini atoll, where the explosion "ejected several million tons of radioactive debris into the air." Although Bikini was then uninhabited, residents of other atolls were left with radiation poisoning, which in some cases proved fatal.

At least this time, Oppenheimer, who was initially skeptical about the H-bomb, would not have to say that he had become death. But his attitude was deemed unpatriotic, and his belief that the United States should share its nuclear knowledge with the Soviets resulted in accusations that he was a communist sympathizer. It was not until 1963 that Oppenheimer was vindicated, only to die four years later.

In *The Story of Mankind* (Warner Bros., 1957), news of a "super bomb" causes consternation in the heavens. A tribunal is convened in outer space to determine—by measuring its achievements against its failures—whether humankind is worth saving. Warner Bros. assumed that if a crash course in world civilization did not attract audiences (it didn't), the cast of moderately well known actors—playing cameo roles and traipsing through the centuries—might (it didn't). The movie's perverse fascination lay in wondering who will pop up next: Virginia Mayo as Cleopatra, Hedy Lamarr as Joan of Arc, Agnes Moorehead as Elizabeth I, Reginald Gardiner as Shakespeare, Helmut Dantine as Napoleon, Marie Windsor as Josephine, a bloated Peter Lorre as Nero. Arguing on behalf of the species is the Spirit of Mankind (Ronald Colman), and for its annihilation, Vincent Price as the bomb's creator, Mr. Scratch (Stephen Vincent Benet's name for Satan in his short story, "The Devil and Daniel Webster"). Scratch's identity is evident from his red accouterments: cravat, pocket-handkerchief, notebook, and telephone. The bomb, then, is literally an infernal machine.

It was rather daring in 1957 to attribute the H-bomb to the devil, although there is no further mention of such a connection in the film. The studio need not have worried about being branded un-American. *The Story of Mankind* is popcorn history, slavered with butter and sprinkled with salt for viewers to munch on during their history tutorial. The spirit invokes the achievements of Moses, Socrates, Plato, Aristotle, Hippocrates, da Vinci, Galileo, Shakespeare. Scratch counters with examples of humankind at its worst: Neronian Rome, the Salem witchcraft trials, the slave-holding South, two world wars, and Hiroshima—the latter, an image too iconic for comment. The spirit calls a final witness, a toddler representing the world of tomorrow. "Let there be a tomorrow for the planet Earth," the spirit pleads. Although he argues eloquently that evil, when crushed, has made humankind stronger, the tribunal is unimpressed. The scales of history are balanced, with neither good nor evil outweighing the other. The species is given another chance to redeem itself. "The choice is entirely up to you," the chief judge warns, looking straight at the camera and leaving the audience less hopeful than they were when they arrived. At least they may have had a few laughs: Harpo Marx appears as a harp-playing Isaac Newton, hit on the head by an apple, and Groucho delivers one-liners as Peter Minuet. When an Indian chief greets him with "How!" Groucho replies, "Three minutes and leave them in the shell." Corny, but it was moments like these that made sitting through this "history for dummies" bearable.

"The choice is entirely up to you" mandate was very much in keeping with the ethics of the age, reflected in the court's ruling that humankind's capacity for good equals its capacity for evil. By invoking free will, *The Story of Mankind* allied itself with *The Next Voice You Hear* and *The Day the Earth Stood Still*, which also challenged humanity to redeem itself, ignoring the fact that a tribunal would not have been necessary—and *The Story of Mankind* would not have been made—if the bomb had not been created.

The bombing of Hiroshima was first seen in movie theaters. In August 1945, a typical bill consisted of a movie, a short subject, previews of coming attractions, and a newsreel. In some theaters, particularly in large cities, double features were common. Saturdays were special. In addition to the main attraction and a below-the-title movie, there was also a newsreel, a chapter of a serial, perhaps a travelogue or short subject, and a cartoon, making it possible for kids to spend the entire afternoon in the thrall of the daylight dream. Hence, the incongruity of a bill with a comedy like *Out of This World* (1945), followed by a newsreel on the bombing of Hiroshima, or, earlier in 1945, footage of the liberation of Auschwitz on the same program as *Bring on the Girls*. Hiroshima had become an epochal event captured on film—but purely as part of the program, not the main attraction. Still, the bomb could be a main attraction; in fact, it could become a versatile plot generator.

In World War II movies, falling bombs carried no symbolism; they simply killed people, like bullets in crime movies and arrows in westerns. For the post-Hiroshima moviegoer, explosions were no longer simply a burst of fire and smoke. They were a cumulonimbus of death, over which hovered the mushroom cloud. Hiroshima had become a lower-case holocaust. In his interview with director Raoul Walsh, Richard Schickel brought up the climax of *White Heat* (1949), with Cody Jarrett (James Cagney) screaming, "Made it, Ma! Top of the world!" amid exploding chemical tanks. Schickel asked Walsh if he intended the explosion as a metaphor for Hiroshima, or at least a reminder of the first atomic bomb. Walsh pondered the question, never answering it fully but suggesting that, unconsciously, he may well have. Explosions were not the same after Hiroshima. They were louder, more ominous, and uncomfortably atavistic, reflecting the "fear of the cata-clysmic destruction of civilization, mayhem of an unimaginable higher or-der than we had ever seen before, the beginning of the end of life as we know it." That kind of paralyzing fear was at the heart of Ingmar Bergman's *Winter Light* (1963), in which the news that China had the bomb drove a simple fisherman to suicide. *Winter Light* is haunted by Christian symbol-ism and existential questioning of religion's ability to assuage humankind's fear of annihilation. American filmmakers, more commercially oriented, avoided the overwhelming question—or answered it with a homily. They preferred to dramatize the effects of the bomb, largely in terms of the mon-strosities it produced: the giant ants, grasshoppers, and sea creatures of the science fiction film. But if the bomb's progeny are so grotesque, what does that say about the parents?

Chapter 4

CREATURES FROM THE ID

THE BROADWAY MUSICAL *JAMAICA* (1957) STARRED LENA HORNE AND RI-
cardo Montalban, and had a score by Harold Arlen that set Calypso to a
Broadway beat and used wickedly satiric lyrics by E. Y. "Yip" Harburg. Josephine Premice stopped the show with "Leave De Atom Alone," making light
of the specter of nuclear war:

> If you want Mississippi to stay where it is
> If you want to see Wall Street and General Motors continue in biz
> If you want Uncle Sam to keep holding what's yours and what's his
> If you're fond of kith and kin in their skin and bone
> Don't fool around with hydrogen
> Leave de atom alone.
> Bad for the teeth, bad for the bone
> Don't fool with it, leave it alone.

The lyrics were black humor, forcing a laugh—a nervous one, perhaps—
out of our deepest fear. And yet, as in most black comedy, reality seeped
through the darkness. Who would not be "most exasperated" when "radio
activated," or agree that becoming "fissionable material" would leave "big
smog in the atmosphere?" But Hollywood would not "leave de atom alone."
It was a plot point, and plot points never die; they are only recycled. The
bomb proved to be an all-purpose plot point, especially for science fiction.

Except for humanitarians like Louis Pasteur (*The Story of Louis Pasteur* [1936]), Marie Curie (*Madame Curie* [1943]), and the Australian nurse,
Elizabeth Kenny, who pioneered a treatment for polio victims (*Sister Kenny* [1946]), Hollywood's scientists were a colorless lot. That is, unless they
were dabbling in the black arts, which made them alternately fascinating
and repellent. They devised formulas to detach their dark side from their

better self (*Dr. Jekyll and Mr. Hyde* in its various versions) and created life out of inert matter (*Frankenstein* and its successors). Science was put to demonic use in the B movies of the 1940s, strangely mirroring the equally demonic experiments being conducted in the Nazi death camps. Scientists turned themselves into apes (*The Ape Man* [1943]), apes into women (*Captive Wild Woman* [1943]), men into wolves (*The Mad Monster* [1942]), rivals into zombies (*The Mad Ghoul* [1943]), and Nazi spies into respectable American citizens (*Black Dragons* [1942]). They could disfigure the innocent (*The Monster Maker* [1944]) and implant a human brain into a gorilla (*The Monster and the Girl* [1941]). One could argue, of course, that such films did not present science as a force for good. But audiences can take only so much nobility. Pasteur and the Curies were humanitarians as well as scientists, whose stories are edifying. So is Dante's *Paradiso*, yet no other part of the *Divine Comedy* has had the universal appeal of the *Inferno*. Sin has always been more marketable than virtue because, as Chuck Tatum (Kirk Douglas), the unprincipled reporter in Billy Wilder's *Ace in the Hole/ The Big Carnival* (1951) proclaimed: "Bad news sells, because good news is no news."

When the horror films of the 1950s reverted to their gothic roots, replete with baroque embellishments, science fiction picked up the slack, exploring the effects of a more disturbing kind of experimentation. In July 1945, less than a month before the bombings of Hiroshima and Nagasaki, a dress rehearsal took place in New Mexico. In 1946, underwater detonations were conducted at Bikini Atoll. In 1951, nuclear testing resumed in Nevada and would continue there for forty years. And in November 1952, the first hydrogen bomb was exploded at Eniwetok atoll. The bomb provided screenwriters with fresh fodder. It was as if—by generating its own mushroom cloud of movies that imagined the after effects of the bomb, taken to the extreme—Hollywood were making America pay for Hiroshima. What if nuclear testing produced giant ants (*Them!*), locusts (*Beginning of the End*), and leeches (*Attack of the Giant Leeches*)? What if it created sea monsters (*It Came from Beneath the Sea*), and evicted prehistoric creatures from their lairs (*The Beast from 20,000 Fathoms*), revivifying and freeing them to wreak havoc? If Hiroshima heralded "The Dawn of the Atomic Age," it was an age that did not bear the name of a metal, but a particle. It was as if the advent of the bomb were a grim parody of Hesiod's account of creation in the *Theogony*, which began with Gaia (Earth) producing Uranus (Sky) out of herself without a male consort, and then mating with her male offspring. Although the coupling of Earth and Sky was a necessary stage in the evolutionary process, it was also an incestuous one that gave birth to the hundred-headed monsters Briareos, Kottos, and Gyges. Analogously, could not the bombing of Hiroshima, the tests in the American Southwest, and the detonations at Bikini and Eniwetok produce their own race of monsters? Hollywood answered with a ringing "Yes." The studios did not wait for the continuation of the Greek version of Genesis, which culminated in the reign of the Olympians. For the Greeks, it was a long haul from chaos to order, each stage less barbaric than the previous one, but none totally free of violence. Hollywood did not care about the Olympians; monsters sold tickets.

Although the MGM classic *Forbidden Planet* (1956) has nothing to do with the bomb, it offers a way of interpreting atomic mutant offspring. The film is richly allusive. Its point of departure is Shakespeare's *The Tempest*, with the setting transferred from "an uninhabited island" to the star Altair, designated Altair IV, whose sole human inhabitants are Dr. Morbius (Walter Pidgeon) and his daughter Altaira, aka Alta (Anne Francis), interstellar incarnations of Prospero and Miranda. Their factotum, Robby the Robot, is not a sprite like Ariel, but a more inventive creation, capable of doing everything from making bourbon to whipping up a diamond-studded dress for Alta. Alonso's son Prince Ferdinand, in love with Miranda, becomes Commander Adams (the pre-*Airplane!* Leslie Nielsen), who is equally attracted to Alta. Caliban, Shakespeare's "savage and deformed slave," does not appear as a character, but rather as a planetary force: a remnant of the Krel, an advanced people who perished in one night, surviving only as a demonic presence, invisible and deadly. Capable of renewing its molecular structure, the force is immune to ray guns and atomic blasters. It is "the monster from the Id," as "Doc" Ostrow (Warren Stevens) declares before he dies. Only the destruction of Altair will annihilate it.

Names are significant in *Forbidden Planet*. Morbius's ship, which landed on Altair, is the Bellerophon, named for the rider of the winged steed Pegasus of Greek mythology. Morbius's own name is derived from the Latin *morbus* ("disease"). He is an anti-Prospero "in pursuit of forbidden knowledge." Altair is a double star in the constellation Aquilla. We are in a darkly magical world, one of doubling. In attempting to transcend the material world through reason by choosing the Apollonian over the Dionysian, the Krel failed to control the monster from the id that burst forth in internecine slaughter. Such was the uninhabited Altair that Morbius found on his arrival—uninhabited, that is, except for the monstrous id, which he channeled into himself, becoming the Dr. Jekyll and Mr. Hyde of Altair.

For those whose Freudianism is rusty, Adams defines the id in layperson's terms as the "mindless beasts of the unconscious," which, if unleashed, can cause destruction. These "beasts" are "the drives and instincts common to humankind, whose existence cannot be denied, but whose power, if uncontrolled, can produce chaos." The language corresponds roughly to Freud's "dark, inaccessible part of our personality," "a cauldron full of seething excitations," unaffected by logic and the passage of time. Most frighteningly of all, the id is amoral. Finally, Adams, who is as good a Freudian as he is a commander and romantic lead, confronts Morbius with the truth. In his determination to establish a utopia for himself and his daughter in order to shield her from the outside world, he has drawn the Krel force into himself, becoming as much of a double being as Henry Jekyll, whose id was Mr. Hyde. The force is Morbius's döppelganger, which he, like the Krel, tried to overcome by privileging ego over id, which retaliated like a scorned lover. Morbius must perish, along with Altair 4, for a new beginning to arise from the ashes of the past. Just as Ferdinand and Miranda presumably embark for Naples at the end of The Tempest, Adams and Alta head back to Earth, which will probably strike Alta as terra incognita.

Altair IV might have been destroyed, but the monsters from the id were not. They reside in the interstices of any weapon of mass destruction, codenamed Thanatos, the death instinct, one of the id's many manifestations. The id, as embodied in the bomb, is amoral and ambivalent. It was used to shorten a war and save the lives of American service personnel, but it brought death and devastation to the innocent. Although created by great minds, it was capable of returning life to the state in which it began. Ironically, the bomb intended to save American lives ended up destroying the lives of others. The anthropomorphic names of the first atomic bombs, Fat Man and Little Boy, were palliatives that downplayed their lethal nature. They sounded like toys or playthings, inanimate twins ready for a mock christening. Hollywood found the monsters from the id in science fiction without having to resort to euphemism. The studios gave the audience its frissons and perhaps some food for thought—not too rich, but substantial enough to make some question the ingredients.

Hollywood in the 1950s was stuck in a time warp, exactly where the Greeks were after the mating of Earth and Sky, which, on 6 August 1945, became the violation of Earth by Sky, producing a new kind of enemy capable of destroying civilization. The bomb even caused mutations in insects. Ants, once household pests, became a menace in Them! (1954). Unlike any other film of the 1950s, Them! was site-specific. It identified the culprit: the bomb that was tested in New Mexico on 16 July 1945. The film opens four years later. A traumatized girl wanders aimlessly along a stretch of road in the New Mexico desert. A police car arrives, and then the child is taken away in an ambulance. The "them" that left her in shock are mutated killer ants, whose presence is heralded by shrill chirping reminiscent of frenzied cicadas. The humongous ants prey on the locals, injecting formic acid into their bodies. When the formic acid is placed before the child, she screams, "Them," thus validating the title. The ants are not just bomb-generated; they are also a totalitarian colony, whose workers are dominated by queens that have established nests beneath the streets of Los Angeles.

Them! is atypical in other respects. The scientists are a father-daughter team (Edmund Gwenn and Joan Weldon). Anyone assuming that a romance would develop between the daughter and the FBI agent (James Arness) was disappointed. What matters is the destruction of the nests, which is accomplished with flamethrowers. At least the bomb that caused the crisis is not used to resolve it. If it were, Los Angeles would have been reduced to a heap of cinders. But the 1945 bomb test was only a point of departure, not the crux of the film, which is a warning that apocalypse may be near. "The beast shall reign over the Earth," Dr. Medford (Gwenn) intones, invoking the seven-headed beast from the *Book of Revelation* (13:1–8). Medford delivers the grand summary: "When man entered the atomic age, he entered a new world. What he will find in that new world, nobody can predict." The unknown was a challenge to writers, who envisioned the worst.

The Deadly Mantis (1957) did not allude to Hiroshima, but the opening image, a volcanic eruption in the Arctic Circle, clearly evoked the atomic bomb. The documentary-style prologue about America's radar defenses, which do not figure in the plot, reassures us that "radar is everywhere" and "designed to defend us against attacks"—especially from the Arctic. But attacks from whom, or what? This time, the enemy is a "what," spawned by a volcanic eruption of such magnitude that it melted the polar ice caps, releasing a long-buried carnivorous mantis capable of circling the globe, attacking planes, wrecking trains, and demolishing buses. Eventually, it sets down in Washington, DC, where it mounts the Washington Monument, and then proceeds to New York, where it takes refuge in a tunnel. Bullets and grenades do the trick, destroying the mantis without disrupting traffic—so much for radar and our defense system. At least moviegoers knew that the system existed, although one doubts that anyone remembered the prologue by the end of the film.

The mantis looked like a crane with a bulbous head, glassy eyes that occasionally glowed, and appendages resembling metallic prostheses. It was too synthetic to be frightening. Even its leitmotif—a buzz that swelled into a laryngitic roar—simply grated on the ear. More impressive was the scientific talk, which was layperson-friendly. *The Deadly Mantis* treated science and the military impartially. Although the military solved the problem with explosives, they would not have known their enemy were it not for the paleontologist, who concluded that what appeared to be a hook was a piece of the mantis's cartilage.

Scientists are not always as helpful as the paleontologist in *The Deadly Mantis*. Initially, Jack Arnold's *Tarantula* (1955) appeared to be a straightforward science fiction film set in Arizona, where a renowned biologist (Leo G. Carroll) is experimenting with laboratory animals, hoping to discover an inexpensive nutrient to combat world hunger and increase longevity. White rats and rabbits, injected with a serum, increase in size at an astonishing rate. To test the serum's effect on humans, the biologist's longtime colleague injects himself, resulting in facial disfigurement and death. A graduate student does likewise, and although he is disfigured, he does not die. Maddened by his transmogrification, the student injects the biologist with the same serum, trashing the lab and inadvertently releasing a gigantic tarantula. The biologist's face rots away until he looks like a sickly Cyclops, and the tarantula terrorizes the community, eventually destroying the biologist's home, as if in retaliation for the experiments conducted there. When neither bullets nor dynamite can destroy the creature, it is napalmed—as Tokyo was by American bombers in 1943 and North Korea in 1950.

Tarantula's tie-in with the bomb is introduced so casually that it can easily be missed. Mutant movies of the 1950s skirted the issue of responsibility. Since the Cold War was in progress, atomic testing was performed for the common good, regardless of the consequences. "Ban the bomb" was a slogan in waiting. Although the bomb itself did not produce the monstrous tarantula, the biologist admitted that he and his colleague had been together at Oak Ridge. It was a throwaway line, but anyone who caught it realized that the two were part of the Manhattan Project at Oak Ridge, Tennessee, known as the "home of the atom bomb." The serum they devised contained radioactive isotopes that increased the size of animals and insects, but produced acromegaly in humans. The experiment, however well intentioned, was not simply a failure, but one with disastrous consequences.

Tarantula is one of the subtlest of the bomb-centered movies of the 1950s. The creature, lumbering towards its prey, its spindly legs extending outward like pincers, was indirectly the product of the Manhattan Project. The biologist would not have experimented with radioactive isotopes if he had remained a college professor. "Oak Ridge" was shorthand that did not require translation.

Beginning of the End (1957) also featured a scientist (Peter Graves) with a noble goal: averting world hunger by subjecting fruit and vegetables to radiation. The result was gargantuan produce. The process is not without risks. Radiation left his assistant hearing- and speech-impaired, the scientist (really, an entomologist, as the plot requires) dispassionately informs a reporter (Peggy Castle). Amazingly, the assistant takes his disability in stride and is irritatingly good-natured, until he is attacked by a monstrous locust, part of a plague sweeping through Illinois.

When the reporter learned that the locusts have broken into a warehouse and eaten the radioactive grain that was also part of the scientist's nutrition experiment, she reacted the way the audience would to such an aberration, inquiring if there is an "atomic installation" nearby. By 1957, moviegoers knew that the atom's offspring were many and varied. If giant ants, why not giant locusts?

Beginning of the End absolves the scientist of culpability. In fact, the thought that he indirectly caused the mutations did not cross the mind of any character, including the reporter. What alone can redeem him—at least in the minds of thoughtful moviegoers—is finding a way to destroy the monstrous fruit of his experiment, although nothing can compensate for lives lost and towns leveled. When the locusts reach Chicago, the military is ready to evacuate the city before bombing it, as if that were the only solution. General Hanson (the ubiquitous Morris Ankrum) outlines his plan so clinically that he seems as much a threat as the locusts. The scientist saves the day, if not the film, by coming up with a solution worthy of an entomologist: a simulation of a mating call transmitted to a launch on Lake Michigan that would lure the locusts into the water, where they would drown. The plan worked, but, as T. S. Eliot asked in "Gerontion," "after such knowledge / what forgiveness?" *Beginning of the End* is not an either-or film, which is why it is so disturbing. The boy-man scientist may have saved the day, but he did so but at terrible cost. He is unfazed by the devastation the experiment has caused. The general believes that the solution to any extraordinary problem is the bomb, as if Chicago were another Hiroshima or Nagasaki. Rebuild and get on with it. Things could be worse. And forget about the irreplaceable masterpieces in the Art Institute; they're only paintings.

In science fiction, radioactivity can cause anything. Witness *Attack of the Giant Leeches* (1959), a cut-rate movie with a ghoulish script by Leo Gordon. Since audiences had already been exposed to gigantism in various species, Gordon, who also wrote the original story, settled on leeches in the Florida Everglades. The Everglades was not an arbitrary choice, although such would not become apparent until the end. Gordon intercut two narratives: monsters from the muck and lust vs. love, the latter, a diptych with an unfaithful wife and her lover, and a game warden and his girl friend, who are as chaste as the lovers are horny. Sex and venality are a prelude to death. Not only does the adulterous couple fall victim to the leeches, so do two locals interested only in grabbing the reward for the creatures stalking the swamp. The film is not for the faint-hearted. The leeches drag their victims down to an underwater cave, where they exsanguinate them—in effect, torturing them to death. "No more," the wife moans, as a leech sucks out her blood.

Knowing that the audience is entitled at least to a one-word explanation for the mutants, Gordon supplies it: the community's next door neighbor, Cape Canaveral, now Cape Kennedy, where the first rocket launch took place in February 1950, and from which a ballistic missile was fired in February 1959, eight months before the movie was released. "Cape Canaveral" is a heavily encoded name. Cape Canaveral equals missiles equals radioactivity equals mutants. According to the film, every launch left a radioactive spoor that could wend its way into a swamp. But Gordon does not end by targeting radiation. The warden, originally opposed to using dynamite for fear of killing off marine life, finally accedes. If TNT can do the trick, so be it. Marine biologists might have to look elsewhere for rare species.

Attack of the Giant Leeches is an issue-layered script in a cheesy production—quite the opposite of Jack Arnold's masterpiece, *The Incredible Shrinking Man* (1957), a faithful adaptation of Richard Matteson's novel, *The Shrinking Man*. Scott Carey (Grant Williams) is sunbathing on a yacht with his wife, when he notices an approaching cloud that expands into a mist, spraying his chest with specks of dust, later determined to be radioactive fallout. When exposure to an insecticide exacerbates his condition, causing the realignment of his molecules, Scott begins losing height, until he becomes a homunculus reduced to living in a dollhouse. The cat, once a household pet, becomes his enemy, driving him into the cellar, where he must contend with an ordinary spider that, to him, is as terrifying as the tarantula in Arnold's earlier film (which he is obviously quoting). Any hopes for Scott's rescue are dashed when his wife and brother, who assume he is dead, make a trip to the flooded cellar, which to Scott is an ocean. Since they can neither see nor hear him, Scott is doomed to a subterranean and solitary existence, literally becoming an underground man.

What is extraordinary about *The Incredible Shrinking Man*, and what makes it unique among the science fiction films of the period, is the coda, an eloquent voiceover monologue. The movie does not end on a note of despair, although anyone in Scott's condition might question the existence of a benevolent God. Scott realizes he belongs to a new world, larger than even his cellar-home. More important, he senses that he is not alone in the universe: "If there were other bursts of radiation, other clouds . . . would other beings follow me into this vast new world?" He inhabits the world of the infinitesimal, which, joined with the infinite, closes the circle of creation. Although "smaller than the smallest," Scott has a place in the cosmos. His final words are an affirmation of faith: "To God there is no zero. I still exist."

The Incredible Shrinking Man is the most theological—as distinct from religious—of science fiction films. Others invoked religion. In *The War of the Worlds* (1953), the survivors of a Martian attack take refuge in a Catholic church; in *The Next Voice You Hear* (1950), God takes over the airwaves to preach a gospel of brotherhood. And *The Incredible Shrinking Man* was not a jeremiad like *The Day the Earth Stood Still*, in which an extraterrestrial arrives in Washington, DC, with a message for Earth: Desist from nuclear war, or write your own epitaph. "The decision rests with you."

A few science fiction films of the period portrayed scientists as reasonable human beings, interested in the new species, but not so as to endanger human life, which was already imperiled. And it was only fitting that they came up with a way to destroy the mutants indirectly created by members of their own profession. Hollywood did not adopt a quid pro quo approach. The bomb was the villain, and implicitly its creators were villainous. But Hollywood was savvy enough not to indict the Manhattan Project. The burden, if not the blame, falls on the next generation of scientists to solve the problems caused by their predecessors.

The Thing from Another World (1951) posed a different question: Should a scientist, in his quest for knowledge, endanger others by attempting to study a new and lethal species? It is an unusual film in several respects. Purportedly directed by Christian Nyby and produced by Howard Hawks, *The Thing* seems more like a Hawksian venture into an alien genre—but with traces of his imprint that confirm what several of those associated with the film maintained: "Chris Nyby didn't direct a thing." In typical Hawks fashion, cues are disregarded as actors intentionally step on each other's lines.

The overlap provides a sense of reality in a film that grows progressively more fantastic, yet is presented so compellingly that everything that happens is believable. The most Hawksian moment occurs in a scene that has little to do with the plot. Captain Pat Hendry (Kenneth Tobey) and Nikki (Margaret Sheridan), secretary to the Nobel-Prize winning scientist Dr. Carrington (Robert Cornthwaite), recall their last night together, when she crept out of bed to catch a cargo plane, leaving him with a departure note that made the rounds. Hawks turned their banter into verbal Ping-Pong, which was explicit for 1951 and is still titillating today. Nothing is made of their liaison, except that later it is implied that it will lead to marriage. The sexually charged badinage (which may have been written by Hawks, whose contribution to the screenplay is uncredited) evokes memories of Cary Grant and Rosalind Russell firing barbs at each other in *His Girl Friday*, and Lauren Bacall informing Humphrey Bogart in *To Have and Have Not*, that, if he's interested, he can whistle: "You know how to whistle, don't you, Steve? You just put your lips together and blow."

The battle of the sexes is only a diversion in *The Thing*. The real battle is twofold: the first, between man and an alien, and the second, between the lone scientist desperate to communicate with "the thing" and the others who realize it must be destroyed. The quest for knowledge only produces disorder. A twenty-thousand-ton UFO has crashed in the Arctic, leaving its tail fin jutting through the ice. An attempt to dislodge the aircraft with thermite bombs only succeeds in destroying it, sending a gusher of smoke into the sky—less awesome than a mushroom cloud, but just as threatening. The UFO's pilot is discovered to be an eight-foot alien encased in ice, the same size Victor Frankenstein specified for his creation in Mary Shelley's novel. In the interests of science, the icebound creature is carted back to a research facility, where it thaws out and runs amuck, leaving enough evidence to convince the scientists that they are dealing with an anomaly, a being without animal tissue and nerve endings, incapable of emotion. In short, the creature is a vegetable, "a super carrot with a brain" capable of flying a space ship. Since the vegetable needs blood for its seedpods to germinate, it attacks the sled dogs and slits the throats of two of the scientists, draining off their blood.

At first, *The Thing from Another World* seems unrelated to offspring-of-the-bomb films, yet there are a few intimations that the anomalous creature and the mutants are kin. Dr. Carrington, the acclaimed scientist, had been at Bikini, although nothing more is said of that. This piece of information is just a bit of exposition for the plot police. The creature is also radioactive, which suggests that in some way it had been exposed to radiation, either from tests conducted by the United States or from Russia's first detonation in east Kazakhstan in August 1949. One of the axioms of 1950s science fiction is that the bomb affected every form of life, including extraterrestrials. The scientists assume that the radioactive "thing" is a Martian, Mars being Hollywood's outer planet of choice. If so, the Manhattan Project could claim the "thing" as offspring. The film, however, did not resort to scapegoating. The closest it comes to criticism is an offhand comment by one of the crew that America succeeded in splitting the atom, evoking the cynical reply, "And that made the world happy."

Because the actors underplay, speaking naturally and often inaudibly, many of the points that are raised but not developed (culpability, the effects of radiation) are caught up in the narrative undertow. Still, *The Thing from Another World* only raises points worth pondering without offering solutions. But on one point, the film is clear: If scientific research endangers human life, the interests of humankind take precedence.

Carrington may be a genius with an impressive scientific vocabulary, but he is a loose cannon, determined to make contact with the creature. To Carrington, "the thing" is superior to homo sapiens and must be treated humanely. "He is a stranger in a strange land," he pleads. Carrington is also a throwback to the mad scientist of the horror film and comes perilously close to being the villain of the piece. He would have endorsed Victor Frankenstein's attempt to "bestow animation on lifeless matter" even if doing so meant becoming a grave robber. But Carrington would never have recanted, as Frankenstein did: "Learn from me . . . how dangerous is the acquirement of knowledge and how much happier that man is who believes his native town to be the world, than he who aspires to become greater than his nature will allow." Carrington believed that knowledge is power, and that having been born great, he wielded greater power than lesser beings.

If *The Thing from Another World* has a hero, it is Captain Hendry, who, frustrated by his superiors' classification of the alien as a "prisoner" to be safeguarded, realizes that his prisoner must be annihilated before claiming any more lives. When one of the men asks what one does with a vegetable, Nikki replies nonchalantly, "Boil it, stew it, bake it, fry it." That was all Hendry needs to hear. After a trap was rigged up to electrocute the creature, Carrington, who had even stolen plasma to keep the seedpods germinating, attempts to turn off the generator in order to save his specimen. Coming forward, he cries, "I'm your friend . . . . You're wiser than anything on Earth." His flattery gets him nothing but a broken collarbone. The creature is electrocuted in a sound and light spectacle—a lesser version of the bomb—and reduced to ash. The electrocution is a tribute to human ingenuity, which steps in when science fails. That is the point of the film: A species capable of destruction is better destroyed than studied.

The film's coda is almost a trailer for other science fiction movies. A reporter files his story over the air, engaging in clever word play, by noting that just as humankind was once saved by Noah's ark, now it has been saved by an "arc" of electricity. But salvation comes with a warning: "Tell the world. Tell this to everyone, wherever they are. Watch the skies everywhere. Keep looking. Keep watching the sky." And the studios did. They also watched the oceans.

The trailer for *The Beast from 20,000 Fathoms* (1953) posed the question of the decade: "Are we delving into mysteries we were never meant to know?" The answer was "yes," and audiences eagerly took the plunge. True horror would not return to the screen until *Psycho* (1960). Meanwhile, moviegoers needing icy fingers moving up and down their spines looked to science fiction for that old black magic.

Beast owes its title—and nothing more—to Ray Bradbury's 1951 *Saturday Evening Post* story of the same name, which underwent a title change to "The Fog Horn" so it would not be confused with the film. The story was a tale of the supernatural, which, as a movie, would require such a makeover that the original would have been unrecognizable. Bradbury's beast is a dinosaur-like sea creature that responds to the plaintive sound of a lighthouse foghorn, thinking it comes from one of its own species. Mistaking the lighthouse for an avatar and frustrated by the lighthouse's lack of response, the creature retaliates by destroying it. But a happy ending guaranteed the reader a good night's sleep. The lighthouse is rebuilt, and the monster is seen no more. The movie, on the other hand, begins in the Arctic, where atomic testing sends the snow cascading in an eerie half-light. Unlike the blinding blizzard at the beginning of *The Thing*, here the swirling snow is strangely beautiful, hypnotic but disturbing, as if nature was daring humans to marvel at the spectacle of whiteness, yet at the same time posting a "remain at your own peril" notice. The tests yield their forbidden fruit: a prehistoric reptile, one of animator Ray Harryhausen's creations, emerging from the shower of snow with a kind of primeval grandeur, as if he were reclaiming his domain. The snow gave the beast the trappings of royalty. On land, he looks like a refugee from Skull Island, lethal but no longer regal.

Beast conforms to the atomic age template: the eyewitnesses vs. the skeptics, romance (female and male scientists, female scientist/male professional/military man), a couple of deaths, a seemingly indestructible creature, and its spectacular demise. *Beast* shows both respect and sympathy for scientists who, true to their calling, act only on empirical evidence. When they are convinced, they set out to study the specimen, regardless of the dangers—until the specimen becomes so deadly that it must be destroyed. When the world's leading paleontologist (the cherubic Cecil Kellaway) steps into a diving bell, excited about viewing a creature that has been extinct for one hundred million years, we hope he will return safely. But the beast is indifferent to credentials, and the paleontologist becomes another of its victims.

The beast makes its way to land, eventually reaching Manhattan Beach, a stand-in for Coney Island. The finale—stunningly photographed in sharp black and white, with a silver-glazed roller coaster set against an onyx black sky—has its own terrible beauty. The beast begins dismantling the roller coaster, stopping only when it is finished off by a radioactive isotope, a lesser form of the technology that released it from its Arctic grave.

It Came from Beneath the Sea (1955), the follow-up to *The Beast from 20,000 Fathoms*, adheres to the same formula, but with a twist. Now it is the military that is skeptical of the scientists, who have reported that a radioactive sea monster is capsizing ships and causing mass drownings. The situation changes when the creature—a giant squid, the offspring of the H-bomb detonation at Eniwetok atoll (never mentioned by name, but clearly implied)—reaches the California coast and coils itself around the Golden Gate Bridge before being destroyed by a jet-propelled torpedo.

It Came from Beneath the Sea recycled the two men-one woman plot, the woman being a brilliant marine biologist (Faith Domergue) who is not above using her feminine wiles to extract a confession from a survivor afraid of being scoffed at. The film's distinctiveness lay in Ray Harryhausen's visual effects, Harry Freulich's stark black-and-white photography, and omniscient voiceover narration that at times makes it seem like a documentary. Unlike the beast from twenty thousand fathoms, which conformed to the popular image of a dawn-of-creation reptile, the squid or octopus (it has been called both) is merely repulsive, with tentacles equipped with suction cups resembling open sores. Radiation made the squid look grey and unhealthy, as if suffused with black bile. It is characteristic of atom-spawned progeny that they do not entirely belong to genus "monster." Universal's monsters—Frankenstein's, the Wolf Man, the Mummy, and Dracula—did not threaten civilization. In the 1940s, the threat originated elsewhere, in Nazi Germany or imperialist Japan. It was different in the 1950s, when one left a theater wondering if perhaps nature could exact its own form of revenge for the horrors wrought by the bomb—even in the form of another world war, this time with an anomalous enemy.

The two films, although made by different studios (*The Beast from 20,000 Fathoms* by Warner Bros., *It Came from Beneath the Sea* by Columbia), complement each other. Warner's lavished more money ($215,000) on *Beast*, which was a more elaborate production, while Columbia only spent $150,000 on *Sea*. Yet each turned a handsome profit, $2.25 million and $1.7 million, respectively. The link between them is Ray Harryhausen's stop motion animation, which followed the classic principle of making the creature fit the habitat. The reptile looked as if it came from twenty thousand fathoms and the squid from beneath the sea.

The most iconic creature in American science fiction was the appropriately named Gill Man, the half human, half fish antagonist in Jack Arnold's *Creature from the Black Lagoon* (1954). Since the script suggested some kind of contact between the Gill Man and Julie Adams, Joe Breen, who upheld the Production Code as if it were the Ten Commandments, demanded that "intimate parts of the body—specifically the breasts of women—be fully covered at all times." It was an easy mandate to observe, since the studios had been adhering to it since the enforcement of the Production Code in 1934. What Breen did not know, and Jack Arnold did, was that a white bathing suit, worn by the right actress, can be more erotic than exposed breasts.

Although the creature is not an offspring of the bomb, the film reflects the questionable view of scientific inquiry characteristic of the genre. The Gill Man, in his scaly suit of armor and with his helmet-like head, is even more frightening than mutated insects and giant octopi because, like the centaur, he embodies two forms of life. He was happy in his Amazon digs until the arrival of a research team, intrigued by the discovery of a hand with webbed fingers that points to an unusual type of amphibian. Curiosity is one thing, but the pursuit of the creature is not that different from the "bring 'em back alive" motto of Carl Denham (Robert Armstrong) in *King Kong*. This was not a case of "leave de atom alone," but "leave the creature alone." The male half of the Gill Man is activated when Julie Adams, added to the expedition to bring some sex to the plot, dons a tight-fitting white bathing suit to go swimming in the most sensuous scene ever to appear in a science fiction film. Ginger Stanley (Julie Adams's double) swims above while the Gill Man does a backstroke below, their movements synchronized in rhythmic foreplay that only activates his libido—which had not abated by the time the sequel, *Revenge of the Creature*, was released in 1955.

Just like *Frankenstein* (1932), *Creature from the Black Lagoon* proved so popular that it demanded a sequel. The Gill Man is presumably asleep in the deep at the end of the first film. He was too marketable to die—besides, Universal-International reasoned, who would remember that he sank into his watery grave at the end of the movie? In *Revenge of the Creature*, the team returned to the "tributary on the upper Amazon," using dynamite to capture the Gill Man and cart him off to Florida, where he is put on exhibit in a tank, as if he were an attraction in a freak show. *King Kong* illustrated the folly of relocation. Not meant for urban life, Kong ran amuck in New York, as does the Gill Man in Florida. Like Kong, he wants his blonde (Lori Nelson) so badly that he crashes a party and carries her off. But Lori is meant for John Agar, who will make her a very dull husband. At least the Gill Man had a sex drive.

Jack Arnold never intended for there to be a Gill Man trilogy, but like John Ford's three westerns dubbed the "Cavalry Trilogy" (*Fort Apache*, *She Wore a Yellow Ribbon*, *Rio Grande*), the third Gill Man movie completed the story, signaling the end of the most empathetic of creatures. In *The Seven Year Itch*, after seeing *Creature from the Black Lagoon*, Marilyn Monroe and Tom Ewell discuss the movie as they walk along Lexington Avenue. Before the familiar shot of Marilyn standing over a subway grating, she expressed her sympathy for the Gill Man, who was the object of an unwarranted eviction and treated as a specimen. When Marilyn spoke so compassionately about the creature and his objectification, it seemed as if she were speaking of herself.

In the *Revenge of the Creature*, the Gill Man is last seen swimming away in a "to be continued" ending. It would have been better if he had returned to the Amazon, where he would be remembered as Julie Adams's swimming partner and Lori Nelson's abductor. But UI was bent on a trilogy, even if Jack Arnold could not direct the third installment. That dubious honor went to John Sherwood. In *The Creature Walks Among Us* (1956) the head scientist (Jeff Morrow) is obsessed with the Gill Man's evolutionary potential and jealous of his wife's attraction to another member of the expedition. A fire destroys Gill Man's scales, leaving him a mammal with a rubbery face—like Orson Welles at the end of *Citizen Kane*, but more grotesque—and chambered ears like those of the god Pan. He is even imprisoned in a goat pen. The film is open-ended, but those who identified with Gill Man, the ultimate displaced person, can only hope that, as a humanoid, he will find a substitute for his former aquatic home, perhaps in another film. But this last was not an option; without his scaly body suit, he would be just another monster. The artificial trilogy was complete, but the message was disturbing. Pursuit of Gill Man led only to death and terror, culminating in the transformation of a semi-human being into a misfit, at home neither on land nor in water. Moviegoers may have gotten their kicks, but they did so at the expense of someone who—like Greta Garbo in *Grand Hotel* (1932)— only wanted to be left alone.

The most unusual creatures in science fiction were the pods in *Invasion of the Body Snatchers* (1956). Director Don Siegel insisted they were not aliens, even though the trailer portrayed them as coming from outer space, which by then had become the designated launching pad for the paranormal and preternatural. Pods are everywhere—particularly in the movie business, as Siegel slyly suggests: "Many of my associates are pods, people who have no feeling of love or emotion." He singles out pod directors, who shoot as if they were on autopilot. "They have no dark moods, but neither do they have moments of exaltation that I might have." The Hollywood pods are the least dangerous. Far more deadly are the ones in the film that infiltrate communities, hijacking the personalities of residents, absorbing their minds and memories, and reducing them to automatons devoid of feeling, whose only resemblance to their former selves is superficial.

The film was supposed to open with Dr. Binnel (Kevin McCarthy) returning to his hometown, the fictitious Santa Mira, after a medical convention and discovering that a strangeness has settled in. A woman insists her uncle is an imposter. A boy says the same of his mother. After a preview left audiences confused, a frame narrative was added, which, despite Siegel's objections, worked to the film's advantage. Siegel was blessed with a skilled screenwriter, Daniel Mainwaring (the pseudonym of Geoffrey Homes), who turned his novel *Build My Gallows High* into one of the great film noirs, *Out of the Past* (1947). The released version of *Invasion* opens with Binnel, restrained by hospital aides and insisting he is not insane, as he stares, eyes bulging, into the camera lens. "Listen to me before it's too late," he insists. In a sense, it is too late, as one by one, the residents of Santa Mira accept pod life, welcoming it as a release from anxiety and turmoil and reveling in the communal homogeneity it brings. Podism is the great equalizer. It is not a matter of "from each according to his ability, to each according to his needs." In Podland, ability does not matter, and need is nonexistent.

Invasion of the Body Snatchers blurs into horror. There is nothing in sci-fi comparable to the sequence in which the pods in a hot house break open in a parody of birth, as primordial fluid oozes forth, revealing incipient clones. At first, reports that relatives have become simulacra are dismissed as mass hysteria, attributable to the "What's going on in the world?" syndrome. The explanation is a variation on alien invasion, with an assist from the bomb. Perhaps—and only "perhaps"—the cause was the atomic radiation of plant or animal life that sent seeds drifting through space, forming pods that drained humans of their humanity, leaving them incapable of loving or being loved, and reducing them to a common denominator. Even Binnel's inamorata (Dana Wynter) succumbs. In a death-defying sequence, Binnel weaves in and out of heavy traffic, desperate to tell his story and encountering only disinterest. Finally, he is picked up and taken to a hospital, where it seems certain he will be committed. Then another patient is brought in, the victim of a collision between a Greyhound bus and a truck carrying pods. Binnel's story is confirmed. The ending is a deus ex machina that avoids the big question: Even if Santa Mira can be saved, what about the rest of the country?

Invasion of the Body Snatchers carries with it a weighty subtext, a not-so-veiled critique of McCarthyism and a reductio ad absurdum of communism. And politically astute audiences might have interpreted the film that way. They would have been the same ones who saw *High Noon* as "a parable for the Committee's onslaught on Hollywood, and for the timidity of the Community," screenwriter Carl Foreman's rebuke of the silent majority that failed to come to the defense of the victims of the witch hunt, shunning them as the town did Gary Cooper, who needed support when his life was in danger. After Foreman was blacklisted, *High Noon*'s anti-HUAC subtext seemed even more apparent, at least to the knowledgeable. These are also the kind of viewers who sensed political undercurrents circulating in *On the Waterfront* (1954). The film was written and directed by HUAC informants Budd Schulberg and Elia Kazan, who blurred the distinction between testifying before a commission investigating waterfront crime, and testifying before a committee investigating communism in Hollywood, even though crime is punishable and membership in the Communist Party is not—unless the times determine otherwise. As Jeff Smith has brilliantly shown, *On the Waterfront* is so politically ambiguous that it can even be interpreted as an anti-HUAC allegory. Kazan must have known that HUAC was a minotaur in search of sacrificial victims, not a serious investigating committee like the Estes Kefauver crime committee. The tactics of union boss Johnny Friendly (Lee J. Cobb, himself a HUAC informant) and his mob bear an uncomfortable resemblance to HUAC, with its strong-arming and browbeating tactics that stopped just short of a shakedown. If Friendly's mob is an evocation of HUAC, it is as un-American—and anti-American—as the committee. In *On the Waterfront*, a dock worker describes the waterfront to Father Barry (Karl Malden) by saying "the waterfront's tougher, Father. Like it ain't part of America," which also serves as an apt description of HUAC. The film's ambivalence becomes even more pronounced. To Johnny Friendly, Terry Malloy (Marlon Brando) is an unfriendly witness testifying against a corrupt union (think HUAC), but a friendly witness for the crime commission. He is willing to cooperate with a legitimate investigation into waterfront crime, but not with one solely concerned with crushing dissent.

Many of the films that Smith discusses (e.g., *Johnny Guitar, Silver Lode, The Robe, Spartacus*) take on a richness when viewed in a political context that may not have been evident at the time. Thus *The Robe* emerges as an antifascist allegory about a lunatic emperor persecuting a minority sect. The historical parallels are obvious, the irony being that the persecuted are Christians who, in 1930s Germany, persecuted another minority. But at the time, *The Robe* was Fox's first CinemaScope production, which provided a grand spectacle on a screen two and one-half times wider than it was high. Compare *The Robe* to Cecil B. DeMille's *The Sign of the Cross* (1932), which dramatized the persecution of the Christians under Nero. In DeMille's film there was no subtext, no metaphorical level—only prurience, sensuality, and torture, all in the name of religion. *The Robe* did not pander to its audience, which was given a spectacle that left ample room for speculation. *The Robe* would really have resonated with 1953 audiences if a suggestion from Darryl F. Zanuck had been incorporated into the screenplay. To create a contemporary parallel, Zanuck proposed a senate committee on un-Roman activities, headed by a Roman senator who must investigate his own son. The Roman version of HUAC never made it into the script; however, Zanuck may still have influenced the script. The son, a military tribune (Richard Burton), has become a Christian, making him a member of a subversive sect. When the emperor Caligula offers the tribune the choice of recanting or death, he chooses the latter, as does his beloved (Jean Simmons), who believes in Christ (although, technically, she has not converted). To complete the parallel, "like the Rosenbergs, the couple march proudly to eternity." And, one might add, to paraphrase Lillian Hellman, they refused to cut their conscience to fit the fashions of 1 A.D as prescribed by committee. But subtext and metaphor are elusive. One may sense their presence without being able to articulate it, only say that the film is about something other than what it purports to be about. There is an infra-narrative threatening to rise up from the depths, but never getting far enough to confirm one's suspicion of a secondary level of meaning more interesting than the primary one.

If *Body Snatchers* had been made in the late 1930s, it would have been considered an allegory of fascism, with the police, who revel in enforcing podism, serving as proxies for Hitler's Brown shirts. Oddly, in 1956, the same year the film was released, *Auntie Mame* opened on Broadway with Rosalind Russell starring as a freewheeling bohemian, who provides her orphaned nephew with an unconventional upbringing—including enrollment at an experimental school, where the children romp around in the nude, playing fish families. Mame's message was a song of the self: "Live! Live! Live! Life is a banquet and most poor sons of bitches [changed to 'suckers' in the 1959 movie version] are starving themselves to death." Following the herd stultifies; separating from it revivifies. Both *Invasion of the Body Snatchers* and *Auntie Mame* argue, in different ways, for individuation, the only way human beings can preserve their essence—that unique aspect of the self that distinguishes each from the other. The alternative is podism.

In refusing to have Binnel, or anyone, pray for divine assistance, *Body Snatchers* is reminiscent of film noir, in which darkness is so pervasive that the light-bearing Deity is loath to make an appearance in a world unhinged, ruled by chance, as is evident from the accident that constitutes the dénouement and confirms Binnel's sanity. It is God's silence in the face of a metamorphic plague that makes the film so disquieting, and the resolution so sadly ephemeral. In a play with a similar theme, Eugène Ionesco's *Rhinoceros* (1960), mindless conformity reaches the level of the absurd, as an entire town collectively sheds its humanity to become rhinoceroses. Only one person refuses to join the herd, the "little man" Berenger, who proclaims, "I'm the last man left, and I'm staying that way until the end. I'm not capitulating!" Both Siegel's film and Ionesco's play make a case for selfhood—with the variance that in *Rhinoceros*, Berenger is the last man standing, destined for an unknown fate. But in the film, Binnel is spared institutionalization through a deus ex machina. He was lucky; Berenger only had his convictions.

Chapter 5

WORLDS ELSEWHERE

IN 1946, THE YEAR THE IRON CURTAIN FELL ON EASTERN EUROPE, UN-
identified flying objects were reportedly seen in the skies over Scandinavia.
Then, in early July 1947, aliens were sighted in Roswell, New Mexico. The
front-page headline of the 8 July 1947 *Roswell Daily Record* read, "RAAF
(Roswell Army Air Field) Captures Flying Saucer On Ranch In Roswell
Region." Was it a flying saucer or, as the army claimed, a weather balloon
from which was suspended a hexagonal disk? As for the aliens, they were
phantasms, spawned by an overheated imagination. The believers put their
credence in the cosmos, not in a government that discredited anything suggesting a world elsewhere and offered an explanation so speculative that it
had to be suspect.

Of the more than eight hundred UFO sightings reported in July 1947,
the one that generated the greatest amount of publicity involved an Idaho
pilot, Kenneth Arnold, who, as he was nearing Mount Rainier in the state
of Washington on 24 June 1947, saw nine saucer-shaped objects flying in V
formation. The *Chicago Daily Tribune* (26 June) quoted his description of
the objects as "silvery and shiny" and shaped like pie plates. The *East Orego-
nian* (25 June) called them saucer-like, thus adding the term "flying saucer"
to the vernacular. Three years later, on 7 April 1950, when Arnold appeared
on Edward R. Murrow's radio program *Hear It Now*, he insisted that he
merely said the objects flew in "saucer-like fashion." By then, however, it was
too late to amend the description. Arnold was naturally bitter that the military dismissed his experience as a mirage. Since communism had become a
real threat, extra-terrestrials were relegated to the recesses of the collective
unconscious.

But there could be a connection. If UFOS existed, as many believed,
where were they coming from? Another planet, it would seem—or rather
the only planet that had any cachet, Mars, which became part of pop culture

after Orson Welles panicked America with his Mercury Theatre on the Air broadcast of H. G. Wells's *War of the Worlds* on 30 October 1938. World War II made Mars a low priority, but after Hiroshima, the Red Planet loomed large in the national consciousness. To paraphrase the opening of the popular radio show *The Shadow*, "Who knows what evil lurks in outer space?" Hollywood knew: aliens.

There will probably never be an end to alien sightings or theories about abductions by extraterrestrials. The government may discredit them, but Hollywood does not. Aliens are potential moneymakers, either in a B movie like *It Came from Outer Space* or in an epic like *Close Encounters of the Third Kind*. Their existence was a given in Hollywood, regardless of government skepticism.

Fifty years after the Roswell incident, the air force issued a report on 24 June 1997, stating that the so-called aliens spotted in July 1947 were anthropomorphic test dummies. But UFO stalwarts, like conspiracy theorists, would have none of it. The very fact that, after half a century, the air force felt the need to bring the matter to closure implies dissatisfaction with the way the case was handled in 1947, when anyone who saw an "alien" was termed delusional. The next day, The *New York Times* printed a summary: no aliens and no cover-up, just an experiment. Faced with a conflict between science and popular belief, Hollywood preferred the latter—especially after America entered the UFO age, presented as an offshoot of the Cold War. UFO sightings and extraterrestrial travel were not incompatible with the Red Scare. Had the Soviet Union drawn the Red Planet into its orbit, making it another of its satellites? Or, even more intriguing, is the Deity using aliens to alert complacent earthlings to their possible annihilation?

Flight to Mars (1951) portrayed the planet as anti-democratic and, in fact, totalitarian, despite appearances to the contrary. The film was a Monogram quickie filmed in Cinecolor in about eleven days—and looked it sometimes. On other occasions, the film suggested what a creative director might have done with sets that flattened space, making Mars into a labyrinth of angled walls and narrow stairways.

For purely scientific reasons four scientists and a lone reporter board a rocket ship to Mars, even if doing so means they may not return. The expedition is heralded as a cause célèbre, as if the country were readying itself for a confrontation with the unknown. America seemed to be on war alert. Even the language, a carryover from the pre-Pearl Harbor days, had bellicose overtones. Congress is divided between the isolationists, who want the scientists to remain in their laboratories, and the interventionists, who urge them to proceed. "Interventionist" and "isolationist" had not been used since World War II broke out in September 1939, when the nation was divided between those urging it to join the fight against fascism and others arguing against becoming embroiled in a European war. Such polarization implies that the expedition can either bring about a thaw in the Cold War or cause a deep freeze. The writers can only toss around ideas, having neither time nor budget to develop them. Imagine what could have been done with the senior scientist's theory that we are all universes unto ourselves. Such dialogue promises a film of a strongly intellectual nature. But unable to deliver, the writers settled for a rocket ship romance, with the reporter wooing a female scientist away from her supposed beau, the chief engineer. This arrangement makes it possible for the latter to find his sole mate, Alita, a lovely Martian (Marguerite Chapman), dressed like a chorus girl in an abbreviated outfit that emphasized her slender body and shapely legs.

Once the rocket ship crash lands on Mars, the plot takes a nosedive into cliché. The team is greeted by a welcoming committee headed by Ikron (Morris Ankrum), council president, whose first words are, "We have been expecting you." The Martians have not only picked up and deciphered radio broadcasts but, *mirabile dictu*, have also mastered English. Politically, Mars purports to be a model democracy, with business conducted by a council and motions brought to a vote. But the democratic trappings are a front for a dictatorship, with Ikron holding sway over the majority. Knowing that Mars is facing extinction, Ikron allows the space travelers to repair their rocket ship, which he plans to appropriate in order to conquer Earth.

Flight to Mars is an amalgam of World War II history and 1950s paranoia. Mars is a totalitarian society. Its council members are draped in red, which may be the color of their planet or their political model. Theirs is a sham democracy, with a council dominated by an autocrat. If Mars could be transplanted anywhere, it would be to Hitler's Germany or Stalin's Russia. In his plan to resettle the Martians on Earth, Ikron sounds like Hitler demanding Lebensraum for his master race. And Stalin would have regarded Mars as another jewel in his iron crown. Today, satellites; tomorrow a planet— and a red one at that.

Like Paris in World War II movies, Mars has an underground, headed by Alita and her father. Its small size is due to budget. Of the six Martians seen in the film, three are resistance members. Audiences expected the explorers to outwit the Martians and return to Earth. They did, with the help of Alita and her father. Then the film ends abruptly with a take off and a fade out.

And what did *Flight to Mars* prove, except that—cinematically—the planet was ripe for the picking?

Red Planet Mars (1952) is one of the few science fiction films of the fifties featuring Soviets as characters sharing America's determination to communicate with Mars. A California scientist (Peter Graves) is trying to establish contact with Mars. After discovering that the Martians have melted the ice caps to irrigate their planet, he regards Mars as superior to Earth. His wife (Andrea King) feels differently, comparing her husband's research to "sitting on a volcano." Meanwhile, the Soviets have conscripted a former Nazi, Franz Calder (Herbert Berghof) to make contact with Mars. At this point, the Christianization of the film begins. Calder operates out of a hideaway in the Andes, in the shadow of the famous statue, Christ the Redeemer of the Andes. As he laughingly informs his Soviet handlers, "You can find me only through finding Christ."

Mars is the promised land, powered by cosmic energy. Its inhabitants have a three-hundred-year lifespan and enjoy such an abundance of food that rationing is unnecessary. The realization that Mars is the new Eden and Earth is a garden gone to seed results in global chaos, as coalmines and steel mills close and banks default. Mars, believing that humankind has suffered enough, delivers an ultimatum: "Love goodness and hate evil." Forget the galaxy and follow the star of Bethlehem. The voice emanating from Mars is none other than God's, the man of Nazareth and the man of Mars being the same. Suddenly, church attendance swells, and miracles abound. The Soviet Union, which "denied God's word and worshipped false gods," abjures communism, and the patriarch of the Orthodox Church becomes head of the provisional government.

Just when it seems that a new order has arisen, Calder arrives at the scientist's laboratory, claiming that the messages were his own transmissions, intended for the gullible. Although the scientist's wife insists they were from Mars (and thus from God), Calder is unmoved and intends to divulge the truth at a press conference. Rather than see the gospel of Mars dismissed as a hoax, the wife asks for a cigarette, setting off an explosion that immolates the three of them. And in case anyone in the audience believes the messages were fakes, a new one comes through, beginning with the words, "Ye hath done well." It is incomplete, but the text is Matthew 25:23: "Ye hath done well, good and faithful servant . . . . Enter into the joy of your master."

For a film purportedly washed in the blood of the lamb, the dénouement was bloody in a different sense. The wife lighting a match is not much different from a suicide bomber pulling a switch. Each action is not so much an act of martyrdom (although in some circles it would be) as a self-immolation that affects others in the vicinity. The wife boasts to Calder that she possesses free will, and she proves it by reducing the three of them to charred bones. Of course, one could argue that that the lighting of a match is morally neutral, but the laboratory setting makes the act at least morally questionable. Was she merely trying to frighten Calder, who panicked when he saw the match? Did the tactic backfire, literally? The biblical text approves her action ("Ye hath done well"), elevating it to a sacrificial act. Since Calder identified with the Satan of Milton's *Paradise Lost*, preferring to reign in hell than serve in heaven, his wish was granted.

In May 1952, when *Red Planet Mars* was released, the utopian universe conjured up at the end of the film was at odds with what was happening globally. Although *Red Planet Mars* is set in the future, there was as much a disparity between the world of the early 1950s and the earthly paradise to come as there was between 1950—declared the Holy Year by Pope Pius XII—and the events of that year. On 25 June 1950, while pilgrims were streaming into Rome, some even traversing the entire Appian Way to reach the Eternal City, North Korean armies crossed the thirty-eighth parallel dividing the Soviet-dominated North from the American-controlled South, resulting in the United Nations police action better known as the Korean War. The American military was convinced hostilities would be a short-lived, certainly not on the scale of World War II, and would end in a few months. But China's entry into the war that October prolonged the conflict, which did not end until July 1953, when it concluded in a stalemate, euphemistically called an armistice.

Anyone other than a cockeyed optimist seeing *Red Planet Mars* in spring 1952 would have considered it more of a fantasy film than science fiction. Newsreels kept moviegoers up to date about Korea, showing roads clogged with refugees whose country was being devastated by rockets, bombs, and the incendiary of choice—napalm—and men, unshaven and grim-faced, braving the cold that left them frostbitten. Some may have believed that they were fighting for America, as President Truman insisted. Others might have concluded that partitioning the Korean peninsula was an act of expediency, which only fueled the Nationalists' goal of uniting the two Koreas under the aegis of the Soviet Union, and therefore justified America's involvement. Either way, the country was mired in what at the time was America's most unpopular war, soon to be termed "the forgotten war."

Mars should have been off limits, especially after *Red Planet Mars* made it clear that it is ruled by God, but that did not stop the four-person crew of *Angry Red Planet* (1960) from taking off in the name of science. What they discover is a hand-drawn, animated dreamscape bathed in orange (another color associated with Mars), with flesh-eating plants, a long-legged flying creature with a rodent's face, and a giant amoeba that engulfs its prey and can only be destroyed by electricity, like The Thing. Mars is a fantastic storybook, with illustrations that suddenly spring to life, threatening the intruders who force open its pages.

The expedition ends in death and trauma. One crewmember is consumed by the amoeba. Another dies of heart failure. And the captain incurs an infection that leaves his arm looking as if it had been coated with tar. The sole female requires narcosynthesis to explain what has happened. The only reason the ship is allowed to return to Earth is that a stern but well-meaning voice—God's, no doubt—comes through the transmitter, warning humans to stay on their own turf. The planet is restricted: Martians Only, No Visitors Allowed. And if one should end up there, he or she would have to be eminently resourceful, like Robinson Crusoe.

The idea of a castaway on Mars was intriguing enough for director Byron Haskin and producer Aubrey Schenck to commission screenwriter John C. Higgins to prepare the final draft of Ib Melchior's preliminary screenplay for *Robinson Crusoe on Mars* (1964). The inspiration was Daniel Defoe's novel, but with Crusoe as a navy astronaut, whose space ship is forced out of orbit by Mars's gravitational pull. Melchior's Crusoe figure had the emblematic name Robin Cruze; his fellow astronaut, the less emblematic one Dan McReady. When a magnetic storm creates shorts in the electrical circuits, Cruze is ejected from his escape hatch and lands safely. McReady's hatch, however, does not open. The ship crashes, and Cruze finds himself alone in a bleak and barren world with grotesquely shaped rock formations and a menacing array of horned reptiles, ants with pincers, and giant centipedes. He also discovers a companion in Marea, a Martian monkey, who leads him to a source of water. Soon, there is a new arrival, a man from another solar system, Alpha Centauri, six trillion miles from Earth, whom Cruze christens Friday. Melchior had no intention of having the trio languish on Mars. A rescue ship arrives, and they are brought back to Earth, but not before Cruze has the last word: "I am coming home and with me comes a man from another world, Friday, my friend." Cruze has realized "man's greatest dream ever since he first looked up into the sky and at the stars and planets and wondered." But the true epiphany was Cruze's "contact with a new, a great alien civilization."

Melchior's script reads like a novel and is lavishly detailed, including a dictionary of Yagor, Friday's native tongue. Although Melchior's was not the kind of screenplay that Haskin and Schenck were after (they specifically wanted a Mars without monsters), it provided Higgins with a blueprint from which he could work. Although "Robinson Crusoe on Mars" sounds like the title of a comic book or a graphic novel, it is a visually mesmerizing, if overlong, story of survival, with a nod to Defoe, and a deep bow to the National Aeronautics and Space Administration (NASA) and Alan B. Shepard Jr., who in 1961 became the first American to venture into outer space. Shepard's voyage in the Freedom 7 spacecraft was only the point of departure. It was as if Higgins were asking, "What if Shepard crash landed on Mars and had to fend for himself?" Higgins also knew that, between 1948 and 1961, the first astronauts were monkeys, few of which survived the flight. Appropriately, Marea became Mona, a monkey in an orange space suit, on board with Commander "Kit" Draper, formerly Robin Cruze, (Paul Mantee) and Colonel Dan McReady (Adam West, who became a household name as Bruce Wayne/Batman in ABC's popular television series, *Batman*). With McReady's death, Mona becomes Draper's sole companion until the arrival of Friday. Crusoe's situation was the same in the novel, except that he had more company: a dog, two cats, and a parrot that he taught to speak.

By the 1960s, the survival film, a sub-genre at best, had acquired a set of recognizable conventions, popularized by Cecil B. De Mille's *Four Frightened People* (1934), John Farrow's *Five Came Back* (1939) (which he remade as *Back from Eternity* [1956]), and Frank Launder's *The Blue Lagoon* (1949). These conventions included resourcefulness (starting a fire, finding drinkable water and edible food, making clothes), omnipresent danger, close calls, an unexpected arrival, and an ingenious escape or a climactic rescue. Thus, Draper discovers that yellow rock can burn like coal, and water can be extracted from quartz crystals. Defoe's Crusoe was more fortunate. From the wreckage, he was able to salvage tools, ammunition, pistols, clothes, and even liquor, so that he could live "mighty comfortably, my mind entirely composed by resigning to the will of God." Draper's habitat is a cave, outside of which he has hung an American flag, which he salutes each morning—a touch Haskin demanded, much to Mantee's displeasure. But that was part of Haskin's concept of the material: a tribute to American ingenuity, endurance, and—with the arrival of Friday—tolerance of the Other, with allusions to an American past in which "others" constituted three-fifths of a person. Significantly, Draper cobbles together a makeshift bagpipes, on which he plays "Dixie," which one would like to think was Haskin's idea of irony.

Robinson Crusoe on Mars differs from the typical survival film, in which the setting is a jungle or an island. Draper is on a planet devoid of life, where no other human appears until midway through the film, in keeping with Friday's belated arrival in the novel. Draper's chief enemy is the hostile environment, made deadlier by UFO attacks from another (unnamed) planet, the film's equivalent of Defoe's cannibals. Draper preserves his sanity by talking to himself or Mona. And like Crusoe, who kept a journal, he tape-records his observations for posterity—or so he hopes.

The powdery ridges of California's Death Valley stood in for Mars, which production designer Al Nozaki replicated in the studio, creating a chain of chalky hills that at times looked glazed. Mars is an anomaly, a desert with slab-like rocks and gorges caused by volcanic eruptions, with a few pools and an underground network of dry canals. It is sinister and awesome, even dreamlike—particularly in Nozaki's rendering of a hollow of striated rock, a study in stillness masterfully delineated by a hand skilled in the lineaments of silence.

Eventually, another human arrives, whom Draper dubs "Friday," adding "with apologies to Robinson Crusoe." Physically, the new arrival conforms to Defoe's description of Friday: "a comely, handsome fellow, perfectly well made, tall and well-shaped," with black hair and tawny skin. He is also twenty-six. Although Friday (Victor Lundin) looks twenty-six, he claims to have lived for seventy-eight years, sixty-two of them as a slave. Since the film began production in 1963, Friday would have been born in 1864 or 1865. Apparently, news of the Emancipation Proclamation had not reached outer space.

At this point, the political subtext, perhaps originally intended to be open-ended, becomes increasingly specific. Draper learns that Friday had been enslaved by a super planet that used its captives to mine Mars's natural resources. Like the others, Friday has been fitted with an electromagnetic manacle enabling his enslavers to track his whereabouts, an interplanetary version of the Fugitive Slave Act of 1850. Slave labor has always existed, but certainly viewers were not reminded of ancient Greece or Egypt in this context—maybe Nazi Germany or the Soviet Union, but more likely, owing the bits of Americana woven into the film, they were reminded of the slave-holding and segregationist South.

By the time *Robinson Crusoe on Mars* was released in early summer 1964, the country had witnessed the bombing of the Sixteenth Street Baptist

Church in Birmingham, Alabama, that left four girls dead. Fire hoses had been turned on civil rights demonstrators, who also had dogs sicced on them. And blacks had been denied admission at the University of Alabama and the University of Mississippi. It was the era of freedom marches and freedom riders, climaxing in Dr. Martin Luther King Jr.'s vision of a new order, which he described in his immortal "I Have a Dream" speech at the Lincoln Memorial on 28 August 1963. But it was an order that was imperiled three months later, when President John F. Kennedy was assassinated in Dallas. Since Draper had already Americanized Mars, it is difficult to think of the enslaving planet as anything other than an intergalactic metaphor for an America that may have shed the vestiges of its slave-holding past, but had not escaped its segregationist present. But further speculation is discouraged by the arrival of the rescue ship.

To expunge the stigma of racism, Higgins, taking his cue from the novel, in which Crusoe instructs Friday in Christian doctrine, has Draper and Friday discourse on God, with each possessing his own concept of a supreme being. Draper is very much a believer. After surviving an attack from UFOs that leaves him covered with soot-like pellets, he recites the Twenty-Third Psalm. The religious elements in the film are no doubt sincere, but they are embedded in a script that raises issues more political than spiritual. That Draper and Friday accept a divinely ordered universe is not controversial; enslavement of one race by another is.

Chapter 6

AMID THE ALIEN CORN

CAN A BOND EVER BE FORGED BETWEEN HUMANS AND ALIENS? AND IF so, does it have a broader effect on society at large? Hollywood offered a shaky "yes" to the first question—with any bond being portrayed as tenuous at best—but a resounding "no" to the second. Racial integration is one thing, alien integration something else. That was the message of Jack Arnold's *It Came from Outer Space* (1953), in which well-meaning aliens, presumably from Mars (or so the residents of Sand Rock, Arizona, suspect), crash land on Earth. Intellectually superior to earthlings, the aliens consider the planet neither a nice place to visit nor to live, but merely an inconvenience to be tolerated until they can repair their spacecraft. Based on a Ray Bradbury story, *It Came from Outer Space* does not seem to be bomb-inspired, even though it is set in Arizona. Still, when what seems to be a meteor tears into the earth, hollowing out a gigantic crater that looks like a conical inferno, the black cloud of Hiroshima looms over it. When an amateur astronomer (Richard Carlson) descends into the crater, he realizes that the "meteor" is really a space ship. The locals are at first skeptical and soon turn hostile, especially when some of them are reported missing. The aliens merely want time to repair their ship so they can continue planet hopping. Knowing that audiences expected to see one of the aliens, Arnold acquiesced— but only fleetingly. An alien's presence is announced by a Theremin-produced motif, eerie and shrill, accompanied by the image of an eye-like drain, ready to suck in whatever is approaching. The aliens have the ability to assume the form of the locals, mingling with them so as not be detected, as they steal clothes and break into hardware stores for supplies. Once the sheriff (Charles Drake) realizes that the aliens are responsible for the disappearances, he forms a posse to advance upon the mine they have taken over for their repairs. The astronomer tries to ward off a confrontation, reminding the sheriff that he has fallen into the trap of believing that the aliens are evil because they are "other." "We kill what we do not understand," the astronomer argues, using as an example a spider—which the sheriff admits he would stomp on. The sheriff has reverted to the kind of primitive impulse that William Hazlitt describes in his essay "The Pleasure of Hating," in which he uses a spider as an object of irrational hatred.

The astronomer alone can reason with the aliens, offering to help them leave if they release the captives they have taken. The dialogue between the astronomer and the aliens' leader is strangely moving. When the astronomer urges the leader to appear before the sheriff and his posse as he is—and not as a human clone—the leader replies, "You would be harmed by the sight of us." Nevertheless, he reveals himself to be a cyclopean creature with an all-seeing eye, thus clarifying the ocular image that heralded an alien's presence. Even the astronomer is horrified, knowing what would happen if the trigger-happy posse saw the alien in his natural state. "We must stay apart," the alien insists. The space ship blasts off, leaving behind a trail of fiery smoke. "They'll be back," the astronomer predicts. Hollywood concurred; aliens were in for the duration.

Once George Pal announced that *Destination Moon* (1950) was going into production, Robert Lippert was determined to release the first Cold War interplanetary travel film. Lippert, originally the owner of a California theater chain, entered production with Screen Guild Productions in 1945, which was renamed Lippert Pictures three years later. *Destination Moon* was an innocuous fantasy, intended to alarm viewers without challenging them. Lipppert envisioned something more provocative. *Rocketship X-M* (1950), written and directed by Kurt Newman—with an uncredited contribution by the blacklisted Dalton Trumbo—used space travel to make a statement about the precarious condition of planet Earth in the atomic age.

The film opens with a press conference, staged prior to the launching of a rocket ship to the moon. The head scientist (Morris Ankrum, again) explains the experiment. Five people have volunteered for space travel: four men and a female scientist, the latter a recurring figure in the 1950s science fiction film. The primary purpose of the expedition is not merely to acquire scientific data, but to establish a center for world peace. The implication is that if America reached the moon first, it would have a lunar ally—and the Soviet Union, a potential enemy.

The team's initial optimism abates as the script goes into perilous journey mode. The ship is thrown off course and lands on Mars. The leader of the expedition, Dr. Karl Eckstrom (John Emery), announces awesomely, "It seems something infinitely greater has taken over." If the Mars landing is the will of the Deity, it is intended as a lesson for humankind: Stay in your own backyard. Mars turns out to be a wasteland of rock and sand, with cratered mountains and the stark replica of a rocket rising from a desolate plain like a totem. Mars is also highly radioactive, the result, Eckstrom concludes, of an atomic war that has reduced the Martians, once beings of superior intellect, to cave dwellers, who throw boulders at the explorers, leaving two of them dead and one badly injured. The three—the female scientist, the navigator, and the astronomer—return to the ship, but insufficient fuel precludes a safe return to Earth. This time, the Deity does not intervene. Before the ship crashes, the scientist (Osa Massen) and the chief engineer (Lloyd Bridges) embrace like doomed lovers in an opera, awaiting their reunion in eternity. Back on Earth, the expedition is not written off as a failure; another is planned that will herald "the salvation for our own world." Interplanetary travel will save the planet—with an assist from the Deity. The next time, the blastoff will succeed. This coda was a sop to optimists, seeking some reassurance about America's embryonic space program. But for sober-minded moviegoers, the film ended with the crash. The message was clear: It was tragic enough that no one survived the mission, but the possibility that an atomic war could turn humans into cave dwellers was even more daunting.

The uncredited Dalton Trumbo clearly played a major role in shaping the script. The working title was "None Came Back." A decade earlier, Trumbo collaborated with Nathanael West and Jerome Cady on the script of *Five Came Back* (RKO, 1939), in which a plane with twelve passengers is blown off course and forced to land in a South American jungle teeming with headhunters. Once the aircraft is repaired, it can only accommodate five. "None Came Back" must have been Trumbo's preferred title. Lippert decreed otherwise, settling on the trendier *Rocketship X-M*. Trumbo is best known for his antiwar novel, *Johnny Got His Gun*, in which Joe Bonham returns from war with a gaping hole for a face, armless and legless, unable to speak or hear, and kept alive by intravenous feeding. Unlike *Johnny Got His Gun*, *Rocketship X-M* did not dramatize the horrors of war (the war had already occurred), only its aftereffects.

Destination Moon (1950), on the other hand, was unintimidating. Suspense was minimal, except for a brief moment at the end. It seemed that one of the astronauts must be left behind because the ship could not jettison anything necessary for the return voyage. But more equipment is dumped, and the rocket ship heads home. Although the film was suggested by Robert Heinlein's *Rocketship Galileo*, the writers—including Heinlein—discarded the novel's revelation that there was a colony of Nazis on the moon. In fact, there is no one on the moon, which may have disappointed audiences expecting lunar creatures. Like many other science fiction films, *Destination Moon* is cobwebbed with ideas that are never spun into anything resembling a pattern, instead remaining mere wisps of thought. The expedition is not funded by the military, but by an industrialist from the private sector. "Preparedness is not always military," General Thayer (Tom Powers) remarks. Neither is interplanetary travel something the government can pursue in peacetime, an argument that would have struck a 1950 audience as ironic. In August 1950, when *Destination Moon* was released, the Korean War was in its second month.

The film is curious for other reasons. The four astronauts are all men. The lone female in the movie, played by Erin O'Brien-Moore, appears briefly as an astronaut's wife, then vanishes from the plot. Although the Soviet Union is never mentioned, its presence is felt. General Thayer's warning, "We are not the only ones knowing that the moon can be reached," does not require parsing "we." Audiences knew. They would also have agreed that whoever controls the moon can control the Earth, and that for the good of humankind, it had better be the United States. But the Soviet threat only appeared in the dialogue; once the line was spoken, it was blastoff time.

The ingenious animator and producer George Pal created a moon that is uninhabited, rocky, and mountainous. The terrain is uneven, parched and cracked. Depressions suggest the existence of hot springs that have dried up. Even so, Pal gave the moon the haunting beauty of ancient ruins at twilight. Still and primeval, it is a site for reflection, not fear. And, as the *pièce de la résistance*, the moon has uranium deposits, which should endear it to the Atomic Energy Commission.

The moon is ours—or rather the free world's. The astronauts claim it "in the name of all mankind." But since they are Americans, the ownership is obvious. Perhaps some moviegoers responded to the political subtext, but for those who did not, there were always the special effects—including sky walking astronauts and a moonscape more fascinating than frightening. Pal strove for otherworldliness, and on that score *Destination Moon* delivered. Instead of the traditional "The End," *Destination Moon* closed with, "This is the End of the Beginning." The beginning of what, one might ask? Obviously, more movies about outer space.

Audiences disappointed at the absence of human—or at least extraterrestrial—life on the moon would eventually get a look at lunar denizens, none more bizarre than the ladies in *Cat Women of the Moon* (1954). The title is nonsense. The handful of moon women (the men have died off) are dressed like dancers in rehearsal clothes. Their slinky movements may be feline, but their attire is ballet school. The moon is a matriarchy, where the women have mastered mind control, communicating telepathically with Helen (Marie Windsor), the sole woman on a five-person lunar expedition, whose space ship lands near the women's cave. The moon is another flattened landscape, looking like a chalk-white riverbed. It is truly a moon for the misbegotten. The women, three of whom have Greek alphabet names—Alpha, Beta, and Lambda—need the space ship to emigrate from the dying moon to Earth, where they plan to establish a society devoid of men. Naturally, they do not succeed, although some radical feminists might have wished otherwise. Although *Cat Women* is pure hokum, it was refreshingly nonideological. Neither the Soviet Union nor the United States military figured in the plot, which is sheer escapism and at times outrageously funny—especially when one of the astronauts sighs, "I love you, Lambda," as if he were pledging a fraternity.

In its refusal to haul the god out from the machine, *Rocketship X-M* remained steadfast in its dark vision, brightened slightly by a feel-good epilogue that is best ignored. Thus, it differed from movie allegories of the 1950s, which seemed like New Testament parables. In *The Next Voice You Hear* (1950), God usurps prime time on radio for six days in order to deliver a homily in installments about the need for love and understanding. Expecting a broadcast on the seventh, listeners are disappointed until they remember that was the day the Deity rested. But the film made its point: The Almighty is displeased with humankind, as nations race to see who can blow up whom first.

The most strikingly Christian science fiction film of the 1950s was Twentieth Century-Fox's *The Day the Earth Stood Still* (1951), which captured the mood of an America searching for a way out of the crater of fear left by the bomb. Sensing that science fiction would be a popular genre in the 1950s, Darryl F. Zanuck wanted his studio's contribution to be in a class by itself, notches above creature features and SFX-driven movies. First, there must be "an exciting and provocative title." Since the script implied that the United Nations was unable to handle a crisis brought about by a visitor from another planet, Zanuck warned against portraying the United Nations as "a failure" or even suggesting "that it has already failed." The UN is simply impotent, as is the army. Neither is science the answer. Rather, Zanuck insisted, scientists must "understand the need for 'spiritual presence' because scientific answers cannot resolve every problem." For the most part, Zanuck got what he wanted, except for a documentary style requiring "narration—how they (UFOs) were first seen—how their existence was denied by the War Department—how other reports continued to come in." Zanuck seems to have wanted a voiceover prologue that traced the history of flying saucers, which would have made *The Day the Earth Stood Still* another semi-documentary. Zanuck realized he had an unusual property on his hands and backed off.

After an uneventful beginning, the plot takes off when a space ship, circling the Earth at supersonic speed, lands on the Washington Mall. A male in a silvery space suit and a robot that looks like a metallic colossus (actually, aluminum-painted foam rubber) emerge from the ship. "We have come to visit you in peace and good will," the alien announces. Extending an object that is later revealed to be a device for learning about other planets, he is greeted with a bullet in his shoulder. The shoot-to-kill response to Otherness was not limited to the jittery 1950s; it is man's knee-jerk reaction to objects that look threatening but really are not. The visitor from an unnamed planet 250 million miles from Earth is the well-spoken Klaatu (Michael Rennie), whose impeccable English is the result of monitoring broadcasts from Earth—similar to the "I have studied at your university" cliché in World War II films that explained a Japanese officer's bilingualism. Unlike Earth, Klaatu's planet uses atomic energy constructively, not for war, which does not exist there. What Klaatu fears is that humans' misuse of the atom will affect other planets. And since his people are technologically superior to humans (as always in sci-fi), he offers a demonstration of his power. He creates a worldwide blackout for thirty minutes, affecting everything except hospitals and planes in flight.

The Day the Earth Stood Still is not just a congeries of biblical references; it is a true allegory. Oddly, the director, Robert Wise, admitted in an interview with Nicholas Mayer that, during the filming, he was unaware of the Christian parallels, a response that surprised Mayer, who enumerated them. Descent/ascent images bookend the film, with Klaatu's arrival at the beginning and departure at the end paralleling the descent of the logos, the word of God made flesh in the person of Jesus Christ, and his ascension into heaven forty days after his resurrection. Like Christ, Klaatu has a mission, which cannot be thwarted by a mere wound. After he applies a special balm, the wound is immediately healed. The balm's magical properties are the stuff of myth, not scripture. Jesus rarely resorted to anything material. He usually cast out demons, raised the dead, or cured the sick with a statement ("Your faith has saved you," Matt. 9:22), an action (the healing of the centurion's servant, Matt. 8:13), or a command ("Rise, pick up your stretcher and go home," Matt. 9:6). On a few occasions, he cured the blind by touching their eyes (Matt. 9:29) and healed others by imposing his hands (Mark 8:23–25; Luke: 4:40, 13:12–13). However, on one occasion, he shocked the Pharisees by not only healing on the Sabbath, but also using a mixture of saliva and clay to do so. He smeared the mixture over a blind man's eyes and ordered him to wash it off, after which the man's sight was restored (John 9:1–7). Klaatu had it easy; he did not have to mix his curative.

The real clue that Klaatu is a Christ figure comes with a suit he has procured (or purloined), which previously belonged to a "Major Carpenter." Klaatu is an avatar of the master carpenter ("major," derived from the Latin "maior," meaning greater), Jesus, and is indeed greater than the ordinary craftsman. He takes a room at a boarding house, where he meets a widow (Patricia Neal) and her son (Billy Gray). The latter shows no fear, and in fact, looks up to Klaatu as a father figure, causing him to respond in kind. Christ often invoked the child as a symbol of the kind of docility and trust he desired in his followers, even making it a requirement for salvation: "Unless you turn and become like children, you will not enter the kingdom of heaven" (Matt. 18:3). Unfortunately, the rest of Washington does not have the boy's innocence or his trust.

The obstacles to cosmic brotherhood are a fear-ridden public and a trigger-happy militia. Klaatu suffers another bullet wound that would have proved fatal to any human, though Gort carries him back to the space ship and resurrects him with a form of radiation that does more than shrink tumors. The resurrection is really a revivification, as Klaatu informs the widow. His lifespan, like everyone's, is determined by the Almighty. Like Christ after his resurrection and on the eve of his ascension, Klaatu delivers a homily. But unlike Christ's envoi to his disciples, in which he prophesied the coming of the Holy Spirit who would inspire them in their evangelizing, Klaatu's speech is a variation of a jeremiad. He belongs to an interplanetary confederation, with a race of robots patrolling outer space, enforcing peace and punishing aggression. Unless humans cooperate for the good of their planet, it will be reduced to cinders. One almost expects him to start quoting Jesus's description of the last days: "Nation will rise against nation, and kingdom against kingdom; there will be famine and earthquakes from place to place ... the sun will be darkened, and the moon will not give its light, and the stars will fall from the sky, and the powers of the heavens will be shaken" (Matt. 24:7, 29). "The decision rests with you," Klaatu warns, entering the spacecraft, which then takes off with awesome majesty.

The fear-inspiring homily, with its reference to an interplanetary UN, seems to have overtones of totalitarianism. Big Brother is watching you, so learn to coalesce—or else. But Christ also delivered his share of mandates. It was not enough to love your neighbor as yourself: "Whoever is angry with his brother is subject to judgment" (Matt. 5:22). An unforgiving servant is handed over to torturers: "So will my heavenly father do to you, unless each of you forgives his brother from his heart" (Matt. 18:34–35). At the last judgment, the righteous will be rewarded with eternal life and evildoers condemned to everlasting punishment (Matt. 24:31–46). Refusal to accept Christ's message portends a bad end.

Despite Edmund H. North's screenplay, with its scriptural overtones, Robert Wise's masterful direction, and the otherworldly score by the great Bernard Herrmann—who used the Theremin for a motif as eerie as Miklós Rozsa's in *Spellbound* (1945)—*The Day the Earth Stood Still* is unsettling, which may have been the point. *The Next Voice You Hear*, by contrast, ends benevolently, with a shot of the transfigured face of a mother (Nancy Davis) who has successfully given birth, although she feared she might die of a false pregnancy like the other women in her family. *The Day the Earth Stood Still* is less optimistic, despairing of any human organization's ability to achieve world peace, including the United Nations. Instead, humans are accountable to a watchdog confederation in outer space that will step in when fools tread on dangerous ground. The message that Earth is doing a poor job securing the peace would have not been lost on 1951 audiences. The Korean War was in its first year, and the body count was rising. Nuclear tests were being conducted in Nevada. Ethel and Julius Rosenberg were convicted of espionage. And a hydrogen bomb was detonated at Eniwetok atoll. War, as Klaatu observed, is indigenous to Earth. It is nonexistent on his planet, but since we never learn about life there, we can only assume that Klaatu's home has found a way to end war without waging one—something humans have failed to accomplish. In a sense, the less prestigious *Rocketship X-M* was subtler, suggesting what nuclear war would mean for Earth, with Mars serving as an example of a planet bombed back to the Stone Age.

The oddest "alien comes to Earth" movie of the 1950s was Columbia's *The 27th Day* (1957), which John Matley converted into a seventy-five-minute movie based on his 1956 novel, a Book-of-the-Month Club selection. Matley managed to retain his novel's plot lines: an alien's abduction of five people; the doomsday boxes they are given; a suicide; a tepid romance between a British woman and an American journalist; a race to keep the Soviet Union from opening the boxes; mass hysteria at the prospect of a nuked America;

last-minute salvation from a physicist whose powers of deduction rival both Aristotle's and Sherlock Holmes's, and a "brotherhood of man" finale. Matley wastes no time in setting the plot in motion. In Cornwall, England, Evelyn Knight (Valerie French), fresh from a swim, lies down on the beach, as the shadow of a man passes over her. A voice, grave but unthreatening, tells her to come with him. The same happens to a Chinese peasant woman, a California journalist, a German physicist, and a Russian soldier. A flying saucer transports them to outer space, where a well-spoken alien (Arnold Moss) informs them that in thirty-five days his planet will become extinct. Since his people practice non-violence, they cannot attack Earth. However, if humans destroy their planet, the aliens will colonize it. The alien gives each of the five a box with three cylinders capable of mass destruction, which can only be opened through thought waves. If the boxes remain un-opened for twenty-seven days, they will become inactive. The alien is antici-pating a race between the world's Pandoras—specifically the United States and the Soviet Union, each eager to wipe out the other. And if they do, his planet stands a chance.

The alien does not make it easy for the humans. Perversely, he goes on the air, like the Deity in *The Next Voice You Hear*, informing the world about the boxes and their owners. The journalist becomes a "man on the run." He and Evelyn, now in Los Angeles, take refuge at a racetrack. The Russian soldier is injected with a truth serum. Once his superiors learn the secret of the capsules, they demand the immediate withdrawal of all Americans from Europe and Asia, causing pandemonium in the United States as doomsday approaches. But before the Soviets can act, the German physicist, allied with the United States, deactivates the capsules, allowing them to be used only to destroy "the enemies of human freedom," a group left unnamed but infer-able. Ironically, someone from a country that was our former enemy has prevented our present enemy from blowing us up. One might also wonder what the physicist did during the war, but *The 27th Day* does not encourage that kind of speculation.

Audiences in 1957 would have found nothing threatening about the film. The Soviets beat the United States into space when they launched the ar-tificial satellite Sputnik I that October, and Sputnik II, carrying a dog, the following month. America's attempt in December failed when an explosion in the fuel tanks destroyed the rocket. America's failure may have been an embarrassment, but it did not cause an increase in tension. On the plus side, Sputnik inspired educators to add Russian to the modern languages curriculum. Fordham University went even further, establishing a Russian institute. The reason—implicit, as usual in academe—was not just that the language was worthy of study, but that it was also the language of the enemy, later known as "the evil Empire," and therefore well suited to diplomacy and espionage.

The 27th Day was a not so much political as conciliatory, affirming the bonds of friendship uniting all who believe in freedom and democracy and, by implication, excluding the Soviet Union. Although the alien has put the country through a nerve-fraying ordeal, it is now "forgive and forget" time. Magnanimous America invites the alien and his people to relocate in the uninhabited parts of the country, and the alien graciously accepts. With the forging of a grand alliance between humans and aliens, one would think that the "creature from another planet" movie had reached its apogee. And perhaps it had, in terms of the Cold War, but not permanently. Two of the greatest alien films, Steven Spielberg's *Close Encounters of the Third Kind* (1977) and *E.T. The Extra-Terrestrial* (1982), had nothing to do with the Cold War. They brought the relationship between humankind and the Other to an interpersonal level—especially *Close Encounters*, in which a five-note musical theme became the means of communication between the two races. The suggestion is that music, toward which—as Walter Pater observed—all art constantly aspires, is truly the universal language. Perhaps aliens can even hear the music of the spheres. They should; they're closer to it.

Chapter 7

APOCALYPSE THEN

AFTER *DESTINATION MOON*, GEORGE PAL BEGAN THINKING DARKER thoughts. Just five years after the end of the Second World War, America was involved in a euphemistically designated "police action" in Korea. The Soviet Union signed a defense treaty with China. President Truman wanted a bigger and better bomb, later known as the H-bomb. Senator Joseph McCarthy was making alarming (and unfounded) accusations about two hundred-plus State Department employees he considered communists. China entered the Korean War, and General Douglas MacArthur would have retaliated by bombing China, triggering a nuclear free-for-all, except that President Truman relieved MacArthur of his command the following year. It seemed time to dust off *When Worlds Collide*, a novella by Edwin Balmer and Philip Wylie that Paramount purchased in 1932.

By 2 October 1950, Sidney Boehm had a script that was bleaker than anyone at Paramount anticipated. In it, a South African scientist discovered two new heavenly bodies, one of which will enter the solar system. Drawn into the orbit of the sun, it will cause massive floods and earthquakes. A League of Last Days is formed, hysteria is rampant with rumors of Martian invasions and flying saucers, and the pope chants the *Kyrie* in St. Peter's Square. Evacuations begin amid widespread looting, and the lucky ones file into a space ship headed for the other—apparently habitable—planet.

Pal thought that the film would work better as an allegory of Noah and the ark. In fact, the ship that transports the chosen is called an "ark," despite having an atomic jet in the stern to hurl it into space. The opening title establishes the biblical connection: "And God looked upon the Earth, and behold, it was corrupt . . . . And God said to Noah, 'I will destroy them with the world,'" which is more or less the gist of Genesis 7:11–13. The new planets, originally named Bronson Alpha and Bronson Beta after their discoverer, have been rechristened Bellus and Zyra, names that sound more authentically sci-fi. Since Zyra is habitable, it is the last refuge of human-kind. The space ship is ready, but who will board it? Only forty can be taken, and they will be the best and the brightest, who, one assumes, will increase and multiply, supplying Zyra with a master race. The film softens the Hitle-rian association by implying that much of humankind has reverted to sav-agery. Even so, the film's attitude towards those who must remain behind is—as Bosley Crowther remarked in his *New York Times* review (7 February 1952)—"disturbing." There is not even an indication that the space ship will operate as a shuttle between Zyra and what is left of Earth. The scene is reminiscent of General MacArthur heading off to Mindanao on a PT-boat and leaving the "battling bastards of Bataan" to their fate. The fortunate forty may have a tough time ahead, but at least it will be scenic. Zyra is a Technicolor Eden in green and pink. "The First Day on the New Earth Has Begun," the end title declares.

Far superior to *When Worlds Collide* was George Pal's production of *The War of the Worlds* (1953), one of the most popular and commercially suc-cessful science fiction films of the 1950s. It was also a masterful updating of H. G. Wells's 1898 classic, with Southern California as the target of Mars's first worldwide blitzkrieg, campaigns that would eventually leave the planet devoid of human life, ready to be populated by Martians. What they would do with such a wasteland is another question. One point is frighteningly clear: Mars is capable of rendering Earth obsolete.

The War of the Worlds opens with a mock Paramount newsreel that shows clips of the two world wars, followed by the announcement of a war that will not so much end war as end human life. In a voiceover prologue, Sir Cedric Hardwicke, sounding like an accomplished storyteller from a class higher than those his listeners inhabit, delivers the essence of Wells's opening chapter, "The Eve of the War," beginning with the author's sober-ing warning, "[T]his world was being watched keenly and closely by intelli-gences greater than man's, and yet as mortal as his own"—the qualifier por-tending things to come, when the Martians are felled by bacteria to which humans have grown immune. Before that happens, havoc reigns. Mars is a dying planet, searching for greener pastures. Pluto, Neptune, Saturn, and Uranus are too cold. Mercury has no air, and Jupiter's atmospheric pressure cannot sustain life. The only possibility is Earth.

All the film owes to Wells is a bit of voiceover prologue and the expla-nation in the penultimate chapter that the Martians succumbed to ordi-nary bacteria. The screenwriter, Barré Lyndon (Alfred Edgar, pseud.), ig-nored Wells's depiction of the Martians. At first, Wells described them using serpentine imagery as dark-eyed, snake-like creatures with tentacled, V-shaped mouths, dripping with saliva as they wriggle out of the space cylinders in which they landed. Later, Wells added further details. The Martians are sexless, budding like flowers and resembling octopuses with two sets each of eight tentacles. Fidelity to the source would have relegated the film to the lower echelon of horror.

In Wells, the Deity is either absent or watching from on high. The only church mentioned in the novella is destroyed, as the curate panics. Later, the curate, hungry and raving, falls prey to a Martian, who lassoes him with a tentacle and presumably absorbs his blood into its veins. In the film, a courageous minister replaced the pusillanimous curate. The minister is convinced that Martians are more advanced than humans because they are nearer to their Creator. Holding up a Bible and reciting the Twenty-Third Psalm, the minister fearlessly approaches a Martian, only to be zapped with its high-power rays. The Deity has not yet chosen to make an entrance.

In the film, the Martians' spacecraft have the saucer-like contours of UFOs with which 1950s moviegoers were familiar, even though the craft are occasionally referred to as "cylinders," and at other times as "machines." At first, the cylinders appear to be meteors. When they crash, they leave behind a radioactive crater, indicating that they are fueled by atomic energy. The meteoric spacecraft and their cargo are the creation of Pal, director Byron Haskin, and art directors Hal Pereira and— especially—Al Nozaki. The machines that subsequently emerge are cobra-headed, resembling gooseneck lamps and discharging rays of such potency that they produce instant annihilation.

Lyndon added a romantic subplot involving an atomic scientist who had worked at Oak Ridge—a reference that goes nowhere—and the minister's niece, and religious symbols that were strikingly visualized. The Martian possesses an electromagnetic eye with three lenses, whose colors—red, green, and blue—match those of the spacecraft. The number three and its multiples are ubiquitous in Christianity—for example, the Trinity; the cardinal virtues of faith, hope, and charity; Christ's third-day resurrection; the twelve apostles, seventy-two disciples, and nine-day novenas. The electromagnetic eye that operates like a surveillance camera evokes an all-seeing eye, a common representation of the Deity. A scientist observes that it would take six days for the Martians to destroy Earth, the inverse of the six days it took to create it. And at the end of the film, an alien's arm falls out of the spacecraft. It is a shriveled, three-fingered appendage—triune Christianity transmogrified.

The Martians are the anti-Christ, the apocalyptic beast, a parody of Christianity and its symbols. But they are no match for Earth's bacteria and the power of faith. In the final scene, those who have not fled Los Angeles or perished take refuge in various churches. In one, a minister prays for deliverance. In another, which is clearly Catholic, a priest recites the rosary in Spanish. In a third, a choir sings "Abide with Me." The spacecrafts collapse as if in a state of exhaustion, suggesting that they, too, have been brought down by the germs in the Earth's atmosphere. But the final shot, of a cathedral looming over the ruins, implies that bacteria alone did not destroy the Martians, that a higher power cooperated in their demise. If the rest of the world resembled the war zone that Los Angeles had become, it would be years before even minimal rebuilding would be possible. But the film did not explore that point. Believe in God and bacteria, and all will be well. And *The War of the Worlds* ignores another significant issue. When the Martians prove immune to ordinary weaponry, the government hauls out the A-bomb. This bomb leaves a spiral of white smoke that is less ominous than a mushroom cloud, and perhaps conveys a sense of the rightness of the act with its color—as if the bombing of Los Angeles were a lesser form of the devastation the Martins were wreaking on the city. But in 1953, the bomb was the answer to anything imperiling America. Lyndon's script had its loopholes, but the production was so spectacular—and has remained so—that one is inclined to invoke the laws of verisimilitude and echo Aristotle's response (*Poetics* 4, 5) to a representation that is uncannily lifelike: "That's it." Pal got it right. That is the way the world ends: with a bang, a whimper, and a renewal.

In the doomsday film, the extinction of the species is a sobering possibility, but rarely a reality. For the most part, the genre avoided the unthinkable. There was always a last-minute reprieve: emigration to a new planet (*When Worlds Collide*), or a fatal miscalculation by the invaders (the Martians' susceptibility to ordinary bacteria in *The War of the Worlds*). In *Earth Dies Screaming* (1965), the planet may be in its death throes, but there are survivors, willing to venture on to the proverbial worlds elsewhere. Even the first postwar nuclear disaster film, *Five* (1951), followed the pattern, imagining a nuclear war (the cause of which is unspecified) that left the planet devoid of life except for five humans who, for various reasons, managed to survive.

Five was written, produced, and directed by playwright-screenwriter-novelist Arch Oboler, who began his career in radio with *Lights Out*, a mandate that a generation heeded by listening under the covers. Oboler's most famous *Lights Out* script was *The Chicken Heart*, in which tissue from the heart of a chicken kept growing until it swallowed up the world. Bill Cosby, who heard *The Chicken Heart* in his youth, later recounted the plot so vividly in one of his monologues that it brought back memories of the shivers it sent up the spines of listeners back in the 1940s. *Five* would have worked better as a radio play. As such, it would have gripped the imagination better than it did by appealing to the eye on film.

Five began promisingly enough with credits accompanied by the now emblematic mushroom cloud and the boom of detonation, followed by a title, "A story about the day after tomorrow," and an excerpt from the *Book of Revelation* about the last days. Next followed a montage of major cities—London, Moscow, Paris—reduced to smoking ruins and accompanied by the sound of wailing sirens. Yet for all its darkness shot through with occasional slivers of light, *Five* is neither particularly unnerving nor reflective. The survivors—a pregnant woman; a Dartmouth MA with mechanical skills made for such a crisis; a bank manager and one of his employees; and an explorer who has climbed Mt. Everest and espouses a Darwinian philosophy of survival of the fittest—may not enjoy life's creature comforts, but with empty stores and homes, they live in nuclear style. The Dartmouth grad has taken over a hilltop house (Oboler's own in Santa Barbara, designed by Frank Lloyd Wright), which he makes habitable, finding a generator to power it and seed to plant corn. The explorer is the villain, believing that there are other survivors elsewhere (the nearest metropolis is Los Angeles) and setting off to find them. To make *Five* compatible with *Genesis*, Oboler must reduce the quintet to a duo. First, the bank manager dies. Then the explorer, after killing the bank employee, develops radiation poisoning, leaving the Dartmouth grad and the woman as the next Adam and Eve. The end title, from the *Book of Revelation* (21:1), promises a new order: "I saw a new heaven and a new earth." It will certainly be a meatless earth. Since there are no animals, the couple and their descendants will be vegetarians.

Columbia's *Invasion U.S.A.* (1952), released the following year, envisioned a nuclear war instigated by a power known as "he" (a pronominal synonym for the Soviet Union) that left the Pacific Northwest and California in the hands of the enemy. Then Boulder Dam was bombed, much of New York was in ruins, and the nation's capital was under siege. However, the phantasmagoria depicted in the film never actually happened. In the opening sequence, a mesmerist twirls a snifter of brandy in front of five people in a Manhattan bar, presenting them with a vision of what could—not would—happen to the United States if the government made cuts in military spending and reduced the armed forces by half, as an Illinois congressman has proposed. Just when it seems that New York will fall to the communists—who spout Marxist clichés about a people's republic on American soil—the heroine (Peggy Castle), to avoid being raped by a Russian soldier, jumps out of a window. As she falls through space, her image is reduced to a speck floating in the mesmerist's brandy snifter, thus bringing the action back to the bar, the five back to reality, and the film back to its didactic end title from George Washington: "To be prepared for war is one of the most effectual means of preserving peace." The prospect of nuclear war between the United States and the Soviet Union prompted the congressman—who in the vision is shot when the Soviets overrun the Senate—to change his mind about reducing the defense budget. Coincidentally, the defense budget rose from $224.3 million in 1951 to $402.1 million in 1952. *Invasion U.S.A.* is wildly implausible (Soviet paratroopers in American uniforms rain down on Washington and barge into the Senate, looking and sounding like ex-Nazis who had discarded *Mein Kampf* in favor of *Das Kapital*). In the end, one is obliged to respect *Five* for not pulling the same stunt—presenting mass devastation as a bad dream that vanishes at dawn, or as a hypnotic state that ends with a click of the fingers or the twirl of a snifter.

On the Beach (1959), on the other hand, posed the unthinkable by dramatizing the end of civilization, with Australia as the termination point and no hope of a deus ex machina. The film, released in December 1959 and set in 1964, premiered in a year that was not particularly tension-ridden, as compared to 1962 and 1963. In 1959, the United States welcomed Fidel Castro as Cuba's liberator after the overthrow of the Fulgencio Batista regime—although the welcome mat was rolled up after Castro allied himself with the Soviet Union. *Rawhide, Bonanza*, and *The Twilight Zone* made their television debuts. Barbie dolls went on sale. Pope John XXIII announced the convening of a council later known as Vatican II. The Ford Edsel proved to be a bust. *Gypsy* and *The Sound of Music* dominated the Broadway scene. And on 17 December, just in time for Christmas, *On the Beach* opened simultaneously in the United States, Australia (naturally), Sweden, and West Germany. Although the United States had been living with the possibility of nuclear war since the late 1940s, the threat seemed remote in 1959. When President Eisenhower played host to Soviet Premier Nikita Khrushchev at Camp David, the presidential retreat in Maryland, optimists even thought that rapprochement with the Soviet Union was possible.

If *On the Beach* had come out during the crucial weekend of 26 October 1962, audiences would have reacted differently. This was the height of the Cuban Missile Crisis, when the presence of surface-to-air missiles in Cuba, supplied by the Soviet Union and aimed at the United States, kept the nation on tenterhooks as the world wondered if Cuba would be the Sarajevo or Pearl Harbor that triggered another world war. Armageddon was averted by a diplomatic pas de deux, the upshot of which was the dismantling of the missiles and their return to the Soviet Union. Even when the crisis ended on Sunday, 28 October, there was still the fear that such incidents were not over and would, in fact, increase. If *On the Beach* had come out after the Kennedy assassination, the film would have had an even greater impact—first a president, then the world. The knowledge that the alleged assassin, Lee Harvey Oswald, had sought residence in the Soviet Union would have given the conspiracy theorists more strands to spin in their ever-growing web of intrigue. And if, by chance, someone who was politically astute had seen *On the Beach* in 1964—the apocalyptic year according to the film—he or she would have realized that extinction was unlikely, but war in Southeast Asia was not. Those who believed that Vietnam was the next Korea were vindicated when President Lyndon Johnson used an incident in the Gulf of Tonkin—when North Vietnamese gunboats fired on an American destroyer—as justification for requesting authorization from Congress to prosecute the war in Vietnam without a formal declaration. The details of the incident were muddied, but that did not matter. Nineteen sixty-four was a year for waiting—not knowing exactly what, except for the one event that would reveal what is to come. Americans had become so used to postwar arrhythmia that a scare here or there suggested the result would be another confrontation/trade off/show of force/police action/undeclared war—but certainly not a pax Americana.

Whenever one sees *On the Beach*, the effect is devastating—more so after 9/11, when a terrorist attack could be the spark that ignites the powder keg. It was a film for all seasons. The fact that it has brought in over $5 million in rentals suggests that doomsday pays off. America had been living under the mushroom cloud since 1945, when the genie had sprinted out of the bottle, ready to bedevil humanity and haunt its dreams. But those who simply dismissed *On the Beach* as an end-of-the-world flick failed to recognize the art with which producer-director Stanley Kramer invested it. With the unofficial Australian national anthem, "Waltzing Matilda," serving as a leitmotif that becomes more dirge-like as the film progresses, Kramer presents the last bastion of civilization as a place where some engage in business as usual—hosting dinner parties, lounging in leathery men's clubs, racing sports cars, hitting the bottle, and engaging in one last romance before the final tolling of the bell. Kramer's last outpost is a cross section of types one would expect to find anywhere at zero hour: a submarine captain (Gregory Peck) resigned to the inevitable, but still speaking of his dead wife and family as if they were living; the functional alcoholic (Ava Gardner) who loves him, knowing that their relationship will be short-lived; a scientist (Fred Astaire) who gives his sports car a tune up before competing in the Australian Grand Prix, believing that if he wins, which he does, death will be an anticlimax; and a lieutenant (Anthony Perkins) with a wife and child, who knows that when the inevitable occurs, they must die as a family—and not from radiation poisoning. When suicide pills are available, he has no choice other than to provide them with the gentlest death available. To placate the Legion of Decency, which frowned on suicide, the wife utters a final prayer, "My God forgive us."

Always the moralist, Kramer could not help but end the film with a shot of a drooping banner, "There Is Still Time, Brother," strung up when the Salvation Army held a revival-type rally. Now the banner is part of a wasteland of deserted streets and empty buildings. In 1959, there was still time, as there was in the years that followed. Armageddon has been predicted so often that when it comes, it will seem like just another battle. If it culminates in total destruction, we will never know it.

Unlike Nevil Shute's novel, in which the war of wars began with Albania bombing Italy, no one in the movie seems to know how the war started. When asked who started it, one of the captain's crew says facetiously, "Albert Einstein." This statement is true only indirectly; more likely, the end of the world comes from a miscalculation, a miscommunication, a pressing of the wrong button, or some such human error. But on one point, the crew is in total agreement and totally correct: Weapons designed for protection became weapons of destruction. Humankind has destroyed itself, a frightening thought that one would rather not contemplate—except in a movie theater from which one could exit onto streets thronged with people with more mundane concerns than the planet's last days.

Chapter 8

RED SKIES OVER CHINA

THE RED SCARE EVEN MADE ITS WAY INTO B MOVIES, WHICH, IN THE late 1940s, with the rise of television as the new mass medium, were often the main attraction in theaters that once showed them on the bottom half of a double bill. *State Department File 649* (1949), released by Film Classics, was a quickie (and looked it). It opened at New York's Globe Theater on Broadway and 43rd Street, the home of low-budget movies, which no one would confuse with a movie palace. Bosley Crowther, chief film critic for the *New York Times*, dismissed the movie, but it is still available for both purchase and download, garnering some astute observations from viewers. *State Department File 649* seemed to derive from a leftover World War II template: Find a historical event; populate it with the heroes and villains of the day; set it in the volatile Far East; inject some local color; add a romantic subplot—and audiences will think it's Yellow Peril time again. The film, released in early February 1949, was shot hurriedly in late 1948 in Cinecolor, a less expensive process than Technicolor, with some colors strikingly rendered and others pastel. The editing was crude, with an inordinate number of fade-outs, making the movie seem like a slide show. At the beginning, a solemn newsreel voice extolled the bravery of the men and women in the foreign service, who risked torture and death for their country—particularly in 1948, when the Iron Curtain, which had already fallen on eastern Europe, was about to descend on China.

Nineteen forty-eight, the year in which the film is set, was critical for China. The Chinese civil war between Chang Kai-Chek's Nationalists and Mao Zedong's Communists, which had been raging since 1927, ceased temporarily in 1937 when both factions joined forces to counteract Japanese aggression. The fighting resumed after World War II. By late 1948, after Mao's armies scored significant gains in North China, a communist victory was inevitable. Today, the North; tomorrow, China—which is exactly what happened.

The film is set before the fall of Peiping (Peking), soon to be renamed Beijing. The new American attaché, Ken Seeley (William Lundigan), is sent to North China, where, as the consul gravely notes, "[A]n iron curtain has been lowered between us and the North." Since Seeley was born in Mongolia of missionary parents murdered by bandits, he is transferred to Ming-Goo province as vice consul, just in time to clash with Marshal Yun Usu (Richard Loo), a Mongolian warlord who, asserting his hereditary rights, plans to set up an autonomous province. Although it may seem that the writers have taken a side trip to Mongolia, the Red Menace was still the main route. Mongolia was not a diversion, but a transition from China, which would soon fall to the communists, to the Soviet Union, which had been allied with Mongolia since 1921, and to which Mongolia was indebted for warding off a Japanese takeover during World War II. The marshal's name is Chinese, his soldiers are dressed like Maoists, and the fiefdom he plans to establish would be a police state as repressive as any communist satellite. Yun Usu is little more than a power-hungry thug, whom Seeley denounces ("You represent murder, rape, and slavery") before he blows up the marshal's trailer, killing them both.

Many 1949 moviegoers would have recognized the Hawaiian-born Richard Loo from World War II films, in which he frequently played a suave Japanese sadist (*The Purple Heart, Prison Ship, Tokyo Rose, Back to Bataan, Betrayal from the East*). He was similarly ruthless as the marshal in *State Department File 649*, ordering the hands of a radio operator to be lopped off for trying to warn the Peiping embassy about the plight of the captive Americans. But audiences, exposed to World War II propaganda movies, would have seen the marshal as the latest version of the Japanese militarist who tore out tongues, gouged out eyes, raped women, bayoneted Chinese babies, and inserted bamboo shoots under fingernails. The marshal just had more finesse than his Japanese confreres.

Anyone following the news in the late 1940s would have found Milton Raison's screenplay uncanny, even though it drew on the lexicon of the World War II movie. In January 1949, two weeks before *State Department File 649* was released, Peiping came under communist control and was renamed Beijing that October. America now had another potential threat: Communist China, a new villain in an ever-growing repertory.

Communist China did not bring out the best in filmmakers, perhaps because the country was so xenophobic that, as a setting, it could only evoke the same clichés that the propaganda films of World War II perpetuated: humorless autocrats who greet each other as "comrade," subordinate personal needs (except their own) to those of that anomaly called "the people," rape with impunity, and torture with glee. Newsreels reduced the Chinese communists to a collective mass. If prime matter could be visualized, it would be Communist China, where individualism, if it existed, was practiced secretly—like an outlawed religion.

The Left Hand of God (1955) is set in North China in 1947 during the civil war, of which little is made in the film. Jim Carmody (Humphrey Bogart), a mercenary, assumes the identity of a priest, Father O'Shea, who had been killed before he could take up his post at a Catholic mission. Since the mission is expecting a priest, Carmody obliges, passing himself off as Father O'Shea. As a Catholic, he knows what a rosary is, delivers an effective New Testament reading, and simplifies the marriage rite: "I join you together in marriage in the name of the Father and of the Son and of the Holy Ghost. Amen." Since there are no communion wafers, he is spared the embarrassment of saying Mass, and Twentieth Century-Fox is spared the ire of the Catholic Church. This deception is only the point of departure for the story of a man with a shady past who dons a Roman collar, functions as an effective clergyman, finds God, and realizes that his relationship with a nurse (Gene Tierney) is becoming decidedly profane. But there are more important considerations. To prevent the village and the mission from falling into the hands of Mieh Yang, a warlord (a strangely unmenacing Lee J. Cobb, looking as he did in *Anna and the King of Siam*), Carmody cuts a deal with Yang. A toss of the dice will determine whether Carmody serves Yang for five years, or Yang withdraws his forces from the village. Happy ending, of course. Two legitimate priests arrive, and all we have experienced is the spiritual regeneration of a soldier of fortune in a country that needed regeneration of another kind.

John Ford ended his career with *Seven Women* (1966), set in China in 1935. Ford's envoi is a well-acted melodrama about seven women—missionaries, staff members, and a pregnant wife—isolated in a North China mission, where they are threatened by a Mongolian warlord—who, with an update, could easily have been a communist general. Nineteen thirty-five was not a good year for missionaries in China. They were often imprisoned by communists and subjected to maltreatment and even torture. In 1935, Arnolis Hayman, a New Zealand missionary, was captured by communists and forced to accompany the Sixth Red Army on the Long March. A year earlier, husband and wife missionaries, John and Betty Sam, experienced a worse fate: a twelve-mile forced march, followed by execution. Mongolia, then a satellite of the Soviet Union, was not receptive to religion. Buddhist monks were victims of mass purges, and most of their monasteries demolished.

The prospects for Christianity were just as dim in 1935 as they would be in 1949 with the founding of the People's Republic of China. *Seven Women* could easily have been set in China after it had fallen to the communists. As it was, there was nothing exactly 1930s about the film. Witness the American Dr. Cartwright (Anne Bancroft), behaving very much like an emancipated woman of the 1960s, who smoked, swore, and drank. Dr. Cartwright is a Fordian woman, feminine yet tough-minded like Dallas in *Stagecoach* and Mary Kate in *The Quiet Man*. With her abrasive humanity, Dr. Cartwright recalls Doc in *Stagecoach*, with whom she shares a fondness for alcohol. In lieu of the Indians from *Drums Along the Mohawk*, who were portrayed as savages, Ford substitutes the Mongols, who are even more barbaric, delighting in murdering and breaking necks.

The ending is a double cross at its most perverse. Dr. Cartwright offers herself to the warlord, played by Mike Mazurki in a Mongolian getup that makes him look ridiculous. Toasting him with a cup of poisoned tea, the doctor purrs, "So long, ya bastard," and then drinks the brew herself. Her suicide is not redemptive like Brünnhilde's immolation in *Die Götterdämmerung*. But in 1966, as the Vietnam War was escalating, audiences cheered when Bancroft delivered the climactic line. To them, Mongolians, the Viet Cong, Chinese communists, and North Koreans were all alike. Moviegoers could leave the theater feeling they had seen the enemy—and it was not themselves.

Chapter 9

"BETTER DEAD THAN RED"

ON 18 FEBRUARY 1951, THE *NEW YORK TIMES* REPORTED THAT HELEN Hayes, who hadn't made a movie since *Vanessa: Her Love Story* (1935) (unless you count her cameo in *Stage Door Canteen* [1943]) would be returning to the screen in *My Son John*, produced and directed by Leo McCarey from his original screen story. Questioned about the plot, McCarey became evasive: "The story is so simple that if it got out someone else could have made it before I finish." The closest he came to a plot synopsis was calling the film a story of hardworking parents who provided a college education for their three sons, "one of whom gets too bright" and embraces atheism. "But who's the brighter in the end—the mother or the son?" Helen Hayes, cast as the mother, was even less informative. "Leo has sworn us all to secrecy," she declared. However, on 13 February the *Times* noted that despite the vow of silence, word had leaked out that Hayes would be playing Lucille Jefferson, a mother on trial for shooting her son John (Robert Walker), the one who got "too bright" and became a communist. McCarey would neither confirm nor deny the rumor. The leak was not far from the truth. Originally, Lucille was supposed to shoot John, but not fatally.

By 20 December 1950, John Lee Mahin, who like McCarey was a staunch anti-communist, had completed a first draft screenplay in which Lucille, realizing that John is a communist, refuses to give him the key to the apartment of Ruth Carlin, a fellow spy and also his lover. When John rushes upstairs to retrieve the key from her purse, Lucille grabs a shotgun off a rack and confronts him. "Put down the key," she demands. John complies, but then tells her he must flee the country. As he rushes from the house, Lucille follows him onto the porch, shooting him in the legs as he reaches the gate. The wounds are superficial, but the press brands Lucille "the trigger mother." A devout Catholic, Lucille goes to confession to Father O'Dowd, who cannot break the seal of the confessional. John, desperate to escape imprisonment, describes his mother as mentally unstable, suggesting that she turned against him when she saw him in civilian clothes, while his two brothers were in uniform. Lucille has a meltdown on the witness stand, as she strings together verses from "The Battle Hymn of the Republic," the ditty that she sang to John as a child ("Deedle, deedle dumpling, my son John"), and football cheers (her other two sons were star athletes). Finally John, unable to endure his mother's mad scene any longer, confesses that he is guilty of treason: "My offense is not against the people of this state but of every state in the union." With "radiant joy and pride in her expression," Lucille, having regained her sanity, embraces her son. Fade out to draft two. But this one was not written by Mahin, whose script was so shamelessly melodramatic that it would have had audiences laughing in the wrong places.

Mahin provided the template for the final screenplay, the work of Mc-Carey and (especially) Myles Connolly, a practicing Catholic and anti-communist like McCarey. But what really endeared Connolly to McCarey was *Mr. Blue* (1928), Connolly's highly influential book about a present-day (uncanonized) saint, known only as Mr. Blue, who becomes a Christ figure, living a life of poverty and devoting himself to the service of others. *Mr. Blue* had been recommended to generations of young men in Jesuit prep schools—including New York University president John Sexton. For many students, it was a life-changing experience. Connolly was McCarey's soul mate, and *My Son John* (1952) was the fruit of their collaboration.

McCarey's decision to make a movie about domestic communism in 1950 suggests that "godless, atheistic communism," denounced in pulpits across the land, had become an obsession with him—an obsession that was magnificent only in terms of its magnitude. He appeared as a friendly witness when the House Committee on Un-American Activities visited Los Angeles in May 1947, believing that communist propaganda had been inserted into films by leftwing screenwriters. He appeared before HUAC again in Washington, DC, that October, again as a friendly witness. By 1950, McCarey was convinced that the Red Menace was real; *My Son John* would prove it.

From the outset, McCarey only wanted Helen Hayes for the role of Lucille Jefferson. When she showed no interest, even asking McCarey to stop pestering her, he would not relent. Traveling to her home in Nyack, New York, he read her the revised script, playing all the parts, as Louis B. Mayer once did to persuade Greer Garson to play the title role in *Mrs. Miniver* (1942). Although McCarey implied that his virtuoso reading did the trick, the actress had her own reasons for signing on. After the sudden death of her daughter, Mary MacArthur, in September 1949, Hayes sought refuge in work. She returned to the theater, starring in Joshua Logan's production of *The Wisteria Trees* (1950), a transplanting of Chekhov's *The Cherry Orchard* to the Deep South. She won favorable reviews for herself in a play that one critic dismissed as "Southern fried Chekhov." *The Wisteria Trees* closed after five months, but the void left by Mary's death did not. *My Son John* was a stopgap measure, as was Mary Chase's *Mrs. McThing*, which opened on Broadway around the same time that *My Son John* went into release. Although *Mrs. McThing* was written by a Pulitzer Prize-winning playwright, and *My Son John* was the work of an Oscar-winning director, neither was a milestone in the actress's distinguished career.

Because she was still grieving for her daughter, and would continue to do so for many years, Hayes did not scrutinize the script as carefully as she might have. Yet she sensed something was not quite right; it kept getting changed. "We've only shot one scene that was in the original script," Hayes told reporters. McCarey admitted as much: "The script isn't yet finished because it became bigger than I thought. We're developing it as we go along." Dean Jagger (Dan Jefferson, John's father), honoring McCarey's wishes, was also close-lipped about the plot; however, in the *Los Angeles Times* (31 May 1951), he praised the director for keeping the script fluid by avoiding a "cut and dried scenario" approach. Since McCarey wanted the script to reflect— at least indirectly—the most recent atomic espionage cases, he had to work without a completed screenplay. He conceived the idea for *My Son John* in 1950: the year Alger Hiss was convicted of perjury; the year Klaus Fuchs, the German-born British physicist, admitted he was a Russian spy; the year Julius and Ethel Rosenberg were arrested for conspiring to commit espionage; and the year the conviction of Judith Coplon, another spy, was overturned. Although none of these individuals appears as a character in the film, or is even mentioned by name, all their cases clearly influenced the way McCarey shaped the character of John Jefferson.

Consider Alger Hiss, a graduate of Johns Hopkins and Harvard Law School and president of the Carnegie Foundation for International Peace, who passed classified information on to the Soviets. His was the familiar story of a brilliant mind derailed by communism's utopian promises. John Jefferson was also an intellectual seduced by the communist dream of leveling the distinctions between the classes and closing forever the gulf between the haves and the have-nots. Although McCarey does not name the universities John attended, they were prestigious enough to lead to a high-level job in Washington that gave him access to classified material. Hiss denied that he was ever a member of the Communist Party; John not only denied that he was, he also swore on his mother's Bible that he wasn't. Hiss was eventually convicted of perjury and sentenced to five years in prison. John confessed in the form of a commencement address, which he recorded before he was murdered by the party.

Klaus Fuchs worked on the Manhattan Project, which was responsible for developing the atomic bombs dropped on Hiroshima and Nagasaki in August 1945. He also had a female contact, the Soviet spy Ruth Werner (née Ursula Ruth Kuczynski). There is a fellow agent with whom John is in close contract, Ruth Carlin, who may also be his lover—or so he implies to his mother. Carlin does not appear as a character, only as a headline. Whether or not they were lovers, John had a key to her apartment.

Ruth Werner may have been one of the models for Ruth Carlin, but there was another woman who was much in the news at the time: Judith Coplon, a prime example of an intellectual taken in by communism's promise of equality for all. Coplon enjoyed a privileged education courtesy of a full scholarship to Barnard College, where she was a member of the Young Communist League (although she later claimed that she never was a communist). She graduated with a BA in history, cum laude, in 1943, and the following year she joined the Justice Department as a political analyst. There, like Hiss, she had access to classified information that she passed on to her Soviet contact. She was charged with treason and espionage, but her conviction was overturned because of illegal wiretapping and the F.B.I.'s failure to procure an arrest warrant. John Jefferson, then, is a composite, an Alger Hiss-like spy in league with a female agent, who may have been a colleague, a contact, a lover—or all three.

The Rosenberg case also influenced McCarey. Like the Jeffersons, the Rosenbergs seemed like an ordinary couple with two sons. Julius graduated from the City College of New York in 1939 with a BS in electrical engineering. Within a few years, he was the head of a spy ring. By 1951, the charge was not just espionage, but treason. *My Son John* started filming on 1 March 1951. The Rosenbergs were sentenced on April 5 and were to have been executed sometime during the week of May 21, although their execution did not occur for two more years. Still, the Rosenbergs were making headlines in 1951. McCarey envisioned a family that would be the antithesis of the Rosenbergs: the Roman Catholic Jeffersons, with two sons, Chuck (Richard Jaeckel) and Ben (James Young), serving in the military, and John (Robert Walker) on the threshold of a brilliant political career. But John, his mother's favorite, has abandoned his faith and—like Julius Rosenberg, Alger Hiss, and Judith Coplon—has become a Soviet agent, believing that communism serves the needs of minorities exploited by capitalism.

The exteriors were filmed partly in Washington, DC, where John worked (perhaps in the State Department), and which is the home base for an FBI agent (Van Heflin) monitoring his activities. Nearby Manassas, Virginia, doubled as the Jeffersons' hometown, although it is never identified as such. While in the DC area, McCarey discovered other sites he wanted to use, not knowing exactly how they would figure in the script. A Catholic church proved especially appealing to him, and he spent a day filming inside it. As coauthor of the screenplay, McCarey found a place for the church in the first scene, when the Jeffersons attend Sunday Mass.

Although *My Son John* began as a script in progress, it eventually developed into a model of beginning-middle-end construction, with a tranquil opening that gradually turns crepuscular and darkens into tragedy. But plotting and story line are not the same. The story—and especially the moralistic dialogue—turned *My Son John* into a message movie. Although the message was a timely one, this was a classic case of overkill that detracted from the tautly structured script and the fine performances of the four principals.

My Son John begins uneventfully. Tired of waiting for his wife to finish dressing for Mass, Dan Jefferson calls out, "Lucille," the cue for Hayes's entrance. She rushes onto the second-story porch in her slip, perhaps the closest the actress has ever came to appearing in a state of undress. Expected to show up later for Sunday dinner, John sends a telegram explaining his absence with the usual cliché, "official business." Lucille has not given up hope. When she hears the bell the following Sunday, she goes to the door, only to see Dr. Carver (Minor Watson), who presents her with a bottle of pills for her dizzy spells. The bell rings again, and this time it is John. When he enters the foyer, his father comes into the frame, his image reflected in the hall mirror. It was a brilliant touch on McCarey's part; the reflection makes father and son—Dan, the patriot father, and John, the traitor son—mirror images of one another.

John wears his education as if it were the torch of knowledge, useful for shining in the faces of the unenlightened. Being in the presence of simple folk only intensifies his sense of superiority. Discovering that Dr. Carver is as conservative as his father, John baits him. "Nobody can ever say that we weren't brought up on those good old American bromides," John comments dryly. Oblivious to his son's cynicism, Dan agrees: "Well, bromides can come in pretty handy sometimes, can't they, Doc?" To which the good doctor replies, "Yes, even when our thinking gets shaky, there's nothing better than the good old bromides." Both the doctor and Dan are concerned about the threat of nuclear war and the spread of communism.

The times suggested there was cause for concern. In spring 1949, China fell to the communists. That August, the Soviet Union demonstrated its nuclear capability by detonating its first atomic bomb. American troops were fighting in Korea, where Chuck and Ben are headed. Atomic espionage was front-page news. Loyalty oaths were required of college professors. *Red Channels* identified supposed communists or communist sympathizers on the flimsiest of evidence, in some cases ruining or disrupting careers. And HUAC was still holding hearings about communists in the film industry. Air raid drills were conducted in schools, with the students crouching under their desks, and bomb shelters were the latest in home improvement. "See you in the bomb shelter" are the doctor's parting words. The time was indeed out of joint.

After Mass, which John considers a penance he must endure when at home, he asks to be dropped off at the local college to see a former professor. The professor, who is not a character, only appears in an extreme long shot, but Dan's dismay suggests that he has had a negative influence on John, who was educated out of his faith and into atheism. Dan, educated to the extent of being qualified to teach in the local grade school, is not overly awed by higher learning. Much to John's amusement, he espouses a literal interpretation of the Bible. Father and son are indeed reverse images.

Distracted by John's indifference to his family, Dan rear- ends a car driven by a stranger, who is really an FBI agent (Van Heflin). The accident was an ingenious way of working the agent (later identified as Mr. Stedman) into the plot. He is in town for one reason, to keep tabs on John, who is under suspicion for espionage.

Gradually, Dan realizes that John does not share his views on communism. Suspecting that John is opposed to everything he stands for, Dan launches into "If you don't like your Uncle Sammy / Then go back to your home o'er the sea." John doesn't like his Uncle Sammy, preferring Uncle Joe—as the mass murderer Josef Stalin was sometimes called at the time— and finds the hammer and the sickle more appealing than Old Glory.

John does not even spare his mother. In a nostalgic moment, she recalls the song she sang to him as a child:

Deedle, deedle, dumpling, my son John,
Went to bed with his stockings on;
One shoe off, and one shoe on,
Deedle, deedle, dumpling, my son John.

When she reminds him that he would always ask her to repeat it, John says perversely, "Do it again, Mother." Hurt, she accepts his derisiveness as a vestige of his education, not understanding that it has produced a John Jefferson who is a far cry from the son who stole pennies and was the pastor's favorite altar boy.

Stedman uses the accident as a pretext for gaining entrance to the Jeffersons' home. He arrives with a bill for damages, hoping to learn more about John. But he is genuinely taken with Lucille, who boasts that John will be delivering the commencement address at his alma mater, which, coincidentally, is the agent's. The agent, pretending that he has just put the names "John" and "Jefferson" together, remarks that her son is very well known in Washington circles. An enigmatic phone call for John from Washington interrupts their conversation.

When Lucille informs John about the call, noting that it was from a woman who did not give her name, he is curious but acts unconcerned. Lucille, however, is delighted, thinking that John is dating, to her a sign of normalcy. Actually, the call came from Ruth Carlin, with whom, as John later tells his mother, he is "intimate." Lucille still senses John is undergoing a crisis of faith, which accounts for his bemused attitude toward matters that she and Dan take seriously. She doesn't know he has abandoned his faith. McCarey implies that even as a boy John, the scholar in the family, was more attracted to secular learning than to the scriptures. Lucille recalls how she would cajole him into reading the New Testament: "I'll make cookies, pies, cakes and jam / If you'll learn Matthew, Mark, Luke, and John." Whenever she can, Lucille introduces religion into the conversation. When John tells her she should take the tablets Dr. Carver prescribed, she replies, "What about Moses and his tablets with the prescriptions on them?" It's a weak rejoinder, but it reflects what is uppermost on her mind: John's lack of faith, or worse, his repudiation of it. She presses John for some sign that he is still "my son John." For the first time, John becomes serious: "I love humanity, the downtrodden. I love the helpless minorities." Lucille is overjoyed at what she misinterprets for her son's acceptance of Christ's message. But to John, only socialism in its most extreme form, the Soviet form, can help the downtrodden by raising their status and substituting the state for

God. When John swears that he is sincere, that's all Lucille needs to hear. She brings out the Bible. John, knowing what comes next, puts one hand on it, raises the other, and swears, "I am not now, or have ever been, a member of the Communist Party." Given John's indifference to scripture, the oath has no meaning. But Lucille is satisfied—for the moment.

Dan shares his wife's fear that John has moved too far to the left. When he asks John to take a similar oath, John refuses because it comes from a man he does not respect. Dan becomes so furious he brings the Bible down on his son's head, causing him to fall over a table, tear his pants, and bruise his knee. John had previously received a call (probably from Ruth Carlin) telling him to return to Washington at once. He just has time to change his trousers, telling his mother to get rid of the torn pair. McCarey made the trousers an important plot point. He needed something to convince Lucille that her son is a communist. In the back pocket of John's pants is the key to the apartment of Ruth Carlin, who has just been arrested. "Ruth Carlin Sentenced," a headline later reads. However, by then Lucille had donated the trousers to the parish clothes drive and was obliged to retrieve them. Finding them, she feels the fabric and discovers the key. Unbeknownst to her husband, she flies to Washington with the trousers, expecting to receive some kind of explanation from John.

John conceals his anxiety, first insisting the key is his key to his apartment, but then admitting the truth. A summons to an urgent meeting prevents further discussion. John leaves, expecting his mother to wait until he returns, but she decides to spend the time sorting out her thoughts on a bench by the Potomac. Stedman passes by, making his presence seem accidental, although Lucille has been under surveillance since her plane landed. He appeals to her patriotism, pointing out the Jefferson Memorial and mentioning other landmarks like the Washington Monument, the Lincoln Memorial, and Arlington Cemetery. Finally, he shows her a headline, "Girl Accused of Betrayal." Realizing the "girl" is Ruth Carlin, Lucille agrees to cooperate and accompanies him to the jail where Ruth is being held. But Lucille is unable to identify Ruth's voice as that of the woman who made the strange phone call. Knowing that the key in her possession is to Carlin's apartment, Lucille sets out to see if it fits the lock, her every move captured on hidden camera. It fits. Lucille, devastated and on the verge of a breakdown, flies home.

But so does John, who wants the key. When his mother refuses to hand it over, he threatens her with institutionalization because of her erratic behavior. Boasting that he has millions on his side, John grasps her hand, expecting to find the key. He finds only her rosary. "There are millions on my side," she boasts, holding her rosary in front of him, as if he were Dracula. "And what a fight you'll have on your hands."

John is not the only one who has returned home. Stedman has, too. He begins by interrogating Lucille, triggering a bravura mad scene from Hayes, in which she evades his questions, speaking if she were distracted by something else. She reminiscences about the football games she and Dan attended, cheering on Chuck and Ben. Even though John was not athletic, she urges him to "get into the game," one that he can play, by admitting his guilt. "Take the ball, John. Time's running out. We can't stop that clock. Go take the ball. I'm cheering for you now, John. My son John! My son John!" Realizing her efforts are futile, she collapses on the sofa, sighing in disgust, "Take him away. Take him away. He has to be punished."

McCarey had been guiding the action steadily toward a climax, yet to be determined. Will John confess or be killed? Or will he confess and then be killed? The last day of shooting was 8 June 1951, which seems right since the film went into production on 1 March, and *My Son John* was the kind of movie that could be wrapped up in three months. But that did not stop the director from tinkering with the film. Supposedly, the movie was to end with John's repudiating communism in his commencement address, after which he's murdered by party members.

Then, on 28 August 1951, Robert Walker died unexpectedly from a combination of pills and liquor. He had never recovered from his divorce from Jennifer Jones, whom he married in 1939. The marriage was short-lived. In the early 1940s, she became the protégée of the legendary producer David O. Selznick and soon after, his lover. She separated from Walker in 1943, sued for divorce in 1945, and married Selznick in 1949. Walker was not suicidal, but only the sedative amobarbital and alcohol could alleviate his depression. Walker's death posed some problems that were easily surmountable. His death did not necessitate a different ending. According to the *Daily News* (14 April 1952), on the Saturday before he died, Walker returned to Paramount to record the commencement address as a sound test. But why a sound test, if the speech was to have been delivered in person? If Walker's death resulted in a new ending, it did so because McCarey didn't like the old ending. Here was a case of destiny cooperating with the director. Whether or not McCarey wanted a voice from the grave, he got one. Even before Walker's untimely death, McCarey decided it would be more dramatic if John—sensing his days were numbered—recorded his speech and then was killed, with the tape played at the commencement.

McCarey was a master of the art of plot resolution, often ending a film with a coda that lingers in the audience's memory long after leaving the theater. In *Make Way for Tomorrow* (1937), a couple (Victor Moore and Beulah Bondi), married for fifty years, must part. He is going to California to live with his daughter; she is headed for a nursing home. As they take leave of each other, the husband says to his wife, "In case it should happen that I don't see you again, it's been very nice knowing you." The wife replies, "And in case I don't see you—for a while—I want to tell you that it's been lovely. Every bit of it. The whole fifty years." An inferior director would have had Moore and Bondi pull out the stops and activate the audience's tear ducts. McCarey, respecting the material and his actors, chose restraint. He did the same at the end of *Going My Way* (1944), when Barry Fitzgerald is reunited with his ninety-year-old Irish mother, and again in *The Bells of St. Mary's* (1945), when Father O'Malley and Sister Benedict (Bing Crosby and Ingrid Bergman) say their farewells, which are really an expression of their deep affection for each other.

Similarly, in *My Son John*, McCarey gave audiences an ending that was both dramatic and reflective. John, realizing the FBI is closing in on him, decides to fly to Lisbon. At the airport he has a change of heart. He calls Stedman, stating that he wants to make "a big decision." When Stedman asks if anyone know his whereabouts, the shadow of a man appears alongside the phone booth. John has been followed, and not by the FBI. He returns to his office, where he finds a telegram informing him that he will be receiving an honorary degree at commencement. He thinks of his mother and her fear that his address will infect the minds of the graduates with his philosophy. John recants, recording his speech in the form of a confession. He then calls Stedman, who hears a click. Realizing that the phone has been bugged, he urges John to leave his office. John hops a cab, but another car follows it, then catches up with it and riddles it with bullets. The cab overturns, symbolically, on the steps of the Lincoln Memorial. The driver is unhurt, but John, trapped inside, has only enough life in him to tell Stedman that the speech is on the tape recorder in his office. John expires, and a close up of his face dissolves to a scene of the student-filled auditorium where the speaker's podium is spotlighted as the recording is played.

The commencement—with a shaft of light streaming down on the speakerless podium and recording machine, and John's voice seeming to emanate from eternity—is pure theater. John confesses to substituting faith in man for faith in God, warning the graduates that, as educated men and women, they are prey to the same corrupting influences that deflected his moral compass.

Flattered when he was courted by intellectuals, he did not realize that he was also being ensnared by them. John's peroration is brief: "I am a living lie. I am a traitor. I am a native American Communist spy and may God have mercy on my soul. This is my commencement day, the beginning of a new life, so help me God." But John's new life is not on this earth.

Robert Walker's death was tragic, ending a career that was on an upswing after he amazed critics with his performance as the psychopath Bruno Anthony in Alfred Hitchcock's *Strangers on a Train* (1951). Had he exorcized his demons, he might have had a career playing a range of characters: heroes, misfits, villains, lovers, and rogues. Were he alive when Hitchcock was looking for a Norman Bates in *Psycho* (1960), he surely would have been considered. What is Bruno but the flip side of Norman, with a mother complex that stops just short of necrophilia?

McCarey had seen some of *Strangers on a Train* shortly after he started shooting *My Son John*. He told the *New York Times* (18 March 1951), "[Hitchcock] even ran off the first four reels of his new film for me." Since the *My Son John* script was incomplete, McCarey could make whatever additions he chose. It is not coincidental that Walker wore the same kind of grey flannel suit in *My Son John* that he wore in *Strangers on a Train*. Both films portray sons more comfortable with their mothers than with their fathers, whom they either hold in contempt (John) or want murdered (Bruno). But Lucille is not a caricature like Bruno's dotty mother (Marion Lorne). Lucille's obsession with her faith may be devotion in the extreme, yet she wins our sympathy, while Bruno's mother remains a freak.

Strangers on a Train proved handy when McCarey needed some closeups of Walker for *My Son John*. Bruno, believing that tennis pro Guy Haines (Farley Granger) has agreed to his bizarre plan to swap murders—Bruno killing Haines's wife, and Haines killing Bruno's father—calls Haines from a phone booth, telling him he has completed his part of the bargain. In postproduction, McCarey felt that he needed a shot of John phoning his mother about the trousers, even though the dialogue, as Helen Hayes delivered it, made it clear what he wanted. McCarey used the scene of Bruno in the phone booth and edited out the dialogue. All we see is Walker in the phone booth, with an anxious expression on his face. But presumably, John is telling his mother about the trousers. The context did not matter, only the shot. The same shot appears left of frame when John phones Stedman from the airport. When Stedman, fearing for John's life, tells him to leave his office, John hails a cab. To show that John was in it, McCarey selected a shot from *Strangers* with Bruno in a cab headed for Union Station.

At the end, when John is pinned under the taxi, McCarey used a shot from the climax of *Strangers*, when Bruno and Guy are fighting on a carousel that has gone out of control. A workman crawls under the ride and shuts it down, causing the carousel to career off its base and Bruno to be thrown off and crushed beneath it. Dying, he still refuses to exonerate Guy, even thought he has the key to Guy's innocence: his cigarette lighter. Bruno dies with a smile on his face, believing that Guy will pay the price for not fulfilling his share of the bargain. McCarey transferred the shot of Walker's smiling face from the carousel to the wrecked taxi, erasing the dialogue and adding voiceover (McCarey's own), so that it seems John dies peacefully after telling Stedman the whereabouts of the speech. Skillful editing enhanced McCarey's morality tale of sin and salvation, even though, in *Strangers on a Train*, Bruno seems to die happily because he thinks Haines will be accused of murdering his wife— until his fingers relax in death, revealing the crucial lighter in the palm of his hand.

My Son John preaches to the converted, but in a way that does not detract from the direction and performances. The Academy of Motion Picture Arts and Sciences bypassed Hayes, Walker, Jagger, and Heflin when Oscar nomination time came around. McCarey was nominated for best original screen story, which went to *The Greatest Show on Earth*, also voted best picture. Original, *My Son John* was; it was also an accurate depiction of America in the early years of the Cold War.

McCarey's hatred of communism carried over to his last film, *Satan Never Sleeps* (1962), in which he transferred the generational conflict between an old priest and his successor—epitomized in his Oscar-winning *Going My Way* (1944)—from New York to Communist China. The script, to which McCarey contributed and which, as producer, he shaped, was allegedly based on a novel by Pearl S. Buck. The novel was published in paperback simultaneously with the film's release, suggesting that McCarey and Claude Binyon, who coauthored the screenplay, had prior access to Buck's work. In its published form, *Satan Never Sleeps* reads like a novelization of the film. There was clearly a symbiotic relationship between Buck, McCarey, and Binyon.

Although the time of the film's action is unspecified, it is probably 1949, after the end of the Chinese civil war and the establishment of the People's Republic of China. *Satan Never Sleeps* begins comically, as Father O'Banion (William Holden), en route to replace Father Bovard (Clifton Webb), the retiring pastor of a Chinese mission, stops to rescue Siu-Lan (France Nuyen) from a flood. Out of gratitude, she attaches herself to him, unaware of his priestly vows. Thus, when O'Banion arrives at the mission, he must explain her presence to the unamused Bovard. The comedy ends abruptly when the communists prevent Bovard from leaving his mission, forcing the two priests to occupy the same space. The initial tension relaxes into camaraderie when they realize they have a common enemy: Colonel Ho-San (Weaver Lee), a former Catholic and (for the moment) a committed communist, who harasses them and desecrates the mission church, toppling the altar and hurling the crucifix into the fire. The scene is intentionally horrifying, emphasizing the helplessness one feels when forced to witness a sacrilegious act that goes beyond vandalism.

The colonel's parents retrieve the crucifix, but are eventually shot when returning it to the church. The desecration was a prelude to rebellion. Father Bovard, after having been imprisoned and tortured, agrees to recant publicly, using the occasion to affirm his faith, and inspiring the villagers to turn against their oppressors and storm the mission (now communist headquarters) and tear down Mao's image.

If only it were that easy. *Satan Never Sleeps* is McCarey's wish fulfillment, losing credibility with every scene as the narrative races towards resolution. Ho-San rapes Siu-lan, impregnating her. She then knifes him in the back, but the wound is not fatal. Demoted for his inability to control the villagers, Ho-San experiences an epiphany and returns to the faith of his youth. Escaping to freedom with Siu-Lan, the child she bore him, and the two priests, Ho-San shoots his pursuers. Since Ho-San has reconverted, he has no qualms about killing Reds. When the group realizes a helicopter is hovering over them, Bovard jumps into a car and takes off with the helicopter in pursuit, firing away and sending the car over a cliff. Unlike Dr. Cartwright's suicide in *Seven Women*, Father Bovard's death illustrates the principle of double effect. Even though death was almost a certainty, he did not intend to kill himself. Rather, he wanted to divert attention from the others to himself. His death was a byproduct of his altruism. "Greater love than this no man hath than he who lays down his life for his friends" (John 15:13). And Father Bovard did exactly that.

The coda is the inevitable culmination of a logic-defying and emotionally manipulative film. The trio reaches Hong Kong, where Fr. O'Banion officiates at the marriage of the rapist and his victim, and legitimizes their union by baptizing their son. When O'Banion asks what name they have chosen, Siu-Lan smiles and replies, "O'Banion," causing William Holden to look embarrassed but flattered—and causing the audience to wonder about McCarey. How could the same director—responsible for such classics as

Duck Soup, Make Way for Tomorrow, The Awful Truth, and *Going My Way*; who humanized Mae West in *Belle of the Nineties* (1934), in which she sang "My Old Flame" with a heartfelt yearning that she never exhibited before or again; and who, in *The Bells of St. Mary's*, suggested that a nun and priest could be spiritual lovers without breaking their vows—bid farewell to the screen with such an inferior example of his art?

McCarey admitted as much. When Peter Bogdanovich interviewed him shortly before his death in 1969, McCarey had nothing good to say about the film. McCarey originally intended O'Banion to be the driver of the car that plunged over the cliff. Realizing that his passion for Siu-lan is bringing him dangerously close to violating his vow of celibacy, O'Banion prays for guidance, which comes in the form of his decision to sacrifice himself for the others. Holden, however, refused to appear in a picture in which he died. Disgusted, McCarey revised the script so that Bovard drove the death car. When Bogdanovich inquired about his relationship with the three principals, McCarey was characteristically blunt. He disliked all of them: Holden, Webb, and Nuyen. As for the picture, "[I]t was a nightmare."

Things might have turned out better if McCarey and Binyon had adhered to Buck's ending, in which neither priest dies. Ho-san, who is even more villainous than the Japanese occupiers in Buck's *Dragon Seed*, makes a 180-degree turn when he discovers he is the father of a boy. (One wonders if he would have felt the same about a girl.) Deciding to flee to Hong Kong with his parents (who are not killed in the novel), the priests, Siu-lan, and their child, Ho-san diverts attention by driving off in the car, with the helicopter in pursuit, and then leaving the car in a bamboo grove, so that the others can continue on to Hong Kong after he has been captured. He asks only that the boy be baptized and given his name. This would have been a more edifying coda, and certainly one that would appease staunch Catholics. But the film's ending is not only unedifying, it's infuriatingly optimistic in its portrayal of a Catholic who turns communist, rapes a woman, sires a child, reconverts, marries the woman, and has the child baptized with the priest's name. This is a film that provokes sheer disbelief, which can in no way be suspended.

Chapter 10

COMMIES, COMMIES EVERYWHERE

AMERICA IN THE 1950S SEEMED TO BE A NETWORK OF COMMUNIST sleeper cells. If they can operate out of Washington, DC, why not San Francisco, lush Hawaii, and blue-collar Boston? The hit men from the Party who murdered John Jefferson formed a shadowy group, but if they ever appeared in the flesh, they would look like thugs from a gangster movie, tough-talking goons from the syndicate with a snarl for a smile and a cigar for a pacifier. Such were the Reds of *I Married a Communist* (1949), Howard Hughes's contribution to postwar alarmism. After Hughes, a megalomaniac and rabid anti-communist, purchased RKO in 1946, he was determined to make his own Red Menace movie. If, as World War II movies claimed, wartime America was infested with Nazi spies and saboteurs, why should postwar America be any different—except that the enemy agents are now communists? It was hysteria time again, with Hughes sounding the alarm, which was not heard at the box office. When the original title, *I Married a Communist*—designed to strike fear into the hearts of women who may have made a similar mistake—proved to be a turn-off, it was changed to the more provocative and politically neutral *The Woman on Pier 13*, which only made sense in terms of the setting, San Francisco, where communists were plotting a takeover of the shipping industry.

One could have been watching a crime movie, as the communists ordered hits and punished defectors with death, always varying the means: drowning, a hit and run, a fall from a window, and a good old-fashioned bullet. The situation in which Brad Collins (Robert Ryan) finds himself is no different from that of the guy in the crime movie who wants to go straight, except that the mob won't let him. In Brad's case, it was because he is really Frank Johnson, an ex-party member, who, like so many progressives in the 1930s, believed that capitalism was an economic behemoth and only communism could balance the scales of justice—then weighted in favor of the affluent. Much to his regret, Brad had a fling with a gorgeous blonde (Janis Carter, presumably the title character), who is still a party member, but one more interested in resuming her relationship with Brad than helping the urban poor. What is irksome about the film is the party members' total disinterest in social justice; they behave as if they never read Marx or Engels. They are nothing more than crime bosses barking orders, issuing threats, and carving out turf. *The Woman on Pier 13* could have ended with Collins either triumphant or dead. The writers chose the later, with Collins giving his wife (Laraine Day) his blessing to marry a more deserving man (Richard Roper), his friend and her first beau.

What makes the film watchable is Nicholas Musuraca's black and white cinematography. Musuraca could give black the sheen of coal, and white, the look of ivory or silver. When the blindingly blonde Janis Carter appeared on the screen, you felt you had to shield your eyes. Musuraca approached the film as if it had been slated for Val Lewton's horror unit at RKO, where he had lavished his art on *Cat People*, *The Seventh Victim*, *The Ghost Ship*, *The Curse of the Cat People*, and *Bedlam*. He infused *The Woman on Pier 13* with a visual richness that was at odds with its subject matter, its sleek and streamlined look adding a touch of class to a script that lacked it. But his art could not conceal the film's poverty of imagination, which reduced communism in postwar America to a series of gangster movie clichés, none of which had anything to do with the threat the country was facing at the time from the Soviet Union.

Had *Red Snow* (1952) been about Alaskan communists attempting to radicalize Eskimos, it would have been offbeat enough to command interest—particularly since Alaska seemed to be in our own backyard, and Stalinist Eskimos would strike moviegoers as a unique breed. Instead, there is an Eskimo villain (the Korean American actor, Philip Ahn, who could be cast as either friend or foe), a Siberian who has supposedly escaped from the Russian side, but has really been sent as a spy.

Although Guy Madison was nominally the star, appearing as an air force lieutenant, he was upstaged by the Eskimos who, despite having to speak in the uninflected English forced upon Indians in Hollywood westerns, became the true heroes of the film. The tired premise of *Red Snow* was that the United States was attempting to track down a weapon of mass destruction the Soviets were testing in Siberia. It should have been a simple matter, with crosscutting between activities on either side of the strait and a romance between Madison and a female lieutenant. Instead, there is an ethnographic detour depicting Eskimo rituals and a walrus hunt, which add a modicum of interest to a film that seems to be stranded on an ice floe. The Eskimos prevent the weapon from being tested when the plane carrying it crashes. An Eskimo couple rubs noses at the fade out, and what might have worked as a (literally) Cold War thriller with a tauter script and less ethnic cuteness, became a lukewarm travelogue with disarmingly patriotic Eskimos.

Columbia Pictures showed an unusual interest in the Cold War in the early 1950s, releasing a number of films about communism (*Assignment Paris, Walk East on Beacon, Invasion U.S.A., The 27th Day, The 49th Man, Red Snow*) and the Korean War (*Mission over Korea, The Bamboo Prison*). It was not merely that the studio's president, Harry Cohn, wanted to prove he was a loyal American. Although Cohn—like the other studio heads—knew that a communist takeover would destroy the capitalistic foundation of the movie industry, he had other reasons for his display of patriotism. Three of the studio's Oscar nominees—screenwriter Sidney Buchman (*Mr. Smith Goes to Washington*), writer-director Robert Rossen (*All the King's Men*, nominated for both direction and screenplay), and actor Larry Parks (who created a sensation as Al Jolson in *The Jolson Story*)—were tainted by charges of communism. Rossen and Parks were two of nineteen members of the Hollywood community (all screenwriters and directors, except for Parks) who vigorously opposed the 1947 HUAC hearings and were stigmatized as the "Unfriendly Nineteen." It was time for Columbia to wave the flag.

The May 1951 issue of *Reader's Digest* carried an article by J. Edgar Hoover, "Crime of the Century," about the atomic spies Klaus Fuchs and Harry Gold. At the end, there was a note stating that Louis de Rochemont's "forthcoming feature production, *Walk East on Beacon*, will be based upon the FBI's current revelations of Communist espionage." Columbia's *Walk East on Beacon* (1952) was the Cold War companion piece to de Rochemont's earlier semi-documentary, *The House on 92nd Street* (1945), and operated from the same premise: a city infiltrated by enemy agents, now communists and part of a "worldwide conspiracy," whose existence was vouched for by the omniscient narrator (the voice of gravitas itself, *The March of Time*'s Westbrook Van Voorhis), citing the chief authority on the subject, J. Edgar Hoover. There was a problem, however. The film had nothing do with Hoover's article, which, if fleshed out, could have been made into an engrossing melodrama about the Swiss-born, American-educated Harry Gold, whose exposure to socialism made him sympathetic to its ideals. That his parents were Russian sparked his interest in stories about that "downtrodden country where millions of honest men and woman starve because they don't have enough to eat." No one ever mentioned that the widespread hunger was largely due to collectivization, only noting that Russia needed all the help it could get to compete with the industrialized West. Asked how he could contribute, Gold was instructed to filch industrial processes and formulas from the Pennsylvania Sugar Company, where he worked, and to pass them on to an assigned agent.

The double life appealed to Gold, whose own lacked excitement until he discovered the thrill of espionage. It also appealed to Klaus Fuchs, who described his compartmentalized life as "controlled schizophrenia," prompting him to adopt an outgoing persona that hid the spy behind it. The climax of Gold's twelve years in espionage occurred in June 1945, when, as Fuchs's courier (code name Raymond), he met the physicist in Santa Fe. Fuchs, who then held a top-level position at Los Alamos, handed Gold a bulky envelope containing atomic secrets to turn over to his Soviet contact. Gold would meet with Fuchs one more time that September, six weeks after Hiroshima. Before handing Gold his last envelope, Fuchs confided that he had "grossly underestimated the industrial potential of the United States." The Manhattan Project obviously convinced him that America meant business. Gold and Fuchs believed that they had done nothing wrong; they were only helping Russia enter the twentieth century, ignoring the fact that the country's performance in World War II left no doubt that it had.

What is not mentioned in "Crime of the Century" is Gold's stopover in Albuquerque to meet with David Greenglass, an army corporal and machinist at Los Alamos, who also had information for him. When questioned, Greenglass readily admitted that he provided Gold with details about installations at Los Alamos. Then he implicated his wife Ruth (who was never convicted), his brother-in-law Julius Rosenberg, and his sister Ethel, although he downplayed her involvement in his grand jury testimony.

The entire case had the makings of a great film, with moles, couriers, handlers, street corner meetings, tokens of recognition, and characters running the gamut from idealism to disenchantment, loyalty to betrayal, friendship to enmity. Such a film has yet to be made. *Walk East on Beacon* did not even come close.

Hoover, who sold the "Crime of the Century" rights to De Rochemont for $15,000, realized *Walk East on Beacon* had nothing to do with his article and returned the fee. Like *The House on 92nd Street*, *Walk East on Beacon* was a semi-documentary with a similar McGuffin—this time, a computer-based system for updating America's defense system, code name Falcon. The star was George Murphy, playing FBI inspector Jim Belden in his last film role. MGM's popular song and dance man, equally at home in light comedy and drama, parted ways with the studio after completing *Talk about a Stranger* (1952), released two months before *Walk East on Beacon*. Fans might have been impressed that Murphy had two movies out within months of each other; the rest was silence, at least in Hollywood. There was, however, another role waiting for George Murphy: Republican senator from California (1965–71).

Walk East on Beacon was a tissue of familiar givens. Anyone can be a communist—even a funeral director, a florist, a cab driver, a photographer, or a scientist's wife in a tailored suit. Any business can be a communist front, including a photo shop, whose blonde proprietor (Virginia Gilmore) is a committed party member. "Once a communist, always a communist," with defectors punished by death. Communists will resort to blackmail, kidnapping, and even murder to transmit secrets to Moscow. In *The House on 92nd Street*, one could understand the eagerness of Nazi agents to acquire the formula for the atomic bomb. But in *Walk East on Beacon*—except for the head scientist (the wonderfully avuncular Finlay Currie) and his peers—no one seems to know exactly what Falcon is, except that it looks like a series of equations on a physicist's blackboard.

Despite the authentic "shot on location" look of the film, the narrative's pressing urgency, and the FBI's ingenious (for 1952) surveillance methods (cameras hidden behind bushes, in headlights, even in cigarette lighters), *Walk East on Beacon* is an unstable union of faux documentary and fiction film. The latter generates more interest, especially in the kidnapping of the head scientist and the uncertain fate of his son in Berlin's Russian sector. After the communists are rounded up, the scientist is rescued, and his son is flown back to America, one wonders if Cold War espionage doesn't work better as cloak and dagger melodrama without documentary footnoting.

De Rochement fared better with his next Columbia production, *Man on A String* (1960), which was at least inspired by an actual case, which was embellished—as one might expect in a thriller—but still a vital part of Cold War history. In 1959, the Russian-born Boris Morros—a onetime music director at Paramount (*Make Way for Tomorrow, The Trail of the Lonesome Pine, Easy Living, Zaza*) and movie producer (*Second Chorus, Tales of Manhattan, Carnegie Hall*)—published his account of working first as a Soviet spy, then as an FBI informant, and finally as a double agent, a role that suited him because of his familiarity with the language and his Soviet connections. The memoir, published by Viking, was appropriately entitled *My Ten Years as a Counterspy* (1959). Among his revelations was the outing as Soviet agents of Martha Dodd, a woman of affairs and daughter of

William E. Dodd, who had been ambassador to Germany from 1933–37, and her affluent husband, Alfred Stern. Rather than stand trial for espionage, Dodd and Stern fled to the Soviet Union, where they were grudgingly given asylum. The couple may have been ardent communists, but their value to the party was minimal. They were not in the same league as Cambridge spy Kim Philby, who also defected to the Soviet Union and was eventually given a hero's burial there, despite his eventual disillusionment with communism.

De Rochemont and his writers turned Morros's memoir into a semi-documentary on the order of *The House on 92nd Street* but with less voiceover, delivered by former war correspondent and TV news reporter, Clete Roberts. Boris Morros became Boris Mitrov (Ernest Borgnine), a film producer with his own studio, who had worked for the Soviets in exchange for his father being allowed to immigrate to America. Like Morros, Mitrov was recruited by the Central Bureau of Intelligence, a sound-alike for the Central Intelligence Agency (CIA). Real names were not used in the film. Martha Dodd and Alfred Stern became Helen and Adrian Benson. Unlike Martha, whom even the Soviets knew was promiscuous, Helen has only one lover.

In 1960, moviegoers still thought of Ernest Borgnine (it is difficult to think of the actor as Boris Mitrov) as Marty Piletti, the title character of his signature film, *Marty* (1955). But Borgnine's character is no longer phoning a girl for a date or wondering how to spend a Saturday night; he is learning to fire cyanide-coated darts from a cigarette lighter. The most chilling moment in the film occurs when he witnesses an espionage class session, in which the students demonstrate their mastery of English—including a Southern accent—for when they infiltrate the United States. *Man on a String* may lack the éclat of *The House on 92nd Street*, but it is far more suspenseful and disturbing than *Walk East on Beacon*.

Another film that is more cloak and dagger than documentary is *I Was a Communist for the FBI* (1951), which showed as much respect for truth as the Hollywood western did for history in its mythologizing of outlaws like Billy the Kid and the James brothers. The "hero" of *I Was a Communist for the FBI* is Matt Cvetic (Frank Lovejoy), a Slovenian Catholic, who for nine years posed as a party member for the FBI to ferret out communists in his native Pittsburgh. That much is true, but little else in the film is.

Communists are only interested in the good life, expecting it to continue "after we take over." The party honchos are snazzy dressers in sharp-looking suits, Upon his arrival from New York, Gerhardt Eisler, a high-ranking member, is feted at a cocktail reception, a harbinger of things to come made possible by the sweat of the proletariat, which will never enjoy such perks.

Historically, that was the way Soviet-style communism operated—dachas for the bigwigs, cramped apartments for the workers. At least the film is correct on one point: Gerhardt Eisler was a real person, who was deported in 1947 after vociferously objecting to the wearisome "Are you now or have you ever been" question.

Cvetic is lionized in the film as a model patriot, who plays his role so well that he is shunned by his family and denounced by his brother as a "slimy Red." Ordered by the party to incite a riot during a steel strike, Cvetic must remain above the fray when his brother is brutally beaten. When a secondary schoolteacher (Dorothy Hart), a onetime party member now disenchanted with its methods, defects, a goon squad is dispatched to prevent her from leaving by train. "Nobody leaves a star," as Gloria Swanson proclaimed in *Sunset Boulevard* (1950). Likewise, nobody leaves the party—and lives. Fortunately, Cvetic intervenes. He and the teacher get off the train and flee into a tunnel, where Cvetic sends one of the goons toppling down the stairs onto the tracks to meet his fate in the form of an oncoming train.

At the end of the film, Cvetic appears before HUAC, portrayed as a serious-minded committee and not the publicity hound it was. When he admits that he was an FBI mole and characterizes the party as a spy system operated by American traitors in league with Moscow, he emerges as a hero to his son and brother. But as Daniel L. Leab has shown, the historical Cvetic was a far cry from the noble crusader of the film. Alcoholic, abusive, and money-grubbing, Cvetic was not even a bona fide agent. Instead, he was simply a plant, one who expected to be compensated for his services and balked when he did not receive his due. He was also indiscreet about his undercover work, boasting about it to his cronies when his tongue was loosened by alcohol. When his fifteen minutes of fame were over, he went on the lecture circuit, eventually suffering a heart attack at fifty-five.

Sensing that *I Was a Communist for the FBI* would contain more fiction than fact, the FBI refused to cooperate with the filmmakers. But lack of cooperation did not stop the Academy of Motion Picture Arts and Sciences from nominating the film for an Oscar in the feature documentary category—that is, as a full-length film rather than a short subject. *I Was a Communist for the FBI* lost to *Kon-Tiki*, which dramatized the 101-day odyssey of an inexperienced crew from Peru to Polynesia. *Kon-Tiki* is a classic; *I Was a Communist for the FBI* is an artifact.

The mythologizing of Matt Cvetic did not end with the film. From 1952 to 1953, *I Was a Communist for the FBI* was a syndicated radio series carried by over six hundred stations and starring Dana Andrews as Cvetic. Hearing some of the episodes makes one wish that Andrews had starred in the film. His voice had a baritone fullness (the actor once aspired to be an opera singer), and his face conveyed a stoicism that suggested a man without a sense of humor, only a sense of the absurd. Frank Lovejoy's Cvetic was a tough guy, whose basic expression was midway between a smile and a sneer. Since the FBI dropped Cvetic when his usefulness ended, it also refused to be involved with the radio series, which, oddly, seemed more credible than the movie. Each episode began with the rich-voiced Andrews announcing, "I was a communist for the FBI." The inaugural episode, "I Walk Alone" (23 April 1952), set the mood, portraying the loneliness of a man forced to lead a double life, attending cell meetings when an important commissar came to town, and inhabiting a nether world in which "we go together but we walk alone." Instead of comradeship, Cvetic discovers paranoia. Skepticism is widespread, party members spy on each other, and booking a single room at a hotel does not guarantee privacy. Cvetic checks into his, only to find that he has been given a roommate. Milton Geiger's scripts for the radio series are more compelling than Crane Wilbur's screenplay, which seems as if it had been fashioned for a gangster movie. If Geiger had written the screenplay for *I Was a Communist for the FBI*, it would never have been nominated for best documentary feature. It would have been a feature film—a real movie.

In *I Was a Communist for the FBI*, a Soviet spy network is active in Pittsburgh. In Republic's *The Red Menace* (1949), a communist cell recruits the disaffected in downtown Los Angeles. Republic, always eager to be in the vanguard of topicality, as it proved with *Remember Pearl Harbor* (1942), was not interested in making a fact-based film. The communists in *The Red Menace* are crime bosses in suits, more fascistic than the fascists they purport to hate, and interested solely in winning converts they can conscript for any cause or demonstration that needs a window-smashing mob. Oddly, the Red Angelenos are not interested in stealing atomic secrets. *The Red Menace* is not a film about atomic espionage or the dictatorship of the proletariat. It is about the proletariat under the dictatorship of the party.

The Red Menace opens with the title set against a deliberately crude drawing of an octopus, with an atonal version of "The International" on the soundtrack, jarring and dissonant—a marching song that bodes ill for anyone getting in the way of the marchers. Structured as a frame narrative, it begins with two people, Bill Jones (Robert Rockwell) and Nina Petrovka (Hanne Axman), driving through the night to an unknown destination. Nina is near panic, convinced they are being followed. "Why are these two running away?" an off-screen voice asks. Cue for a flashback to a disgruntled ex-GI (Jones), the victim of a real estate scam, whose appeal to the Veterans Affairs Office proves fruitless. Then he is approached by a sympathetic stranger claiming to have experienced the same rebuff. One gets the impression that communists were planted in such places, ready to ensnare the disaffected. Without a crop of newcomers, *The Toilers*, the local Marxist paper, would go out of business.

Jones is introduced to a labyrinthine world that is difficult to exit once entered. There he meets a group of walking clichés: a former Irish Catholic, who embraced communism because she believed that capitalism is the exploiter of humanity and responsible for her parents' poverty (eventually, she returns to the fold in both the political and the religious senses); the man she loves, a Jewish poet, ostracized because he wrote that Marx was not an original thinker, but owed much to Lenin, Engels, and Democritus (he commits suicide); an African American news writer, who joined because communists boasted about the good they were doing for "his people" (he quits after his father reminds him that slavery ended with the Civil War, except in communist countries where it persists); and a vociferous female commissar, who calls an Italian dissenter a "dago." The dissenter is beaten to death. The commissar, when unmasked as a German national, starts raving maniacally, envisioning the masses on the march, with an off-screen off-key "International" reflecting her mental state.

What began with a man and woman on the run veered off into a phantasmagoria. After the film reached the end of its litany of horrors, it returned to the fleeing couple, now in a small Texas town. Feeling guilty for having betrayed their American heritage, they surrender to a sympathetic sheriff. After hearing their story, he reacts like a priest who has heard a sinless confession and sends the couple on their way. Spiritually renewed, Jones asks a boy the sheriff's name. The boy replies that the locals call him "Uncle Sam"—a cue for the grand finale—a shot of the Statue of Liberty, accompanied by an unseen chorus singing "My Country, 'Tis of Thee" with patriotic fervor. Uncle Sam forgives—but only the repentant.

After seeing *The Red Menace*, the ingenuous might have looked suspiciously at their Russian neighbors and boycotted borscht. But as transparent as the film is, it accomplished its purpose, dramatizing the way the party violated its own philosophy of universal brotherhood through deception, intimidation, and violence. On one point, *The Red Menace* is deadly accurate: Anyone deviating from the party line is disciplined. If the offender does not recant, his or her membership can be revoked.

Albert Maltz was one of most talented of the Hollywood radicals. A novelist, short story writer, playwright, screenwriter, ardent communist, and one of the Hollywood Ten—who stood by what they thought were their First Amendment rights, refusing to answer the "Are you now, or have you ever been" question—he wrote an article entitled "What Shall We Ask of Writers?" for *New Masses* (12 February 1946), arguing that writers should be judged on the basis of their art, not their politics. Otherwise, art is vulgarized, and the writer straitjacketed. The article infuriated communist critic Michael Gold, who denounced Maltz as a Trotskyite aesthete—and worse, "non-political." Desperate to remain in the party's good graces, Maltz published a retraction in the same journal on 9 April 1946, admitting that he was guilty of revisionism and distortion of Marxist thought, even though he must have believed he was right. For many, the party was a home, but one in which you lived by your parents' rules even if you were old enough to go off on your own.

Many years later, Maltz admitted that he was caught in a dilemma: "Expulsion over *this* matter was completely unacceptable to me. I felt the Party was the best hope of mankind; that it would be the force which moved the world toward brotherhood." The poet in *The Red Menace* felt similarly. He was too intellectually honest to write that Marx was an original thinker, and too insecure to split from the party and pursue a new life with the woman he loves. In despair, he hurls himself through a window, shattering the glass and plunging to his death. The woman, realizing that the party was responsible for his suicide, returns to her old parish church, where the pastor is waiting to welcome her home.

Maltz and the poet faced expulsion differently. Maltz did not despair, and suicide was not an option. After Premier Nikita Khrushchev denounced Stalin and catalogued his crimes at the twentieth party congress in February 1956, Maltz left the party, which at the that time feared that Khrushchev's demonization of Stalin would cost it members. The party then did an about-face, admitting that Maltz was right in affirming that a work should be judged on the basis of its art, not the author's politics. Although Maltz lived until 1985, his best days were over. Blacklisted, he wrote the script of *Broken Arrow* (1950), using Michael Blankfort as a front. The removal of his name from the screenplay of *The Robe* (1953) shows how meretricious the blacklist was. *The Robe*, based on Lloyd Douglas's inspirational novel, was Twentieth Century-Fox's first CinemaScope release, although it was never intended as such. In 1945, Maltz was asked to adapt the novel for RKO. When the production proved too costly, Fox acquired the property. By then, Maltz was unemployable. His name was removed from the script, which was passed on to Philip Dunne, who revised it and received sole screenplay credit. In a happier time, Maltz and Dunne would have shared credit. In 1997, Maltz was acknowledged posthumously by the Writers Guild of America. The corrected credit for *The Robe* now reads, "Screenplay by Albert Maltz and Philip Dunne."

The blacklist did not end at the same time for every writer. For Dalton Trumbo, it ended in 1960 when Otto Preminger hired him to adapt Leon Uris's *Exodus*, and Kirk Douglas hired him to adapt Howard Fast's *Spartacus*. For Albert Maltz, the blacklist ended a decade later. After *The Naked City* (1948), he did not receive another credit until 1972 (*Two Mules for Sister Sara*), with a final one in 1973 (*Scalawag*). It was not until 1956 that Maltz realized that his career, which began promisingly, had been abbreviated by his involvement with the party. For a long time, comradeship seemed more important to him than art, despite his insistence on the primacy of artistic integrity in evaluating a work. Maltz's was a career derailed by radicalism. When he awoke to the truth, the energy that had been sapped did not return.

Despite its shrillness and dime store symbolism, *The Red Menace* explained, in rudimentary terms, why ordinary Americans joined the party. Unfortunately, their reasons (brotherhood, camaraderie, racial and social equality, the extirpation of capitalism) made them seem like stock characters in a left-wing propaganda movie, repeating the same revolutionary clichés. Set to music, these would sound exactly like an atonal arrangement of "The International."

One might expect communists in Los Angeles—but in a rural community in Minnesota? And not only communists, but a germ warfare center headed by a former Nazi scientist, who disappeared from Germany in 1946 and resurfaced in the Soviet Union, where he put the knowledge he acquired from death camp experiments at the disposal of his new homeland. In *The Whip Hand* (1951), a magazine writer (Elliot Reid) vacationing in the mythical Winoga, once known for trout fishing, discovers that a mysterious virus has killed off the fish. Except for the general store owner (who is murdered when he tries to help the writer), the locals are a glum-looking lot, obviously harboring a secret that is not revealed until two-thirds into the film. They are all in league with the ex-Nazis turned communists, who have purchased a lodge for research that includes experiments on human beings, which leaves them looking like the walking dead. The head scientist, wanted for war crimes, is more Nazi than communist in his inhumanity— and more communist than Nazi in his allegiance to the Soviet Union. The climax is reminiscent of the end of a chapter in a serial like *Nyoka and the Lost Secrets of Hippocrates* (1942), with Nyoka on a conveyer belt headed for a buzz saw. We know she will not be shredded, but we will not know for certain until next week. Similarly, federal agents arrive before the heroine receives her injection, which her doctor-brother was supposed to administer. He reneges at the last moment and is shot, but not before taking out one of the commies. Federal agents storm the lodge, and the cadaverous victims pummel the scientist—if not to death, then close to it.

The Whip Hand was released by RKO, which, at the time, was owned by the anti-communist Howard Hughes. For a B movie, it had a propulsive script that kept the action from faltering and the audience from second-guessing the outcome. The director was the eminent William Cameron Menzies, better known as the production designer for such classics as *Gone with the Wind, For Whom the Bell Tolls,* and *Kings Row. The Whip Hand* was photographed by Nicholas Musuraca, a master of the art of black-and-white filmmaking, with its tonal gradations that brought out the rich palette of monochrome, showing that black and white were not polarities but a spectrum of light and dark, sunlight and shadow, that could be calibrated to fit the mood. "Dark" and "light" to Musuraca constituted a range, whose variety may not have been infinite, but seemed so. Because of the setting, rural Minnesota, *The Whip Hand* does not allow for a visually elegant production, yet it is a strikingly photographed and tightly constructed film. It was also supposed to have been about Hitler.

The Whip Hand originated as a script entitled "The Man He Found," the man being Adolf Hitler, who did not commit suicide in his Berlin bunker on 30 April 1945, but made his way to America, finding a hideaway in a New England village to begin preparing for the Fourth Reich. But when the mercurial Hughes saw a rough cut, he decided that Hitler movies were passé. He ordered the film to be scrapped, except for scenes that could be salvaged for a different project, one set in a Minnesota fishing village taken over by communists, who co-opt the locals and set up a base of operations for germ warfare on America. A much-underrated film of escalating suspense and striking cinematography, *The Whip Hand* failed to break even; it cost $376,000 to make and brought in only $225,000. RKO's 1951 moneymakers were *The Blue Veil, Payment on Demand,* and *The Racket.* The problem may have been the title. "Whip hand" is not a particularly common idiom. It refers to a wielder of power, which in the film would be the mad scientist. But his power is short-lived, as is he. "The Man He Found" might have drawn a bigger audience.

By 1955, communist agents could be anywhere in the United States, even in a greasy spoon in Malibu, the setting of *Shack Out on 101* (1955), 101 referring to Pacific Coast Highway 101. Unremittingly brutal, *Shack Out* is filled with red herrings, plot reversals, and a harpoon death, enough to keep the audience riveted for eighty minutes.

Shack Out on 101 does not open like a spy thriller. In a shallow focus shot, Kotty (Terry Moore, in a two-piece bathing suit) is seen lying on the beach, as a male in the distance starts moving toward her. He comes into focus in all his sculpted virility, bending over her, kissing her passionately, and then engaging in some roughhousing. If rape isn't on his mind, one wonders what is. Kotty is a waitress at the diner, who hopes to pass a civil service exam to move on to a better job. The man (Lee Marvin), a short-order cook at the same diner, is nicknamed Slob because of his dress and manners. But this is a "things—and people—are not what they seem" movie. Slob is actually Mr. Gregory, the mastermind of an atomic spy ring and a devoted communist. At least the audience is spared a "we shall bury you" speech like the one in *The Whip Hand.* And who would have believed it if Lee Marvin had delivered it? Accepting Marvin as a communist puts enough strain on credulity. Even when he reveals his identity in coldly cultivated English, he just seems to be delivering his lines in a different voice. Marvin was more convincing as Slob the vulgarian than Mr. Gregory, which presumably was a code name.

Slob is not the only deceiver. Deliverymen are federal agents in disguise. A nuclear scientist (Frank Lovejoy), with whom Kotty is in love, seems to be in league with the spies, but is really working with the FBI to expose them. The screw is turned and loosened so many times that one forgets that the owner of the diner (Keenan Wynn) and his ex-army buddy (Whit Bissell) are planning a vacation in the Caribbean, where they will snorkel and spear fish with a harpoon. The harpoon comes in handy when no other weapon is available to dispatch Slob.

Because the action is largely confined to the diner, *Stake Out* has the unventilated look of film noir, where claustrophobia spells entrapment, and the dark is light enough. Anyone unaware that *Shack Out* was an original script might think it was an adaptation of a single-set play like *The Petrified Forest* or *Watch on the Rhine*, which only allowed for minimal exteriors. But the cast worked well within the circumscribed setting, confirming the impression that many diner regulars have of servers like Kotty, who do their begrudging best until something better comes along. For Kotty, it is the physicist and, perhaps, a desk job in her future husband's office.

Chapter 11

MICROFILM MANIA

MICROFILM, USUALLY THOUGHT OF AS A MEANS OF PRESERVING DOCU-
ments that might otherwise be subject to disintegration, took on a different
meaning in the 1950s. Then, it was a method that Soviet agents used for recording classified information. David Greenglass informed the FBI that his
brother-in-law, Julius Rosenberg, had two apartments, one in Greenwich
Village, the other on the Lower East Side, where he microfilmed whatever
he received from his sources.

But the best known case of microfilm used in service of espionage was
what came to be known as the "Pumpkin Papers," an umbrella coinage for a
cache of secret documents and two developed—and three undeveloped—
rolls of microfilm. Whittaker Chambers, a former Soviet spy who broke
with the party in 1938, kept them in his possession as bargaining chips in
case his life were threatened because of his defection. Chambers deposited the microfilm in a hollowed out pumpkin on his farm in Westminster,
Maryland. But since the microfilm dealt with events that occurred in the
mid 1930s, its value was negligible.

A strip of microfilm with instructions for assembling a portable atomic
bomb figures in the plot of Columbia's *The 49th Man* (1953), a dizzyingly
convoluted and morally disturbing thriller in the semi-documentary style of
Walk East on Beacon, narrated authoritatively by Gerald Mohr, as if the film
were reenacting a real-life incident. *The 49th Man* opens on a young man
driving at a dangerously high speed. The car crashes, exploding in flames.
At the crash site, a case with suspicious metal parts is retrieved, sparking the
curiosity of the Security Investigation Division. One of the agents (John Ireland) brings the satchel to Los Alamos, where his suspicions are confirmed:
The parts are components of an atomic bomb. After other such cases are
discovered, the spy hunt is on, and an agent is dispatched to Marseilles, cinema's favorite port of shadows and a likely spot for uranium trafficking.

The 49th Man is a "things are not what they seem" movie—with a twist. The agent's French interpreter and two naval officers, who seem to be in league with the enemy, are really players in a war games scenario scripted by the military, in which the agent is the lead. Even the head of the division (Richard Denning) is out of the loop, pointing to a military establishment that has become recklessly autonomous. If everything is just a game, everyone is expendable—including the hot rod kid and the agent, whose life is in danger after coming upon a terrorist cell in Marseilles that was not part of the endgame.

The villains are two disaffected World War II vets, one of whom had been labeled a subversive by the military. Before they can detonate the bomb in San Francisco, they are apprehended, and the bomb is dropped on an atomic testing site in Nevada, killing no one, but increasing radioactivity in the area. Implicitly, *The 49th Man* argues that the end justifies the means. If a war games maneuver unmasked a terrorist organization and kept San Francisco from being nuked, it was worth it, despite the loss of a couple of lives and the creation of more radioactive fallout in the Southwest. Better that than a city in ruins. This is not a film to be overly analyzed. The screenwriter, Harry Essex, working from an original story by Ivan Tors, did not wag a finger at the military, but gave the audience reason enough to do so.

The ruthlessness of Soviet agents and their obsession with microfilm were not lost on screenwriter-director Samuel Fuller, whose *Pickup on South Street* (1953) revolved around a double theft: A strip of microfilm stolen by an agent is then inadvertently filched by a pickpocket. *Pickup*, which raised pulp to high melodrama, had exactly what the anti-communist movie needed: old-fashioned urban realism, for the most part studio-created, and New York in a sweltering summer, with an air of oppressiveness that had less to do with the temperature than the net of entrapment thrown over Candy (Jean Peters), a onetime call girl and now an unwitting courier for Joey, her communist lackey-lover (Richard Kiley). In a densely packed subway car, Candy brushes up against Skip McCoy (Richard Widmark), an experienced pickpocket, who deftly opens her purse and removes her wallet, unaware that it contains the microfilm. McCoy is breezily amoral and proudly apolitical. He is unimpressed when told that by not relinquishing the microfilm (containing a patent application for a chemical formula, about which nothing further is mentioned), he is "as guilty as the traitors that gave Stalin the A-bomb." It was a weak analogy. McCoy was not in the same league as Klaus Fuchs and Harry Gold. He probably would not even have known who they were. Unlike the communists in *Walk East on*

Beacon, who professed allegiance to the Soviet Union, those in *Pickup on South Street* are straight out of the hoodlum empire, a mix of lowlifes and mobsters. These so-called agents are go-betweens, devoid of ideology. They are merely in the rackets, and if the latest racket is secret microfilm, they're in for the long haul.

Fuller structured the plot along classic lines of recognition and reversal, with ignorance yielding to knowledge, knowledge to regeneration—and, in one case, to death. When Candy is summoned before Joey's associates to explain the loss of the microfilm, she suddenly realizes that she is caught up in an espionage ring. Without saying a word, Peters, a much-underrated actress (and not Fuller's first choice), adopted a vacuous expression that masked her fear.

Women are expendable in *Pickup on South Street*. Although they may not get grapefruit pushed in their faces or hot coffee thrown at them, they are still victims of misogyny. It is bad enough that Candy is manhandled by McCoy, who at one point knocks her unconscious after he finds her in his waterfront shack. McCoy's behavior is ungentlemanly but understandable. Joey, on the other hand, brutalizes Candy, even shooting her in the back (but not fatally). Joey is the ring's one-man goon squad. Richard Kiley—who that same year showed another facet of his art by playing the romantic lead in the Broadway musical *Kismet* (1953), in which he introduced "Stranger in Paradise"—had the face of an aesthete, dreamy and vulnerable, which made his sadism even scarier. In the most emotionally devastating scene in the film, he makes himself comfortable in Moe's furnished room. Moe (Thelma Ritter, in an Oscar-nominated performance) is a police informant who sells neckties for a dollar and is on familiar terms with fences and pickpockets, including McCoy. Moe is literally preparing for the end. For her, it's not a matter of being "tired of living and scared of dying," as it is for Joe in *Show Boat*, but of being tired of living and resigned to dying—if she can be buried in a private cemetery, not in a potter's field. When Joey demands McCoy's address, she refuses, adding that she wants nothing to do with commies. Like Candy and McCoy, she is politically naïve: "What do I know about commies? Nothing. I know one thing: I just don't like them." Realizing that Joey means business, she faces him, unafraid: "So I don't get to have the fancy funeral after all .... Look, Mister, you'll be doing me a big favor if you blow my head off." Joey obliges—off camera, with the sound of gunshot substituting for the visual nobody wanted to see. McCoy provides Moe with her funeral of choice, and then he realigns himself on the right side of the law and finds true love with Candy, who plans to keep him out of trouble.

In his autobiography, Fuller describes the film's reception. Conservatives found *Pickup on South Street* pro-communist, perhaps because the three principals were not gung ho patriots in an era when it was "us" or "them." J. Edgar Hoover loathed the movie. He considered McCoy anti-American, thereby missing the point that McCoy, like Candy and Moe, is oblivious to world affairs. For McCoy, a newspaper's sole purpose is to distract subway riders while he picks their pockets. Candy knows basic morality. Giving the microfilm to Joey is wrong, and returning it to the authorities is right. And Moe does not even have a radio in her room, just a phonograph on which she plays "Mam'selle," the only record she seems to own. They are three basically decent human beings on the periphery of New York's netherworld, too busy trying to make a buck to fret about Korea, the Rosenbergs, or Alger Hiss. Yet when it is time to show their allegiance, they put their lives on the line—in Moe's case permanently.

In France, where the Communist Party was thriving, *Pickup on South Street* was retitled *Le Port de la Drogue* ("*Port of Drugs*"), with a drugs shipment replacing the microfilm and a corresponding loss of context. Even so, *Pickup on South Street* won the Bronze Lion at the Venice Film Festival.

Chapter 12

MADNESS RISEN FROM HELL

CORROSIVE COMMENTARY ON BOTH ANTI-COMMUNIST AMERICA AND
the Korean War are perversely united in a plot that gives new meaning
to "layered," in *The Manchurian Candidate* (1962), a crazy theorem with a
"given" and a "to prove." The given is a prologue in the form of a pre-credits
sequence and an opening title: "Korea 1952." A patrol led by the unpopular
Sergeant Raymond Shaw (Laurence Harvey) is betrayed by an interpreter
(Henry Silva), later revealed to be in the service of the North Koreans. The
patrol is ambushed, rendered unconscious, and carried off on stretchers,
destination unspecified. That much makes sense. We assume we will see
the men, or at least some of them, later. But there is something puzzling
about the interpreter, who looks more Mediterranean than Korean, which
is understandable since Silva was half Sicilian and half Spanish. A Red, or a
red herring? A step in proving the theorem? A matter to be clarified later?
Or a sign that we are in a world where reason no longer prevails, and the
irrational holds sway?

After the credits roll, Shaw is being welcomed with great fanfare for
having saved the lives of his men, routing the enemy, and, after three days
during which the patrol had been reported missing, leading them back to
safety—acts of heroism that merit the Congressional Medal of Honor. This
account of Shaw's bravery is the first of many such mind-teasing incidents.
When did Shaw perform these heroic acts, if he did? After he and the patrol
had been carried off on stretchers—and to where?

At the ceremony, Shaw is upstaged by his mother, Eleanor Shaw Iselin
(Angela Lansbury), who uses the occasion to campaign for his stepfather,
Senator Johnny Iselin (James Gregory), a vice presidential candidate. Shaw
loathes them both, but he is especially contemptuous of his stepfather, who
is in the thrall of his manipulative wife. (The backstory, which is not in
the film, can be found in Richard Condon's novel of the same name. Iselin

139

had been the law partner of Raymond's father and the lover of the power-obsessed Eleanor, who divorced her husband when he resisted her machinations and married the malleable Iselin.) Eleanor and her puppet spouse pose as rabid anti-communists, even though Iselin cannot keep straight the number of communists he claims are in the State Department. In that respect, he is not unlike Senator Joseph McCarthy, except that Iselin is more stupid than sleazy.

Another member of the patrol, Captain (later Major) Bennett Marco (Frank Sinatra), is plagued by a recurrent nightmare in which the members of the patrol are at a New Jersey garden party where a woman is extolling the virtues of hydrangeas. An extraordinary circular shot tracks left to right, from the lethargic looking men to the garden club ladies, then reverses direction, as if to close the circle. Eventually, we realize that during the three days the men were reported missing, they had been flown to Manchuria, where they were brainwashed—or "dry-cleaned," as a communist doctor gleefully remarks. Marco is reliving a demonstration that took place before an audience of communist functionaries, in which Shaw was singled out as an example of successful brainwashing. Another indication that something is amiss occurs when Shaw is asked to identify the person he dislikes least. When he names Captain Marco, the hydrangea expert insists he pick another: "That won't do, Raymond. We need the captain to get you your medal." But Shaw is unworthy of the medal. He did not save his patrol; in fact, he kills two of its members. To illustrate the effectiveness of the experiment, Shaw is ordered to strangle one of the men, then shoot another, tasks he performs with the dispassion of a somnambulist.

Shaw has become a programmed assassin. The procedure setting him in motion never varies. He receives a call telling him to play solitaire, which he does unquestioningly. When the queen of diamonds—the red queen, the symbol of his controlling mother—keeps turning up, he is ready for his next assignment. At present, that task is murdering the liberal editor of the newspaper for which he works. Shaw kills unfeelingly, unable to remember what he has done and experiencing no guilt.

Gradually, we realize Shaw's mother has something to do with her son's programming, but exactly what? Initially, she was opposed to his relationship with Jocie, the daughter of a senator who does not conceal his contempt for Iselin, whom she denounced as a "communist tart." But when Mother Shaw realizes that a marriage between her son and Jocie could bring the senator into her orbit, she stages an elaborate costume ball, at which Iselin dons a fake beard in order to look like an Amish farmer, accompanied by Mother Shaw costumed as a cross between a shepherdess and a matronly Little Bo Peep. Raymond is dressed as a gaucho, Jocie, as the queen of diamonds—which may mean either that she is part of the conspiracy or that her choice of costume was accidental. Tragically, it was the latter. When Mother Shaw realizes that the senator is committed to blocking her husband's nomination, it is elimination time. The situation becomes more complicated when Shaw and Jocie elope. It is then time for a game of solitaire, with the senator as victim. Unfortunately, Jocie appears at the crime scene and is murdered as well. (In the novel, both murders are ugly. Raymond shoots the senator in the forehead, and Jocie gets one bullet in each eye.) Raymond Shaw has killed his father-in-law and his wife. He has two more to go.

The Manchurian Candidate has the dazzling unreality of a work like Ayn Rand's *Atlas Shrugged*, which is so grippingly preposterous ("Who is John Galt?") one keeps turning the pages in disbelief, hoping that eventually it will all make sense. *The Manchurian Candidate* (both the novel and the film) is also hypnotically improbable. To use E. M. Forster's phrase, it is an "and then" type of story, in which motivation gives way to chronology. Instead of cause and effect, there is a series of "and this happened," followed by "and then that happened," with "this" alternating with "that" until the last link in the narrative chain has been forged, with "The End" in place of a resolution.

As *The Manchurian Candidate* approaches what would normally pass for closure, the truth is disgorged from the clotted mass of story lines awaiting some kind of unification. Mother Shaw divulges the truth, which she articulates so chillingly, each syllable ice-coated, that we hang on every word she utters. She coldly informs her Pavlovian killer-son that he is to dress as a priest to gain access to Madison Square Garden, where a political convention is taking place. He must then shoot the presidential nominee through the head, making it possible for Iselin to steal the spotlight and deliver a speech that is a model of rhetoric—a speech that, she rhapsodizes, has been "worked on" in the United States and the Soviet Union, implying that there are communist cells in America in league with Moscow. The speech will sweep her and her mannequin husband into the White House, where they will replace the republic with a totalitarian state. She then kisses Raymond as she would a lover. The incestuous implications would not have shocked readers of the novel, in which the adolescent Eleanor has sex with her father in the attic of their home. Her incestuous relationship with her father, which naturally is not mentioned in the film, comes close to explaining why

Mother Shaw, having broken the incest taboo with her father, could easily break it again with her son. However, neither mother nor son will live long enough for the unspeakable to occur.

At this point in the film, logic begins to buckle—but not snap apart. Mother Shaw has been anti-communist from the start, yet she has worked with the Soviets and North Koreans to produce a robotic assassin, not realizing that it would be her son. Once she and her spouse are safely ensconced at 1600 Pennsylvania Avenue, she intends to make the brainwashers pay for what they have done, vowing, "[T]hey will be pulled down and ground into dirt for what they did to you and what they have contemptuously done to me." Apparently, what they have done to her takes precedence over what they have done to him. Clearly, she understands that her son is the human equivalent of a computer program. One wonders if she would have had Raymond deprogrammed after the assassination, or, more likely, kept him as he is so she could have a personal hit man. Perhaps she never intended to be her own son's controller, but that is exactly what happened. One wonders if this wasn't a perverse joke the Soviets and North Koreans played on her. They must have known Raymond Shaw was her son. *The Manchurian Candidate* invites all sorts of speculation, little of it conclusive.

Mother Shaw's dream of turning America into a fascist state is not far-fetched. Only her chosen means are. She adopts the Soviet model and then discards it, along with those she colluded with—but she retains her original model's totalitarian features. In the early years of the Great Depression, when capitalism seemed to be a failed philosophy, fascism or some sort of dictatorship appeared to be an alternative. And after Hitler became chancellor of Germany, Fritz Kuhn, head of the pro-Hitler German-American Bund, embarked on a campaign to emulate the Nazis' demonization of Jews by characterizing them as an alien race and enemies of the United States. Although Kuhn denied that he wanted a Nazified America, this was his goal. Mother Shaw's would have been an American police state that owed more to Stalin's Russia than Hitler's Germany.

Marco deprograms Raymond by showing him that he was playing solitaire with a force deck, one that contains fifty-two replicas of the same card, the Queen of Diamonds. Raymond now knows who must be killed, and it is not the nominee. He dispatches his mother and stepfather before turning the rifle on himself. He has thus committed matricide, uxoricide, suicide, and—if stepfathers and fathers-in-law qualify—patricide. Marco's final thoughts in the film differ from those in the novel, in which he mutters, "No electric chair for a Medal of Honor man." Unless Marco divulges the truth, Shaw will be remembered as a deranged killer, not the son of a mother who dreamed of turning America into a dictatorship. The film ends with Marco's personal commendation for Shaw's Congressional Medal of Honor, which, if it ever saw print, would have validated Shaw as the hero he had originally been made out to be—but in a different way: "He had been made to commit acts too unspeakable to be cited here by an enemy who had captured his mind and his soul. He freed himself at last, and, in the end, heroically and unhesitatingly, gave his life to save his country." Then Marco, played brilliantly by Sinatra in his best screen performance, says despairingly, "Hell, hell." Thoughtful moviegoers would have nodded assent. "The End" then appears on the screen, leaving the audience speechless or pensive, depending on their reaction to a film about tragic waste.

The movie version of *The Manchurian Candidate* is far more critical of America than the novel. If one assumes that brainwashing can produce assassins like Shaw and leave men with their minds and souls in disrepair, the fault lay not with the lunatic fringe—of which Mother Shaw is the paradigm—but with a nation so obsessed with communism that it would wage a war in Asia to keep the red tide from traveling westward. The Korean War resulted in fifty-four thousand American casualties. Raymond Shaw might have been one if them if he had not been chosen for a different role. Either way, he died.

The Manchurian Candidate belongs to the tradition of cautionary tales, which includes *The President Vanishes* (1934) and *Gabriel over the White House* (1933). In the former, an isolationist president, refusing to involve America in a European war, incurs the anger of the public, which equates neutrality with cowardice. To drive home his rationale, the president allows himself to be kidnapped and held captive by the right wing Grey Shirts (a composite of Hitler's Brown Shirts and William Pelley's Silver Shirts). An FBI agent kills the Grey Shirts leader with the transparent name of Lincoln Lee, freeing the president to preach non-intervention and implying that it took his kidnapping to bring the country to its senses. In *Gabriel over the White House*, a seemingly incompetent president undergoes political regeneration after an auto accident and embarks on a campaign to purge the country of undesirables, even if doing so means executing criminals (which it does). In short, he strives to convert the republic into a dictatorship so powerful that—dispensing with the Constitution and individual liberties—he will be able to accomplish his goal of world disarmament. All three are troubling films. Although what they depict never came to pass, their night-marish plots unfolded so naturally that one could easily imagine these sce-narios coming to pass.

The Manchurian Candidate opened in New York on the eve of the tense weekend of the Cuban Missile Crisis. In his *New York Times* review (25 Oc-tober), Bosley Crowther could not take the film seriously, but he admitted that it could "scare some viewers half to death." He hoped they would not be foolish enough to believe it. But this was a time when one could be-lieve anything, even global war precipitated by a missile buildup on an is-land some ninety miles from the Florida mainland. When John F. Kennedy was assassinated a year later, Sinatra, out of respect for the late president, purchased the rights to the film and had it withdrawn from circulation—even though Sinatra himself played "a would-be presidential assassin" in *Suddenly* (1954). Sinatra overreacted. A president is not assassinated in *The Manchurian Candidate*, only a power-crazed woman and the buffoon she intended to install in the White House. Another explanation given for the film's withdrawal was Sinatra's dissatisfaction with the way the profits were allocated by United Artists—not that this mattered much, since the movie failed at the box office. Whatever the case, *The Manchurian Candidate* did not resurface for a quarter of a century.

The ideal 1962 double bill would have been *The Manchurian Candidate* and the half-hour short, *Red Nightmare* (1962), produced by Warner Bros. "under the personal supervision of Jack L. Warner," and in cooperation with the Department of Defense, whose seal appears at the end. If Mother Shaw could achieve her dream, the United States would be the police state de-picted in *Red Nightmare*, in which the main character, a Joe Smith Ameri-can type, experiences the dream to end all dreams: He goes to sleep in a democracy and wakes up in a dictatorship.

Narrated by a grim-voiced Jack Webb, *Red Nightmare* opens with what looks like a small-town street, except that there is an armed guard patrol-ling an area cordoned off by barbed wire. The setting, Webb informs us, is a mock-up in Soviet Russia, complete with a college where students learn the American way of life, which they will abandon once they become the future commissars of a Stalinist United States. The message, with its "it can happen here" warning, is far from subtle. To prove his point, Webb subjects a typical American father of three to a nightmare in which he awakens to a world where his church has become a "people's museum"; his wife has turned into a party diehard; his teenage daughter is off to a collective farm; and his younger children have chosen to attend a state school. Worse, he is put on trial for the triple crime of subversion, deviation, and treason. Just before he is about to be executed, he is jolted into waking, having learned that freedom is not a gift, but a right that must be earned. It was a kind of *Father Knows Best* meets *Invasion U.S.A.* movie, at thirty minutes mercifully short, which was about all the homily could sustain without going into overdrive. *Red Nightmare*, seen in conjunction with *The Manchurian Candidate*, would have provided a gloss on the latter. Mother Shaw learned enough about communism to be able to convert the republic into a dictatorship, American style, without the Soviet trappings and the abhorred "c" word. When Angela Lansbury describes her vision of the new America to her son, one does not need to experience the red nightmare. Mother Shaw, harshly lit, as if in a horror film, was the nightmare.

Seven Days in May (1964), filmed with President Kennedy's support and released a year after his assassination, is a more reliable guide to Cold War tensions. The film dramatizes the seemingly impossible, when a president successfully negotiates a disarmament treaty with the Soviet Union, calling for the dismantling of nuclear missiles. In 1964, such a treaty would have been devoutly to be wished for—at least by Americans tired of living under the ever-increasing threat of nuclear war. But the film, adapted by Rod Serling from the novel by Fletcher Knebel and Charles W. Bailey II, was set in 1970 after another war—this time with Iran—which, like the Korean War, ended with an armistice. The public's mood is hardly joyous, recalling the response to disarmament in *The President Vanishes*, in which any form of détente was considered a sign of weakness. Certainly the joint chiefs of staff think so, going so far as to plan a coup "in the interests of the nation's safety," the assumption being that disarmament does not ensure safety. Actually, the conflict goes deeper. Jordan Lyman, the president (Fredric March), is a Democrat and a dove, unlike his would-be nemesis General Scott (a chillingly self-righteous Burt Lancaster), who is primed for a takeover. Unbeknownst to the president, a training base, code name ECOMCON (Emergency Communications Control), has been set up in the Texas desert, where an elite paramilitary force is ready to spring into action.

By setting the action in 1970, Serling was altering the time frame of the novel, published in 1962, but set in 1974. In both cases, the time change moved the action into the future, a feature of science fiction. But the time-shifting was also a way of reassuring us that what is being depicted is not happening now and that just before the point of no return, the crisis will be resolved without the country going into red alert. Cold comfort, perhaps, but better that than a radioactive shower.

Unlike *The Manchurian Candidate, Seven Days in May* was doubly time-specific: 1964 audiences were watching a movie set in 1970. *The Manchurian Candidate*, released in 1962, was set after the Korean War, which ended a decade earlier and had little to do with either the time of the film's release or the time of its action, remaining at the level of horror fantasy. Certainly anyone who saw *Seven Days in May* in 1964 would never have associated the film's president, Jordan Lyman, with Lyndon Johnson, a hawk who called opponents of the Vietnam War "nervous Nellies." Johnson mired the country in an unwinnable war that encountered such resistance that he was forced to announce on nationwide television that he would not seek reelection—as if that were possible.

While anything was possible in the days after the Kennedy assassination, a year later the nation's problems were mostly domestic, except for the looming specter of Vietnam. By the time *Seven Days in May* opened in February 1964, President Kennedy and civil tights leader Medgar Evers had been assassinated; protests against the Vietnam War were mounting, often accompanied by the burning of draft cards; three civil rights activists had been murdered in Mississippi; race riots had broken out in Harlem, despite passage of the Civil Rights Act, which supposedly had ended segregation; and Dr. Martin Luther King Jr. had been awarded the Nobel Peace Prize, even though peace seemed remote.

Like *The Manchurian Candidate, Seven Days in May* blurred the distinction between politically charged melodrama and science fiction. Each operated from the "what if?" premise. What if a Korean vet could be programmed into becoming an assassin? What if the nation—which preferred the continuation of the Cold War to disarmament—had become so polarized by a peace-seeking president and a war-happy military that it would ignore a government take-over if the United States could maintain its superiority in the arms race?

Once the president learns what has been planned in his absence, he announces that he will be going fishing for a few days. But instead, he stages a counter-coup and gives a press conference in which he anticipates Dr. King's "I Have a Dream" speech: "We will remain strong and proud and we will see a day when on this earth all men will walk out of the long tunnels of tyranny into the bright light of freedom." Dr. King was more eloquent, but the point was the same. Significantly, the president does not condemn Scott for his refusal to compromise. Neither Scott nor the Soviet Union represents the enemy: "The enemy is the nuclear age and out of this comes a sickness." It is a simple explanation of what occurred on 6 August 1945, for which the world has paid hundreds of times over. The age claimed its victims, dead and alive. Among the latter is General James Scott. Forced to resign his command, Scott can remain in the military, his sickness untreated and perhaps untreatable.

Chapter 13

CURTAIN UP!

THE END OF WORLD WAR II MANDATED NEW VILLAINS. THE NAZIS AND the Japanese would never go out of vogue, but they would no longer be the satanic incarnations they were in the 1940s. Then, Nazis ranged from sadistic (*None Shall Escape* [1944]) to stupid (*Desperate Journey* [1942]). The Japanese were not even worthy of a range. They were Yellow Peril grotesques who inserted bamboo shoots under fingernails (*Behind the Rising Sun* [1943]), gouged out eyes and pulled out tongues (*Manila Calling* [1942]), and gang raped Chinese women (*China* [1943], *Dragon Seed* [1944]).

A year after Churchill's Iron Curtain speech, the House Committee on Un-American Activities, convinced that left-wing screenwriters were inserting communist propaganda into their films (e.g., "Share and share alike" in *Tender Comrade* [1943]), launched an investigation in October 1947 into the alleged communist subversion of the movie industry. In February that year, a four-part series, Igor Gouzenko's "I Was Inside Stalin's Spy Ring," began in *Cosmopolitan* magazine, concluding in May just as HUAC engaged in a dress rehearsal in Los Angeles for a full-scale, media-covered witch hunt in the fall. If Gouzenko had been in the movie business, he would have been HUAC's poster boy.

In 1943, the Ukrainian born Gouzenko was flown to Ottawa, Canada, to work as a cryptographer at the Soviet Embassy. It was his first trip abroad. He would not be returning to Russia. Initially, Gouzenko observed the protocols, learning to answer questions by providing only basic information. With the locals, he was courteous but aloof—in short, a model apparatchik. He began to change when he discovered messages that he encoded and others that he decoded revealed the existence of a Soviet spy network run by a military attaché at the embassy. The spies included some high-ranking Canadians, even a member of Parliament. At first, the classified material only piqued Gouzenko's curiosity, but over the next two years, he became increasingly disenchanted with communism. Living in Canada had awakened him to the freedom enjoyed by others, who, unlike himself, were not government automatons. He was also loath to return to Russia, where he would be a low-level code clerk. Defection was the only alternative. He also knew how he could make himself useful to the Canadian government.

On 5 September 1945, a month after the bombing of Hiroshima, Gouzenko stuffed 109 classified documents under his shirt. These contained enough evidence to arrest thirty-nine people and convict eighteen of them. But defection was not as simple as Gouzenko thought. The Royal Canadian Mounted Police did not believe him, and the *Ottawa Journal* was not interested in the documents. Finally, through the intervention of the undersecretary for external affairs, Gouzenko and his family were granted asylum, which came with a price: The family lived under an assumed name outside of Toronto, and Gouzenko always wore a hood when interviewed on television.

Shortly after the first installment of "I Was Inside Stalin's Spy Ring" appeared, Twentieth Century-Fox purchased the movie rights, changing the title to *The Iron Curtain* (1948). Since Fox was going through its semi-documentary phase, *The Iron Curtain* was conceived as a companion piece to *The House on 92nd Street* (1945), with authenticity provided by on-location filming and a visual style that combined features of the documentary and the fiction film. Martin Berkeley had a story outline ready by 22 April 1947. Berkeley was ideally suited to the task. Once a party member, he had now become an informant, providing HUAC with a record 155 names. Zanuck hired Milton Krims to write the screenplay. Krims was a logical choice, since he had written *Confessions of a Nazi Spy*, which came off as a fact-based espionage film, for Warner Bros.

Zanuck might have achieved his goal if Henry Hathaway, *The House on 92nd Street*'s director, had been assigned to *The Iron Curtain*. Instead, Zanuck put William Wellman in charge. Since the semi-documentary was alien to Wellman, he treated the script as a melodrama with off-screen narration by the sober-voiced Reed Hadley (who performed a similar service in *The House on 92nd Street*) and on-location filming in Ottawa's Parliament Building, the Ministry of Justice, the National Research Council, and the Royal Canadian Mounted Police Headquarters. In Wellman's hands, *The Iron Curtain* became a thriller in which the intrigue-riddled embassy is so fearful of leaks that Shostakovich's music is played full-volume in the code room to prevent anyone from hearing what went on in the adjoining office.

But this scenario was quite the opposite of Ottawa, where people moved freely and did not have to censor their thoughts before speaking. The distinction is also apparent in the lighting: low-key lighting, dark and shadowy, for the embassy; natural light for outside.

Filming began on 23 November 1947 and ended on 13 January 1948. Krims's screenplay was faithful to the source. Dana Andrews was the perfect Gouzenko, the model bureaucrat, square-jawed and unsmiling, obedient to a fault. When his wife, Anna (Gene Tierney), arrives from Russia, he changes momentarily but warns her against socializing with their neighbors. As they walk through Ottawa, they seem to be breathing in the air of freedom that Canadians take for granted. In one scene, they realize what they have lost when they pass a Catholic church. They look at each other, their faces reflecting a longing they cannot articulate but can only convey through their eyes. One senses it is only a matter of time before they become Canadian citizens.

Expatriation was gradual. Gouzenko's work gave him access to memos revealing the existence of a spy ring that included a number of diverse Canadians, including an MP, along with members of the Royal Canadian Air Force, the National Research Council, the Department of Internal Affairs, Marxist study groups, and an atomic scientist who believed in sharing information about nuclear weapons with an ally. Although most Americans at the time were unaware of Canada's role in the creation of the atomic bomb, the uranium used for it came from Canada.

In the film, Gouzenko's reasons for defecting are not just disillusionment with the party and exposure to the free world. The order for his return to Russia and the bombing of Hiroshima are the deciding factors. As a new father, Gouzenko fears his son will grow up under a form of government in which he longer believes. Equally disturbing is the prospect of the Soviet Union developing nuclear capabilities, as it eventually did. The coda is a masterful mounting of suspense undone by a last-minute rescue. Gouzenko's story falls on deaf years at the Ministry of Justice, Parliament, and the Ottawa Journal, whose desk clerk writes him off as a "crackpot." Finally, the Royal Canadian Mounted Police arrive, like the Seventh Cavalry at the besieged fort, leaving the Soviets threatening but powerless. The Gouzenkos are now free, but free to do what? To live in protective custody under the name "Brown," which did not prevent Igor from writing books and appearing on television, albeit with a hood. At least Igor Gouzenko had the satisfaction of knowing that it was his confession that started the Cold War. Churchill's speech was only the curtain raiser—literally.

When Hollywood raised the curtain in 1948, audiences were treated to an array of films set in the Soviet Union's newest satellites. Some were rooted in times and places; others combined the fictitious and the factual, giving audiences a movie and a mini-history lesson at the same time. There would also be movies like *Sofia* (1948), in which a Soviet bloc country like Bulgaria had only a tenuous connection with the plot. In 1946, Bulgaria was absorbed into the Soviet Union and renamed the People's Republic of Bulgaria. The following year it became a Stalinist paradigm with the inauguration of five-year plans and nationalization of industries. In *Sofia*, however, Bulgaria's capital was only used as the setting for a Cold War espionage movie. In the *New York Times* (5 September 1948) Bosley Crowther dismissed *Sofia* as a "spy and fly" melodrama about an American operative who helps a nuclear physicist and his wife escape to freedom. A chanteuse, who is also a double agent, poses a threat, but nothing—much less a femme fatale—will prevent American ingenuity from triumphing over Soviet bureaucracy.

Guilty of Treason (1950), on the other hand, could not have been set anywhere but Hungary. It is a deeply felt film about the show trial of Joszef Cardinal Mindszenty, who spoke out against the Nazi occupation of Hungary during World War II, and was equally vocal about the communist regime that came to power afterwards. His criticism resulted in a sentence of life imprisonment. Since the film deals only with the period after late 1948, when the Cardinal was tried and declared an enemy of the state, to early 1949, it ends with his trial. But after eight years of incarceration, torture, and degradation, the cardinal was released in 1956 and granted asylum in the American embassy in Budapest. Later, he was allowed to return to Vienna, where he died in 1975.

Guilty of Treason is imbued with a strong Catholic sensibility, not merely because of the subject matter, but also because the script was written by Emmett Lavery, a well-known Catholic layman, screen writer (*Hitler's Children, Behind the Rising Sun, The Court Martial of Billy Mitchell*), television writer (*Dr. Kildare, Mr. Novak*), and playwright (*The First Legion, The Magnificent Yankee*). Charles Bickford, the stern but compassionate Father Peyramale in *The Song of Bernadette* (1943), played the cardinal. The Catholic actress, Bonita Granville, was cast as a music teacher tortured seemingly to death for refusing to betray the cardinal, and Paul Kelly played a journalist in Hungary at the time of the trial. *Guilty of Treason* was co-produced by Granville's husband, Jack Wrather, who, along with his wife and Kelly, is buried at Holy Cross Cemetery in Culver City. Lavery's funeral Mass was held at Our Lady of Grace Cathedral in Encino, California.

The film is a frame narrative, beginning and ending at the Oversees Club, where journalist Tom Kelly (Kelly) is reporting on conditions in Budapest at the time of the trial, the axis around which revolves the story of the hopeless love of a Catholic music teacher (Granville) for a Russian colonel (Richard Derr). Their religious differences are irresolvable and can only end in death: hers probably by torture, and his by being thrown from a window like the Czech foreign minister, Jan Masaryk. Although the teacher and the colonel are fictitious characters, Lavery made them representative of a people's republic that is really a police state, where the innocent are tortured until bogus confessions are extracted from them or they die. Neither Lavery nor director Felix Feist resorted to torture by suggestion. In fact, the torture scenes recall exploitation films like *Hitler's Children* and *Behind the Rising Sun*, both written by Lavery, who did not shy away from atrocities if they exposed the oppressors as marble-hearted fiends. The cardinal's secretary is lashed, and the music teacher is subjected to various forms of torture, including being placed under a shower and bombarded with water. Even when chained to a wall, she refuses to sign a false confession, her head dropping in exhaustion and suggesting death.

There was little difference between Hungary under the Nazi occupation and after the Soviet takeover. Hungarians who had collaborated with the Nazis transferred their allegiance to the Soviets, covering both bases by signing their messages "Heil Hitler! Heil Stalin!" as if there were no difference between one dictator and another. And, according to the film, there wasn't.

At the trial, Bickford—in a towering performance in which he seems to be looming over everyone even after he has been subjected to physical and psychological torture—finds his voice, which otherwise had been muted. Before he was apprehended, the cardinal had left a note stating that any confession attributed to him is "a consequence of human frailty." Although the cardinal broke under pressure, only a simpleton would have believed his confession. And with Bickford delivering the peroration, as if he were in a pulpit, the audience could not. Like so many anti-Soviet movies, *Guilty of Treason*, despite its modest production values and low-end distributor (Eagle-Lion), did not stint on truth. It may not have been gospel truth, but one doubts the Evangelists would have protested.

The most prestigious of the early anti-Soviet movies was MGM's *The Red Danube* (1949), with a starry cast that included Walter Pidgeon, Peter Lawford, Ethel Barrymore, Louis Calhern, Angela Lansbury, and the young Janet Leigh. It was adapted from Bruce Marshall's novel, *Vespers in Vienna*

(1947), which, like Emmett Lavery's *Guilty of Treason* screenplay, was Catholic to the core. Marshall was a Roman Catholic convert active in church affairs. The film's Catholicism is muted until the end, when it is worked into the dénouement to circumvent objections to the suicide of one of the main characters. Set in the aftermath of World War II, when Vienna, like Berlin, was a divided city with British, American, French, and Russian sectors, *The Red Danube* dramatized the plight of Russians living in the British zone, who were about to be repatriated to the Soviet Union. A ballerina (Leigh), the daughter of anti-communist Russian parents, is performing in Vienna under the name Maria Buhlen. A British major (Peter Lawford) falls in love with her and nearly succeeds in saving her from deportation. When his efforts fail, Maria leaps to her death from a window.

The ending posed problems for the adapters, Gina Kaus and Arthur Wimperis, who had to ensure that the film would pass muster with the Roman Catholic National Legion of Decency, founded in 1934 for the purpose of rating films in terms of their moral content. In 1949, there were four categories: A-I (morally unobjectionable for general patronage), A-II (morally unobjectionable for adults and adolescents), B (morally objectionable in part for all), and C (condemned). Later, an A-III category (morally unobjectionable for adults) was added. When *The Red Danube* was released, many Catholics still followed the legion's ratings and falsely assumed that seeing a "B" or "C" movie was sinful. That misconception was the result of a pledge that was administered each year around 8 December during the Feast of the Immaculate Conception. The congregation was asked to "condemn indecent and immoral motion pictures," "form a right conscience" about movies that are morally dangerous, and avoid venues that exhibit such movies. The pledge was non-binding, but many assumed it was binding because of the way in which it was administered.

The legion was especially critical of movies that employed suicide as a plot resolution, unless there was some indication that the act is morally wrong. Such films were generally rated "B." The legion ignored classics like *Julius Caesar* (1953), with the double suicides of Brutus and Cassius. But Arthur Miller was not Shakespeare, and although *All My Sons* is a major American play, the legion slapped a "B" rating on the 1948 movie version because of "suicide in plot solution." *All This and Heaven Too* (1940) was rated "B" for the same reason: "Suicide presented in a sympathetic and heroic manner." In *The Red Danube*, a Russian professor shoots himself rather than return to an uncertain fate in a detention camp or a gulag. Maria Buhlen committed the same act, but more dramatically. Maria is also a Catholic, residing in a Catholic convent. To the legion, her religion is incompatible with her action, unless there is a deathbed repentance. Oddly, suicide to avoid rape did not seem to bother the legion. In *So Proudly We Hail* (1943), Red Cross nurses stationed on Corregidor ponder their fate under the Japanese, aware of what happened in Nanking when Japanese soldiers raped twenty thousand Chinese women. One of the nurses comments soberly, "I was at Nanking. I saw what happened to the women there. When the Red Cross protested, the Japanese called it the privilege of serving his Imperial Majesty's troops. It's an honor you die from." One of the nurses (Veronica Lake), knowing that all of them could suffer a similar fate, places a grenade under her shirt and walks out of their compound, her hands raised in surrender. When the Japanese soldiers surround her, she pulls the pin, blowing them up along with herself, but enabling the others to escape. The Legion of Decency did not object. This was war, after all; it was also a case of one sacrificing her life for many. *So Proudly We Hail* was classified A II.

In *Vespers in Vienna*, Maria shoots herself through the breast and, like an operatic heroine, lives long enough to bid a "you must not weep" farewell to her beloved. Aware of the gravity of her action, a nun summons a priest, who hears Maria's confession and administers last rites. The novel did not specify the nature of Maria's confession, but the film did. Maria not only confesses, but also begs forgiveness. Mother Auxilia (the saintly Ethel Barrymore) gently admonishes Maria as she lay dying: "My child, you have been guilty of a grave sin, but Our Lord in His mercy has given you time to ask for forgiveness." Maria replies, "I have asked forgiveness for my sin. I am sorry, very sorry, for what I have done," Reverend Mother prays in German, repeating the last of Christ's words on the cross, "Into thy hands I commend my spirit."

The legion classified *The Red Danube* A-1. It is amazing what repentance can accomplish—but not at the box office. Audiences preferred a Danube that was blue.

The communist (Greta Garbo) and the count (Melvyn Douglas), who introduces her to the joys of capitalism in *Ninotchka* (1939). MGM/Photofest. © MGM. Photographer: Milton Brown.

A faceoff between collective farmers in Ukraine and the Nazi invaders in *The North Star* (1943). RKO Radio Pictures Inc./Photofest. © RKO Radio Pictures Inc.

Robert Taylor testifying before HUAC in 1947. Photofest.

Ayn Rand testifying before HUAC in 1947. Photofest.

A lobby card for *The Red Menace* (1949). Republic/Photofest. © Republic Pictures.

Dana Andrews and Gene Tierney as a Russian defector and his wife in the fact-based *The Iron Curtain* (1948). Twentieth Century-Fox Film Corporation/Photofest. © Twentieth Century-Fox Film Corporation.

Osa Massen and Lloyd Bridges, who have landed on Mars instead of the moon in *Rocketship X–M* (1950). Lippert Pictures Inc./Photofest. © Lippert Pictures Inc. Photographer: Buddy Longworth.

Michael Rennie as Klaatu in *The Day the Earth Stood Still* (1951). Twentieth Century-Fox Film Corporation/Photofest. © Twentieth Century-Fox Film Corporation.

Frank Lovejoy as Matt Cvetic in *I Was a Communist for the FBI* (1951). Warner Bros./Photofest. © Warner Bros.

Gene Evans as Sergeant Zack in one of the best Korean War movies, *The Steel Helmet* (1951). Lippert Pictures/Photofest. © Lippert Pictures.

A lobby card for *The Thing* (1951). RKO Radio Pictures/Photofest. © RKO Radio Pictures.

Robert Taylor as Colonel Paul Tibbets, the pilot of the Enola Gay, and Eleanor Parker as his wife, in *Above and Beyond* (1952). MGM/Photofest. © MGM.

Robert Walker swearing to his mother (Helen Hayes) that he is not a communist in *My Son John* (1952). Paramount/Photofest. © Paramount Pictures.

Frank Sinatra as Major Bennett Marco and Laurence Harvey as programmed assassin Raymond Shaw, in *The Manchurian Candidate* (1952). M. C. Prods/UA/Photofest. © M. C. Prods/United Artists.

Richard Kiley as a communist thug brutalizing Jean Peters in *Pickup on South Street* (1952). Twentieth Century-Fox/Photofest. © Twentieth Century-Fox.

The beast running amuck in *The Beast from 20,000 Fathoms* (1953). Photofest.

Richard Carlson as Herbert J. Philbrick in the popular television series *I Led Three Lives* (1953–56). Photofest.

William Holden and Grace Kelly as a navy lieutenant and his wife in the Korean War drama *The Bridges at Toko-Ri* (1954). Photofest/Paramount Pictures. © Paramount Pictures.

Paul Mantee as a Robinson Crusoe figure and Victor Lundin as Friday in *Robinson Crusoe on Mars* (1954). Paramount Pictures/Photofest. © Paramount Pictures.

Gaby Rodgers opening the Pandora's box in *Kiss Me Deadly* (1955). Photofest.

Kevin McCarthy and Dana Wynter in flight in *Invasion of the Body Snatchers* (1956). Allied Artists/ Photofest. © Allied Artists.

Bette Davis as a librarian who refuses to remove a controversial book in *Storm Center* (1956). Columbia Pictures/Photofest. © Columbia Pictures.

Cary Grant and Eva Marie Saint descending Mt. Rushmore in *North by Northwest* (1959). MGM/Photofest. © MGM.

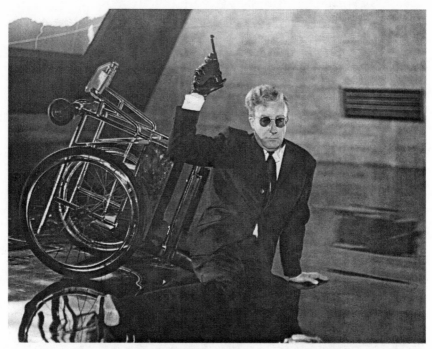

"Mein Führer, I can walk!" Peter Sellers in *Dr. Strangelove* or: *How I Learned to Stop Worrying and Love the Bomb* (1964). Columbia Pictures/Photofest. © Columbia Pictures.

Gregory Peck and Ava Gardner as doomed lovers in the apocalyptic *On the Beach* (1959). United Artists/Photofest. © United Artists.

Gregory Peck as the historical Lieutenant Joe Clemons in *Pork Chop Hill* (1959). United Artists/Photofest. © United Artists.

John Saxon as a sociopath turned serial killer in *War Hunt* (1962), the most powerful of the Korean War movies. United Artists/Photofest. © United Artists.

Henry Fonda faced with the prospect of nuclear war in *Fail-Safe* (1964). Columbia Pictures/Photofest. © Columbia Pictures.

John Wayne as Colonel Mike Kirby in *The Green Berets* (1968). Warner Bros./Photofest. © Warner Bros.

Richard Burton as the dissipated title character in *The Spy Who Came in from the Cold* (1965). Paramount Pictures/Photofest. © Paramount Pictures. Photographer: Bob Penn.

Paul Newman and Julie Andrews, safe after escaping from East Germany in *Torn Curtain* (1965). Universal Pictures/Photofest. © Universal Pictures.

A French intelligence agent (Frederick Stafford) and his anti-Castro lover (Karin Dor) in *Topaz* (1969). Universal Pictures/Photofest.
© Universal Pictures.

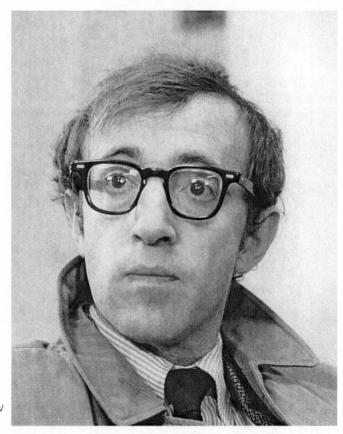

Woody Allen, playing a front for blacklisted television writers, appearing before HUAC in *The Front* (1976). Columbia Pictures/ Photofest. © Columbia Pictures.

Keri Russell as KGB operative Elizabeth Jennings in FX's *The Americans* (2013–). FX Network/Photofest. © FX Network.

Hope Davis and Scott Cohen as the imperiled couple in NBC's short-lived *Allegiance* (2015). NBC/Photofest. © NBC.

Chapter 14

WALKING A TIGHTROPE

ON 11 APRIL 1952, A PAID ADVERTISEMENT APPEARED IN THE *NEW YORK Times* bearing the name of director Elia Kazan, who the previous day had appeared in executive session before HUAC. In the ad, Kazan admitted that he joined the party in summer 1934 and left eighteen months later. He was initially attracted to communism because it "claimed to have a cure for depressions and a cure for Nazism and Fascism." He then learned to his dismay that the cure consisted of police state tactics and thought control. Without using words like "inform" or "informant," which at the time had taken on Dantean connotations of betrayal and treachery, Kazan called upon those in possession of the "facts" about communism "to make them known, either to the public or to the appropriate government agency," insisting it was their "obligation" to do so. The ad was a circumlocutory way of saying that if you know anything—or rather, anything about anyone—say so. In other words, inform.

On 10 April, Kazan was so cooperative that at the end of the session, Representative Francis E. Walter thanked him for helping the committee alert "the American people to the machinations of this Communist conspiracy for world domination." One would have thought that the ad was sufficient, except that Kazan had given testimony before HUAC on 14 January 1952, stating that he would not divulge the names of any party members. Three months later, he had second thoughts, requesting that the committee give him the opportunity to complete his testimony by providing information he had previously withheld.

One can understand why Kazan asked for a rehearing. A year earlier, actor and Oscar nominee Larry Parks, after expressing his reluctance to identify party members, broke down after a day of interrogation and named twelve. Writer Budd Schulberg did not have to be grilled; he offered fifteen names. And then there was director Edward Dmytryk.

On 25 April 1951, Dmytryk—who, in June 1950, had been sentenced to six months in Mills Point Prison Camp in West Virginia for refusing to answer the "Are you now, or have you ever been" question—realized after his release (he only served four and a half months) that a screenwriter can use a pseudonym or a front, but a director must show his face on the set. It was a matter of either recanting or working abroad until the witch-hunt ended. He had already made two films in England before he was sentenced and was eager to be reinstated in Hollywood, where he had roots. Dmytryk came before HUAC offering his full cooperation and admitting that he had joined the party in early summer 1944 and left in fall 1945. During his testimony, he named twenty-six individuals, some of them members of the Hollywood Ten, of which he was once a member. But since they had already been indicted, he felt he was only repeating common knowledge. Neither did he think it wrong to name his friend, Adrian Scott, who produced four of his RKO films: *Murder, My Sweet, Cornered, Crossfire,* and *So Well Remembered.*

Eighteen days after Dmytryk's justification of his volte-face was published in the *Saturday Evening Post* (10 May 1951), Albert Maltz responded in a letter. Maltz wondered why, if Dmytryk left the party in 1945, he didn't say so in 1947 when he first appeared before HUAC. Then, he could have named names and gone on with his career, avoiding the stigma of the blacklist. In his autobiography, *It's a Hell of a Life but Not a Bad Living,* Dmytryk never explained his actions, which were especially puzzling since at the time he was not a communist. His reasons were complex. Dmytryk believed in the right of free expression, which was being undermined by HUAC. To him, that was an issue that had nothing to do with communism, only with safeguarding First Amendment rights, which in less parlous times would have been taken for granted. His gesture of solidarity linked his communist past with his colleagues' present, making him one of them intellectually, but not politically—a distinction that Dmytryk could not make in 1947 without separating himself from the group. Although Dmytryk could have endorsed their position while separating himself from their politics, he chose solidarity. Perhaps it was fear of being branded a coward that motivated him to stand with the others. Dmytryk had developed a sense of brotherhood, which may have come from his brief period in the party, but more likely came from the common bond shared by a group of men who had all been subpoenaed to appear before HUAC and had met earlier to formulate plans to present a united front. That sense of commonality gave him a high that no drug can induce, not even the opiate of the party.

In 1947, Dmytryk believed in unity. Four years later, he was a separatist, ready to cooperate. By 1952, he was back at work, directing some of Hollywood's biggest stars in mid- and late career films—for example, Kirk Douglas in *The Juggler* (1952), Spencer Tracy in *Broken Lance* (1954), Deborah Kerr and Van Johnson in *The End of the Affair* (1954), Humphrey Bogart in *The Caine Mutiny* (1953) and *The Left Hand of God* (1955), Clark Gable in *Soldier of Fortune* (1955), Elizabeth Taylor in *Raintree County* (1956), Marlon Brando in *The Young Lions* (1957), Bette Davis and Susan Hayward in *Where Love Has Gone* (1964), and Gregory Peck in *Mirage* (1965). He was vilified by his former comrades, but at least he was working at his craft.

Kazan knew that in the climate of the times he would have to do what Dmytryk did. He could have continued in the theater, which was not affected by the blacklist. Film was another matter. Kazan's movie career was thriving, and he had no intention of jeopardizing it over a brief excursion into radical politics. He had received an Oscar for *Gentleman's Agreement* (1947) and was nominated for another for *A Streetcar Named Desire* (1951). Kazan had more movies to make, more plays to stage. If purging himself before HUAC was the price, it came cheap.

Kazan's biographer believed that the *New York Times* ad was "a huge mistake." It was really overkill, but it served a purpose. Although it seemed like an addendum to Kazan's testimony, which was in the form of a prepared statement, it was really a clarion call to others to follow his example and reveal what they knew. If an Oscar-winning director could turn informant, naming eleven names, so could the less credentialed.

The sworn statement ended with a list of Kazan's stage and film work, emphasizing their American character. The first play he directed, *Casey Jones* (1938), was "thoroughly and wonderfully American." His first film, *A Tree Grows in Brooklyn* (1945), was "a typically American story . . . and a glorification of America not in material terms, but in spiritual ones." *Gentlemen's Agreement* (1947), an unsubtle expose of anti-Semitism, "is in the healthy American tradition [and] opposite to the picture which Communists present of Americans." *Pinky* (1949), in which a young woman of mixed race refuses to pass for white when she returns to the Deep South, was generally well received, except by "Communists, who attacked it virulently." And despite its quasi-leftist slant, *Viva Zapata* (1952) is "an anti-Communist picture."

If Kazan had come before HUAC a year later, he could have added *Man on a Tightrope* (1953) to the list. The film was anti-communist, but with a deeply felt humanity and a refreshing lack of shrillness, both of which were rare in Cold War films. *Man* was shot on location in Bavaria with a cast capable of the kind of realistic acting for which Kazan is noted. One could even believe that Hollywood types like Terry Moore and Gloria Grahame were members of a traveling circus. The screenplay was the work of the Pulitzer Prize-winning playwright Robert E. Sherwood (*Idiot's Delight, There Shall Be No Night, Abe Lincoln in Illinois*), who also received an Oscar for his screenplay for *The Best Years of Our Lives*. Sherwood avoided the temptation to ennoble the members of the Circus Cernik, a provincial troupe traveling through communist-controlled Czechoslovakia. The manager of the circus, Karel Cernik (Fredric March), is apolitical. Since he can do nothing about the nationalization of his circus, he agrees to add some Marxist skits, but removes them when they fail to get laughs. Essentially a proud but conciliatory man, Cernik maintains his dignity even when negotiating with communist functionaries. But gradually he develops contempt for a regime that has deprived him of the rights he once enjoyed. When he learns that there is a spy in his company, he realizes he must find a way to cross the border into Bavaria. His opportunity arises when Fesker (Adolphe Menjou), a member of the Soviet secret police who had been informed of Cernik's plan, issues him a travel permit, intending to have him apprehended at the border crossing.

From the outset, Kazan had been monitoring the suspense, gauging its rise until it can go no higher. The finale begins as the caravan makes its way past the Soviet guards, who are distracted by the antics of the clowns, finding them a welcome diversion from their humdrum routine. Cernik makes a dash to the border, with the caravan rattling across the bridge to Bavaria— but with one casualty. Cernik is shot by Krofta (Richard Boone), who had been with the circus for twenty years before defecting to the Soviets. Cernik's wife, Zama (Gloria Grahame), takes over as manager: "He's dead. He got us across but he paid for it. He was glad to pay. We give a performance tonight."

Among the great ironies in the history of casting are Richard Burton and Rex Harrison cast as a gay couple in *Staircase* (1969), Frank Sinatra as a Catholic priest in *Miracle of the Bells* (1948), Shirley Temple as a neurotic teenager in *That Hagen Girl* (1947), and Adolphe Menjou as a communist in *Man on a Tightrope*. At the HUAC hearings, Menjou was a friendly witness, who told the committee (21 October 1947) that if there ever were a communist takeover, "I would move to the State of Texas . . . because I think the Texans would kill them on sight." Kazan enjoyed emphasizing the disparity between Menjou and his character, admitting that it was one of his "private jokes," but at the same time commending Menjou for playing a communist "perfectly."

Like Dmytryk, Kazan worked steadily after his second appearance before HUAC. He admitted that "the only good and original films" he made came after his testimony. He was partially correct, although *Boomerang!* (1947) and *Panic in the Streets* (1950) are exemplary semi-documentaries. In addition, *A Streetcar Named Desire* is a model of adaptation, except for the ending. And Marlon Brando's performance in *Viva Zapata* made one forget that the movie was really about a revolutionary icon of the Left. Audiences may be more familiar with the later Kazan because the films dating from that period appear more frequently on television: *On the Waterfront, East of Eden, Baby Doll, Splendor in the Grass, A Face in the Crowd,* and *America, America.* He also continued working in the theater (*Tea and Sympathy, Cat on a Hot Tin Roof, Sweet Bird of Youth, The Dark at the Top of the Stairs, J. B., After the Fall*). *Cat* and *J. B.* were Pulitzer Prize winners, but the others, fine plays all, were not of the same stature as *The Skin of Our Teeth, All My Sons, Streetcar,* and *Death of a Salesman.* But few directors in film or theater can boast of uniform excellence throughout their careers. Regardless of what one thinks of his stand before HUAC, Elia Kazan is one of our greatest film and stage directors.

Conversely, Edward Dmytryk did his best work before recanting. His 1940s films partake of a reckless vitality, characteristic of a young director who did not shrink from the sensational and, in fact, reveled in it (e.g., *Hitler's Children, Behind the Rising Sun, Captive Wild Woman*). Two of his collaborations with producer Adrian Scott, a tragic victim of the blacklist who resorted to pseudonyms and fronts for the rest of his career, reveal Dmytryk's mastery of scorching realism: *Murder, My Sweet* (1944), textbook noir with extremes of black and white (it opens in an interrogation room with a tabletop that looks as if it were made of Lucite); and *Crossfire* (1947), which laid bare the roots of anti-Semitism in a pathological hatred of otherness. Dmytryk's later films may have had big name stars, but except perhaps for *The Caine Mutiny,* the stars twinkled more than they shone.

Chapter 15

THE FORGOTTEN WAR

WAR IS DECLARED BY NORTH KOREANS; FIGHTING ON BORDER
The Russian-sponsored North Korean Communists invaded the
American-supported Republic of South Korea and their radio
followed it up by broadcasting a declaration . . .
—*New York Times*, 25 June 1950

THE NEWS WAS ONLY A SURPRISE TO THOSE WHO THOUGHT THAT THE
war to end all wars was World War II, not its disastrous predecessor, the
Great War, which was only the prelude to more war. But the Soviet Union's
detonation of an atomic bomb at the end of August 1949, and the formation of the People's Republic of China three weeks later, did not encourage
optimism. Korea had already been partitioned at the thirty-eighth parallel
in 1945, resulting in a Soviet backed North and a United States supported South. A line of demarcation between two states—one communist, the
other allegedly democratic—resulted not only in a geographically divided
peninsula, but an ideologically divided one as well.

The free elections that were to have been held in 1948 only occurred in
the South, with the election of the American-educated Syngman Rhee as
president of what was designated the Republic of Korea. The Soviets merely
installed their puppet, Kim-Il-Sung, as head of North Korea. The only difference between the two strongmen was political. Both were dictators, one
less oppressive than the other, and each working to bring about reunifica-
tion under his own form of government. Border clashes were inevitable.
First, there were skirmishes. Finally, there was all-out war. The American
withdrawal from Korea in June 1949 left its ally weak. The South Korean
army was too busy routing out communist guerillas, and Rhee was too involved in jailing communists and communist sympathizers to give much
thought to war. The Soviet Union, on the other hand, supplied the North

Koreans with arms and military advisors, making them a superior fighting force.

The events of 25 June 1950 pointed to a civil war of an unusual kind, a United Nations police action, which involved 1,319,000 Americans, of which "33,629 did not return."

On 27 June 1950, the *New York Times* made it official: "Truman orders U.S. Air/Navy Units to Fight in Aid of Korea; U.N. Council Supports Him." There was no need for Congress to declare war. The president had already done so as commander-in-chief of the armed forces. And whenever there is war, declared or otherwise, Hollywood signs up. A Korean War plot template was unnecessary; the one for World War II would do: home front/combat/home front cum combat/home front romance/combat romance.

Samuel Goldwyn decided that the public needed a follow-up to *The Best Years of Our Lives* (1946), which portrayed the adjustment problems of three returning World War II veterans: a banker (Fredric March), a former soda fountain attendant (Dana Andrews), and a sailor who had lost both arms (Harold Russell). *I Want You* (1951) would begin four years later with a family adjusting to the start of a new war, in which their sons will have to serve. The follow-up was no *Best Years*. The new trio did not command the same interest or sympathy as the men in *Best Years*, who felt more at home in the military than in civilian life. There was little screenwriter Irwin Shaw could do with a World War I veteran (Robert Keith) with two sons, one of whom (Dana Andrews) had shown his patriotism by serving in World War II, while the other (Farley Granger) tries to dodge the draft until he realizes that his selfishness could cause him to lose the respect of the girl he loves. *I Want You* was little more than a self-ennobling recruitment film. One could predict that the draft dodger would have a change of heart, and that his older brother would re-enlist rather than have his children ask, "What were you doing, Daddy, when the world was shaking?" (As if any child would use such an expression. Usually, it's "What did you do in the war, Daddy?") There was no shaking at the box office. *I Want You* was a great disappointment to Goldwyn, who expected at least a nomination for best picture. It was only nominated for sound recording, losing to *The Great Caruso*, which had the most glorious soundtrack of any movie that year.

Hollywood knew how to divert attention from a porous script by interspersing montage sequences, newsreel footage, and staged combat, thus providing enough action to cover the gaps in the narrative. One simply waited for the fighting to cease so the story could resume—not that there was much of one in *A Yank in Korea*, released by Columbia in February

1951. This "Yank" (Lon McCallister) had nothing in common with Americans who went abroad to study (*A Yank at Eaton, A Yank at Oxford*) or join the Royal Air Force (*A Yank in the RAF*). He was a cocky kid who wound up in Korea after a reporter mistakenly identified him as his hometown's first enlistee. Rather than lose face and the love of his life, the protagonist finds himself with men who do not know why they're in a strange land, except that "somebody has to do the job."

There is more combat than plot, with McCallister graduating from callow youth to war hero. At the end, he visits the family of a dead buddy, who had left behind a letter for his children in case he did not return. With emotions in check, McCallister reads the letter, making no attempt at eloquence. The letter was a plot resolver, with "The End" coming on so fast that one wonders if anything was accomplished—except that some of the enemy were killed, a munitions dump was destroyed, a locomotive was repaired, and a boy became a man. *A Yank in Korea* made no attempt to justify the war. It's a job that has to be done, and if "your conscience tells you something is right," you do it. But what was "right" about Korea is never explained. And by all means leave a letter for your family, telling them that if you don't return, you're up there helping God.

A "job" is what it was. There was no Pearl Harbor to remember, no hit song like "Praise The Lord And Pass The Ammunition." No glory, either—only drudgery captured in black and white photography that gave the landscape a bleak, wintry look, even when the action took place in another season. It was not just a dirty war. It was a visually drab one without calibrations of tone. There was also nothing cosmopolitan about Korea—no Paris, London, or Lisbon; no OSS operatives, French resistance fighters, ladies with a past, or men without a future; no actors on the order of Clark Gable, Errol Flynn, Cary Grant, Spencer Tracy, Robert Taylor, Ingrid Bergman, Greer Garson, Claudette Colbert, Hedy Lamarr, Gene Tierney, or Ann Sheridan, who all served their country so memorably on celluloid during World War II (and Gable in the Air Corps as well) and whose star power made an allied victory seem inevitable, even when the headlines suggested otherwise. If Korea evokes any cinematic memories, it is of grim-faced soldiers with rags wrapped around their feet, trudging through unforgiving terrain and making the best of a questionable job.

The early Korean War films were World War II retreads, using such standard plot templates as men at odds with one another (*Retreat, Hell!*, *The Steel Helmet*): a lost patrol in search of a leader (*The Steel Helmet*): the gung-ho youth tested in the refining fire of combat (*Retreat, Hell!*); the kid next door who becomes a war hero (*A Yank in Korea*); wives left behind (*Retreat, Hell!, Sabre Jet*); and boy meets girl in wartime (*One Minute to Zero*). Inferior films like *Tank Battalion* (1958) and *Marines, Let's Go* (1961) simply used Korea as background for action movies that would have been programmers in the 1940s. The best of them were site-specific, whether filmed in Griffith Park in Los Angeles (*The Steel Helmet*), Camp Pendleton in North San Diego County (*Retreat, Hell!*), or on a Twentieth Century-Fox soundstage (*Fixed Bayonets*), so that the characters seem to have stepped out of World War II and into Korea without any alteration of personality. The enemy was now the North Koreans, and as of October 1950, the Chinese, who had entered the war.

The Korean war films of 1951–52 were, understandably, short on details, since history was being made on a daily basis. It was the same in the early days of World War II. Wake Island fell to the Japanese two weeks after Pearl Harbor; then Paramount released *Wake Island* in August 1942. The battle could only be the climax; it was preceded by a story of male bonding between characters from different social and military strata—a major and a construction engineer—and for comic relief, two privates who die together, sharing the fate of their superiors. By 1942, audiences were familiar with the "band of brothers" plot, which they had seen in movies as varied as *What Price Glory?*, *The Dawn Patrol*, *Gunga Din*, and *Beau Geste*. The same was true in the early days of Korea. In the absence of facts—at least facts that could be dramatized—*A Yank in Korea* fell back on war as rite of passage, tracing the main character's journey to manhood, which was not peculiar to Korea. In fact, the film could have been made ten years earlier as "A Yank at Pearl Harbor."

But unlike the American World War II film, which got off to an unmemorable start with Republic's *Remember Pearl Harbor* (1942), the first film about Korea was a masterpiece. *The Steel Helmet* was written, directed, and produced by Samuel Fuller. More accurately, it was "written quickly" (reportedly in a week) and shot in ten days in October 1950, opening in January 1951, a month before the programmer *A Yank in Korea* was released. In fact, *Yank* did not open in New York until 1 April. *The Steel Helmet* had its New York premiere at Loew's State on 24 January. Although *The Steel Helmet* cost a mere $104,000, it ended up grossing $6 million. *Remember Pearl Harbor*, remembered today for the patriotic song that inspired the title, was made by a studio, albeit one on Poverty Row. *The Steel Helmet* was an independent film, produced by Deputy Corp. and released through Lippert Pictures, the creation of Robert L. Lippert, who graduated from organ accompanist for silent movies to exhibitor, and finally to producer with his own distribution company.

After a dedication to the United States Army infantry, *The Steel Helmet* opens, appropriately enough, with a shot of a helmet. The bullet-riddled helmet belongs to Sergeant Zach (Gene Evans), whose eyes slowly come into view, as he drags himself up to the top of a hill, his hands bound behind his back, zigzagging along the ground. As yet, there is no dialogue. The next shot is of a pair of legs belonging to someone carrying a M-1 rifle. The "someone" is a boy, who speaks the first words in the film: "South Korean." But to the bound Zach, the boy is a "gook." The boy, whom he names Short Round, then asserts that he is not a "gook" (apparently he has heard the racial slur before), but a South Korean. After freeing Zach, the boy insists upon accompanying him, despite Zach's objections. Short Round explains that when a Buddhist saves another's life, they must travel together, because the life that was saved is in the other's hands. Short Round is so endearing that even the misanthropic Zach cannot deny him.

Prejudice in its various forms permeates *The Steel Helmet*, which is a recreation of the World War II scenario of unity in diversity, best exemplified in *Bataan* (1943) with a patrol consisting of whites, a Moro, a Latino, and an African American. *The Steel Helmet* has an even more diverse mix, consisting of an African American medic; a racist sergeant; a lieutenant who realizes that the sergeant, crude as he is, is a better leader than himself; a World War II conscientious objector with the literary surname of Bronte; a bald private obsessed with hair-growing remedies; and a Japanese American sergeant who massages the private's head with mud, claiming the treatment worked for his bald mother. Tempers flare, insults are traded, but differences—racial and otherwise—are resolved as the men band together to fight a common enemy.

Like many war movies, *The Steel Helmet* revolves around a single operation: this time commandeering a Buddhist temple as an observation post. Although the temple seems deserted, the statue of the Buddha that greets them is so sinisterly awesome that it suggests otherwise. Danger is lurking. A North Korean major hiding on the second level will soon emerge for the kill. As the men enter the temple and see the statue confronting them—as if questioning the appropriateness of their being in a place of worship where none of them belongs except Short Round—they realize they are in a sacred space. One by one, they remove their helmets in respect. Since Fuller knew that the Buddha was too powerful a symbol to use just once, he cuts to it periodically to emphasize the irony of a temple being used as a military outpost that eventually becomes a charnel house. The Buddha exudes a stony serenity, neither sanctioning nor condemning what takes place within his sacred precinct, but letting it play out at his altar as he observes from on high the violence that men wreak on each other. *The Steel Helmet* is a war film without a villain. The North Korean major, who looks like a teenager in uniform, is a hard- line communist, who (don't ask) speaks perfect English and knows enough about racism in America to remind the African American medic that he has to ride in the back of the bus. The medic admits he's right, but "a hundred years ago, I couldn't even ride a bus. At least now I can sit in the back. Maybe in fifty years, sit in the middle. Someday, even up front. There are some things you just can't rush, Buster." To the post-civil rights generation, the medic may seem like an Uncle Tom, but Fuller is implying that in the army he acquired both a skill that made him the equal of any white man, and a sense of self-worth that made racial injustice at least bearable. The North Korean then baits Sergeant Tanaka about the internment of Japanese Americans during the last war. Tanaka admits that major "struck a nerve," but goes on to say that he served with one of the most highly decorated units in World War II, the 442nd Regimental Combat Team, comprised of second-generation Japanese Americans.

The military was upset about the reference to the internment camps, claiming that this was the first time a film referred to their existence. The allegation was untrue. Five months after President Roosevelt signed Executive Order 9066 on 19 February 1942—which authorized the internment of West Coast Japanese Americans in relocation camps in remote sections of California, Arizona, Idaho, Wyoming, Colorado, and Arkansas— Twentieth Century-Fox released *Little Tokyo, USA* (1942). At the end of the film, a newspaper headline barrels on to the screen: "All Japs to Be Evacuated / Manazanar Settlement for Japanese Evacuees in Owen's River Valley." Brenda Joyce, best remembered as Jane in the Tarzan movies of the 1940s, justifies the evacuation:

> And so, in the interests of national safety, all Japanese, whether citizens or not, are being evacuated from strategic military zones on the Pacific Coast. Unfortunately, in time of war, the loyal must suffer inconvenience with the disloyal. America's attitude toward this wholesale evacuation can best be summed up, I believe, in the last four lines of a poem by Robert Nathan, entitled, "Watch, America": "God, who gave our fathers freedom / God who made our fathers brave, / What they built with love and anguish / Let our children watch and save. Be vigilant, America."

The poem has nothing to do with the internment—unless the vigilance that Nathan stresses is to be directed at the Nisei, who were rumored to be ready to spray produce with arsenic, blow up dams, and poison the water supply.

The military was also disturbed by the killing of the North Korean major, technically a POW, as if Americans had never killed POWs before. If one views the major as the villain, his villainy is the villainy of war, in which each side tries to kill the other. To the major, the Americans are the enemy. When Short Round is killed, Zach shows no emotion, until he realizes the major is responsible. Then, in one of his frequent irrational moments, he shoots the major. When the lieutenant excoriates him for killing a POW, Zach realizes what this act will do to his career, the only one he has. "If you die, I'll kill you," he shouts at the soon-to-be corpse. Zach's killing of the POW unhinges him. He becomes as stone-faced as the Buddha, imagining he is back at Normandy. The extreme close-ups of Evans's eyes staring into space, as if there was no horizon—a kind of ocular stupor—was a perfect metaphor for war itself. When a platoon arrives at the temple, the four survivors straggle out, becoming members of another march into the unknown. Before he leaves, Zach pauses at the lieutenant's grave, marked by his helmet set atop his rife. Earlier, the lieutenant had asked Zach to exchange helmets, thinking that Zach's would bring him good luck. Zach refused. Now, in a silent gesture of repentance, Zack replaces the lieutenant's helmet with his own. "There Is No End to This Story," the end title reads. The war was far from over, and Fuller had more to say about it.

Fixed Bayonets (1951), Fuller's second Korean War film, was released eight months after *The Steel Helmet*. This time, the studio was Twentieth Century-Fox, with which Fuller had a seven-picture arrangement. *Fixed Bayonets* is another rite of passage movie, concerning not the change from smart aleck to hero, but from follower to leader. Early in the film, Corporal Denno (Richard Basehart) admits he can only take orders, not give them. He is so eager to avoid assuming command that when Sergeant Lonergan (Michael O'Shea) is wounded, he risks his own life crossing a minefield to rescue him, only to have Sergeant Rock (Gene Evans in a role similar to Zack in *The Steel Helmet*) inform him that he has brought back a corpse. Lonergan's death leaves only Rock in charge. Rock does all but hold a mirror up to Denno, forcing him to see what he is and what he must be: "Nobody goes out looking for responsibility. You're not a corporal for nothing." When Rock is killed, Denno becomes a leader by default, ordering the sergeant's body to be stripped of "everything we can use" before he is buried.

Since the military was unhappy with *The Steel Helmet*, Fox made certain that *Fixed Bayonets* had the Pentagon's imprimatur. Thus, the opening title was in the form of a dedication to "the Queen of Battles—the United States Infantry." "King" would have been more appropriate, but the Pentagon was pleased, particularly with Fox's expression of gratitude for its cooperation.

Fuller did not exploit the film's point of departure: a rearguard platoon left on its own to protect a division that had been ordered to retreat. The forty-eight men of the platoon were the equivalent of the "Battling bastards of Bataan, / No mama, no papa, no Uncle Sam," left on their own. On 11 March 1942, General Douglas MacArthur boarded a PT boat with his wife and son and left Corregidor for Mindanao, vowing, "I shall return." But by that time, many of the battling bastards had died on the Bataan Death March. Similarly, in *Fixed Bayonets*, the platoon is expendable; the division, like MacArthur, is not.

Fuller served in the First United States Infantry Division ("The Big Red One") during World War II, and he gave *The Steel Helmet* and *Fixed Bayonets* a real sense of place—even though Griffith Park doubled as Korea in *The Steel Helmet*, and *Fixed Bayonets* was filmed entirely on a Fox soundstage. Neither film could be mistaken for a World War II movie in disguise. Korea was a war of guts, not glory. In each film, the enemy is the communists. A captive in *The Steel Helmet* identifies himself as a "North Korean communist." In *Fixed Bayonets*, the men know they are fighting "Reds" and "commies." Fuller's heart is clearly with his foot soldiers; one senses that if he could, he would have joined them.

Fuller's achievement is even more impressive when contrasted with Columbia's *Mission over Korea* (1953), in which the army fliers are clean shaven, the photography is evenly textured with varying shades of gray, foxholes are non-existent, testosterone is mid-level, and actresses like Maureen O'Sullivan (as the uncomplaining wife of a captain on a mission [John Hodiak]) and Audrey Totter (as a nurse attracted to a playboy lieutenant [John Derek]) serve purely decorative purposes, like happy faces on a refrigerator. The plot is a World War II clone. A carefree lieutenant and swinging bachelor teams up with a serious-minded captain and family man in a war that everyone despises, but no one abandons. "I hate this police action. I'm no cop," one of the men complains. The war film, unless it was an adaptation of a classic novel like *All Quiet on the Western Front* or *From Here to Eternity*, followed a simple course: The hero either lives or dies, and wars are either won or lost, with defeat masked as bravery in the face of insurmountable odds. Within each possibility, there is a variety of plot permutations. In *Mission over Korea*, the lieutenant could survive after performing an act of heroism (Gene Kelly in *For Me and My Girl*), or return to civilian life with a disability (John Garfield in *Pride of the Marines*). The lieutenant could perform a selfless act that results in his death (Ronald Reagan in *International Squadron*), while the captain could be reunited with his wife and children (Fredric March in *The Best Years of Our Lives*). One could live, the other die (Pat O'Brien and Randolph Scott, respectively, in *Bombardier*). The writers of *Mission over Korea* chose the last scenario. The captain dies, despite the lieutenant's attempt to save him. The ending deprived audiences of seeing Maureen O'Sullivan again. But at least they saw what Tarzan's mate looked like in her early forties, which was not all that different from the way she looked in *Tarzan's New York Adventure* (1942), her last appearance in the series.

Retreat, Hell! (1952) contrasted the youthful desire for combat with the wariness of seasoned professionals, as the war entered its first phase. The script was a throwback to the "men–at–odds–with–each-other–who–grow–into–mutual–respect" plot. The men here are an unmarried colonel (Frank Lovejoy), whose family is his battalion, and a captain (Richard Carlson) with a family of his own. There was no way *Retreat, Hell!* would have been considered a World War II transplant, although it had the same kind of measured rhythm, whereby the plot was suspended periodically so the grenades could be lobbed, the screen could smoke up, tanks could roll, and bodies could drop, after which the plot would continue until it was time for another mortar round. Meanwhile, audiences wondered which of the principals would end up on a stretcher or in a body bag. Neither the colonel nor the captain ends up this way; even the boy-turned-man (Russ Tamblyn) is left wounded but proud. Tamblyn, who had to trace a character arc as if he were crossing the rainbow bridge to Valhalla, gives the best performance in the film.

Although *Retreat, Hell!* had the backing of the Defense Department and the marine corps, it did not shrink from expressing the marines' disillusionment when the rumor that the war would be over by Christmas 1950 proved to be false. Nor did it downplay the danger of frostbite, which in one case is so severe that amputation may be necessary, although that possibility is only fleetingly mentioned. It is also clear that no one had been informed that China had entered the war until the colonel notices that some of the dead are Chinese. Korea may not have been a war fought on two fronts, but it was one against a dual enemy, reducing the chances of an American victory.

Early World War II films such as *Wake Island* and *Bataan* portrayed what were, historically, defeats as preludes to ultimate victory ("Their spirit will lead us back to Bataan," the end title of the film assured us). *Retreat, Hell!* ends on a similarly ambivalent note. After being ordered to withdraw, the colonel passes the news on to the battalion. When one of the marines asks if this means a retreat, the colonel bellows, "Retreat, hell! We're attacking in another direction." The climactic line is a more defiant version of what Major General O. P. Smith said at the time: "We are not retreating. We are merely advancing in another direction." A chorus of "The Halls of Montezuma," which played over the opening credits, is reprised, as if to convince audiences that the war would end triumphantly. History decreed otherwise.

Joseph H. Lewis seemed an odd choice as director of *Retreat, Hell!* His strengths lay in melodrama (*So Dark the Night*) and film noir (*My Name Is Julia Ross, Gun Crazy*), Supposedly, after Jack Warner saw *Gun Crazy*, he put Lewis under contract. When no project was forthcoming, Lewis managed to get out of his contract, only to be offered *Retreat, Hell!* under a separate arrangement. Lewis brought in a profitable film for Warner Bros., despite the interference of producer-writer Milton Sperling, Jack Warner's son-in law. Lewis wanted the Chinese attack, one of the most awesome sights in the film, to be photographed in long shot, with the soldiers streaming down the hill in a suicidal charge, as if they were embracing death. Lewis covered himself with a few close-ups, but not enough for Sperling, who added some of his own. Still, Lewis was proud of the film, another mark of his versatility, which became even more apparent when he moved into television, directing episodes of *Bonanza, Gunsmoke, The Zane Grey Theater,* and *Big Valley.*

Seventeen years before audiences associated the mobile army surgical hospital with Robert Altman's *M*A*S*H* (1970), they learned in MGM's *Battle Circus* (1953) about the makeshift operating rooms that could be dismantled like circus tents when the unit was ordered to move on—or if the enemy was advancing, could be torched in compliance with the military's scorched earth policy. Written and directed by Richard Brooks with front-line realism, *Battle Circus* is a tribute to the doctors and nurses who performed delicate surgery under primitive conditions, never shirking their obligations and even treating prisoners who needed medical attention. In one breath-holding scene, a North Korean prisoner (Philip Ahn, who made a career of playing Asians, both friend and foe) bolts from his bed, seizes a grenade, and threatens to pull the pin as he raves incoherently, mainly out of fear and disorientation. This is the most chilling moment in the film. A nurse (June Allyson), equally frightened but trying to conceal her fear, approaches him, speaking as if to a child, until she persuades him to hand her the grenade.

Filmed at Fort (then Camp) Pickett in Blackstone, Virginia, *Battle Circus* brought the war home in a way that most Korean War films did not. The only false note was the romance between a hard-drinking and equally hard-loving major (Humphrey Bogart) and the nurse, the pert and winsome June Allyson, who seemed as if she should be off playing Nellie Forbush in *South Pacific*, announcing that she's "as corny as Kansas in August" and "as normal as blueberry pie." It was just that Bogart was eighteen years older than Allyson. He had a seen-it-all face, while Allyson looked as if she had never even had a pimple. Their love scenes were not so much May-September as father-daughter. It was not a question of Major Jed Webbe putting the moves on Lieutenant Ruth McGara, but of Humphrey Bogart coming on to June Allyson. The two acquitted themselves professionally, but their improbable romance detracted from a powerful film about a military unit that remained largely unknown until *M*A*S*H* (both the film and the TV series) arrived. If mobile surgical units were as lively in Korea as they seemed in *M*A*S*H*, the war might not have been so unpopular. The men and women in *Battle Circus* lived in constant fear for their lives, yet forged on, as if the specter of death were hovering elsewhere. Unlike the surgeons in *M*A*S*H*, they had no time for sex and football.

Nineteen fifty-four found MGM, once the Tiffany of studios and now surviving in diminished splendor, still programmed in Korean War mode. *Men of the Fighting Lady* (1954), released a year after *Battle Circus*, was one of the few Korean War movies filmed in color. It also had an impressive lineage—at least on paper—along with a seal of approval from the military. The script was a conflation of two stories: the Pulitzer-Prize winning author James A. Michener's "The Forgotten Heroes of Korea," and Commander Harry N. Burns's "The Case of the Blind Pilot." Michener, in fact, appears as a character played by Louis Calhern at the beginning and end of a flashback, replete with authentic footage of bombing raids, air attacks, takeoffs, rockets being fired, and a crash landing on a carrier, all of which had been skillfully edited into the film, thus authenticating it. The footage was taken during the war itself. It was not studio-generated or pulled arbitrarily from some film library to hold the attention of moviegoers interested in action rather than story. As it happened, audiences got both.

Men of the Fighting Lady did not mute the pilots' disillusionment as the war moved into its final phase. A World War II hero (Keenan Wynn) compares the last war, in which he won the Navy Cross, with the present one:

"We knew what we were fighting for then." As for Korea, "We're obsolete. It's a police action. No one wants to hear about it." One of the pilots uses the vernacular, calling the war a "nut house cheese game." In 1954, the war was over—or rather, an armistice had been signed. It was not that it was open season on Korea; it was simply that Korea had besmirched the national image that had been rendered immaculate after Japan's unconditional surrender in August 1945. There would be no more of such days of glory. *Men of the Fighting Lady* was, unintentionally, self-referential. With actors like Walter Pidgeon, Van Johnson, Louis Calhern, and Keenan Wynn, who harked back to the studio's golden age, one could see the difference between MGM in 1944 and the studio a decade later. *Thirty Seconds over Tokyo* (1944) ran 138 minutes; *Men of the Fighting Lady* ran eighty, enough time for a movie that had the usual mix of characters (a sympathetic flight surgeon, a cynic, a daredevil, a recruit) and a climactic Christmas scene, when the men receive filmed greetings from their families, including one from the family of a pilot (Wynn) that had not been notified of his death. During World War II, stock footage augmented the plot. In *Men of the Fighting Lady*, the footage, authentic to the core, was integral to the plot, which could not have proceeded without it. The fusion of narrative and non-narrative was in sharp contrast to the war itself, which was a disconnect between myth and reality. The myth was that Korea was a police action; the reality was that Korea was a war. "Police action" was a euphemism.

The most harrowing scene in *Men of the Fighting Lady* involves Van Johnson giving instructions to a blind and agitated Dewy Martin about how to land his plane on the deck of the carrier. Martin manages, but he will always be sight-impaired. When John Garfield returned home in *Pride of the Marines* (1945), he was blind, but Eleanor Parker was waiting for him. One never knows if the girl Martin left behind will be at the dock when he arrives. That was the difference between the two wars. One was worth fighting; the other was a "nut house cheese game."

The films that came out after the Korean War were not revisionist, yet they posed questions about the war's efficacy, questions that, when challenged, were never answered with a historical overview, but instead with a cliché like "You don't get to pick your war; you get the one that's given to you." Such was the answer in *The Bridges at Toko-Ri* (1954), derived from another Michener work (this time, his novel of the same name) and released seven months after *Men of the Fighting Lady*. Although *Bridges* was also filmed in color (but this time in the more prestigious Technicolor), Loyal Griggs's cinematography avoided the eye-catching lushness of such epics as

Gone with the Wind (1939) and *For Whom the Bell Tolls* (1943). Since director Mark Robson had made only two films in color before *Bridges*, *Return to Paradise* (1953) and *Hell Below Zero* (1954), he approached Technicolor as a process, not a painterly enhancement. *Bridges* was also a better fit for Robson than *I Want You*, which he could not raise to anything higher than domestic drama with a wartime slant. *Bridges* is precise in its documentary-style depiction of bombings and flight deck landings, and one is only aware of color in the few scenes between naval lieutenant Harry Brubaker (William Holden) and his wife Nancy (Grace Kelly). Technicolor brought out Kelly's cool beauty, which did not come through in her black-and-white films, *High Noon* (1952) and *The Country Girl* (1954).

Because it was made a year and a half after the July 1953 armistice that left Korea as divided as it was before the war, *Bridges* had the advantage of hindsight. The war is nothing other than a thankless job that has to be done, with dissent countered by explanations that could easily have been expressed in a single word, expediency. Nancy is convinced that the war is "senseless," until Admiral George Tarrant (Fredric March) explains to her that the bridges are the North Koreans' supply lines and must be destroyed. When Brubaker protests that Korea is a "dirty war" and "militarily, a tragedy," Tarrant replies, "[A]ll though history men have had to fight the wrong war, in the wrong place, but that's the one they're stuck with." And so, it seems, were the men who fought in Korea. This is the closest the film came to questioning America's involvement in the conflict. It's the wrong war and the wrong place, but that is what happens when a fort is fired upon, an archduke is assassinated, a country is invaded, and a line of demarcation is crossed. To use the buzz phrase of the millennium, "Stuff happens."

Men of the Fighting Lady and *The Bridges at Toko-Ri* probably could have been filmed in black and white, but the result would not have been as effective. The same was true of Universal-International's *Battle Hymn* (1957), directed by Douglas Sirk, who had also been a translator of Shakespeare, an art historian, and a painter. Sirk's palette is dominated by blue, often suffused with white, except for the flat and dull landscape of Nogales, Arizona, standing in for Korea and resembling an unending expanse of beige. Even the sky, vibrantly blue in Arizona, looked washed out in Korea.

To Sirk, blue had a sacramental quality. It is the color of the Madonna, with its evocation of purity and spirituality, which he used so creatively in *Magnificent Obsession* (1954). *Battle Hymn* was Sirk's quasi-sequel to *Magnificent Obsession*. The film is loosely based on the autobiography of the same name by Reverend Dean Hess, an air force colonel during World War

II, who later returned to Korea to train pilots. In *Magnificent Obsession*, the self-absorbed Ron Kirby (Rock Hudson) undergoes a spiritual awakening that enables him to put himself at the disposal of others. In *Battle Hymn*, Dean Hess (Hudson again) discovers that atonement for the deaths he inadvertently caused in a bombing raid can be achieved in a way other than self-recrimination.

Battle Hymn opens in the summer of 1950, a month after the outbreak of war. Reverend Hess has just delivered another guilt and repentance sermon in a church with blue stained glass windows. (The Hess bedroom is also bathed in blue.) When the deacon (Carl Benton Reid) gently suggests that he vary his topics, Hess turns the congregation over to him, explaining that he is returning to the air force to train Republic of Korea (ROK) pilots. Hess has been unable to clear his conscience of the deaths of thirty-seven children that resulted from his accidental bombing of a German orphanage during World War II. The silhouette of a cross appears against the blue window of the church, symbolizing the one Hess must carry until he atones by organizing an airlift for Korean children left orphaned by the war.

Battle Hymn may have had its patriotic moments ("The Battle Hymn of the Republic" is played over the opening credits and reprised at the end by Korean children), but it is essentially one man's spiritual journey. Although the Defense Department and the army lent their cooperation, *Battle Hymn* is not a recruitment film like *I Want You*. The pilots Hess encounters in Korea are far from poster boys for the air force. Hess inherits a company of undisciplined men, including his World War II buddy, Captain Dan Skidmore (Don DeFore), that he must make combat ready. After learning that Hess is a minister, the men are dismayed; some are even disappointed, wondering why he isn't a chaplain instead of their CO. After Hess learns that orphans are scavenging for food in garbage cans, he demands that they be fed with the others, signaling the beginning of his spiritual renewal.

When Skidmore flies off course, causing Lieutenant Maples (James Edwards, the fine but undervalued African American actor, featured in other Korean War films such as *The Steel Helmet*, *Men in War*, *The Manchurian Candidate*, and *Pork Chop Hill*) to bomb refugees and children, Hess comforts him as a fellow sufferer. With the help of a Korean ivory carver (Philip Ahn in a white chest-length beard), who explains that war is the lesser of two evils—some lives must be destroyed so that others can be saved—Hess begins to see himself as part of a divine plan,. Hess has his own epiphany as Skidmore lies dying. He lessens his friend's fear of death by describing it as a passing from darkness to light. Then Hess understands the reason for his presence in Korea: "Perhaps through the agony of war, in reaching beyond myself, I found myself."

Although Hess was the film's technical advisor, he did not have script approval. Even so, he must have been flattered by the hagiographic screenplay by Vincent B. Evans and Charles Grayson, who all but made Dean Hess a candidate for canonization. In the film, Hess emerges as the guiding force behind the "Kiddy Car Airlift" of the Korean orphans to Jeju island. But such was not the case, as Dr. George F. Drake has argued, alleging that Hess took credit for a rescue operation that he neither planned nor witnessed. Hess, however, did arrange housing for the orphans before they arrived at Jeju. But with Hudson as an amalgam of Christ and Moses, audiences expected a savior, not a member of the housing authority. Moviegoers were not disappointed; only those who knew the truth were. Sirk, who generally worked closely with his writers, wanted *Battle Hymn* to follow the same plot trajectory as *Magnificent Obsession*, in which Ron Kirby (Hudson, in his third film with Sirk) found redemption by embracing a mystical form of altruism. In *Battle Hymn*, Hess (Hudson, now in his seventh film with Sirk), trying to find peace of mind in the ministry, finds it by bringing peace to others in time of war.

Other Korean War films were not so uplifting. The heroes were not pilots in the wild blue yonder, but infantry contending with the elements and the enemy. Paramount's *Cease Fire* (1953) presented the plight of the foot soldier in Korea in the form of staged realism, part documentary and part feature film. Director Owen Crump flew to Korea in April 1953 with his crew to make a movie that had the texture of a documentary, with real soldiers playing characters who, in most cases, bore the men's real names. Thus "Elliott" is Sergeant Richard Karl Elliott, and "English" is Corporal Harold D. English. The battle scenes were staged like historical reenactments on television's History Channel. Still, there was a visceral authenticity in a number of tense scenes—in particular, a scene involving two soldiers crawling down a path, feeling for land mines.

Cease Fire opens like a traditional war movie. The barrel of a tank gun juts into the screen, an effect that, in the 3-D version released in late November 1953, looked as if the gun were aimed right at the audience. After the credits, the film becomes a quasi frame narrative beginning on the last day of the war, as reporters eagerly await news from Panmunjom, and ending with the birth of a baby, signaling hope for the future despite a past that did little to inspire it. But an armistice had been signed, the boys were going home, and all's right with the world until the next crisis. The film's final words, "Peace is born again in Korea," is laughable in light of a Korea still divided between a totalitarian North with its record of human rights violations, and a jittery South within missile range. Even the withdrawal from Pork Chop Hill was euphemized, with one of the soldiers bitterly commenting that the war was supposed to have ended "when we got kicked off Pork Chop." In 1953, such a statement would not have made much sense to anyone but a Korean War buff.

In his *New York Times* review (25 November 1953), Bosley Crowther complained that the sequence with the reporters was producer Hal Wallis's way of making *Cease Fire* seem more like a typical movie. The attempt was certainly unnecessary, as was "Brothers at Arms," a marching song sung by a chorus of male voices heard intermittently and sounding like something from an operetta on the order of "Stout-Hearted Men" in *Naughty Marietta*. Finally, capitulating to the short-lived 3-D craze detracted from *Cease Fire's* importance as the first Korean War movie shot on location by a major studio. The acting may not have been Oscar-worthy, but casting real soldiers made it clear that *Cease Fire* was not another Hollywood version of Korea—despite attempts to make it so—but a film in which audiences actually heard from the men at war.

Anyone puzzled by the reference to Pork Chop Hill in *Cease Fire* had to wait until the end of the decade to learn about one of the most frustrating battles of the war. *Pork Chop Hill* (1959) made no attempt to downplay the futility of fighting an unwinnable war as it was winding down at a discouragingly sluggish pace. Six years after the signing of the armistice, Hollywood was unwilling to admit that the war had been lost, only that a police action had ended. In 1953, Korea was as divided as ever, and the GIs returned to an America that was in a less celebratory mood than it had been at the end of World War II. In 1954, the Battle of Dien Bien Phu marked the end of French rule in Indo China, and the beginning of American involvement in Vietnam, which, like Korea, was also partitioned between the communist North and the anti-communist South. Since Korea had become the "forgotten war," the newly demarcated Vietnam induced shudders in those with long-term memories. In 1973, the war in Vietnam would also end with an armistice and even greater ignominy, when Saigon fell to the Vietcong two years later. "When will they ever learn?" as Pete Seeger lamented.

Although Lewis Milestone, who directed *All Quiet on the Western Front* (1930)—an indictment of both the Great War and war itself—seemed a perfect choice for *Pork Chop Hill*, it was not a happy experience for him. The film starred Gregory Peck as Lieutenant Joseph Clemons and was co-produced by Peck's Melville Productions. The actor wanted a vehicle that would showcase his ability to play another war hero like Captain Bill Forrester in *The Purple Plain* (1954). But there is little comparison between the two movies. *The Purple Plain*, set in Burma near the end of World War II, had a far better screenplay, as one would expect from Eric Ambler. Peck's Forrester was psychologically complex, like the characters he portrayed in *Spellbound, The Gunfighter*, and especially *Twelve O'Clock High*. The death of Forrester's wife made him suicidal, and it is only through the love of a Burmese woman that he reclaims his humanity.

Pork Chop Hill takes place three months before the end of the Korean War. Unlike Forrester, First Lieutenant Joseph G. Clemons Jr. was a real person, who was in his early twenties when he traveled from West Point to Korea. Peck was in his early forties and wanted to invest Clemons with a heroic aura, which, historically, was impossible. Clemons won the Distinguished Service Cross, but it was given for holding out in an impossible battle that left fourteen of his 135-man company alive. Although Peck affected a heroic persona, he could not deflect the script from the path it had taken as a combat film. Peck was nominally the star, but the battle captured the spotlight. Milestone may have been unhappy with the result, but it was his best war film since *A Walk in the Sun* (1945), with its rough poetry. *Pork Chop Hill* has the same linearity as *A Walk in the Sun*, the same unity of action centering on a single military operation—blowing up a bridge in *A Walk in the Sun*, taking a hill in *Pork Chop Hill*. As Windy (John Ireland) writes in a letter to his sister at the end of *A Walk in the Sun*, "We just blew up a bridge and took a farm house. It was so easy—so terribly easy." Taking—and holding—Pork Chop Hill was not so easy. Clemons knew that the hill had no strategic importance, dismissing it as a "stinking little garbage heap." But the Chinese, who had entered the war on the side of North Korea in fall 1950, captured it to demonstrate their tenacity, holding on to a worthless outpost while peace talks were dragging on seventy miles away at Panmunjom.

Pork Chop Hill also benefited from hindsight, which made it possible for the filmmakers to stand back and view the war critically. Clemons is ordered to retake Pork Chop, a collective term for the area designated as a neutral zone. (The film conflates two battles that took place in April and July 1953.) From the expression on his face (and Peck excelled at projecting stoicism), Clemons would be carrying out an order in which he did not believe. That was bad enough, but the film implies that Clemons did not know that Pork Chop was a bargaining chip the American team at Panmunjom hoped to use to their advantage while negotiating a truce. The chip was a slug. The Americans took the hill but were no match for the Chinese, who persisted in fighting. A withdrawal was ordered, and Pork Chop Hill became a battle won and lost.

Although the film takes certain liberties with history, *Pork Chop Hill* is a worthy addition to the American war film genre. Milestone used his trademark tracking shots to survey the terrain, slowly moving down the ridge to reveal bodies, helmets, weapons, and trenches, as if he were panning a graveyard where the dead had not yet been buried. The battle sequences are thrilling, especially when the Chinese send up a war cry, rushing down the hill with suicidal fervor to keep a worthless piece of land from falling into American hands. To prevent the film from becoming a documentary, screenwriter James R. Webb added a human dimension to the characters, particularly Private Franklin (Woody Strode), a would-be deserter who hides in a bunker. Franklin is ready to kill Clemons, until he realizes that everyone is involved in the same futile operation. Although Private Franklin is fictitious, American, Korean, and Chinese soldiers had been known to take refuge in bunkers to avoid trench warfare. Humor is virtually absent from the film, except when an assistant production officer arrives, hoping to photograph the men's beaming faces as a morale-booster for the folks back home. Clemons was as civil as he could be in the presence of a clueless non-combatant, asking only that he tell the truth about a campaign that was denied sufficient reinforcements.

During World War II, Axis Sally and Tokyo Rose delivered cynical greetings to GIs over the air, and now Webb invented their Chinese equivalent, a well-spoken man broadcasting from the comfort of his bunker and reminding the men that they can have long lives if they withdraw: "Why must you die when you haven't begun to live?" He conjures up the future they could have by playing a recording of the Vernon Duke classic, "Autumn in New York"—an ironic choice, given the verse "Autumn in New York / Is often mingled with pain."

At least in *A Walk in the Sun* a bridge was blown up and a farmhouse taken. In *Pork Chop Hill*, there was no victory, only an exercise in one-upmanship carried out under orders. As co-producer, Peck would not allow the film to end on a negative note, only a false one. His voice, unfaltering and authoritative, admits that while there are no monuments to the fallen at Pork Chop Hill, "[V]ictory is a fragile thing, and history does not linger long." And is it not entirely true that "millions live in freedom today because of what they did." The peninsula is still divided, and South Korean families have little chance of being united with their relatives in the North.

Like American World War II movies, the Korean War movies of the 1950s only portrayed one side of the story, the American side. That there was even a Japanese side to World War II was never dramatized until *Tora! Tora! Tora!* (1970), in which the weekend of 5–7 December 1941 unfolded like made-to-order tragedy, in which a delayed message, a poor typist, and a Sunday that was anything but a day of rest conspired to create the "day that will live in infamy." And while 25 June 1950 was a day of lesser infamy, it was characterized by greater disillusionment, which did not escape the attention of director Anthony Mann, whose *Men in War* (1957) ranks high among great war films. *Men in War* did not look at Korea from a four-year vantage point, which would have allowed a more reflective and perhaps revisionist view of the war. Set three months after the war began, the film is unflinchingly objective in its portrayal of men who will never experience grace under pressure, only the pressure that robs them of grace. The screenplay was attributed to the prolific Philip Yordan, a front for the blacklisted Ben Maddow, who adapted it from Van Praag's novel *Combat* (1950), originally entitled *Day without End*. Short on both heroics and propaganda, *Men in War* is a variation on the odyssey theme, in which Lieutenant Mark Benson (Robert Ryan) leads the remnants of his platoon through enemy-infested territory, with landmines adding to their peril. Maddow's script is scrupulous in its observance of the classical unities of time, place, and action. The action is limited to a single day, 6 September 1950; the setting is the Pusan perimeter; and the platoon's attempt to return to its battalion constitutes the main action. Despite Maddow's leftist leanings, his screenplay is apolitical. "There is no political issue in this film's war. It is a game, a game over space." And the space is another hill that must be taken at the loss of all but one member of the platoon.

Men in War lives up to its title. It is an intensely psychological study of two men: a by-the-books lieutenant (Ryan), trying to do the right thing in a wrong war, and a maverick sergeant (Aldo Ray) from another company, concerned only with the welfare of his traumatized colonel (Robert Keith, of the riveting eyes). The sergeant cares more about the colonel than the protocols of war. The colonel is a surrogate father, whose dying word is "son," the only time he speaks in the entire film. There are few war films in which male bonding is portrayed as selflessly as in *Men in War*.

Denied the military's cooperation because of the fronted script, *Men in War* forged ahead on its own steam, benefitting enormously from Elmer Bernstein's score, which was at times sweepingly orchestrated, at other times, starkly monodic, as when death was in the air. Mann, who early in his career revealed an affinity for film noir in *Two O'Clock Courage* (1945), *T-Men* (1947), and *Raw Deal* (1948), had director of photography Ernest Haller provide some noirish touches, such as shots of trees glazed by moonlight in an otherwise ominously dark forest. At times the screen seemed to be exploding, veiled in white smoke, as if Mann was shielding the viewer from the attack, and then lifting the veil to reveal the carnage left behind. *Men in War* opens with an epigraph: "Tell me the story of the foot soldier, and I will tell you the story of all wars." At the end of *The Unnamable*, Samuel Beckett provides a coda that sums up the foot soldier's lot dramatized in *Men in War*: "You must go on, I can't go on, I go on."

The most ambiguous end-of-war film set in Korea was Columbia's *The Bamboo Prison* (1954), in which Master Sergeant John Rand (Robert Francis) poses as a collaborator—or "progressive" as the North Koreans labeled men who showed (or feigned) sympathy for communism—in order to obtain information that would speed up the peace talks at Panmunjom. Sergeant Rand then passes the information on in ingeniously encoded form to Corporal Brady (Brian Keith). Hitchcock might have done something outstanding with the "people are not what they seem" script (the camp's chaplain is a communist in a cassock). Lewis Seiler was no Hitchcock, but he did his best to keep an engrossing but implausible movie on track, despite the turn offs, dead ends, and erratic rhythm that alternated between slapstick and serious.

The writers, Edwin Blum and Jack DeWitt, were familiar with war movie templates. The camp informer, a bogus priest (E. G. Marshall), was inspired by a similar character, Price (Peter Graves), in Billy Wilder's *Stalag 17* (1953). The POWs mock their captors with double talk and made-up words that sound erudite (like Ronald Reagan throwing around technical sounding gibberish at a befuddled Raymond Massey in *Desperate Journey*). "Comrade Instructor" (Keye Luke) is so literal-minded that he does not realize the men are ridiculing everything he is trying to teach them. The commandant (Richard Loo) is so convinced of Rand's sincerity that he cannot see that Rand's broadcasts denouncing American imperialism and Wall Street warmongers contain hidden messages for his superiors.

The writers did not find their resolution in the catalog of war movie plots, but in an August 1953 news story in which some of the returning prisoners reported that "a few of their fellow Americans had refused repatriation." The number was actually twenty-one, and most of them eventually returned to the United States with dishonorable discharges. If one forgot that Rand is role-playing, his decision to remain in North Korea implied that he had embraced communism. Robert Francis delivered his anti-American diatribe so forcefully that it was easy to come to that conclusion. The reason for Rand's rejection of repatriation in front of American military personnel is never explained, except in the final scene, when he joins a truckload of other progressives. Since Rand has been working as a mole, one assumes that, with the cessation of hostilities, his next assignment will be herding the errant sheep back into the fold. Virtually nothing is known of the progressives. Did they switch allegiance because they had been subjected to thought control sessions? Did they choose collaboration out of fear of torture and privation? Or did communism make more sense to them than the Constitution? And if Rand ever succeeded in reeducating them, how would they be received back home? *The Bamboo Prison* poses more questions than it answers. American POWs who refused repatriation, such as the progressives, were given ninety days to reconsider. However, according to the *New York Times* (17 September 1996), two men who had a change of heart were not only dishonorably discharged, but received prison sentences as well. When Rand tells Corporal Brady, "I'll be back," he means back to the States. One would like to believe that the ninety-day grace period was waived for the progressives after they saw the light; otherwise, they would have been given the turncoat treatment. But their reconversion would mean an additional ten minutes or a sequel, neither of which Columbia had any intention of funding. Despite its unsatisfying resolution, *The Bamboo Prison* is still a provocative film, overly melodramatic at times, but honest—and even daring—in admitting that there were men who were not ready to return home.

The most disturbing portrayal of collaboration during the Korean War appears in *Time Limit* (1957), adapted from the play of the same name (but with an exclamation point for emphasis) by Henry Denker and Ralph Berkey that lasted on Broadway for 127 performances during the 1955–56 season. Denker adapted the play himself, ensuring a faithful stage-to-screen transfer. The director, Karl Malden, in his only stint behind the camera, made certain that the play lost none of its momentum as it moved to another medium. Malden, who had assimilated the mechanics of moviemaking by working with Elia Kazan in *A Streetcar Named Desire*, *On the Waterfront*, and *Baby Doll*, and had been a stage actor since 1937, knew how the essence of theater could be preserved on film. The transfer was not that difficult this time, since the play was a study in escalating suspense, with enough false assumptions and wrong starts that the dangling plot strings could be knotted together in the shattering dénouement.

In the military, collaboration is treason, even if the so-called collaborator served the enemy in order to save the lives of others. Hence the dilemma posed in the film: Is collaboration treason, if sixteen POWs were saved from certain death? Or was it another case of one sacrificing himself for many—who, as it turned out, were unworthy of his magnanimity? The plot pivot is simple enough: POW Major Harry Cargill (Richard Basehart) is accused of making propaganda broadcasts for the enemy and admitting to engaging in germ warfare. As Colonel William Evans (Richard Widmark) probes deeper into the case, he is confronted with contradictory statements made by the unusually self-assured Lieutenant George Miller (a creepy Rip Torn), who shrugs when confronted with an inconsistency. And how to explain the testimony of sixteen men who swore that one of their own died of dysentery, all sixteen sounding as if they had rehearsed the same script? Then there are the major's cryptic utterances: "My brother died that I might live. May I be worthy of his sacrifice," and "Whoever kills one man kills the world. How many worlds have I killed?" These are the sentiments of one who believes in universal brotherhood, but they could easily have been expressed by a communist. There is a suggestion that the major was not so much a collaborator as an infiltrator. Eventually, the ugly truth comes out, illustrating the lengths to which POWs will go when they learn that one of their own has betrayed them. No longer able to bear the hunger, the cold, and the torture, Captain Joe Connors defected to the enemy, an act of treachery that all except the major believe merits death. The men draw lots to determine who will be the executioner. The task falls to Miller, who strangles Connors. After burying him, the men agree to testify that he died of dysentery.

The film poses a dilemma that is irresolvable. If treason is punishable in the military, is strangling a traitor murder or execution? What kind of collaboration is worse: switching sides for better treatment, or doing so to save lives? Everyone in the camp was a collaborator of some sort, even those who worked together—literally collaborate—to kill Connors. Morally, murder is more serious than an act of collaboration that did not result in anyone's death. Neither the play nor the film reached closure. Even when Connors's father learns the truth about his son, he still insists that Major Cargill has committed treason. The ending is moderately hopeful, implying that with Richard Widmark (forget his character) handling the defense, Cargill will have a strong advocate. The viewer is left with Cargill's explanation that the military must understand there is a time limit on courage, beyond which there is only survival. Upholders of the code would say, "Collaboration is still treason, even if the prisoner breaks under pressure." One doubts that even Solomon would have been able to adjudicate such a case. In *Prisoner of War* (1954), the situation was much simpler, with an army captain (Ronald Reagan) infiltrating a Korean POW camp to obtain evidence of enemy atrocities by posing as a collaborator, as do two other prisoners. The atrocities—forced marches, physical and mental torture—are gruesome enough, but in documenting them, *Prisoner of War* became just another atrocity film. There are no atrocities in *Time Limit*, only a challenge to the audience to vote on whether an act of collaboration that saved lives is treason, and whether ridding a prison camp of a collaborator responsible for one death and capable of causing others is murder.

Almost a decade after the armistice, *War Hunt* (1962) arrived with little fanfare, written, produced, and directed by relative newcomers. John Saxon heading a cast that included several stage actors, such as Charles Aidman and Sydney Pollack, the latter going on to become one of the industry's premier directors (*They Shoot Horses, Don't They?, Out of Africa, Tootsie*). *War Hunt* also marked the film debut of another actor who proved to be as comfortable behind the camera as he was in front of it, Robert Redford. The director of *War Hunt* was Denis Sanders, a two-time Oscar winner in the best short subject category for *A Time Out of War* (1954), a reenactment of a temporary truce between two Union soldiers and a lone Confederate during the Civil War, and in the best documentary short subject category for *Czechoslovakia 1968*, now included in the National Film Registry, devoted to the preservation of films of historical and cultural significance. The producer was Denis's brother, Terry. Denis, who came of age during World War II, had a special affinity for the combat film. He and his brother subsequently adapted Norman Mailer's sprawling novel, *The Naked and the Dead*, for the screen in 1958. Except for Bernard Herrmann's score, the movie version fell short of the original, but in 1958, a faithful screen transfer would have been impossible for linguistic reasons alone. It was bad enough that Mailer had to use "frig." But in 1958, what was the euphemism for a euphemism?

War Hunt did not need euphemisms. Stanford Whitmore, who served in the marines in World War II, wrote a screenplay that should have heralded the arrival of a new talent. But in 1962, Korea was still an open wound. World War II was the only war whose scars were proudly displayed. Audiences in need of a war movie fix turned out for *Hell Is for Heroes* (1962), with Steve McQueen and Bobby Darin, whose names, at least, were familiar. Yet *War Hunt* closed the book on the Korean War movie, after which filmmakers would be traversing ground already marked by the footprints of others.

War Hunt inverts the conventions of the war film. The untried Private Loomis (Redford), who also serves as the film's narrator, is assigned to Company E, 2nd Battalion, during the last days of the war. Given the short period between his arrival and the cease-fire, Loomis has no opportunity to grow into a hero, only to enter the war's nether world. This is not a coming of age film in which Loomis loses his idealism upon entering the Korean inferno. Instead, it is a journey to the abyss that brings this 1950s Candide to the edge of civilization, beyond which lies barbarism.

Within the war that is winding down is another war waged between Loomis and Raymond Endore (John Saxon) for the soul of a Korean orphan, who has become Endore's surrogate son and trainee in the art of guerrilla warfare. Endore keeps the boy in the bunker with the other men, who ignore Endore's violations of protocol and even his nightly forays behind enemy lines. When Loomis sees Endore blackening his face and going off into the night, he is naturally suspicious but told to steer clear. The others know what Endore does, but do not report it: He cuts the throats of enemy soldiers as they sleep.

Heroics have no place in *War Hunt*. Captain Pratt (Charles Aidman) informs the company at the beginning of the film that the war is being won at the conference table at Panmunjom, and that the fighting must continue to give the negotiators greater bargaining power. Although Loomis fits in easily, he is increasingly disturbed by Endore's attachment to the boy, suspecting that Endore is making him into a replica of himself. That Endore is more than just a loose canon is obvious. He is prized for his reconnaissance skills, even though they include cold-blooded murder, which if reported would have led to a court martial. The reason for his bloodlust is never explained, but from John Saxon's coldly expressionless face, it is obvious that his conscience has ossified. Either Korea has turned a soldier into a serial killer, or it has activated his potential for becoming one. *War Hunt* does not pass judgment on Endore, but merely allows him to reveal himself through his actions. Endore even has a leitmotif announcing his presence: four plaintive notes orchestrated into dissonance, as a simple theme swells into a danger signal.

Ignoring the truce, Endore takes the boy into the demilitarized zone, forcing a show down. As Endore stands like a warrior atop a hill, Captain Pratt shouts up to him, "The war's over." Endore shouts back, "Which war?" He plans to stay on, continuing his nocturnal throat-cuttings and training the Korean orphan to do the same. A scuffle ensues between Pratt and Endore, resulting in Endore's death. Having peered into the heart of darkness,

Loomis has seen the darkness of the heart. When Pratt asks, "Soldier, are you all right?" Loomis—looking as if he is trying to comprehend the incomprehensible—replies, "No." And he never will be.

Nor will the Korean War—with its hills that cannot, but must be, held; its defeats translated into redeployments; its attitude of eyes opened and minds shut—ever be all right. In act 2 of Jean Giraudoux's *The Trojan War Will Not Take Place*, produced on Broadway as *Tiger at the Gates*, Hecuba is asked to describe the look of war: "Like the bottom of a baboon. When the baboon is up in a tree, with its behind end facing us, there is the face of war exactly: scarlet, scaly, glazed, framed in a clotted, filthy wig." That metaphor makes it possible to see the Korean War from what is literally a different perspective. *War Hunt* anticipates *Apocalypse Now* (1979) and *Platoon* (1986), each of which portrays war as a breeding ground for potential psychopaths who could never find in civilian life what they did on the other side of the divide, where darkness alone is visible. In Joseph Conrad's *Heart of Darkness*, Kurtz looks into the abyss and utters the now legendary response, "The horror! The horror!" Screenwriter-novelist Stanford Whitmore has linked Endore with Kurtz, both of whom are in the thrall of a land where they can reign with impunity. Had Endore survived, one could imagine him, like Kurtz, fortifying himself in a compound with a fence decorated with human heads, the equivalent of a "No Trespassing" sign. Endore had already discovered a deserted village where he could found his kingdom. But even then, he would not have confronted the darkness within himself and recoiled in horror. Like Macbeth, he is so steeped in blood that he has reached the point of no return. Only death remains.

Korea was too ugly a war to be passed off as an appendix to World War II. Movies were not the same mass medium they were in the 1940s. In the postwar years, small town movie theaters gave way to drugstores, supermarkets, and even storefront churches. There was no way Hollywood could portray Korea as anything other than a job that had to be done. "You win or you die," as Captain Skidmore says with a shrug in *Battle Hymn*. Korea was not a war to be won, but a United Nations police action to be fought. Hollywood could not ignore Korea, but it was a no-win situation, historically and otherwise.

Chapter 16

MEANWHILE, BACK IN THE WEST . . .

FILMMAKERS SENSED THAT KOREA WOULD HAVE LIMITED APPEAL. THE landscape was too hostile for anything but battle. Romance at the front might have been possible with Clark Gable and Lana Turner in *Somewhere I'll Find You* (1942) and *Homecoming* (1948), but Bogart and Allyson had a difficult time striking sparks in a hospital tent in *Battle Circus*. Korea was a man's war, and Hollywood knew it. The women must wait until Johnny comes marching home, no matter what shape he's in. Europe was more fertile ground, both in front of and behind the Iron Curtain.

Cold War melodrama made the World War II espionage film look like an early version of Windows—functioning, but in need of an upgrade. There would still be movies with an imperiled heroine awaiting rescue by a knight in a trench coat—or, like Clark Gable in *Never Let Me Go*, in a bathing suit; reporters risking their lives for a scoop; and patriots doing the same, even at the expense of their families (*Assignment, Paris*). It was the people's war all over again. This time the people behind the Iron Curtain were the oppressed, and the communists were the oppressors. No longer were women tied to a flagpole and lashed like Bonita Granville in *Hitler's Children* (1942), or men bound to a chair and beaten like James Cagney in *13 Rue Madeleine* (1946). Communists kidnap and blackmail (*The Man Between*). They excel at brainwashing, leaving Dana Andrews (*Assignment, Paris*) in such a somnambulistic state that one wonders if even sexy Marta Toren can revive his old romantic self.

Cold War Europe was made for melodrama: shadowy figures in the night; gothic-style embassies; posh hotels; Old World restaurants with the observed and the observers; women dressed by Jean Louis; and men in tailored suits and Windsor-knotted ties. The communists were square-faced men in suits that looked like regulation attire from a people's republic, made especially for barrel-chested bureaucrats. The women from Eastern

Europe looked bargain basement drab; those from the West were stylish, sporting the New Look, with its tapered waist and long skirts.

Noir had caught up with the Cold War. The streets were coal black like the night—but the kind of night that augured ill. There were too many blind alleys, too many menacing corners. Europe was like a rogue planet in an alternate universe. Paris was recognizable, but it was no longer the city of light, but the city of darkness. And Budapest was no longer a city where lonely hearts find love, however circuitously, as they did in *The Shop around the Corner* (1940). Instead it was a city in which American reporters are jailed and disappear, or are sentenced to death on a trumped up charge of espionage.

Assignment, Paris (1952) is set in both cities. Dana Andrews plays a danger-defying reporter assigned to the Paris office of the *Herald Tribune*, where, to his delight, the glamorous Marta Toren also works. Toren is following a lead about a proposed alliance between Hungary and Yugoslavia against Russia, one that would radically alter the configuration of the Soviet bloc. The alliance was, in Hitchcock's language, the MacGuffin. All that was missing was proof of an alleged meeting between Hungary's prime minister and Yugoslavia's Marshal Tito.

Such an alliance was not implausible. Tito broke with Stalin in 1948, preferring his own form of communism to the inflexible Soviet model. Tito was too independent for Stalin, who considered the Yugoslav leader a maverick and an ingrate. Tito refused to credit the Russians for saving his country from the Nazis, knowing that his partisans deserved recognition, despite the atrocities they committed. (The Russians did their share, especially after they entered Berlin in 1945.) Hungary had witnessed the effects of enforced imposition of the Soviet model: purges, torture, inferior housing, low wages, food rationing. The country was ripe for rebellion. Resentment of Soviet rule erupted in fall 1956 with a short-lived Hungarian revolution. It is tempting to imagine Tito's capitalizing on Hungary's discontent after he parted ways with Stalin. There is no proof that he did, but speculation often makes better copy than fact.

Assignment, Paris has one of the most unsettling dénouements in Cold War melodrama. Andrews accepts an assignment in Budapest, where, like his predecessor, he is accused of espionage. During his taped interrogation, he repeats, "I am not going to say I came here to act as a spy." The first part of the statement is erased, turning it into a confession: "I came here to act as a spy." The communists will exchange the reporter for a *Herald Tribune* employee, a former member of the Hungarian resistance who has unearthed documents pointing to a Hungary-Yugoslavia federation. This makes for a painful ending, with the Hungarian willing to sacrifice his life for an American. At least the communists got a man with his senses intact. Andrews, looking as if he had been mesmerized, keeps repeating, "I came here to act as a spy." As he is bundled into a car with Toren, his editor (George Sanders), mutters, "He'll be all right." Possibly, after deprogramming. Regardless, it is a morally perplexing ending. The ill-fated Hungarian is the father of two children from whom he will be separated permanently. He was helping an American reporter expose a covert union between two Soviet bloc countries. Is this a case of "Greater love hath no man than this, that a man lay down his life for his friends" (John 15:13)? Sadly, yes. This is the Cold War; the friend is an American, the sacrificial victim a Hungarian. Since both are anti-communists, does one form of anti-communism take precedence over the other? Or, more specifically, is an American's life more valuable than a Hungarian's? A voice over coda—"A story out of the headlines of today, out of the headlines of tomorrow"—comes on so quickly that it is easy to forget there is no resolution. The Hungarian will either be executed or sent to a gulag. Perhaps the reporter will work again, but never in Budapest. But neither man will ever be the same. And what was it all for? A scoop that would expose the cracks in the Iron Curtain?

In *Diplomatic Courier* (1952), released the same year, the former Yugoslavia is still an irritant to Moscow. By spring 1948, Stalin had determined that Tito must die, but assassination attempts proved futile. Tito informed Stalin that if the dictator sends any more assassins, he would retaliate, warning that he would not have to send a second hit man. Such was the historical background of *Diplomatic Courier*, which imagined a Kremlin, exasperated by Tito's socialist reforms, planning an invasion of Yugoslavia, supposedly in April 1950. The screenwriters, Casey Robinson and Liam O'Brien, had done their homework, but the date was actually spring 1949. Cold War movies were often inspired by the Soviet Union's latest muscle flexing, especially when one of its satellites fancied itself a planet. Such was Yugoslavia after World War II. Marshal Tito, flush after his Partisans' victories, cast his eyes on neighboring Trieste, a strategic seaport in northeastern Italy. Tito was behaving like a junior-league Stalin, empire building with less grandiosity and more benevolence. It would be Titoism, not Stalinism.

After the State Department intercepts a message warning of a Soviet invasion of Yugoslavia, a neophyte in the diplomatic corps (Tyrone Power) is dispatched to Salzburg to make contact with the agent in possession of the secret plan, code name Semper. This is the courier's introduction to the first principle of espionage: Nobody is what he or she appears to be. A widow in mink (Patricia Neal) is in league with the Soviets. The woman who appears to be a Soviet spy (Hildegarde Neff) is a double agent—more on the side of the Americans than the Russians—so that she and the courier can find romance in the shadows of Trieste.

The only sympathetic character in the film is the double agent, who has to play both sides of a dangerous game. Her motives may be selfish (she wants a visa to emigrate to America), but her worth is measured by her present status. Alive, she is useful; dead, she is worthless. The courier's life is what matters. And what takes precedence over his is the invasion plan: a piece of microfilm inserted in a watch. The double agent has served America well, but if she is caught, "[S]he's a casualty of the Cold War."

Except for James Bond movies, the romance of espionage is a myth. It is an ugly business where protection can cease at any moment, after which you fend for yourself when your usefulness has been exhausted. There is a deep strain of cynicism in *Diplomatic Courier*, especially when the double agent proves to be as pragmatic as her recruiter. She will offer the microfilm to anyone, American or Soviet, who will guarantee her a visa. With Power and Neff lying on the grass, looking dreamily at each other in the fade out, one suspects that her espionage days are over.

Night People (1954)—the title refers to East Berlin communists who do their dirty deeds at night—is the flip side of *Diplomatic Courier*. The communists have kidnapped an American GI and are holding him in East Berlin, hoping to exchange him for a German couple in the American sector. Nunnally Johnson, who wrote, directed, and produced *Night People*, braided the script with so many strands that each unraveling brings a new revelation. A double agent (Anita Bjork), who seems to be working for the Americans—even convincing an army colonel (Gregory Peck) of her loyalty—is really in league with the Soviets. The so-called German couple consists of a British woman and her German husband, who had been blinded by the Nazis because of his complicity in an abortive attempt to assassinate Hitler. Rather than be sent to East Berlin and an unknown fate, the couple takes strychnine. If they die, there can be no exchange. But American doctors can work wonders, even when based in West Berlin.

Once the colonel discovers the agent's duplicity, he pretends to woo her, reviving their old romance and offering her absinthe, her drink of choice, which he has mixed with sleep-inducing powder. As usually happens in this kind of a film, the colonel drinks the drugged absinthe and needs a stomach pump. Still, the exchange goes through. The Americans get the GI, and the communists get the double agent, reeking of absinthe, wrapped in a blanket, and rolled into a waiting truck on a gurney. And the couple can spend their sunset years without thoughts of suicide.

Night People posed a profound dilemma, which Johnson did not have to resolve, since he steered the film toward a successful resolution. Before that happens, the colonel must determine whether the life of one American is worth the death of a married couple. And when the colonel discovers that the wife is a British subject, he realizes the consequences of such a trade: a court martial and imprisonment. By having the couple attempt suicide, Johnson delays the climax until the "exchange" is accomplished—except that it is now the exchange of a disgraced agent for an American corporal. The irony carries over to the coda, in which a radio announcer reports that the Soviets have returned a corporal (no name is mentioned) to the American sector, signaling further co-operation between the two world powers in the interest of peace, darkening what Milton in *The Reason of Church-Government* called the "bright countenance of truth." The truth is that both sides had to save face. The Russians could not admit one of their spies was an absinthe addict, and the Americans could not reveal the nature of the original exchange. There is at least a grain of truth in the announcement: A corporal was released.

The pit of espionage—with its ever-widening circles of agents, counter agents, controllers, and expendables—would even have challenged the imagination of Dante, who fashioned a mathematically exact hell of nine circles, some with subdivisions. Espionage is not that ordered. The circles of deception expand or contract, depending on the number of newcomers and discards. Everyone is expendable, except Control, the grand master of intelligence, who moves his agents around the chessboard of espionage as if they were pawns. In Mary Renault's novel, *The Charioteer*, Ralph, who has accepted his homosexuality, explains the gay demimonde to Laurie: "Ours isn't a horizontal society. It's a vertical one, Plato, Michelangelo, Sappho, Marlowe, Shakespeare, Leonardo, and Socrates if you count the bisexuals— we can all quote the upper crust. But at the bottom ... believe me, there isn't any bottom. Never forget it. You've no conception, you haven't a clue, how far down it goes." The same is true of British intelligence as portrayed in *The Spy Who Came in from the Cold* (1965), based on John le Carré's bestseller of the same name. Unlike Dante's hell, here there is no ninth circle. Just as the bottom appears, another circle opens, and the descent continues. The hell of espionage is a netherworld without poetry. There are no symbolic beasts or metaphorical punishments; no Virgil for a guide, no sins or sinners. The only sin is failure, which can mean a transfer, a desk job, dismissal, or death. There are no men in trench coats, no women in slinky dresses. Spies, as Alec Leamas (Richard Burton) explains to Nan Perry (Claire Bloom), a British communist, are "seedy, squalid bastards like me . . . drunkards, queers, hen-pecked husbands, people who stammer, civil servants playing cowboys and Indians to brighten their rotten little lives." This is a world in which James Bond would not feel at home.

Photographed in bleak monochrome and directed with unflinching realism by Martin Ritt, *The Spy Who Came in from the Cold* presents a grimly cynical picture of British intelligence. Expediency is all, betrayal is inevitable, and double agents mean double crosses. As Leamas, Richard Burton—his waist thickened and his face rueful—exudes dissipation. Leamas, who had been in charge of intelligence operations in Berlin for nine years, is recalled to London after his best contact—who had supplied him with microfilm of East German intelligence meetings—is killed. Control has worked out an elaborate scenario for Leamas, more dangerous than his previous job. He will supposedly be demoted. Then, after being seen acting unruly in public, he will be briefly imprisoned, then reduced to working for a pittance in a library—all this to attract the attention of East German operatives and convince them he is ripe for defection. The ruse is only clarified at the end of the film. Until then, we believe Leamas has turned into a drunken bully, intimidating and then pummeling a grocer. But what does a trouncing matter to Control, who says matter-of-factly, "We do disagreeable things . . . . We have to live without sympathy."

Control's scheme is even more perverse. He informs Leamas that Hans-Dieter Mundt (Peter van Eyck), an ex-Nazi and now a communist, is a double agent and must be killed—preferably by his subordinate, Fiedler (Oscar Werner), a Jew and a loyal communist. The truth is that Control wants Fiedler killed so Mundt can continue working for the British. A principled Fiedler is a liability; a ruthless Mundt is an asset.

The ending is a *Liebestod*, stark and unorchestrated. Leamas has fallen in love with Nan, who sees communism as the only hope for world disarmament and universal brotherhood. Just when it seems that they are doomed to be executed, Mundt arranges their escape. They are to drive to the Berlin Wall, which they will be allowed to climb and return to the West. When Leamas has almost reached the top, pulling Nan up after him, a shot rings out. Nan falls to the ground. Control only wants Leamas. A guard shouts, "Go back to your own side!" Leamas then realizes that he has been manipulated by the grand puppeteer, who cuts the strings of his marionettes when their performing days are over. Looking down at Nan's body, he begins his descent, leaving the guard no other choice but to kill him. Ritt resisted the temptation to have the lovers' hands touch in death. Leamas and Nan lie alongside each other in front of the most potent and tragic symbol of the Cold War, the Berlin Wall.

Chapter 17

ALFRED HITCHCOCK AND COLD WAR ESPIONAGE

COLD WAR ESPIONAGE SEEMED A NATURAL SUBJECT FOR ALFRED Hitchcock, who in the 1930s, enriched the genre with such classics as *The 39 Steps* and *The Lady Vanishes*. These films were apolitical espionage—or rather, espionage with politics so carefully muted that viewers were free to make their own associations. Hitchcock "cared not a whit for politics," in that he did not identify with any party or fit into any political category, right, left, or centrist.

A plot of mounting suspense mattered more than the reasons for a planned assassination (*The Man Who Knew Too Much*), coveted defense plans (*The 39 Steps*), or an encoded folk melody (*The Lady Vanishes*). In *The 39 Steps* (1935), the spies' objective, acquiring a blueprint for a fighter plane, is only clarified at the end, when it is obvious that "Hitchcock has even less interest in it than we do." In *The Lady Vanishes* (1938), by the time we know why Miss Froy (Dame May Whitty), a British spy, has been kidnapped on board a train traveling from the mythical Bandrika (perhaps a stand-in for Austria) to London, the movie is almost over. The hero and heroine, Michael (Michael Redgrave) and Iris (Margaret Lockwood), have gone from repulsion to attraction, becoming allies in their attempt to expose an ingenious plot to kidnap Miss Froy and pass her off as a heavily bandaged patient in need of surgery. With Hitchcock, people are rarely what they seem. A nun is a fraud in high heels. Dr. Hartz (Paul Lukas), a seemingly benign neurosurgeon with a German accent, is the mastermind behind the kidnapping. And least important in terms of plot—but not in terms of its resolution—is the heroine's decision to stay with the hero, with whom she has experienced the adventure of a lifetime, rather than marry her milquetoast fiancé.

Like most intricately plotted spy films, *The Lady Vanishes* is a tangle of incidents knotted to the point of frustration, but then unlaced, with each strand attesting to the deceptive naturalness of the events as they occurred. That was Hitchcock's genius: to make the weirdly improbable dramatically possible, so that disbelief is not so much suspended as ignored. Once you are caught up in the narrative undertow, you remain submerged until you're deposited on shore. It was also part of Hitchcock's genius to make the MacGuffin, "what . . . the spies are after," a kind of afterthought—a piece of information that is explained once, and only once, to satisfy those more interested in knowing the reasons for the kidnapping than in stringing along with Michael and Iris in their attempt to save Miss Froy and themselves from Hartz's machinations.

What exactly is Hartz after in *The Lady Vanishes*? It is only near the end of the film that Miss Froy explains that she has encoded in a folk tune a vital clause in a secret pact between two European nations. Which two, one might ask? We never know. Hitchcock could not care less. Once the MacGuffin has served its purpose, "[I]t is actually nothing at all." Suspense is everything; the explanation is a freebie.

When *The Lady Vanishes* was released in August 1938, Hitler had already taken over Austria. A month later, British prime minister Neville Chamberlain returned from the Munich Conference, umbrella in hand and brandishing a piece of paper, to assure Britons that there will be "peace in our time." Hitler will make no further territorial demands after acquiring the Sudentenland, the German-speaking part of the former Czechoslovakia. But any optimism was short-lived. The annexation was merely the prelude to his absorption of the entire country. A year later, on 1 September 1939, Hitler invaded Poland, and Britain was again at war.

The Lady Vanishes contains some cryptic fragments of dialogue ("England is on the brink," "conditions as they are now"), which would have disturbed the politically astute. On another, and perhaps deeper, level, the film reflects an uneasy optimism, "a British mood immediately after Munich." The villain with a German accent, whose quarry is British to the core, can only mean one thing: Germany has designs on Britain, and it is only a matter of time before they become apparent. Thus far, Hitchcock has left the enemy unnamed, although there could only have been one possibility. Since Germany had not yet become a belligerent, it was never identified as the country plotting assassinations, stealing blueprints for airplanes, or kidnapping British agents.

The situation was different when Hitchcock made his next espionage (and second American) film, *Foreign Correspondent* (1940). When Hitchcock arrived in Hollywood at the end of March 1939, Europe was five months away from war. Between 18 March and 29 May 1940, when *Foreign Correspondent* was being filmed, the Nazis had overrun Norway, Denmark, Belgium, and the Netherlands. When the film opened in New York on 27 August, the Battle of Britain was raging; on 7 September, the London Blitz began. There was no way *Foreign Correspondent* could end on a tentative note.

Foreign Correspondent portrayed the world on the brink of war. On 20 August 1939, reporter Johnny Jones (Joel McCrea) is elevated to foreign correspondent. The date is significant; the world is two weeks away from war, as headlines and calendars keep reminding us. Hitchcock generates the kind of suspense common in movies in which the outcome is known (for example, *Titanic*; depictions of the crucial 5–7 December 1941 weekend in *Pride of the Marines* and especially *Tora! Tora! Tora!*); however, the incidents leading up to it are dramatized so compellingly that the audience forgets about 1 September. Their attention is focused on what is happening between 20 and 31 August, as Jones is thrown into Hitchcock's unhinged world, where a crypto-fascist poses as the head of a peace foundation; a Dutch diplomat's lookalike is assassinated on the steps of a conference hall; windmills with reverse-turning vanes function as a primitive version of air traffic control; the wing of a plane that crash lands in the Atlantic acts as a life raft; and the MacGuffin—a treaty between Belgium and the Netherlands—proves a moot point. If it was an alliance against Hitler, it did little good in spring 1940, when both countries fell to the Nazis.

When war finally erupts, it is almost anticlimactic. But Hitchcock makes the declaration of war part of the coda, in which Jones delivers a wake-up call to America at a radio station that has lost electricity. Broadcasting in darkness, he reminds Americans that they have yet to suffer Britain's fate: "All the noise you hear isn't static. It's death coming to London . . . . You can hear the bombs falling on the streets and in the homes." London has become a city of darkness, but America's lights have not been extinguished. "Hello, America. Hang onto your lights," he urges. "They're the only lights left in the world." In August 1940, Jones was right. But even America would know its share of air raids and blackouts.

In Hitchcock's spy world, characters must either fend for themselves, or depend upon the kindness of strangers until they are forced to function on their own. Each scenario has a variety of possibilities. In *The 39 Steps*,

Hannay (Robert Donat) must prove his innocence by exposing a spy ring known as "the thirty-nine steps." There is no reason why a crofter's wife should befriend him, much less give him her husband's jacket; why the heroine (Madeleine Carroll) should change from adversary to ally, particularly after she had been handcuffed to him and forced to accompany him on his quest; why an innkeeper and his wife are hospitable to them, when it is obvious they are on the run. The answer is simple: They wear their innocence on their faces and their hearts on their sleeves. In *The Lady Vanishes*, Michael and Iris use their wits—he more than she—to solve the mystery of the vanished lady. They receive no help from their fellow passengers, some of whom deny ever having seen her. Once Johnny Jones—with little help from anyone, including the heroine, who is the villain's daughter—makes the giant leap from innocent abroad to one-man intelligence operation in *Foreign Correspondent*, he becomes a source of light for a world in shadow. For the rest of his career, Hitchcock used the same plot lines, refining or embellishing them. If it was a "wrong man" movie, he needed an actor with the face of a Candide, like Robert Cummings in *Saboteur* (1942). Although Hitchcock would have preferred Gary Cooper—whose "aw shucks" image would have resulted in a different rite of passage (hayseed to spy catcher)—Cummings underwent a similar transition without the burden of a persona, creating a more believable character in an unbelievable but engrossing movie.

Saboteur opens with an explosion in a California defense plant. The explosion results from a fire that burned out of control after Barry Kane (Cummings) handed a fire extinguisher to his friend, who immediately went up in flames because the extinguisher had been filled with gasoline. This act of sabotage was in keeping with Hollywood's vision of a post-Pearl Harbor America overrun with spies and saboteurs, who will stop at nothing to disrupt the war effort. Like Hannay in *The 39 Steps*, Kane becomes a fugitive, but he is so guileless that even the victim's mother does not report him to the authorities. A garrulous truck driver gives him a lift and later misdirects the police so Kane can escape. A blind composer welcomes him into his cottage; the composer's niece, Pat Martin (Priscilla Lane), is ready to turn him in until they meet up with a circus caravan, whose performers sense his innocence—all, that is, except the midget with the Hitler-like moustache whom the others denounce as a fascist. But once the couple reaches New York on their cross-country odyssey, they are on their own. Los Angeles may be the city of angels, but angels fear to tread in New York. Kane must find a way of escaping from his basement prison to prevent a battleship from being blown up at the Brooklyn Navy Yard. Pat must risk her life to trap Frank Fry (Norman Lloyd), the saboteur, at the Statue of Liberty, where Kane confronts him on Lady Liberty's torch, from which one of them will fall—and it will not be Kane.

Hitchcock approached espionage as if it were a branch of affirmative action. The field is open to women, age unspecified and ethnicity subject to popular taste—meaning, for the most part, Caucasian females (Annabella in *The 39 Steps*, Elsa in *Secret Agent*, Miss Froy in *The Lady Vanishes*, Eve Kendall in *North by Northwest*). But no female agent was ever recruited the way Alicia Huberman (Ingrid Bergman) was in *Notorious* (1946), and by Cary Grant no less. Devlin (Grant), an intelligence agent, starts Alicia on a guilt trip because she has an unrepentant Nazi for a father. Devlin intimates—not very subtly—that if she wanted to atone for her father's sins, she should accompany him to Rio de Janeiro to expose a colony of ex-Nazis. Since Devlin treats Alicia like a tramp, frequently reminding her of her promiscuous past, he expects her to seduce Alexander Sebastian (Claude Rains) in order to gain access to his inner circle. When Sebastian proposes marriage, the head of intelligence expects Alicia to accept. How else can she show she is a loyal American, unlike her traitorous father? Rarely has a woman been treated so shabbily by men, who see her only as a channel for information. Devlin taunts Alicia for her willingness to sleep with the enemy, hoping that she will prove herself a virtuous woman by insisting that she loathes her job but places her country before her scruples. Alicia, however, will not degrade herself further by encouraging his inflexible morality.

With Devlin as her contact (but not protector), Alicia can rely on no one. It is she who must put Devlin on the guest list for a party so he can gain access to Sebastian's mysterious wine cellar, which contains more than wine. When Sebastian discovers Alicia's identity, his mother decides to slowly poison her to death. At this point, unless Devlin rescues her, Alicia cannot free herself from the bedroom that will soon be her death chamber. But that is *his* job. She does the hard work, he does the (not especially dangerous) rescuing, and American intelligence (the unnamed CIA) takes the credit.

Hitchcock inverted the male-female dynamic in *North by Northwest* (1959), with Cary Grant as Roger Thornhill, the now familiar wrong man (*The 39 Steps*, *Saboteur*), mistaken for the non-existent George Kaplan. CIA double agent Eve Kendall (Eva Marie Saint) is not a penitent like Alicia, even though her duties requires her to continue to be the lover of Philip Vandamm (James Mason of the measured cadences), a spy working for an unnamed, but inferable, country. And if Eve has to spend the night with the fugitive Thornhill in her train compartment, it is all in a night's work.

"George Kaplan" is a decoy created by the CIA to convince Vandamm that such an agent exists and to deflect attention away from Eve, who Thornhill does not know is Vandamm's mistress—much less a CIA agent. When the head of intelligence, known only as the professor (Leo G. Carroll), learns that Vandamm believes Thornhill is the mythical Kaplan, he realizes the deception is successful. Let Vandamm go on thinking that Thornhill is Kaplan. If Thornhill should meet a tragic end, *c'est la guerre froide*. At least he would have died for his country.

Eve must maintain her credibility with Vandamm, even if it means sending Thornhill to a rendezvous with death, which he narrowly escapes. A one-night stand is no guarantee of fidelity, especially if the lady is working both sides of a treacherous street. Since both Thornhill and Eve are playing a dangerous game (although Thornhill doesn't know the extent of it), they are forced to help each other. To prove she is loyal to Vandamm, Eve shoots Thornhill in public. When Vandamm learns her pistol contained blanks, she is earmarked for disposal "from a great height"—that is, thrown off his private plane.

Although Vandamm seems to be in the employ of the Soviets (who else?) and searching for (what else?) valuable microfilm, *North by Northwest* is not so much Cold War as romantic melodrama, with a hero and heroine who are the essence of cool and a villain who sounds as if he should be giving elocution lessons to Cockney flower sellers. The film includes some extraordinary set pieces, such as the assassination in the lobby of the United Nations; the crop-duster sequence in which what should have been insecticide turns out to be bullets; and the climactic rescue on Mount Rushmore, when Thornhill saves Eve from falling to her death as he pulls her up the face of the cliff and, in a sensuously smooth dissolve, into the upper berth of a train speeding through a tunnel—Hitchcock's idea of consummation by rail. For the most part, *North by Northwest* is a compendium of familiar tropes: wrong man and blonde companion (*The 39 Steps*, *Saboteur*); fashionably dressed enemy agents whose appearance belies their agenda (*The 39 Steps*, *Foreign Correspondent*, *Saboteur*); a MacGuffin (the microfilm); the climax at a familiar landmark (the London Palladium in *The 39 Steps*, the Statue of Liberty in *Saboteur*); and the hand-on-hand finale (Robert Donat and Madeleine Carroll holding hands in *The 39 Steps*; Norman Lloyd holding on to Robert Cummings in *Saboteur*). Hitchcock was a perennial recycler, but the end result is always new.

Hitchcock could have made a Cold War hair-raiser if he had remained faithful to Daphne du Maurier's "The Birds," the second of eight short stories in the collection *Kiss Me Again, Stranger* (1952). "The Birds," set in Cornwall, is told from the point of view of Nat Hocken, a farm worker, who first observes a flock of birds circling restlessly. Assuming the birds are frustrated because the weather has prevented them from migrating, he ignores a portent that the Roman augurs would have considered an ill omen. Even when the birds swoop down without warning and fly through an open window into his children's room, colliding with each other and bouncing off the walls, he is not alarmed, again attributing their behavior to the weather. The locals feel differently, laying the blame on the Russians: "The Russians have poisoned the birds." When the birds attack RAF planes, Britain declares a state of emergency. "Won't America do something?" Nat's wife asks. "They've always been our allies, haven't they?" Meanwhile, one can only wait and wonder, as Nat does, "how many million years of memory were stored in those little brains . . . giving them the instinct to destroy mankind with all the deft precision of machines." For a film version, "The Birds" would have to be fleshed out, with characters added. If Hitchcock had retained du Maurier's plot, the film would have been real Cold War science fiction, a worthy companion to *Invasion of the Body Snatchers*.

For the 1962 film, Hitchcock used only the title and the setting: a coastal community (now California's Bodega Bay) terrorized by birds. Evan Hunter's screenplay is really an original, even though the credits read "based on a story by Daphne du Maurier." Hitchcock was even less interested in the cause of the birds' behavior than he was in what the spies were after in *The 39 Steps, The Lady Vanishes*, and *North by Northwest*. Taken as an allegory of evil, *The Birds* asks one to imagine that if the main characters—a widow who undermines every relationship her son has with a woman, a son incapable of realizing the hold his mother has on him, and a female intruder who comes between them—were birds, their behavior might be just as irrational. However one interprets *The Birds* (Camille Paglia has argued convincingly that Hitchcock "has left the ending ambiguous"), one thing is certain: *The Birds* is not a Cold War parable like du Maurier's short story.

Oddly, two of Hitchcock's less acclaimed films are distinctly Cold War in setting: *Torn Curtain* (1966), set in East Germany, and *Topaz* (1969), set in Castro's Cuba. Although fascinated by espionage, Hitchcock only made one spy film in the 1950s, *North by Northwest*, his last movie of the decade. One would have thought that in the 1950s, when atomic espionage was front-page news, Hitchcock would have considered a film on the order of *My Son John* or *Pickup on South Street*. Yet despite their potential as material for compelling drama Hitchcock ignored the Klaus Fuchs, Alger Hiss, and

Julius and Ethel Rosenberg cases, perhaps feeling that such films could easily become dated. Guy Burgess was another matter. In May 1965, Hitchcock was contemplating a film about Burgess, one of five Cambridge University graduates who became Soviet agents. Perhaps Burgess's death from alcoholism in 1963 revived Hitchcock's interest in the Cambridge Five—or at least in Burgess, who defected to the Soviet Union in 1951. Burgess's sexual orientation was even more challenging. In the 1960s, a director could be less evasive than formerly about a character's homosexuality, although the love that dares not speak its name was still expressed sotto voce. A gay spy would provide an alternative to the straight James Bond, whose franchise was then in its early stages (*Dr. No* [1962], *To Russia with Love* [1964]).

As a rudimentary plot began to take shape, the focus shifted from Burgess—or a Burgess-like spy—to his wife and her reaction to her husband's treason. Since Burgess was unmarried, the character would have to be a composite, perhaps of Burgess and Donald Maclean, another of the Cambridge Five, who was married with three children and who also fled to the Soviet Union in 1951. This Burgess clone would be neither gay nor bisexual, especially if played by Paul Newman.

It was not surprising that Hitchcock envisioned a film about the effect of one family member's actions on another, a theme that ran through his three preceding films. In *Psycho* (1960), the infidelity of Norman Bates's mother drove Norman to murder her and her lover and, in atonement, to take on her personality. In *The Birds* (1962), a mother's unwillingness to sever the silver cord had profound repercussions not only for her grown son and teenage daughter, but also for a woman who has become part of their circle. *Marnie* (1964) traced the title character's kleptomania and frigidity to a childhood trauma caused by her murder of one of her mother's johns. One can only speculate about how Hitchcock might have dealt with a wife's discovery that her husband is a traitor: a slow death (*Notorious*), a confrontation at a landmark (*Saboteur, North by Northwest*), an arranged murder by one party or the other (*Dial M for Murder*). The wife could also alert Scotland Yard, leading to a romance between herself and the inspector assigned to the case (*Stage Fright*).

Believing that the Irish novelist Brian Moore would be sympathetic to his ideas—particularly since Moore created such a psychologically complex female protagonist in *The Lonely Passion of Judith Hearne*—Hitchcock entrusted him with the screenplay, despite his lack of experience as a screenwriter. But Universal, Hitchcock's home studio, had already selected the leads: the Hollywood royals Paul Newman and Julie Andrews. Hitchcock was speechless: Hud and Mary Poppins as a communist spy and his unsuspecting wife? Even Moore knew Hitchcock's premise was unworkable with such casting. What Hitchcock seemed to envision was a film like *Suspicion* (1941), in which the wife would gradually discover the truth about her husband. But unlike *Suspicion*, in which the wife's fears proved groundless, this time they would be confirmed. Such a film would simply be the old Hitchcock, repackaged for the 1960s—but not with Newman and Andrews.

But the two actors could costar in a different type of espionage film, a grand deception in which a distinguished American physicist (Newman) only *pretends* to be a traitor, so that he can travel behind the Iron Curtain and meet his German counterpart in Leipzig, who, he suspects, knows the part missing from a formula for a defense missile that would make nuclear warfare obsolete. Thus the main character must be a male with a fiancée-lover assistant. All that remained of Hitchcock's original concept was a woman's discovery that the man she loves posed as a defector to East Germany, convincing the press that the government's cancellation of his Gamma Five project, which would banish the threat of a nuclear holocaust, was the reason for his defection.

Torn Curtain represents Hitchcock's most extensive use of a support group of ordinary citizens and professionals who help Michael (Newman) and Sarah (Andrews) on each leg of their Norway-Denmark-East Berlin-Leipzig-Sweden odyssey, which they could never have managed on their own. In fact, they do nothing on their own, except escape after others have made the preparations.

Brian Moore, who was unhappy with the film (as were the leads), felt that Hitchcock "simply ransacked his bag of tricks." It would be more accurate to say that Hitchcock repeated familiar motifs, themes, and compositions in a totally new setting. His characters frequently travel long distances (*The 39 Steps, The Lady Vanishes, Saboteur, Shadow of a Doubt, Notorious, North by Northwest*) and in a variety of ways (car, train, boat, plane). But the routes are never the same, and no one's itinerary resembles Michael and Sarah's in *Torn Curtain*, which opens like *Psycho* with two people in a post-coital state. Unlike Sam (John Gavin) and Marion (Janet Leigh) in *Psycho*, who are spending a long lunch hour in a ratty hotel room, Michael and Sarah are cuddling under the covers in their cabin on a Norwegian ship, the site of an international physicists' congress. So we have similar openings, but different couples in different settings.

The mood darkens when Michael receives a radiogram informing him that his book is ready. At first, he refuses the message, but then decides to accept it. In the opening scenes, Michael's behavior is so enigmatic, and Newman's face so unreadable, that one might wonder if *Torn Curtain* is the underside of *Suspicion*, but with a different disclosure. In the earlier film, a wife's fears about her husband prove unfounded, even though she had every reason to suspect him of trying to murder her. In *Torn Curtain*, the crucial book is a mathematics primer, with a marker on the page explaining pi, the Greek letter used to represent the ratio of the circumference to the diameter of a circle. Pi is also, as Michael discovers, the code name of an underground organization devoted to transporting Germans from Leipzig to East Berlin, and from there to the West.

Moore knew the kind of screenplay Hitchcock wanted, one in which a bookmarked page sends Michael on a dark odyssey into the anti-communist resistance. Following instructions, Michael manages to elude Gromek, the "personal guide" the communists have assigned to him, and takes a cab to a farm on the outskirts of the city. There he is greeted by a woman who, like the man with the all-American accent driving a tractor, is a member of the underground. Just as the Christians in imperial Rome used their staff to make the sign of the cross in the dirt to identify themselves to co-religionists, Michael traces the Greek letter on the ground. The woman understands the symbol. Her willingness to help Michael is a Hitchcockian article of faith: There will always be people of conviction who take enormous risks to aid the imperiled hero.

When Gromek discovers where Michael has gone, he heads out to the farm. Michael and the woman have no other choice but to resort to violence. But violence in Hitchcock is ritualized. The passengers on the lifeboat in the eponymous 1944 film descend on a Nazi (Walter Sleazak) in a Dionysian frenzy, pummeling him to death before heaving him over the side. The shower murder of Marion Crane in *Psycho* is stylized slashing. We see Marion step into the shower. Her head turns toward the spray, her mouth open. Then a silhouette appears against the shower curtain, which is violently pulled aside. We next see a slashing knife, a gaping mouth, Marion's body sliding down the shower wall with her head facing the viewer, her staring eye, and the bloody water gurgling down the drain. The fifty-five or sixty-five cut sequence ("depending on where you start counting") is a manual for blood sacrifice, with water serving as a purifying agent that cleanses the perpetrator of the deed.

The killing of Gromek in *Torn Curtain* also occurs in stages. The woman throws soup in his face, and Michael grips him in a stranglehold. She then strikes Gromek with a shovel, but like the undying monster in horror films, he is not felled. She finds a kitchen knife, wielding it at an angle, like Norman Bates in *Psycho*. Gromek is still breathing. Finally, she turns on the gas jets and opens the oven door, so that she and Michael can stuff him inside. After Gromek has been asphyxiated, she turns off the jets, as the two murderers breathe heavily, like Brandon and Philip in *Rope* (1948) who, after strangling their victim, savor the moment as if they were experiencing orgasmic release.

Pi reserves seats for Michael and Sarah on a special bus running between Leipzig and East Berlin. The bus sequence recalls the caravan in *Saboteur*, where the performers in a freak show shelter Barry and Pat, despite the objections of the major, a Hitlerian midget. Similarly, a woman on the bus denounces Michael and Sarah for jeopardizing the enterprise. After some close shaves but no nicks, the bus arrives in East Berlin, where Michael and Sarah encounter a Polish countess (played with seedy bravura by Lila Kedrova), who assists them, hoping that they will sponsor her for a visa to America. But once the police arrive, she is left behind as the couple flees to a travel bureau. There they learn they will be transported in baskets supposedly containing the costumes of a touring ballet troupe. When detected, they swim to a Swedish freighter, where they are taken aboard and given a common blanket. They huddle under it, as the film comes full circle—except that now Michael and Sarah are sitting, rather than reclining.

The extensive network of enablers who leave Michael and Sarah nothing to do but run from one adventure to another reduces them to fairy tale characters guided by clever elves and omniscient birds. The couple also recalls Tamino and Pamina in Mozart's *The Magic Flute*, who are initiated into rituals for which they have been prepared. All they have to do is sing (Tamino must also play his flute) before they are united in the finale. All Michael does on his own is find the missing part of the formula. By the time he does so, the audience has to be reminded of the reason he played traitor in the first place. What does come through, however, is Michael's overriding determination to complete the formula, even if doing so means delaying a carefully planned rescue operation—while he and the German professor play the physicists' equivalent of "Dueling Banjos" at the blackboard. They add and erase, until the professor is so exasperated he provides the crucial piece, which Michael then memorizes. Like Devlin in *Notorious*, who uses a vulnerable woman to expose an enclave of former Nazis, Michael endangers Sarah's welfare and pi's future, until he finds what he is seeking. It is again a case of the end justifying the means. If the end is a good, and the means result in some casualties along the way, *c'est la guerre*, as the professor in *North by Northwest* would say. War, hot or cold, is still war.

Hitchcock depicted the dark side of espionage—isolation, loneliness, ambivalence, and remorse—in the critically undervalued *Secret Agent* (1936) and *Topaz* (1969). In *Secret Agent*, a novelist (John Gielgud, theatrically handsome at thirty-one), whom the world believes is dead, is recruited as a spy and given a new name, Ashenden, and a mission: He is to travel to Switzerland and assassinate a German agent en route to the Middle East via what was then Constantinople, now Istanbul. The dateline introducing the film, May 16, 1916, is not accidental. Turkey was neutral when Archduke Franz Ferdinand and his wife Sophie were assassinated on 28 June 1914 in Sarajevo. A month later, the Ottoman Empire formed a secret alliance with Germany, signaling its eventual involvement in the conflict. By the end of October, it was official. The Ottoman Empire had joined the Central Powers, throwing its lot in with Germany, which hoped to profit from the alliance by gaining a foothold in the Middle East. Since Turkey was now a belligerent, the agent had to be stopped from reaching Constantinople.

Ashenden has been given a colleague known as the Major (a scene-stealing Peter Lorre, with curly hair and one earring) and a "wife," Elsa (the glowingly blonde Madeleine Carroll), who, unlike her "husband," admits she entered the shadow world for thrills. A romantic triangle results when Robert Marvin (the cherubic Robert Young) begins pursuing Elsa. If Marvin comes on as an irresponsible playboy, that was Hitchcock's intention. First impressions, however, are often misleading. Meanwhile, his only clue a jacket button, Ashenden must find the German agent. Although assassination in the call of duty should depend on more compelling evidence than a button, in wartime any lead is a clue, and any clue can be cause for liquidation. When Ashenden and the Major notice that Caypor's jacket is missing a button, they assume he is the agent. After the Major pushes Caypor off an alp, they learn they were mistaken. The agent is still at large. Caypor's murder is atypical of the "wrong man" scenario, in which the accused must prove his innocence. Caypor didn't have a chance.

The tragic error takes its toll on Elsa, who is shattered by the news, and on Ashenden, who deals with his disgust by getting drunk. The Major, on the other hand, finds the situation hilarious. *Secret Agent* does not glamorize espionage, despite Madeleine Carroll's radiant appearance and boutique wardrobe. This is the slimy underbelly of spy world, in which a hiking trip resulting in an innocent man's murder is intercut with scenes of Elsa and Marvin in the Caypors' parlor, conversing with the victim's soon-to-be widow, as the family dog, sensing tragedy, sniffs and whines at the bedroom door. At the moment of the murder, the whine becomes an attenuated *cri de coeur*. What is extraordinary about the sequence is that the dog's telepathic sense affects Elsa and Mrs. Caypor, who share the same tragically prescient moment, as if they had just witnessed the murder.

Secret Agent depicts espionage as a profession only for those willing to perform a high-wire act without a net. Ashenden and Elsa have no guardian angels, yet they must play on to the end after learning that Marvin is the agent they have been seeking. Robert Young tries to exude menace in the final scenes, but his moonlike face beams too brightly. Ashenden, Elsa, and the Major must stop Marvin from boarding the Constantinople-bound train. Conveniently—in a rote-like resolution—British planes strafe the train, which crashes, leaving Marvin with just enough life to kill the Major—and Elsa and Ashenden with enough sense to get out of the spy racket. Although the film ends abruptly, with Elsa and Ashenden resigning from the foreign service in favor of marriage, the imposed happy ending does not mitigate the inhumanity of espionage. *Secret Agent*, along with the much later *Topaz*, exposes the vulnerability of spies who serve their country. When the chips are down, they're on their own. There is no shortage of replacements.

Topaz marked the end of Hitchcock's ventures into espionage. It is also his most unwieldy film, spanning as it does an arc of locations: Copenhagen, Washington, DC, New York, Havana, and Paris. As one might expect from an adaptation of Leon Uris's 1967 novel of the same name about Soviet spies who have infiltrated NATO, the film suffers from narrative sprawl, running an uncommonly long 127 minutes. Its length places it in the same category as *Torn Curtain* (126 minutes) and *North by Northwest* (136 minutes), both of which were more geographically compact. *Topaz* also suffers from Hitchcock's now familiar technique of resolving the MacGuffin near the end of the film. This time, the MacGuffin is not what the spies are after, but who the spies are: highly placed French officials in NATO who transmit vital information to the Soviets. The spy ring is code named Topaz, whose head is "Columbine," and whose second-in-command is a noted economist. One learns about Topaz and the leak in NATO early in the film. The plot keeps branching out like tree roots, and the locales keep changing like a slide show, so that by the time Columbine and his accomplice are unmasked, the film has reached the two-hour mark, making the detection seem more of an appendix.

What is intriguing about *Topaz* is its unusual protagonist, André Devereaux (Frederick Stafford), a French intelligence liaison officer, who works closely with his American counterpart, Michael Nordstrom (John Forsythe). Devereaux, then, is a double agent serving two allies. When the CIA needed information about the Soviet missile buildup in Cuba in July 1962, Nordstrom persuaded Devereaux to fly to the island, as he had done in the past. Arm-twisting is unnecessary. Devereaux has a lover there, Juanita de Cordoba (Karin Dor), the widow of a revolutionary hero. Juanita is now disenchanted with Castro and has become a counter-revolutionary, turning her home into an espionage center with a skilled staff that can hide cameras in poultry and microfilm strips in typewriter ribbons, razor cartridges, and book covers. Hitchcock has come a long way from encoded folk songs and uranium ore in wine bottles.

As the culmination of the director's espionage cycle, *Topaz* is also a recapitulation. With a slim frame, a sleekly masculine wardrobe, and a cool demeanor that conjures up crème de menthe over chipped ice, Devereaux is 007 with traces of DNA from Cary Grant, whose crisply pressed suits served as the inspiration for Stafford's. Despite his jet setting, Devereaux's pants keep their crease. It is as if a phantom Grant were standing behind Stafford and sometimes emanating from him, imposing his persona on Stafford, who, lacking one of his own, slipped back into Grant's. And yet Devereaux is unique among Hitchcock spies. Miss Froy (*The Lady Vanishes*), Ashenden (*Secret Agent*), and Devlin (*Notorious*) were never double agents. Hitchcock's only other double agents are women: Alicia in *Notorious* and Eve in *North by Northwest*, who have to toggle between both sides and literally sleep with the enemy. The agents survive; the fortunes of those who serve them vary. The enablers in *Torn Curtain* go unscathed. Juanita de Cordoba and her staff pay dearly for working against the Castro regime. Two of her servants, Carlos and Rita Mendoza, who had been sent to photograph the missiles during a rally, are apprehended and tortured. In the film's most potent image, Carlos Mendoza lies unconscious across the lap of his wife, her face battered and her eyes glazed, a gruesome pietà. It is a composition that in some prints appears again at the end of the film. Unable to endure further torture, Rita Mendoza betrays Juanita by whispering her name in a belabored gasp to Rico Parra (John Vernon), one of Castro's lieutenants. Although Parra is in love with Juanita, the goals of the revolution supersede affairs of the heart. Rather than see Juanita suffer the Mendozas' fate, he presses her body against his and shoots her. It is stylized death. When Juanita sinks to the floor, her dress fans out like a pool of blood.

In America, civilians involved in intelligence operations fare better. A florist (a brilliant cameo by Roscoe Lee Browne) has a skin-of-his-teeth time microfilming the Cuba-Soviet pact for Devereaux while Castro is holed up at the Hotel Theresa in Harlem. But New York is not Cuba, and even if the florist had been caught, Castro and his entourage could never admit that they had been duped into believing that a florist from Martinique was a reporter for *Ebony* magazine. The defector Boris Kusenov (Per-Axel Arosenius)—a KGB deputy chief who sought asylum in the West in return for information about Topaz—was richly compensated. He and his family were ensconced in a safe house outside Washington, DC, with servants and a housekeeper. His daughter was given a full scholarship to study music at a college of her choice. And Kusenov himself has been promised a job commensurate with his abilities. When Kusenov learns that Devereaux is being recalled after the French discovered he was moonlighting for the Americans, he advises Devereaux to cut as good a deal for himself. Devereaux seems to be doing so at the end of the film, when he and his wife are flying from Paris to Washington, DC. To keep Devereaux's heroic image intact, Hitchcock does not spell out the reasons for the spy's departure. It is clear that America rewards informers, although Devereaux would never have considered himself one. And yet, espionage is informing—or rather, informing in a cause sanctioned by the homeland. What do agents do except pass on the information to their superiors? But if the information prevented the Cuban Missile Crisis from becoming World War III, and if the leak in NATO was sealed after the exposure of Topaz, it was all worth the effort. Again, the end justified the means, as it always does in spy world.

If, after so many divagations, one can remember that *Topaz* is supposedly about French spies transmitting NATO secrets to the Soviets, the resolution is an anticlimax. One of the spies, Henri Jarré (Philippe Noiret), makes a major blunder and ends up face down on the hood of a car. "Columbine" is bon vivant Jacques Granville (Michel Piccoli), with whom Devereaux's wife has been having an affair—an ironic quid pro quo since Devereaux had been having one of his own with Juanita.

Hitchcock experimented with three different endings. The first, which went over poorly with preview audiences, had Granville and Devereaux engaging in an anachronistic duel in a football field. A KGB sniper in the stands shoots Granville, whose usefulness to the Soviets has ended. The second, better ending has Devereaux and his wife departing for Washington, DC, on one plane, and Granville leaving for Moscow on another. Granville waves, shouting "Bon voyage." Devereaux smiles, knowing a true survivor when he sees one. In the third, originally released ending, Granville goes home and shoots himself. The second is the one television viewers will recognize; it is also the ending of the *Topaz* DVD in Universal's *Alfred Hitchcock Collection*. In this version, a newspaper with the headline "Cuban Missile Crisis Over" is tossed on a park bench. Superimposed over this final shot are the Mendoza pietà, Jarré's body on the hood of the car, and Juanita's murder, all grim reminders of the price the world pays for peace, which is just a momentary lull between hostilities.

Although *Topaz* may feel like an intercontinental travelogue with attractive people, lovely scenery, and an implausible story line, it does have a factual foundation. True-life espionage is often so complex that it can cause the head to shake in doubt or disbelief. French intelligence was dealt a severe blow when the Nazi occupation began in June 1940. In 1944, as the tide of the war was turning in favor of the Allies, the Free French created an agency, *Service de documentation extérieure et contra-espionnage* (SDECE), whose primary purpose was to hasten the liberation of Europe. Instead, it became another spy organization polarized by tension between non-communist and communist factions, "spying on French colonies and American allies who were doing all the actual work of liberating France." The communist presence never disappeared. As the Cold War intensified, a Soviet spy ring was formed within SDECE, code name "Sapphire," whose purpose was to penetrate French intelligence and provide the Soviet Union with information—especially about NATO—that it could not otherwise acquire.

Uris was privy to information obtained from Philippe Thyraud de Vosjoli, a former member of the Free French, and later head of French intelligence in the United States from 1951 to 1963. De Vosjoli had also set up a spy network in Cuba a year before the Cuban missile crisis, and was aware of the threat posed by Soviet missiles in Cuba. President de Gaulle, irked by the Kennedy administration's refusal to keep him in the loop, refused to believe that the Soviet Union was establishing a missile base in Cuba. Discredited and ridiculed by de Gaulle, de Vosjoli sought asylum in the United States. The extent of Uris's indebtedness to de Vosjoli was revealed in a brief *Time* magazine notice (21 February 1972) stating that after Uris refused to split the *Topaz* profits with de Vosjoli, the latter went to court and was awarded $352,356, plus interest and half of all future earnings.

De Vosjoli may have been the inspiration for Devereaux, but Uris's creation was never chief of French intelligence in the United States. On the

other hand, Boris Kusenov ("Kuznetov" in the novel) is clearly modeled after Anatoliy Golitsyn, a KGB major who defected in 1961, traveling first to
Helsinki and Stockholm, and then to the United States, where he proved
an invaluable source of information about Soviet espionage—including the
existence of moles in the French government, whom a KBG official termed
"sapphires." In *Topaz*, Kusenov and his family traverse a similar route, Copenhagen to Washington, DC. There was an economist who was a Soviet
mole; he was not French but rather the Canadian Hugh George Hambleton.
Unlike the economist in the film, whose murder was disguised as a suicide,
Hambleton was arrested and given a ten-year prison sentence. However,
Colonel Charles de la Salle, who had been a spy for the Romanians, did
commit suicide by jumping out of his kitchen window and landing on a car.
Uris used his source material along with his imagination to create his characters, some historically based and others composites or inventions. Unable
to use "Sapphire" for the name of the spy ring, Uris chose another gemstone,
topaz. It is clear that he never could have written *Topaz* without the information provided by Philippe Thyraud de Vosjoli.

Hitchcock originally wanted Uris to write the screenplay. By 15 June 1968
Uris had prepared an outline, which Hitchcock found unusable. Uris had
Devereaux operating an espionage ring in Cuba for France, like de Vosjoli.
Juanita also has spies of her own photographing the Soviet ships as they
arrive with the missiles. Uris's Devereaux, realizing the threat posed to the
United States, wanted to share his knowledge with American intelligence.
But Hitchcock did not want a conflicted protagonist; Devereaux is too cool
for pangs of conscience. Hitchcock's agents follow orders up to a point, but
then improvise until circumstances require a different strategy. Devereaux
must have enough self-confidence to assist Nordstrom without seeking permission from his government. Since Uris could not provide Hitchcock with
the kind of protagonist he envisioned, Samuel Taylor, who coauthored the
Vertigo screenplay, inherited the project. Taylor's was the screenplay that
Hitchcock filmed.

Hitchcock showed greater concern for the characters in *Topaz* than he
did for those in *Torn Curtain*. The Mendozas suffer for a cause, and Juanita
dies for a democratic Cuba that has yet to come into being. Devereaux's job
involves frequent separations from his wife, Nicole (Dany Robin), whose
icy glamour, alluring but detached, explains his frequent trips to Cuba,
where he can check on the missiles and enjoy the company of an affection-
ate woman. Similarly, Nicole is attracted to the debonair Jacques Granville,
whose self-fabricated image complements hers. For both of them, artifice is

everything. There is also the irony of Nicole's liaison with the head of the spy ring that her husband is trying to expose, making for political, rather than tragic irony. Critically and financially a failure, *Topaz* remains Hitchcock's most contemporary film, which may explain why those who know or remember the period can be more forgiving of its faults.

Chapter 18

HOLLYWOOD'S COLD WARRIOR: JOHN WAYNE

COMPARED TO JOHN WAYNE IN WILLIAM WELLMAN'S *BLOOD ALLEY* (1955), Clark Gable had it easy in *Never Let Me Go* (1953). Gable starred as a Moscow-based journalist married to a Russian ballerina (Gene Tierney of the sculpted face and cheekbones). As they are boarding a plane for America, he is allowed to leave, but not she. The film's second half is a rescue operation, as exciting as it is improbable, with Gable mastering the art of navigation so he can sail from Cornwall to Moscow and bring his beloved to America, where she can enjoy the benefits of capitalism. *Never Let Me Go* is the kind of a film in which there may be a dead end, but not a dead Gable. Since the Soviets are vodka-swilling buffoons, Gable and his buddies dupe them into believing that Russia is responsible for every known invention of the twentieth century. The climax is a series of narrow escapes, including Gable's. He sheds his swimsuit for a Soviet colonel's uniform and then chucks it when detected. Tierney does the same with her tutu, and the two swim to safety. Destination: America. Where else could they go after such a wild adventure except the land that created the dream factory called Hollywood?

In *Blood Alley* (1955), Wayne is a prisoner of Chinese communists who try to brainwash him, little knowing that nobody brainwashes the Duke. During his incarceration, Wayne conjures up an imaginary companion, "Baby," to whom he speaks in order to maintain his sanity. When he isn't grousing to Baby, he's mocking his non-English speaking captors, who smile when he calls them "lard heads" and "jerks"—a carry over from World War II movies such as *Desperate Journey* (1942) and *Three Came Home* (1949), in which American captives did the same to the Nazis and Japanese, resorting to a form of mockery that gave them a fleeting moment of superiority.

Chinese villagers secure Wayne's release, expecting that, in return, he will ferry the entire village—179 people—three hundred miles down the Formosa Strait to Hong Kong (then part of the British Empire). The riverboat that he commands becomes a Noah's ark, with men, women, children, animals—and Lauren Bacall. Forget her character's name or even why she's in the village. Supposedly, she is the daughter of a humanitarian doctor, which is more an identity tag than an explanation.

Wayne was not Wellman's first choice. After Robert Mitchum proved intractable, Wellman sought out Gregory Peck, who was uninterested, then Humphrey Bogart, who was too expensive. Wellman then approached Wayne, a staunch anti-communist, who was looking for properties for his independent production company, Batjac. *Blood Alley* became a Batjac production released through Warner Bros. Perhaps if Bogart had played the captain, he and Bacall might have heated up this Cold War odyssey. But with Wayne at the helm, hammering out each syllable as if he had been coached by Bette Davis, the cycle of attraction and repulsion that he and Bacall undergo is limited to slapping each other across the face before their obligatory embrace at the end.

Since the Wayne-Bacall combination proved non-combustible, Wellman struck some sparks among the evacuees, some of them communists, who poison the food and attempt a takeover. Although no one starves, and Wayne retains control of the boat, these incidents are only momentary distractions from a script that needed periodic infusions of drama to sustain audience interest for 115 minutes. One assumes the riverboat will reach Hong Kong, and Wayne and Bacall will go into a clinch at the fadeout. But the Chinese alone deserve our sympathy. When the boat arrives in the harbor, a British naval officer looks at the passengers and remarks sadly, "Refugees." These are, one might add, refugees without a country.

Blood Alley was another addition to the mythology of John Wayne, whose image—like that of the protagonist in a serial whose exploits become more daring with each chapter—grew more heroic with each film. Wayne's persona was forged in the fires of World War II, from which Wayne the actor emerged as Wayne the icon, a symbol of America the invincible. Although his best films were westerns (*Stagecoach, Fort Apache, She Wore a Yellow Ribbon, Rio Grande,* and especially *The Searchers*), movie buffs associate John Wayne, more than any other actor, with World War II. That was his war: *Flying Tigers, Reunion in France, The Fighting Seabees, They Were Expendable, Back to Bataan, Sands of Iwo Jima, Flying Leathernecks, Operation Pacific, The Sea Chase, The Longest Day, In Harm's Way.* Wayne was an actor for all wars. But he never did serve in one, although he could have served during the Second World War.

Wayne was not a draft dodger. In the John Ford Papers at Indiana State University, there is a May 1942 letter from Wayne to John Ford in which Wayne beseeched Ford to get him assigned to the OSS Field Photographic Unit, which Ford headed. Wayne wanted desperately to serve: "Can you get me assigned to your outfit, and if you could, would you want me? How about the Marines? You have Army and Navy men under you." Wayne never received a reply, perhaps because Ford realized Wayne was on the verge of becoming a major star and could serve his country best by playing a service man rather than being one. On the other hand, Ford had a perverse streak that might also account for his silence.

A survey of his war films reveals a John Wayne who served his country on land, sea, and air. Since he was never meant to be a grunt, Hollywood gave him officer status. Even before America's entry into World War II, Wayne heard the call to arms and enlisted in the RAF in *Reunion in France* (1942), in which he is shot down in France and befriended by Joan Crawford, with whom he has a brief romance (insofar as two such dissimilar types could have one). But Wayne must return to beleaguered Britain and Crawford to her Resistance leader-lover, who, with her aid, will help liberate Paris, something one must take on faith. The versatile Wayne then became a mercenary in Claire Chennault's Flying Tigers, defending China from Japanese aggression (*Flying Tigers*, 1942) before Pearl Harbor made it necessary for him to return to America and serve in various branches of the armed forces. He did not think working as a construction engineer in the Seabees was beneath his dignity (*The Fighting Seabees*, 1944). His heroic death at the end of the film led to his resurrection in *They Were Expendable* (1945) as a navy lieutenant in a PT boat squadron in the Philippines. He apparently liked the Philippines and stayed on at the rank of colonel to train guerilla units in *Back to Bataan* (1945). After a four-year hiatus, Wayne was back in uniform as a marine sergeant in *Sands of Iwo Jima* (1949), which won him an Oscar nomination. He dies in this one, too. But he had died before, even underwater in two movies, *Reap the Wild Wind* (1942) and *Wake of the Red Witch* (1948), in which he lost to a giant squid.

Wayne remained under water, this time as a submarine commander in *Operation Pacific* (1951), and emerged in *The Sea Chase* (1955) as a German steamboat captain, *sans* accent, who despised Hitler. According to the *New York Times* (11 June 1955), Wayne played the part "as though he was heading a herd of cattle up the old Chisholm Road." After spending some time in the post-bellum West, where he made his greatest film, *The Searchers* (1956), and the equally memorable *The Man Who Shot Liberty Valance* (1962), Wayne inserted himself into history as Lieutenant Colonel Benjamin H. Vandervoort in *The Longest Day* (1962). Unlike most of Wayne's other characters, Vandervoort is a historical figure. He commanded the 2nd battalion, 505th Parachute Infantry of the 82nd Airborne Division during the Normandy invasion. Vandervoort was twenty-seven in 1944; when Wayne played him, the actor was fifty-five. And yet the age difference did not matter. To see John Wayne hobbling around with a broken ankle—an injury Vandervoort sustained during the Normandy landing—is to see the embodiment of the fighting spirit that led to an allied victory.

In his end was his beginning. Wayne's last World War II film, *In Harm's Way* (1965), is a recap of the conflict, beginning just before Pearl Harbor and lasting to the war's end. John Wayne saw it all—on sound stages and on location. Yet it always seemed he was in the thick of it, in both the European and Pacific theaters. World War II was Wayne's war, but he would have one more: Vietnam.

Wayne bypassed Korea, with *Blood Alley* as a substitute that seemed to be set in the early 1950s—or so Lauren Bacall's wardrobe suggested. Yet no other Hollywood star was so identified with anti-communism as John Wayne. In fact, Stalin sent two hit men disguised as FBI agents to assassinate him. The FBI learned of the plot and intervened, although one suspects the Soviets would have bungled the job as badly as the German saboteurs did in 1942, when they landed by submarine on Long Island and Florida, intending to blow up America. Instead, they were sentenced to death or, in two cases, imprisonment.

In 1944, three years before HUAC began holding hearings, the Alliance for the Preservation of American Ideals was formed. Its members included, among others, the organization's first president, director Sam Wood, Walt Disney, Robert Taylor, Gary Cooper, Hedda Hopper, Adolphe Menjou—and John Wayne, who became president after Wood died of a heart attack in 1949. The purpose of the alliance, as one member put it metaphorically, was to "turn off the faucets which dripped red water into film scripts." When producer Walter Wanger assumed the chair of the Los Angeles division of Crusade for Freedom in September 1950, Wayne sent him a letter of congratulations, noting that six years earlier Wanger had accused the alliance of making "unsupported charges of Communism in the motion picture industry." In September 1950, the Korean War and atomic espionage vied for headlines. Without lording it over Wanger, Wayne wrote, "We didn't make

'Hollywood' and 'Red' synonymous—the Communists, their fellow travelers and their dupes did that damaging job. We foresaw this result and tried to persuade our fellow workers of the need for cleaning our own house." Wanger was now willing to let bygones be bygones.

At 10:35 am, 21 March 1951, Larry Parks, Oscar-nominated for his brilliant impersonation of Al Jolson in *The Jolson Story* (1946), testified before HUAC that he had been a member of the Communist Party, but he initially declined to name names. By 4:00 pm, the interrogation had so worn him down that he named twelve, including Anne Revere, Gale Sondergaard, Karen Morley, Lee J. Cobb, Dorothy Tree, and Morris Carnovsky. At a meeting of the alliance the next day, Wayne criticized Parks for waiting so long before admitting that he had once been a party member. That evening, Wayne made his and the alliance's position clear: "Let no one say that a Communist can be tolerated in American society and particularly in our industry." Sadly, that included Larry Parks, whose film career was virtually over, despite his recanting and soul bearing. He made two more films, both British productions: *Tiger by the Tail* (1955) and *Freud: The Secret Passion* (1962). Parks died of a heart attack in 1975. He was sixty years old.

If Wayne could not be a member of HUAC, he could at least play a HUAC investigator in *Big Jim McLain* (1952), which he co-produced. The lowbrow title matched the script, which had Wayne as the title character and his buddy (James Arness) investigating a communist cell in pre-statehood Hawaii. That much was at least plausible. HUAC had amassed enough evidence about communists in Hawaii to hold hearings there in 1950. Seventy subpoenas were issued. Thirty-nine of the subpoenaed, dubbed "the reluctant thirty-nine," refused to testify and were cited for contempt. But unlike the Hollywood Ten, who went to jail for standing on their First—not Fifth—Amendment rights, the reluctant thirty-nine never served time. The following year, the FBI rounded up seven prominent Hawaiian communists. They were convicted of conspiring to overthrow the territorial government, but escaped imprisonment when the convictions were overturned. If the script had dealt with some of the thirty-nine, or even the seven, which included a former teacher and a newspaper editor, *Big Jim McLain* might have had some credibility. But the facts were fictionalized, and the communists, present and past, were portrayed as either unreconstructed Stalinists or repentant sinners.

Except for a secretary (Nancy Olson), who provides the love interest, and a rooming house owner (Veda Ann Borg), who provides some sex, everyone else is either a present or former communist. The latter admit the error of their ways as if they were in a confessional seeking absolution. One former member describes communism as "a vast conspiracy to enslave the common man." The communists themselves are a mix of professionals (a commissar in a white suit, a bacteriologist, a psychiatrist), labor leaders and their henchmen, and locals representing "the common man," who sit passively when informed they are expendable, and that, if apprehended, they should plead the Fifth Amendment. The cell has more important work to do paralyzing the shipping industry by staging a strike and causing an epidemic. Except for the epidemic, the scenario was not farfetched. Hawaiian communists were known for fomenting labor unrest. In the film, after the traitors are apprehended, two get off by taking the Fifth. Their rights are not questioned. Wayne glowers, but a constitutional right is upheld. A film can be jingoistic without being erroneous, but *Big Jim McLain* errs in its zealousness. HUAC's ostensible position, announced at the outset—that anyone who is a communist after 1945 is essentially a traitor—is incorrect. In 1952, the Communist Party had not been outlawed, and it never would be. The film's assertion was wishful thinking on the part of the star and co-producer.

Wayne's first Cold War movie should have been the Howard Hughes production *Jet Pilot*, which was finished in 1951 but not released until 1957. The delay had nothing to do with *Jet Pilot*'s mediocrity (it was atrocious), but with Hughes's determination to make it the successor to his World War I aviation epic, *Hell's Angels* (1930). Hughes insisted on filming *Jet Pilot* in color, so that the yonder is not wild but serenely blue, giving the aerial sequences a majesty that may please the eye but tranquillize the mind. The film's release coincided with the closing of RKO, the first of the major studios to shut its doors owing to Hughes's mismanagement. In fact, *Jet Pilot* was released under the auspices of Universal-International, as were all of RKO's final productions.

By 1957, the stars, John Wayne and Janet Leigh, did not look as they had six years earlier. Wayne's face had become craggier, and Leigh was no longer a fresh-faced ingénue. Hughes, who was attracted to big-bosomed women, had Leigh wear what Amanda in *The Glass Menagerie* calls "gay deceivers" ("falsies," in the vernacular) that made her breasts look like torpedoes. (Hughes did the same with Janis Carter in *Flying Leathernecks* [1951]). Director Josef von Sternberg showed his indifference to the disjointed script by not having Leigh, playing a Soviet pilot, use a Russian accent. Wayne played an air force colonel attracted to Leigh, supposedly a defector from the Soviet Union, who is as good an aviator as he. That should have tipped him off that she is a spy and out to recruit him. He falls in love with her, and she falls in love with him, as well as haute couture, sirloin steak, and champagne in romantic Palm Springs. Since a charge of espionage would result in her imprisonment, followed by deportation, the pair flies off to the Soviet Union, where it will be his turn to do the spying. Leigh, now in her Soviet uniform and speaking perfect English, is torn between Mother Russia and John Wayne. Naturally, she chooses the latter, along with haute couture, sirloin steak, and champagne.

Wayne and Leigh were two immovable objects, neither being an irresistible force. There was more sensuousness in the aerial photography, which, as Andrew Sarris observed, had the planes doing what their pilots do not, so that "the film soars in an ecstatic flight of speed, grace, and color"—all of which are lacking in the performances.

In Vietnam, Wayne found a war that was as meaningful to him as World War II, but in a different and less global way. The enemy was no less pernicious, and the stakes were just as high—or so he thought. Wayne may have personified America—a global commodity epitomizing the nation's values—but in the mid-1960s, America also had a growing involvement in Vietnam. It was another war, with the North Vietnamese as the oppressors, and the South Vietnamese as the oppressed. In short, it was Korea, part 2.

Hollywood paid little attention to Vietnam at the time of the first French Indochina War (1946–54), the prelude to America's involvement in what was originally a colony of French Indo-China, which also included Laos and Cambodia. It was a war of liberation waged by the Viet Minh under Ho-Chi-Minh to free Vietnam from French rule. In 1952, the Korean War was dragging on, and there were enough Korean War films in the pipeline to satisfy audiences interested in America's attempt to prevent South Korea from being absorbed by the communist North. Vietnam seemed remote at the time. The United States was not involved, except for covert military aid to the French. Yet the war there seemed topical enough for *A Yank in Indo-China* (1952), a quickie that resembled a World War II movie except in one detail: an enemy that denounced Americans as "capitalistic imperialists."

A Yank in Indo-China was set during a war that was already in progress, but little known to early 1950s audiences who, if they grooved on war movies, munched their popcorn while watching *Mission over Korea* and *Fixed Bayonets*. For World War II buffs, there was John Wayne in *Operation Pacific*, taking out Japanese and wooing back his ex-wife, thus satisfying the high testosterone crowd and the distaff side.

Yanks tended to be around whenever there was war: in Britain (*A Yank in the RAF*), in North Africa (*A Yank in Libya*), in Korea (*A Yank in Korea*), and now in the former Indochina. The Yanks, played by John Archer and Douglas Dick, are an entrepreneurial duo running a cargo operation transporting supplies to French troops and Vietnamese loyalists. Considering themselves American nationals and thus unaffected by the present war, they nonetheless find themselves caught up in it when they are forced to fly ammunition to a communist outpost. *Yank* then takes on the features of a Saturday matinee serial, as the group—including two women, one of whom is pregnant, and a traumatized geologist—manages to outwit its captors. The group then makes its way to Hanoi, where the women and the geologist are left with the French before the others go off to destroy the communist hideout, which looks like Vultura's cave in the serial *Nyoka and the Lost Secrets of Hippocrates* (1942). *A Yank in Indo-China* arrived too early to alert Americans to a war that was a decade away from becoming theirs. The best the screenwriters could do was a Yellow Peril replay, with the Chinese communists behaving as barbarically as the Japanese in World War II movies, shooting anyone who defies them and ignoring the needs of a woman in labor. It is also the kind of film in which a Vietnamese orphan is so endearing (he even helps deliver the woman's baby) that you pray he will survive (he doesn't). While some films can be remade, *A Yank in Indo-China* is not one of them. It is a relic of a time when France was fighting its war in Indochina, and the United States fighting its own in Korea. And who would have thought that, with American aid, the French would lose—or that, in 1975, America would, too, and Saigon would undergo a name change and become Ho Chi Minh City? By February 1954, "[T]he United States was paying a third of French costs, shipping arms to Indochina and providing two hundred U.S. Air Force technicians." It was money spent on a dubious cause. Three months later, on 7 May, the French garrison at Dien Bien Phu fell to the communists after a fifty-seven day siege, marking the end of Vietnam as a French colony. Vietnam was partitioned into North and South at the seventeenth parallel. Now it was up to America to keep Laos and Cambodia out of the communist orbit. Otherwise, who knows? "Tomorrow the world," as Hitler used to say.

By 1963, there were fifteen thousand "military advisors" in Vietnam. Hollywood still ignored the possibility of a war in Southeast Asia. America was still recovering from the assassination of John F. Kennedy and the end of Camelot. Vietnam was not a topic that appealed to the major studios.

Although *A Yank in Indo-China* came out under the Columbia Pictures trademark, Columbia was only the distributor. *Yank* was a production of Esskay Pictures, which released through Columbia. Similarly, *A Yank in Viet-Nam*—released in early 1964 through Allied Artists, the former Poverty Row studio, Monogram—brought the war in Southeast Asia into the theaters. This *Yank* was actually filmed in South Vietnam, with Vietnamese and Filipino actors and an authenticity that was lacking in *A Yank in Indo-China*. Marshall Thompson, who, in his early days at MGM, was a male ingénue, was both star and director, playing a marine pilot captured by the Viet Cong, then rescued by a band of guerillas led by a young woman with whom he falls in love. Like the previous *Yank*s, here love and survival take precedence over fact. And like the Seventh Cavalry in a western, paratroopers drop down like gods from the machine to rescue the few survivors. *A Yank in Viet-Nam* left no doubt in anyone's mind that a war being waged in Vietnam involved Americans. By the time *Yank* premiered in February 1964, there had been 118 American casualties, with more to come.

By 1965, the American presence in Vietnam had reached 170,000; by the end of 1966, it would be almost 400,000. In June 1966, Wayne visited Vietnam as part of a USO-sponsored tour. Looking more like a construction worker than a movie star, he awed the troops, who were given a rare glimpse of John Wayne without his hairpiece. Wayne moved easily among the men, shaking hands and signing autographs with a pen that also wrote under water. Before going to Vietnam, he had read Robin Moore's bestseller, *The Green Berets* (1965), which introduced readers to the army's special operations unit known for its distinctive brimless cap and specialty in unconventional warfare. Despite its factual basis, *The Green Berets* was published as a novel. The United States special forces did not welcome Moore's proposal of a fact-based account of the Green Berets' activities in Vietnam. Attorney General Robert Kennedy intervened, enabling Moore to join the unit as a civilian. The army made an additional demand that Moore undergo training, even though he was then thirty-seven. Moore agreed, survived the ordeal, went to Vietnam, and amassed enough material for a work of non-fiction. What Moore uncovered was considered so controversial that *The Green Berets* had to be marketed as a novel, although in no way did it condemn America for intervening in a civil war.

Moore's novel and the Vietnam tour convinced Wayne that audiences needed a movie justifying American involvement in Southeast Asia. That movie would be *The Green Berets* (1968), inspired by, rather than adapted from, Moore's novel. "The Ballad of the Green Berets," the most popular song of 1966, which honored the "fighting soldiers from the sky, / fearless men who jump and die," thrilled Wayne so much that he had a choral version sung over the opening credits. The somber ballad is both a tribute and a eulogy, ending on a note of death and renewal. In the last two stanzas, the wife of a Green Beret becomes a widow, and the balladeer, in the voice of her dead husband, urges her to make certain that their son follows in his father's footsteps and wins his own green beret. That stanza inspired the last scene in the film, in which Wayne places the green cap on the head of a Vietnamese orphan.

When other studios balked at making *The Green Berets*, Wayne stepped in. The film would be a Batjac production released, like *Blood Alley*, through Warner Bros. However, for Wayne to get the army's cooperation—which included equipment, uniforms, and location shooting at Fort Benning, Georgia——Moore could not be involved with the screenplay, which was the work of James Lee Barrett, a former marine. Barrett also coauthored the screenplay of *The Greatest Story Ever Told* (1965), in which Wayne played the Roman centurion at the crucifixion who proclaimed, "Truly this man was the son of God."

The Green Berets was in every sense a John Wayne film. Wayne codirected it; his son Michael produced it; his production company made it. Winton C. Hoch, his favorite cinematographer (*Three Godfathers*, *She Wore a Yellow Ribbon*, *The Quiet Man*, *The Searchers*, *Jet Pilot*) shot it. Wayne played Colonel Mike Kirby, a name intended to conjure up his other Kirbys (Captain Kirby York in *Fort Apache*, Lieutenant Colonel Kirby Yorke in *Rio Grande*). The supporting cast included Bruce Cabot, who first worked with Wayne in *In Harm's Way* and went on to appear in other Wayne films such as *The War Wagon*, *Hellfighters*, *Chisum*, and *Big Jake*. The cast also included Wayne's son Patrick, who had appeared with his father in *Rio Grande*, *The Quiet Man*, *The Searchers*, *Donovan's Reef*, and *McClintock!* The film editor was Otho Lovering, who had cut other Wayne films, such as *Stagecoach*, *The Man Who Shot Liberty Valance*, *Donovan's Reef*, and *McClintock!* Dave Grayson was the makeup artist. He had also done Wayne's makeup in *In Harm's Way* and *The War Wagon*. Wayne was so pleased with the look that Grayson created for him in *The Green Berets* (actually, his face had the sheen of waxen fruit) that Grayson continued in that capacity for most of the actor's last films: *Chisum*, *Big Jake*, *The Cowboys*, *Cahill*, *U. S. Marshal*, *McQ*, *Brannigan*, *Rooster Cogburn*, and his final screen appearance, *The Shootist*. *The Green Berets* was a family gathering, with the Duke at the head of the table.

To use the current designation, *The Green Berets* is "a film by John Wayne." There was no point of view but Wayne's and, by extension, America's. The movie opens with a press conference at which the Green Berets present themselves as a bi- and tri-lingual elite corps, color blind and ready to answer even the most probing questions—one of which concerns American support for a country unable to draft a constitution. The answer is simple—and simplistic: It took the United States six years after the end of the Revolutionary War in 1781 to come up with a constitution acceptable to the thirteen original colonies. (It also took another year before the Constitution was ratified in 1788, a fact that was not mentioned, perhaps because of information overload.) Of course, constitutions are not written overnight, but the difference between Vietnam and the United States is that during most of the Revolutionary War, the colonies had the Articles of Confederation. The analogy is false. A confederation of thirteen states and a country divided at the seventeenth parallel are not similar. The American Revolution was a war of self-determination, the prelude to which was a rationale for severing bonds with the mother country, as articulated in the Declaration of Independence. The Vietnam War was a civil war that America entered in order to halt the spread of communism. The circumstances leading to the drafting of the Constitution grew out of the realization that even a revision of the Articles of Confederation would not serve the needs of a new nation, which would no longer be a confederation but a federation. A wholly unique document was the answer, and the United States Constitution was the result.

Moreover, there was a Vietnamese constitution, written in 1946 and amended after Vietnam was free of French rule. The 1946 constitution only applied to the communist-controlled part of Vietnam, yet it did guarantee, at least nominally, three of the five freedoms guaranteed in the US Constitution's First Amendment (speech, press, assembly). The 1946 constitution was replaced in 1959 by an explicitly communist one intended for the Democratic Republic of Vietnam. On paper, the new constitution mandated a tripartite form of government (executive, legislative, judicial), so South Vietnam could not claim that it had no template from which to work. It could have selected the more democratically representative parts of both texts. And one would think that with such well-educated Green Berets around to help, this could easily have been done. The lack of a constitution was not the issue. One could have been cobbled together and held up as the first stage in the democratization of Vietnam. But that would not happen until the defeat of the communist North, which never occurred. Vietnam was a fiasco. Two years after the 1973 armistice, Saigon fell to the North Vietnamese, and Americans awakened to the realization that they had lost a war.

But in 1968, the war had not been lost. Audiences had to be convinced that if South Vietnam fell to the communists, Laos and Cambodia would be next. And who better to preach the gospel of containment than John Wayne, champion of everything American? Wayne argued in 1971 that westward expansion was justified because "great numbers of people . . . needed new land, and the Indians were selfishly trying to keep it for themselves." Such a mindset makes rational discourse difficult, if not impossible. In the film, when the reporter for an anti-war newspaper (David Janssen) argues that the Vietnamese are engaged in a civil war, another Beret holds up weapons made in China, the Soviet Union, and the former Czechoslovakia, showing that that they were manufactured in communist countries and intended for use by the North Vietnamese. And when the reporter persists, Wayne—it is impossible to think of him as Col. Mike Kirby—asks if he has ever been to Southeast Asia. When the reporter replies in the negative, Wayne grunts and walks away. One knows that it is only a matter of time before the reporter sees the light and becomes so convinced of the need for American involvement that he stays on rather than return to his former job.

The Green Berets, like many combat films, has a trickle of a plot that fancies itself an ocean, but which, if anything, terminates in a puddle. Amid explosions and falling bodies, one is left wondering which Berets will live and which will die—and how. Certainly not the boyish Sergeant Petersen (Jim Hutton), who alone has a character arc. Once Hamchunk, a Vietnamese orphan who speaks adequate English (he was taught by missionaries, as the cliché goes), attaches himself to Petersen, they become inseparable, with Hamchunk regarding the sergeant as both a friend and a father, and Petersen playing big brother to the orphan. Unfortunately, Petersen does not survive. Not only do the North Vietnamese murder, behead, rape, torture, and infiltrate; they also lay booby traps such as a spike-studded bed. When someone sets off the well-camouflaged trap, it springs up, impaling the victim. Petersen is the last Beret one expects to be impaled, but he is.

No matter how hard viewers gird themselves against this 142-minute onslaught of propaganda, they might find themselves shedding a tear at the end. When the helicopters set down after a mission that used a woman as bait to kidnap an elusive North Vietnamese general (the incident, taken from Moore's novel, is the only exciting part of the film), Hamchunk runs from one helicopter to the other, crying out, "Petersen!" Wayne, his face stoically immobile, finally tells the boy the truth, omitting the grisly details. When Hamchunk asks what will become of him, Wayne implies that all manner of things will be well. "You're what this is all about, Green Beret," he says, placing Petersen's cap on the boy's head. One can imagine a sequel with Hamchunk—now known as Mike Kirby Jr.—winning his green beret in America's latest war of intervention.

Chapter 19

HOME FRONT LIBERALS

MCCARTHYISM, DESCRIBED BY ONE HISTORIAN AS "A PHENOMENON that, for at least a decade, disfigured the American political landscape," has now become a generic term, applicable to any attempt to silence the liberal voice singing in a key that is not the choice of the choirmaster. But in the 1950s, McCarthyism was sect-specific: communism. Senator Joseph McCarthy's Permanent Subcommittee on Investigations (PSI) seemed like a spawn of HUAC, which was still holding hearings in 1952, when McCarthy took on the State Department and then, to his detriment, the United States Army. PSI and HUAC had separate agendas that dovetailed: HUAC investigated communism in the movie business, PSI did the same in the government. HUAC's targets were actors, writers, directors, and producers. PSI's were government officials. Liberals, who were once anti-communist and appalled by McCarthy's tactics, realized the vileness of red-baiting. A self-respecting liberal had to take an anti-anti-communist stand. One can be opposed to both communism and committees investigating party members—past or present, card-carriers or sympathizers—who, to avoid being blacklisted and perhaps incarcerated, were required to name names as a sign of their patriotism, even if doing so meant betraying others. Since Congress cannot legislate one's politics, it should not be able to investigate them—or so the reasoning went. A true 1950s liberal would say—as Bette Davis did playing a feisty librarian in *Storm Center* (1956)—that while she hates communism, she will not remove a book called *The Communist Dream* from the shelves, expecting readers to see through its specious arguments. Anti-anti-communism may be a cumbersome term, but as a philosophy it at least allows individuals to maintain their integrity by not compromising their beliefs. Thus one can be anti-communist, anti-HUAC, and anti-McCarthy, and also pro-freedom of expression and the right to dissent.

Storm Center deals explicitly with the ogre of McCarthyism, but in a way that reduces political conformity to the absurd by dramatizing the disastrous effect that a book, an accusation, and child's disenchantment have on a community. The film was written and directed by Daniel Taradash, who won an Oscar for his adaptation of James Jones's *From Here to Eternity* (1953). *Storm Center* was to have starred Mary Pickford as the small town librarian, Alicia Hull. It would have marked Pickford's return to the screen after a twenty-three-year absence. Everything seemed to be set. She had even been fitted for the costumes. Then, suddenly she withdrew for reasons that even Taradash could not fathom, except perhaps that the thought of making a movie after being away for so long caused her to have second thoughts about a comeback—particularly in a film that, in 1956, would have been politically incorrect. Taradash contacted Bette Davis, who stepped in without hesitation. Davis had now become a character actress; that same year she played a Bronx homemaker in *The Catered Affair* (1956). The glamour had gone, but not the art. Heavier than she was in her prime (her suits did not conceal the weight gain), she was still in her element as the fiery Yankee who risks ostracism for her convictions.

Believing that the city council members have invited her to lunch to discuss her children's wing, Alicia discovers that owing to complaints they have received, their purpose is to ask her to remove *The Communist Dream*. At first she declines, but then agrees if the council will authorize the children's wing. A libertarian with a loathing for any ideology that suppresses free thought, she subsequently puts the book back on the shelf. An unscrupulous politician (Brian Keith) compiles a dossier on Alicia, who unwittingly supported liberal organizations that were communist fronts. The press turned a beloved librarian into a communist tool, demoting her from icon to pariah.

The smear campaign polarizes the Slater family. Alicia had been especially close to Freddie Slater, choosing books for him that he eagerly read, much to his father's displeasure. Mr. Slater is not only anti-communist, but also anti-intellectual; he resents his son spending time on books when the two of them could be playing catch. Mrs. Slater's status as an accomplished pianist also irritates her husband, who equates the ability to play classical music with an assertion of superiority. Alicia's firing and the ensuing witch-hunt have a disastrous effect on Freddie. Convinced by his father that Alicia has tried to poison his mind with her books, Freddie burns down the library. The conflagration is a literal book burning, with flames engulfing the works of Shakespeare, Ibsen, Voltaire, and Dickens. Even the Bible is not spared; in fact, the whole library goes up in flames. It is a sickening finale to a film that may seem overwrought—but not if one recalls the book burnings throughout Germany in 1933, when works not only by Jews (for example, Albert Einstein, Sigmund Freud, Walter Benjamin, Karl Marx, Franz Werfel, Stefan Zweig) were hurled into bonfires, but also many written by non-Jews such as Ernest Hemingway, Joseph Conrad, Upton Sinclair, and Theodore Dreiser. All were deemed incompatible with the goals of National Socialism.

The film's coda tries to sweeten the bitter pill, but not enough to make anyone optimistic about the rebuilding of the library and the replacement of the books—not to mention the children's wing, another casualty. Those who think the phoenix will rise from the ashes might feel confident about Alicia being reinstated, although for the present she will be head librarian of a pile of debris. Freddie's fate is undetermined. Clearly neither he nor his parents will ever be the same. To Taradash, that did not matter. The Slaters were an example of McCarthyism gone wild, disappearing from the plot after the devastating finale. Davis gets the fade out line, which she delivers with prophetic vengeance: "And if anybody ever again tries to remove a book, he'll have to do it over my dead body." Famous last words, except that there are still communities in which books are banned, biblical inerrancy is taught, play productions are cancelled, and controversial teachers discharged. Senator McCarthy's ectoplasm has not yet dissipated.

Despite a script that verges on hysteria, *Storm Center* is less dated than *Three Brave Men* (1957), even though the latter was occasioned by the true story of Abraham Chasanow, who was dismissed from the Navy Department as a security risk, despite his exemplary record. The film is another semi-documentary, for which Twentieth Century-Fox was famous, with intermittent omniscient narration and a prologue stating, "[T]he story you are about to see is based on a series of Pulitzer Prize-winning articles by Anthony Lewis." That much is true. Lewis's account in the *Washington Daily News* of Chasanow's travails, which won Lewis a 1955 Pulitzer, was instrumental in clearing Chasanow and forcing the navy to improve its screening methods. The prologue is careful to note that while *Three Brave Men* is "basically true," characters and names are invented. Thus, the film is not really about Chasanow, but about a fictitious character, Bernie Goldsmith (Ernest Borgnine), who underwent a similar ordeal.

While *Storm Center* might strike post 9/11 audiences as a cross between horror and science fiction, *Three Brave Men* seems like a tempest in a thimble. Once the War on Terror replaced the Cold War, "security" took on a different meaning, particularly at airports and public events. Bernie's "crimes" seem inconsequential compared to those of jihadists and suicide bombers. But this was the age of the great communist conspiracy, as the prologue reminds us. Bernie Goldsmith, like Alicia Hull, made the mistake of subscribing to magazines that were communist fronts. When Bernie discovered their nature, he let his subscriptions lapse, but never notified the publishers of his reason. Another mistake was participating in politically dubious discussion groups, which he stopped attending when the topics became pro-Soviet. Again, he never resigned in writing. Then there were Bernie's critics, who accused him of radicalism because, as secretary of a housing cooperative, he insisted that no one should be excluded because of religion, race, or creed—which, as one of his detractors testified, was a well-known communist mantra. With the help of a crusading lawyer (Ray Milland) and the backing of some of the townspeople, Bernie is cleared by an appeals board, which rules that his actions were "clearly consistent with the interests of national security." But that was not good enough for the secretary of the navy (Dean Jagger), who still harbored doubts but agreed to reopen the case, resulting in Bernie's exoneration and an apology from the secretary. The film's title is a misnomer; it should have been "Two Brave Men," referring to Bernie and his lawyer. The third is allegedly the navy secretary, who only changes from inflexible to contrite. Had it not been for his lawyer and supporters, Bernie Goldsmith would have been another victim of a seriously flawed security program.

The liberal home front had a low demographic in the early 1950s, when the Senate Internal Security Subcommittee was investigating organizations such as the Joint anti-Fascist Refugee Committee (JAFRC), the Spanish Refugee Appeal, the Committee to Aid Spanish Democracy, and the American Committee to Save Refugees, all of which were considered communist fronts—the recurring phrase applied to groups that supported the Loyalists during the Spanish Civil War and considered Franco's Spain a totalitarian regime. Remaining anti-fascist after World War II had become a liability. The tag of choice was "anti-communist"—meaning anti-Soviet, anti-Red China, and anti-Soviet bloc. The attorney general had compiled a list of a vast number of organizations, many with star-spangled names implying noble ideals, such as the American League for Peace and Democracy, the American League against War and Fascism, the American Youth Congress, and American Youth for Democracy. That some of these organizations had gone out of existence—such as the League of American Writers, which included William Carlos Williams, John Steinbeck, and Nathanael West—did not matter. The league leaned too far to the left, and that was enough to condemn it.

By the end of the fifties, McCarthyism had entered plot limbo. When filmmakers decided to revisit the era decades later, they realized they would be making period pieces for audiences too young to remember what Lillian Hellman dubbed "scoundrel time." a time of inquisitors—grand and otherwise—of informants, victims, penitents, and blacklisted writers who resorted to fronts and pseudonyms. By the 1970s, HUAC and PSI had receded into the misty past, which, if it were to be brought back, would have to be painstakingly recreated to ensure authenticity—a task more exacting and expensive than making a movie about contemporary life.

In 1950, Walter Bernstein, then a promising screenwriter, found himself blacklisted for, among other reasons, being a member of the Young Communist League when he was at Dartmouth and then joining the party after being discharged from the army at the end of World War II. Refusing to change professions, Bernstein had friends front for him. Even though his scripts bore their names, they still reached the big and small screens. A quarter of a century later, when the time of the toad was a memory, Bernstein decided to acquaint the baby boomers with the decade during which he was nameless. *The Front* (1975), directed by friend and fellow blacklistee Martin Ritt, starred Woody Allen as cashier-bookmaker Howard Prince, who agrees to front for a group of TV writers barred from working in the industry because of their communist pasts. Although the film lovingly recreates the golden age of live television, it also portrays the dilemma executives faced when they were forced to decide between remaining loyal to their actors and writers, and succumbing to pressure from HUAC and the FBI to purge their rosters of subversives. One of the subversives is Hecky Brown (Zero Mostel), the star of a children's show, who attended communist meetings to date girls. Jim Carey gave the same reason in *The Majestic* (2001), although he was more explicit: "I was a horny young man." Fired from his job and confronted with a bleak future, Hecky checks into a hotel and throws himself out the window.

The model for Hecky Brown was Philip Loeb, a highly respected actor who played opposite Gertrude Berg on Broadway in *Me and Molly* (1948), which was based on her popular radio show, *The Goldbergs.* After *The Goldbergs* moved to television in 1949, Loeb continued in his role as Molly's husband, Jake, until 1951, when he was falsely accused of being a communist. When the sponsors and the network insisted Loeb be fired, Berg stood by him, but even she was powerless against the rising tide of anti-communist hysteria. On 1 September 1955, Loeb checked into the Hotel Taft, where he committed suicide with a drug overdose.

Hecky's suicide transforms Howard from an apolitical schlemiel to a committed liberal. When it is his turn to be interrogated by HUAC, Howard balks at naming names. Informed that he could even give the name of a dead person like Hecky Brown as evidence of his good will, Howard looks at the men and says, "I'm sorry, but I don't recognize this committee's right to ask these kinds of questions. And you can all go fuck yourselves." Howard is last seen on a train platform handcuffed to a McCarthy looka-like as he goes off to prison, sharing the same fate as the Hollywood Ten. *The Front* was humorous enough to swell the ranks of Woody Allen's ever-growing fan base, while at the same time holding a dirt-streaked mirror up to a shameful period and accurately capturing its reflection.

Bernstein had not finished with the era that left him nameless. Sidney Lumet hired him to write the screenplay for *That Kind of Woman* (1959). When Bernstein learned that the FBI had recruited former Nazi war crimi-nals and collaborators as informants to spy on communities with large émi-gré populations where there might be communist enclaves, he knew he had the making of screenplay. The FBI was especially interested in scientists and technicians who had found positions at aerospace corporations like Lock-heed, and producers of construction materials like Martin Marietta. The FBI was not the only organization smuggling Nazis into the country. The CIA did likewise, bringing in Nazis as contract agents and "placing them on US payrolls overseas." The reasoning was simple, if specious: "Nazis are regarded as anti-communist, so a Nazi background is not derogatory." In 2014, the CIA's recruitment of Nazis made front-page news: "In the decades after World War II, the C.I.A. and other United States agencies employed at least a thousand Nazis as Cold War spies and informants and, as recently as the 1990s, concealed the government's ties to some still living in America, newly disclosed records and interviews show." Such was the historical back-ground of *The House on Carroll Street* (1988).

Reminiscent of Hitchcock's *Saboteur*, in which two ordinary people un-covered a colony of American fifth columnists, *The House on Carroll Street*, written by Bernstein and directed by Peter Yates, begins with a young pro-gressive, Emily Crane (Kelly McGillis), an assistant picture editor for *Life*, refusing to release the files of Liberty Watch to HUAC. Bernstein may have been thinking of Helen Reid Bryan, JAFRC's administrative secretary, who refused to surrender the "subversive" organization's files to HUAC and was sentenced to three months in prison in 1950. Ironically, Bryan had never been a member of the Communist Party. But she was a strongly principled Quaker.

Emily does not go to jail, but she is fired, eventually finding a job reading to an elderly woman with failing eyesight (Jessica Tandy), who lives in the Carroll Gardens section of Brooklyn. Emily discovers a strange house in back of her employer's, where she overhears people talking in German—except for the non-German speaking HUAC lawyer (Mandy Patinkin), who had been so unctuously condescending to her at the hearing. The Germans are former Nazis, given the names of dead Jews taken from tombstones.

In the Hitchcock tradition of potential lovers working in pairs (*Saboteur, Notorious, North by Northwest*), Emily is given a partner, Cochran (Jeff Daniels), an FBI agent assigned to keep tabs on her. At first he is doubtful of her story, but he becomes convinced after he sees Nazis arriving from Europe being welcomed like visiting royalty. Working as a team, they expose the recruitment of Jew-killers transformed into Jews, as Emily describes the loathsome practice. Since Cochran has acted on his own without the FBI's approval (which is understandable in view of the organization's complicity), he is transferred to Montana. And one assumes Emily will go her liberal way, circulating "Ban the Bomb" petitions and working for nuclear disarmament.

If *The House on Carroll Street* had limited public appeal, it is largely because the movie subverted the conventions of the Hitchcock thriller, while at the same time paying homage to them. Emily ascending the stairs of the house on Carroll Street recalls a similar ascent in *Psycho*, as Vera Miles explored the Bateses' gothic house on the hill. When Mandy Patinkin comes crashing down from the dome of Grand Central Station, landing by the information booth, it was impossible not to think of Norman Lloyd falling to his death from the Statue of Liberty in *Saboteur*. In each case, the fall serves as a fitting death for a traitor.

The Hitchcock thriller is apolitical; *The House on Caroll Street* is not. Although we never learn about the wartime activities of the Nazis in *Notorious*, one of the FBI recruits in *The House on Carroll Street* was a doctor who experimented with inmates at Auschwitz to see how long it would take them to die in freezing water. *The House on Carroll Street* has a clearly defined political agenda that is unabashedly anti-fascist and pro-First Amendment. Set in 1951, the film reflects an age of anxiety with its concomitant neuroses, when belonging to an organization or subscribing to a journal on the attorney general's list of suspect periodicals would make you unemployable and perhaps even a felon. But the greatest deviation from the genre is

the ending. Although Emily and Cochran sleep together (once), their en-
counter is the equivalent of a one-night stand. They both realize they were
only meant to share an adventure and expose a demonic scheme that left
Cochran with his career in limbo and Emily with the stigma of "subversive."
"Oil and water," Cochran says ruefully as he sums up their personalities. In
Hitchcock, the couples are together at the fade out: Robert Cummings and
Priscilla Lane in *Saboteur*; Cary Grant and Ingrid Bergman in *Notorious*;
Grant and Eva Marie Saint in *North by Northwest*. Bernstein did not opt
for a happy ending. He was only interested in showing how following your
conscience in the 1950s could isolate you from the very people who should
be defending your rights.

   Guilty by Suspicion (1991), also set in 1951, was the first film to dramatize
HUAC's investigation into the movie industry. The film contained a mix of
real and fictitious characters, with several of the latter based on real people.
It was written and directed by Irwin Winkler, better known as a producer
(*Rocky*, *Raging Bull*), who chose to make his protagonist a director, David
Merrill (Robert De Niro). Merrill bore no resemblance to any director of
the 1950s, so audiences would not be wondering about the identity of Darryl F. Zanuck's favorite filmmaker, who had consorted with communists but
had never been one. In 1951, there was no one at Twentieth Century-Fox
who closely resembled Winkler's David Merrill, a major director who, after
shooting a film in Paris, returns to a fear-ridden Hollywood. Here, friends
speak sotto voce about "what is going on" and dread a mail delivery that
might include a subpoena. It was also a time of guilt by association; if there
is any evidence that one had attended a few party gatherings, HUAC could
demand a list of all those present, requiring the innocent attendee to supply names. In 1951, the only high-profile director called before HUAC was
Edward Dmytryk, one of the Hollywood Ten, who served four and one-
half months of a six-month sentence at Mill Point Prison Camp in West
Virginia. After his release, he recanted so that he could return to his profession. While a writer could always use a pseudonym or a front, and an actor
could work in the theater, a director had two choices: purge himself, to use
HUAC's phrase— as if confession had become an emetic that would restore
peace to the soul and health to the body—or become an expatriate and
work in Europe.

   Merrill was a fictitious character; Zanuck, of course, was not. Played with
corporate panache by Ben Piazza, Zanuck deplores HUAC's slimy tactics
(as did the historical Zanuck), but insists he is at the mercy of a board that
wants the studio rid of Reds. Zanuck prized good screenwriting, regardless

of the writer's politics. He did not want to fire Ring Lardner Jr., one of the Hollywood Ten, who impressed him with his work on *Forever Amber* (1947). Lardner received screenplay co-credit for the film. Zanuck then assigned Lardner to *Forbidden Street*, which bore his name as sole writer when it was released in 1949. Less than a year later, Lardner was serving a one-year sentence at the federal correctional institution in Danbury, Connecticut, from which he was released after nine and one-half months.

When Winkler tries to forge parallels between his characters and their counterparts, though, the script becomes historically inaccurate, especially to moviegoers with a sense of chronology. In 1951, Merrill's friend, Bunny Baxter (George Wendt), is doing rewrites for a Marilyn Monroe film, later revealed to be *Gentleman Prefer Blondes*, which did not come out until 1953. In 1951, Marilyn was playing supporting roles in such films as *As Young as You Feel* and *Let's Make It Legal* (both 1951). While it may have seemed ingenious to have an actual director (Martin Scorsese) play communist director Joe Lesser, the similarities between Joe Lesser and the historical Joseph Losey are irritatingly tenuous. Lesser, who chooses exile in Europe to testifying, entrusts the editing of his last film to Merrill. The film is Losey's *The Boy with Green Hair* (1948), which was not the director's last Hollywood movie. He made four more: *The Lawless* (1950), *The Prowler, M,* and *The Big Night* (all 1951), the last being the one he was unable to edit. Knowing that he was about to be subpoenaed, Losey called the producer, Philip Waxman, "in the middle of the night" and explained how to cut the film. He then left for London.

But Winkler succeeded in capturing the desperation that prevailed in Hollywood to the point that Bunny Baxter asks Merrill's permission to name him. Winkler clearly had in mind the scene in Arthur Miller's drama, *After the Fall* (1964), between Mickey and Lou, friends and former party members, in which Mickey asks the same of Lou, who becomes morally indignant ("Because if everyone broke faith, there would be no civilization!"). But Merrill is so disillusioned that he does not care. In the final scene, Merrill faces the committee, ready to speak about himself but not about others, taking the same position that Sidney Buchman and Lillian Hellman did, the latter framing her statement as a letter with the famous declaration, "I cannot and will not cut my conscience to suit this year's fashion." Furious at the committee's coercive methods, Merrill shouts, "Shame on you!" as he leaves the room with his wife (the underutilized Annette Bening). Then an epilogue comes on the screen, calling the Merrills typical of HUAC's victims, many of whom remained under the black cloud of anonymity for twenty years. Dalton Trumbo did not have to wait that long. He made front-page news in 1960 when Otto Preminger hired him to adapt Leon Uris's *Exodus*. Kirk Douglas also hired Trumbo to adapt Howard Fast's *Spartacus* for Bryna, the production company Douglas named after his mother. As for the Merrills, one would like to think they joined Joseph Losey and other Hollywood exiles, although Winkler deliberately left their future in doubt.

Chapter 20

THE YEAR OF LIVING DANGEROUSLY

WAS 1964 "THE LAST INNOCENT YEAR," AS ONE WRITER CLAIMED, EVEN though he admits, "there never was an innocent year"? A nation's loss of innocence, if it ever occurred, is not like the biblical fall of man, which, according to Genesis, was the result of a specific act of disobedience. Each generation has its own date for its first glimpse into what, in *Lord of the Flies*, William Golding calls "the darkness of the heart," the moment when innocence yields to experience, and the world no longer seems the same. For the children of the Great Depression, it was the bombing of Pearl Harbor on 7 December 1941. For the baby boomers, it was the assassination of President John F. Kennedy on 22 November 1963. And for the millennials, it was the terrorist attack on the World Trade Center on 11 September 2001.

Whether or not 1964 was the last innocent year, it was certainly an erratic one, alternately vibrant and somber. Technically, America was at peace; in reality, it was engaged in an undeclared war in Vietnam that was destined to escalate to the point that, by fall 1966, men between twenty-six and thirty-five could be drafted if the number of eligible males in the eighteen to twenty-five age category was exhausted. But war was far from Flushing Meadow, Corona Park, in the borough of Queens, the site of the 1964 World's Fair. Major companies like General Motors, Dupont, and General Electric exhibited their newest creations intended to improve quality of life. There was something for everyone: the world's largest cheese at the Wisconsin Pavilion; Michelangelo's *Pietà*, blue-lit, at the Vatican Pavilion; cities of the future, some with moving sidewalks, and others underwater with submarines instead of cars. Films, live entertainment, simulations—everything pointed to a future of limitless possibilities.

Nineteen sixty-four was also notable for the passage of the Civil Rights Act, the surgeon general's warning that cigarettes pose a health hazard, and the Beatles' appearance on *The Ed Sullivan Show* on 9 February, which attracted seventy-three million viewers. Summer 1964 was declared "Freedom Summer." Andrew Goldman, Mickey Schwerner, and James Chaney became freedom riders, traveling to Mississippi to inform blacks about their constitutional rights and the importance of registering to vote. Their idealism ended in death at the hands of the Ku Klux Klan. Black America was still, as Dr. Martin Luther King Jr. described it in his famous "I Have a Dream" speech, "a lonely island of poverty in the midst of a vast ocean of material prosperity." Freedom summer saw little freedom. There were race riots in New York, Jersey City, and Philadelphia.

In August 1964, President Lyndon B. Johnson authorized the bombing of North Vietnam, which signaled the escalation of the war, affecting the 23,310 members of the armed services deployed there. By 1966, the death roll had reached six thousand. It would continue to rise. Nineteen sixty-four was also a presidential election year, with Johnson running against Barry Goldwater. Johnson's team devised a potent television ad, "Daisy," in which a little girl counts as she pulls petals from a daisy. She has not quite mastered sequential order: "One, two, three, four, five, seven, six, six, eight, nine." Next, a voice that has mastered sequential order is heard in a different form of countdown: "Ten, nine, eight, seven, six, five, four, three, two, one, zero," followed by a nuclear explosion. Then Johnson's voice is heard issuing a warning: "These are the stakes: to make a world in which all of God's children can live or go into the dark. We must either love each other or we must die." Then came the kicker: "Vote for President Johnson on November 3. The stakes are too high for you to stay home." Johnson was elected, but the nuclear threat did not abate.

It was not a great year for movies. The best were *The Pink Panther, Mary Poppins, My Fair Lady, The Americanization of Emily, The Pawnbroker*, and two that were in a class by themselves: *Fail-Safe* and *Dr. Strangelove or: How I Learned to Stop Worrying and Love the Bomb*, both of which ended with a nuclear holocaust. The former, directed by Sidney Lumet, was the more harrowing; the latter, directed by Stanley Kubrick, was more popular, although one film scholar found it rather broad and "sophomoric." The essential difference lay in the films' approach to the inexorable. In *Fail-Safe*, brilliantly adapted by Walter Bernstein from Eugene Burdick and Harvey Wheeler's novel of the same name, events mount to a fatalistic climax, like a Greek tragedy. The infernal machine is wound up, needing just a push, a press of a button, or a computer glitch to set it in motion. And once that happens, there is no stopping it. In *Dr. Strangelove*, nuclear disaster could have been averted if the means of preventing it were not in the hands of a lunatic.

"They give birth astride of a grave, the light gleams an instant, then it's night once more," as Pozzo observes in Samuel Beckett's *Waiting for Godot*. Kubrick would agree—but add that we should at least have some laughs before that perpetual night.

Fail-Safe does not begin conventionally. After the Columbia logo of the lady with the torch appears, a title bursts on the screen: "New York City, 5:30 A.M." The first image is not of New York, but of a bullring, where a victorious matador is slaying a bull. A white-haired man in the stands looks petrified, as if he identifies with the slowly dying animal. As yet the connection between the opening scene and the New York setting is unclear—although it will become horrifyingly evident at the end. Then "*Fail-Safe*" appears in bold lettering, followed by the rest of the credits that blast onto the screen like projectiles, suggesting a crisis growing incrementally into a catastrophe. The New York episode is the first in a multipart sequence of events occurring simultaneously in various locations at 5:30 am. The ritual slaying of the bull is a recurring dream of General Black (Dan O'Herlihy), who must rise early to fly to Washington, DC, for an important meeting in the war room, a location that foreshadows darker things to come.

Next we are in Washington, DC, where Professor Groeteschele (Walter Matthau), a political scientist, is still pontificating after an all-night discussion on nuclear war, whose casualties he has estimated at one hundred million. By 5:30 am, he had lowered the number to sixty million, as if the new figure were cause for joy. Groeteschele is the worst type of academic, self-important and supercilious, not so much hating communism as considering it intellectually beneath him. He even believes that after a nuclear war, "culture" may never mean what it once did, yet whatever remains of American culture would be preferable to the Russian variety.

On to Omaha, Nebraska, where Colonel Cascio (Fritz Weaver) enters the plot He is a neurotic who has transcended his lower-middle class background, but not the sense of inferiority that has made him eager to offer proposals that are as irrational as they are dangerous. The last stop is Anchorage, Alaska, where Colonel Grady (Edward Binns) is introduced. Grady will pilot the plane that bombs Moscow after a nuclear alert has been accidentally triggered. The Soviets have jammed the fail-safe boxes in the bombers, making radio reception impossible. Once the bombers have passed fail-safe and are out of United States jurisdiction, nothing can deter them from accomplishing their mission, which, because of a computer error, is the bombing of Moscow. When reception has been restored, and the president orders the bombers to turn back, Colonel Grady refuses; he has been instructed to ignore verbal commands even from the president, since someone could be imitating the voice of the commander-in-chief. Even the pleas of Grady's wife are in vain. The president (Henry Fonda) then orders fighter planes to shoot down the bombers before they reach Moscow, even if it means running out of fuel and plunging into the ocean. This is precisely what happens, and the bombers continue on to their destination.

At this point, the cold irrationality of war becomes transparent. A system has been created, which to succeed requires sacrificial victims who are not even aware they have been designated as such. Operating on the assumption that Russia will be the aggressor in a nuclear war, the United States established a system of preparedness that is really preemptive retaliation: in short, we'll bomb you before you bomb us. And if the system goes into red alert when an unidentified plane invades American air space, we shoot it down. Of course, there was no such system, which is why the Defense Department would not cooperate in the making of the film. *Fail-Safe* is a reductio ad absurdum of Cold War paranoia, which is inevitable in a country conditioned to expect war. The rules of engagement alone matter: If we bomb Moscow by mistake, we will do a quid pro quo and bomb New York. And so a gentleman's agreement will leave two great cities in ruins. But what does it matter if the protocols were observed?

The most unnerving sequence in *Fail-Safe* is the phone conversation between the president and the Soviet premier. In the bunker are the president and Buck, his young translator (Larry Hagman, in the film's most demanding performance). One never hears the Soviet leader, only Buck's translation, delivered haltingly and with a slight hint of an accent, as if he were doing his best to reproduce the premier's inflections and tone. It is chillingly formal, Mr. President speaking to Mr. Chairman. Curiously, there is no bellowing at the other end when the Soviet premier is told that his capital will be bombed. "We're paying for our mutual suspicions," the president ruefully comments. As to the question, "What do we say to the dead?" the answer is a limp, "It must not happen again."

Early in the film, General Black wonders if he will ever know the identity of the matador in his dream. When the president decides to atone for the mechanical failure that triggered the bombing of Moscow by ordering a similar bombing of New York, he assigns the task to Black, even though he knows that Black's family lives there. But he also knows that the first lady is visiting there. Each man will suffer a loss; each will make the supreme sacrifice. But for what? An infernal machine that has acquired a mind of its own, impervious to human considerations? Black was the matador; the slain bull was the dead of New York, which includes his wife and sons. It was an act of patriotic homicide. Just following orders.

The film ends with a montage of New York street life just before the bombing. People in motion freeze into stills, as a three-dimensional world is drained of depth. But *Fail-Safe* does not end with the photomontage. Columbia insisted on a disclaimer to calm anxious moviegoers: "The producers of this film wish to stress that it is the stated position of the Department of Defense and the United States Air Force that a rigidly enforced system of safeguards and controls insure that occurrences such as those depicted in this story cannot happen." *Fail-Safe*, then, is a hybrid: science fiction that spills over into existential horror.

Dr. Strangelove or: How I Learned to Stop Worrying and Love the Bomb is black comedy that blurs into absurdism. Both *Strangelove* and *Fail-Safe* were Columbia releases, similar in theme, but not in treatment. Peter George's *Red Alert* (1958), which he published earlier in Britain as *Two Hours to Doom* under the pseudonym Peter Bryant, left a deep impression on Stanley Kubrick, who had long harbored the desire to make a movie about nuclear war. Originally, Kubrick and George had intended to film a fairly close adaptation of the novel, in which nuclear devastation is narrowly averted, despite a rogue—and probably insane—air force general's order of a massive air strike against the Soviet Union. But as the screenplay progressed, Kubrick felt that the lunacy of war required a lunatic plot, a "nightmare comedy." Although originally Columbia Pictures had no intention of releasing both *Fail-Safe* and *Dr. Strangelove*, it ended up doing so in the same year. One film was stark and somber (*Fail-Safe*); the other, antic and gleefully misanthropic (*Dr. Strangelove*).

In 1961, Eugene Burdick, knowing of Kubrick's interest in a nuclear war film, sent him a rough draft of *Fail-Safe*, thinking it was the kind of material Kubrick was seeking. Since Kubrick's production company, Harris-Kubrick Pictures, had already purchased the rights to *Red Alert*, the director immediately sensed the similarities between his project and *Fail-Safe*. Kubrick, George, and Columbia sued Burdick and co-author Harvey Wheeler for plagiarism, along with the Entertainment Corp. of America (ECA), a new production company that planned to release *Fail-Safe*. The case was settled out of court. Columbia took over *Fail Safe* from ECA so it could control the release dates of both films to keep them from competing with each other.

It is hard to imagine that Burdick and Wheeler had not read George's novel. For example, in *Red Alert*, the president proposes to the Soviet premier that if the B-52s get through to their destination, the Soviets can retaliate by bombing an American city, preferably Atlantic City. Ultimately, neither Moscow nor Atlantic City is destroyed. In *Fail- Safe*, Moscow *is* bombed, and as atonement, the president sacrifices New York. Kubrick persuaded Columbia to take advantage of the publicity generated by the lawsuit and release *Dr. Strangelove* first. He preferred mid-August 1963, even though the film was not ready. The date kept changing; first it was October, then December. With the assassination of President Kennedy on 22 November 1963, Columbia finally decided on 29 January 1964. *Fail-Safe*'s opening was delayed until October of that year, dooming it at the box office, despite impressive notices. After laughing at a global holocaust, few wanted to don the mask of tragedy that was regulation attire for *Fail-Safe*. *Dr. Strangelove* continues to find admirers. It ranks third in the American Film Institute's list of the one hundred best comedies, preceded by *Some Like It Hot* and *Tootsie* in first and second place, respectively.

Compared to the meticulously structured *Fail-Safe*, with its opening sequence of events occurring simultaneously, *Dr. Strangelove* is more of a series of burlesque skits, one more outrageous than the other. Rather than place the "It's only a movie" disclaimer at the end of the film, as Columbia had done with *Fail-Safe* (as if that would have made audiences sleep more easily), the studio inserted it at the beginning of *Dr. Strangelove*: "It is the stated position of the United States Air Force that their safeguards would prevent the occurrence of such events as are depicted in this film. Furthermore, it should be noted that none of the characters portrayed in this film are meant to represent any real persons, living or dead."

The "events" triggered by a deranged mind take on their own form of derangement, as if it was not Stanley Kubrick who was behind the camera, but Victor Frankenstein or Dr. Caligari. General Jack D. Ripper (Sterling Hayden) has sealed off Burpelson Air Base ("Burpelson," a sound-alike for Burleson, Texas, and one of many emblematic names in the film), placing it on condition red. Rabidly anti-communist and pathetically delusional, Ripper has convinced himself of the imminence of a Soviet attack, requiring the implementation of Wing Attack, Plan R, a retaliatory measure against the Soviet Union. Such a weirdly realistic beginning requires a filmmaker to keep upping the ante, making each sequence more bizarre—or nightmarish—than the last. When the message is relayed to the B-52 pilot, Major Kong (Slim Pickens), a Texas Redneck who acts as if he had been a bronco buster in his salad days, there is no turning back. Actually, there cannot be; General Ripper alone knows the recall code, which he is sharing with no one.

Whatever unity *Dr. Strangelove* possesses derives from the inspired casting of Peter Sellers in three pivotal roles as RAF Captain Mandrake, an officer in the exchange program, who plays straight man to Hayden's mad man, the voice of reason vs. the voice of lunacy; Merkin Muffley, president of the United States, a buffoon compared to Henry Fonda's model leader in *Fail-Safe*; and the title character (who does not appear in the novel), a former Nazi scientist recruited to ensure America's superiority in the arms race. Although Sellers was also slated to play Major Kong and worked hard at perfecting a Texas accent, he suffered a leg injury that led to the Texas-born Slim Pickens taking over the part. The film also profited from the addition of Terry Southern to the writing team. Although Southern only worked about six weeks on the script, he imbued it with the darkly comic quality that Kubrick wanted. The screenplay acquired an antic disposition, so that the action seemed frighteningly plausible and at the same time hilariously surreal. Southern, who had both an edgy sense of humor and a disdain for sexual propriety, produced the equivalent of a cartoon for adults, as if he were telling audiences, "It's all right to laugh when the bombs start falling"—particularly when they fall as Vera Lynn is heard singing the World War II classic, "We'll Meet Again," with it's refrain, "some sunny day." This juxtaposition of images of nuclear devastation with an optimistic pop song is bound to evoke a laugh, or at least a smile, because of its utter incongruity. And yet the incongruous is at the heart of comedy, in which there is a disconnect between what should be and what is. The future of civilization should not be in the hands of a wacko, but it is. War should not be a substitute for sex, but it is.

Dr. Strangelove is a specialized kind of comedy. Kubrick called it "nightmare comedy"—but one that is charged with sexuality. War is sex with planes and bombs in lieu of partners, with detonations as the ultimate orgasm. The opening, an ironic fusion of image and music, shows the boom of a tanker jutting into the screen like a steel phallus, as it refuels a B-52 bomber in what looks like mechanical copulation. Yet there is something poetically graceful about the mid-air coupling, which is particularly suited to the soundtrack: an instrumental version of "Try a Little Tenderness."

Southern did not originate the character of Dr. Strangelove, who was the joint creation of Kubrick and Peter George. At first, Dr. Strangelove had a given name, Otto. At one point, the film was even entitled *The Rise of Dr. Strangelove*. Then, the first name was dropped, and the title changed. But the surname remained, as transparent a name as that of any of the characters. "Strangelove" may not have been Southern's idea, but it seems highly probable that he was responsible for some, or maybe even all, of the transparent names in the film. Like many satirists, Southern had a penchant for such names (Candy Christian, Dr. Krankheit, Prof. Mephisto [*Candy*]; Guy Grand, the multi-millionaire, Youngman Grand in *The Magic Christian*).

The transparent (telltale, emblematic) name should say something about its bearer. The telltale name was one of the glories of Restoration Comedy, which featured the likes of Dr. Quack, Margery Pinchwife, Sir Jaspar Fidget, Mrs. Squeamish in Wycherly's *The Country Wife*; and Lady Sneerwell, Mrs. Candour, Sir Benjamin Backbite, Snake, Careless in Sheridan's *The School for Scandal*. Tom Dirks, whose painstakingly detailed analyses can be found on his website, "The Greatest Films," has shown that the characters' names in *Dr. Strangelove* are in some way associated with sex. Jack D. Ripper suggests the Victorian murderer of prostitutes. One suspects that Southern would have wanted the name pronounced as if it were Jack "de" ("de" for "the") Ripper, a hipster version of the formal middle initial. But the name is not a perfect fit for the character, unless one assumes that the general would like to emulate his namesake, perhaps even mutilating his victims sexually, as the Ripper occasionally did. The general is not only maniacally anti-communist, he also believes that fluoridation is a communist attempt to "sap and impurify our precious bodily fluids," including semen. He first came to that conclusion "during the physical act of love," and thus withholds his "essence" from women, meaning either onanism or, more likely, total abstinence—perhaps because the imagined sapping of his bodily fluids has left him impotent. Digging for meaning is not characteristic of the emblematic name, whose associations should be immediate. When a character in Farquhar's *The Beaux' Stratagem* is named Mrs. Sullen or Lady Bountiful, we know immediately that one must be withdrawn and the other benevolent. Not so in *Dr. Strangelove*, where the names make sense only in retrospect.

The group captain's name, Mandrake, derives from a plant considered to have magical properties, including aphrodisiacal. Yet the captain is the epitome of British reserve and decorum. Perhaps the name was meant to suggest that Mandrake could use an aphrodisiac, since sex seems to play no role in his life. In fact, closeness makes him uncomfortable. In a scene with strong homoerotic overtones, perhaps hinting at another side of General Ripper, the General sits uncomfortably close to Mandrake, putting his arm around him as he explains his theory of fluoridation. It is only after Ripper commits suicide that Mandrake, who has figured out the recall code (it is OPE, a permutation of the first letters of Ripper's mantra, "Purity of Essence"), takes charge, despite the interference of Colonel "Bat" Guano, who thinks the base has been overrun by communist "preverts"—one of whom is the group captain. Guano is fertilizer made of bat dung, among other substances. "Bat Guano" does not fit the character, especially as played by a deadpan Keenan Wynn.

The president—Peter Sellers again, looking like Phil Silvers as Master Sergeant Bilko on *The Phil Silvers Show*—is Merkin Muffley. A merkin is a genital covering often made of fur; "Muffley" suggests "muff," slang for female genitalia. But the president is as sexless as Mandrake. That he is also a bit effeminate (note the way he elongates the first name of the Soviet premier, "Di-mi-tri") may explain the name—but not satisfactorily. Still, it a clever juxtaposition of two words referring to the same anatomical area. The pilot of the bomber that will execute Plan R (for "Romeo," which somehow had been changed from the less obvious "Robert") is Major Kong, named after King Kong, that iconic ape who never behaved like a yokel or sounded like a Texan. King Kong was the embodiment of the ideal male—desirous of the female, protective of her, and willing to die for her. Major Kong is a joker, an anti-communist like everyone else and eager to do his bit to rid the world of Russkies. And sex is present in the bomber, where the survival kit contains lipsticks and nylons as enticements for accommodating Russian females and condoms (called prophylactics) for whatever follows. Even the bombs bear suggestive names, Dear John and Hi There, the latest versions of Fat Man and Little Boy. To end a relationship, a young woman would send a "Dear John" letter to her former sweetheart in the military, informing him that she now has a new beau. "Hi there" is a hooker's way of making contact, although one writer calls it "a homosexual advance." Still, it is sexual in one way or another. When Kong manages to open the hatch to detonate Hi There, he sits astride the bomb as it falls toward its target, waving his Stetson as if he were at a rodeo. The detonation is probably the closest Kong ever came to orgasm. Major Kong is as sexless as the other males in the film, with the exception of Buck Turgidson (George C. Scott). Again, the character bears a sexually allusive name: Buck, an adult male animal; Turgidson, from "turgid," meaning "swollen," implying sexual arousal. Turgidson is first seen half dressed with his secretary, who is wearing a bikini, after what was obviously an assignation. His sex life has bifurcated into lust for women and lust for war. He envies the Russians their doomsday machine, which forms the film's climax.

Although the film's opening disclaimer insists that the characters are fictitious, several of them were suggested by historical figures—or rather, historical figures transmogrified into caricatures, with some traces of the prototypes left behind. However, *Dr. Strangelove* is not *cinema à clef* like *Citizen Kane*, in which the similarities between the fictitious Charles Foster Kane and newspaper tycoon William Randolph Hearst are obvious. In his impressive ongoing study of *Dr. Strangelove*, Rob Ager identifies the models for the main characters. To Ager, Buck Turgidson is a stand-in for General Curtis LeMay, a warrior in the literal sense and the bearer of several unflattering nicknames, including "The Demon." In the last months of World War II, LeMay replaced the standard practice of daylight precision bombing with the relentless nighttime cluster bombing of Tokyo and other Japanese cities. After the war, he reorganized the Strategic Air Command (SAC), but could not adjust to Cold War America without a battle plan. In this respect, he is more like General Ripper. Le May, like Ripper, advocated a preemptive nuclear attack policy if there was any indication that the Soviet Union was planning a strike against the United States. LeMay also favored big cigars, like General Ripper. Kubrick often used a low shot to photograph Sterling Hayden, so that the cigar in his mouth extended into the frame like a projectile—or, in keeping with the film's dominant image, a phallus. According to a PBS program about LeMay, after *Dr. Strangelove* came out, the press referred to him as General Jack D. Ripper.

Ager also notes that two of Kubrick's biographers consider Merkin Muffley a composite of Adlai E. Stevenson, United Nations ambassador under John Kennedy, and former President Dwight D. Eisenhower. Stevenson and Eisenhower were bald like Muffley, and Stevenson had also been governor of Illinois and the Democratic Party's presidential candidate in 1952 and 1956, losing both times to Eisenhower. Stevenson was also an intellectual, something Muffley is not. As for Muffley as Eisenhower, one could hardly imagine Muffley at Normandy in 1944, much less planning the Normandy invasion, as Eisenhower did. If anything, Muffley is the antithesis of Stevenson and Eisenhower, possessing neither Stevenson's diplomatic skills nor Eisenhower's military expertise. Muffley is a twit. His natural habitat would have been a burlesque house, where he could have been a Top Banana like Phil Silvers in the early days of his career. If Muffley is anyone, he is Master Sergeant Ernie Bilko in the White House.

The last character to make an appearance is the eponymous Dr. Strangelove, a onetime Nazi and now an anti-communist and member of the president's inner council. The screenwriters—Kubrick, Southern, and George—wove aspects of the life and career of rocket scientist Werner von Braun into Strangelove, creating an anti-Von Braun. The historical Werner Von Braun oversaw the production of the V-2 missiles that rained down on England in 1944. Inmates from concentration camps were conscripted to build the rockets and forced to live underground in tunnels, where they were subjected to widespread mistreatment and physical abuse. Von Braun was appalled by the workers' living conditions but claimed he could do nothing to improve them. Like Strangelove, Von Braun was one of several ex-Nazi scientists brought to the United States as part of the then covert Operation Paperclip. The operation was intended to ensure that America's nuclear superiority, demonstrated at Hiroshima and Nagasaki, remain unchallenged. Von Braun could only do so much, yet without him, there might never have been a moon landing in 1969—one of the ironies of Operation Paperclip.

The wheelchair-bound and presumably impotent Strangelove occupies a special place in the war room during the film's final moments. He advances a plan to preserve what is left of the human race: underground breeding in mineshafts, similar to the tunnels at Mittelwerk, the underground factory where slave laborers built the V-2 rockets. Since the ratio of women to men would be ten to one, monogamy would be discontinued in order to produce a master race. The notion of a polygamous society appeals to the horny Turgidson. Even the Russian ambassador considers it "an astonishingly good idea." The finale is Peter Sellers's last attempt to top himself. Having played a proper Brit and a nincompoop president, he now takes on Strangelove. Gleefully decadent and eerily effete, like an androgynous cabaret performer in Christopher Isherwood's Berlin, Strangelove is also part machine. He has a mechanized arm that he must pull down when it springs up. Sellers' Strangelove is the personification of silken villainy and amoral detachment. To him, humankind is the equivalent of the refueling device seen at the beginning of the film. Energized by his dream of a race of super humans, he suddenly rises from his wheelchair, crying, "Mein Führer, I can walk." Standing upright is the closest he will get to an erection. But it is too late. The doomsday machine goes off, and one wonders who will be alive to populate the world that survives.

The world's future, if it is to have one, lies in an underground metropolis like the one in Fritz Lang's 1927 film of the same name, except that everyone would be living below the earth. (In *Metropolis*, only the workers toil beneath the surface.} But the idea of underground breeding chambers brings the film to the height of nihilism. The strange love that the doctor advocates is sex as work, loveless reproduction. Pushed to the extreme, Strangelove's metropolis would be like Plato's ideal state, with its regulated breeding and communal child rearing. Children never know their birth parents, ensuring that their sole allegiance is to the state. Ironically, the anti-communist Strangelove's plan, if fully implemented, would result in a form of communism that goes beyond the excesses of the Soviet Union. *Dr. Strangelove* may be a classic comedy, but its implications do not inspire laughter.

Chapter 21

AFTER SUCH KNOWLEDGE

COLD WAR MOVIES INSPIRED FEAR—FEAR OF A COMMUNIST COUP d'état, of nuclear devastation, of the end of civilization. They portrayed an America swarming with Soviet agents where no one was safe. An ex-communist who recants is a marked man (*The Woman on Pier 13*, *My Son John*). Withholding information from a communist hoodlum results in a fate worse than refusing to pay protection money to the mob. The mob would send their goons to vandalize your establishment. Communists will blow your head off (*Pickup on South Street*). In McCarthyist America, liberals did not stand a chance. Subscribing to a left-wing publication made you a security risk if you worked for the military (*Three Brave Men*). Refusing to remove a controversial book from a library could cause a kid to burn the building down (*Storm Center*). Marching in a May Day parade could get a television performer blacklisted, eventually causing him to take his life (*The Front*). The films may have exaggerated, but only about the violence inflicted on uncooperative citizens.

There was, in fact, an attorney general's list, and one could get blacklisted or lose a job for something as innocuous as subscribing to the *Nation* or supporting the Joint Anti-Fascist Refugee Committee—the former considered subversive; the latter, a communist front. American communists themselves were not a threat. In 1955, they numbered only about twenty thousand, eighty-eight hundred of whom were New Yorkers. The real threat was to freedom of expression, a threat that came from a Senate subcommittee of dubious authority (HUAC) and an alcoholic senator from Wisconsin, who derailed careers in the name of a cause that was a personal crusade. "The age demanded an image / Of its accelerated grimace," Ezra Pound wrote in "E. P. Ode pour l'election de son sépulchre." In Senator Joseph McCarthy, the age found its image, more grotesque than accelerated. Although America had to maintain its nuclear strength, the science fiction films of the 1950s dramatized the bitter fruit of atomic testing. Moviegoers may not have believed that detonations in the Southwest could produce such mutations as depicted in *Them!* and *Tarantula*, but the notion that they might lingered. The bomb was untrustworthy.

The movies released in the first decade of the Cold War showed an America in a preparedness stage, much as in some of the pre-Pearl Harbor films. Hollywood anticipated America's involvement in the Second World War as early as 1940. In *Arise, My Love* (1940), Ray Milland referred to the Spanish Civil War as "palooka preliminaries" for "the big event." There were also films showing America girding for something impending, but never articulated, films such as *Flight Command* and *Flight Angels* (both 1940), and *Dive Bomber* and *Parachute Battalion* (both 1941).

In the 1950s, America's idea of preparedness was a bomb shelter. It was axiomatic that if any nation could start World War III, it would be the Soviet Union, which would launch a nuclear attack against the United States. In the event of such an attack (preemptive, of course), school children were instructed to "duck and cover," sliding under their desks and clasping their hands in back of their heads. There were also nuclear attack drills, in which students would be shepherded into school basements until the "all clear" sounded. Those who could afford to do so built bomb shelters, accessible either from outside their homes via cellar doors, or preferably, through basements, where they could take refuge in a enclosed spaces accommodating as many as eight persons. The amenities, such as they were, included dry packaged food, fresh water, toilet facilities, an air pump, and a generator— no frills, but supposedly manageable. The down side was the neighbors, who might expect to be accommodated when the bombs started falling. Some homeowners would lie, claiming they were building a wine cellar.

The decade that began with *Five* and ended with *On the Beach* brought the doomsday genre full circle—from a quintet of survivors to none at all. Hope emerged briefly in the early sixties with the election of John F. Kennedy and his short-lived Camelot. But with the Cuban Missile Crisis in 1962 and Kennedy's assassination the following year, it was back to fear and trembling with *Fail-Safe* and *Dr. Strangelove*.

The films of the 1940s, especially those dealing with World War II, were different. They inspired hope, even in the darkest days of the conflict. The most ingenious of filmmakers could never have turned the fall of Bataan into an allied victory. At the end of *Bataan* (1943), Robert Taylor, squatting in the foxhole that will become his grave, is seen firing away at the advancing Japanese. Then a title appears: "So fought the heroes of Bataan. Their sacrifice made possible our victories in the Coral Sea, at Midway, on New Guinea and Guadalcanal. Their spirit will lead us back to Bataan." There is no connection between the fall of Bataan on 9 April 1942 and the victory at Midway two months later, marking the turning point of the war in the Pacific. But at least the epilogue afforded a ray of hope at a time when hope was indeed the thing with feathers.

There was no need to preach conformity in the 1940s. The country was united as it never has been since. There were common enemies: Nazi Germany and imperialist Japan and, until it surrendered in September 1943, fascist Italy. The 1950s, on the other hand, was a decade of conformity in dress and politics. The goal was to look cool. Girls wore ponytails with their poodle skirts and penny-loafers, while boys with short hair wore khakis and button-down shirts. For a male, rebellion meant being a greaser with a duck's ass haircut, black leather jacket, form-fitting T-shirt, and tight jeans. Perhaps those who could interpret subtext got the point of *Invasion of the Body Snatchers* (1956): The think-alikes of society are pod people, eager to make others into plants like themselves. Pod life was simple: You lose your humanity, but think of the peace. No striving, no climb to the top, no drop to the bottom. Regardless of whether one was a Republican or a Democrat, political affiliation meant anti-communism. Support the undeclared war in Korea, even if you can't locate Korea on a map. We were fighting the Reds; that was all you needed to know.

To its credit, Hollywood made no attempt to mythologize Korea in the way it did World War II. The Korean War was an ugly war, a dirty job to be done. No great love story like *Casablanca* (1942) emerged from Korea; no family dramas like *Mrs. Miniver* (1942), *The Human Comedy* (1943), *The Sullivans*, or *Since You Went Away* (both 1944); no classic comedies like *To Be or Not to Be* (1942), *The More the Merrier* (1943), or *Hail the Conquering Hero* (1944). In the 1950s, when your draft notice arrived, you served your country or you would be shamed into doing so (*I Want You* [1951]). The age demanded, and its demands were met.

Cold War films are now part of the past. When they first arrived, there was an immediacy about them. They did not require period costumes or an acting style suited to the era. The only tense was the present; no excavating was required. This was even true of movies about World War II that came out in the late forties and early fifties. *Three Came Home* (1949), based on Agnes Newton Keith's account of her internment in a Japanese prison camp, was in every way a World War II film, right down to the abuse the women suffered at the hands of the guards. Similarly, *Twelve O'Clock High* (1949) and *Force of Arms* (1951)—the latter vaguely reminiscent of Hemingway's *A Farewell to Arms*, but with a happy ending—seemed to be continuations, not appendices, of the World War II film. It was as if the war had not ended. Much had to do with the leading actors in these two films—Gregory Peck in the former and William Holden in the latter—both of whom attained stardom in the 1940s and had not yet lost their luster. You could believe Peck as a rigid brigadier general in 1942 and Holden as an army sergeant in 1944. World War II had not yet ossified into an artifact.

But fifty years later, it had. *Memphis Belle* (1990) (not to be confused with *The Memphis Belle: A Story of a Flying Fortress* [1944], William Wyler's brilliant documentary) had a cast (Matthew Modine, Eric Stolz, Tate Donovan) that did not look, speak, or act like a 1943 bomber crew, but instead brought a thoroughly modern sensibility to their roles. The same was true of Ben Affleck and Josh Hartnett in *Pearl Harbor* (2001), which also suffered from the misuse of two fine actors, Jon Voight and Alec Baldwin, who impersonated FDR and Lieutenant Colonel James Doolittle, respectively, as if they were at a World War II costume party.

As the twentieth century drew to a close, HUAC seemed the stuff of vintage newsreels, black-and-white images of another time. It was commendable that Irwin Winkler wanted to revisit the past in *Guilty by Suspicion* (1991), but having Robert De Niro, one of the finest actors of his generation, play a director who socialized with communists (but was not one himself) was not so much casting against type as casting against period. By 1991, De Niro was so closely associated with such larger-than-life figures as Vito Corleone in *The Godfather, Part II* (1974), Travis Bickle in *Taxi Driver* (1976), Jake LaMotta in *Raging Bull* (1980), and Rupert Pupkin in *The King of Comedy* (1982) that playing a less charismatic figure made both the actor and his character seem ordinary. De Niro did not step into the right time frame; he had not moved from his contemporary comfort zone. When he shouted "Shame on you!" at HUAC, one felt that he would have rather used the obscenity Woody Allen did in *The Front*.

"The past is never dead. It's not even past," as Gavin Stevens explains to Temple Drake in William Faulkner's *Requiem for a Nun*. The line has been quoted so often (and misquoted by Owen Wilson in Woody Allen's *Midnight in Paris* [2012]) that it seems part of the collective unconscious. In Hollywood, right from the beginning, the past was present, conjured into being whenever a filmmaker wanted to flip the calendar pages to get to his period of choice. For D. W. Griffith, it was the Civil War (*The Birth of a Nation*); for John Ford, it was the post-bellum West (*Fort Apache, She Wore a Yellow Ribbon, The Searchers*); for Henry King, it was vintage America (*In Old Chicago, Ramona, Wilson, Margie, Wait Till the Sun Shines, Nellie*). The best recreations had a semiotics of their own, attesting to their authenticity in every detail: physical production, actors, soundtrack, and script. Some films are justly admired for their renderings of the past: Steven Spielberg's *Schindler's List* (1993) and *Lincoln* (2012), Roman Polanski's *The Pianist* (2002), Warren Beatty's *Reds* (1981), Curtis Hanson's *L. A. Confidential* (1997). Others call attention to themselves as restorations. In Clint Eastwood's *Changeling* (2008), Angelina Jolie's cloche hat and painted mouth function as 1920s signifiers, as if to say, "The costume designer and makeup artist have done their homework, and here is the fruit of their research." *Swing Kids* (1993), set in 1938 Hamburg, where teenagers with a love of swing run afoul of authorities who consider this music decadent, starred Robert Sean Leonard and Christian Bale, who looked as if they were members of an American boy band. The best filmmakers know that "it is an art to conceal an art." They also know that the further removed from the present the setting of a film is, the more true-to-the-period it must be in every detail—especially the performances.

While it is hard to imagine anyone reopening the wounds of Korea, the Cold War has not lost its appeal; neither has the "what if?" movie about another world war that leaves some teenagers determined to make a last-ditch stand against the invaders. Although the Cold War was in its final phase in 1984, the possibility of nuclear holocaust was still present. In fact, war might have occurred in late September 1983, when a report came through the Soviet warning system's computer that the United States had launched intercontinental ballistic missiles against Russia. Fortunately, an officer in the Soviet air defense forces discovered that it was a false alarm. The incident was not made known until the 1990s, but had it been reported at the time, it would have made sense in a macabre kind of way. On 1 September 1983, a South Korean airliner en route from New York to Seoul flew through Soviet air space and was shot down, killing all 269 passengers, including a United States congressman. History has shown that it takes little to start a war: Julius Caesar's crossing a stream called the Rubicon; the assassination of an archduke and his bride in Sarajevo; the crossing of a parallel in Korea.

And a war might have occurred—or at least writer-director John Milius thought so. In *Red Dawn* (1984), Milius, who won an Oscar for his screenplay for *Apocalypse Now* (1979), imagined an America in the midst of World War III. The aggressors were the Soviets and their Cuban and Nicaraguan allies, who have nuked Washington, DC, and now taken over a town in

Colorado. A group of high school students dub themselves the Wolverines and retreat to the hills like resistance fighters in a World War II movie. *New York Times* critic Janet Maslin rightly observed (10 August 1984) that *Red Dawn* "may be rabidly inflammatory, but it isn't dull." Invasion movies, including those about extraterrestrial invaders, prey on our fear of the unknown. In the 1980s, this fear concerned the possibility of an occupied America, where a drive-in has become a detention camp, and the local Bijou is showing Sergei Eisenstein's *Alexander Nevsky* (1938). You say to yourself, "It can't happen here," but then you know it could. The young cast—including Patrick Swayze, C. Thomas Howell, Jennifer Grey, Charlie Sheen—was uncharismatic enough to be convincing. They looked like the kids in *The Boy from Stalingrad* who took on the Nazis but were no match for their brutality. One has to fight from tearing up at the end. Near a boulder that the guerrillas have christened "Partisan Rock," there is a plaque with the following inscription: "In the early days of World War III, guerrillas—mostly children—placed the names of the lost upon this rock. They fought here alone and gave up their lives so that 'this nation shall not perish from the earth.'" War films, in which the young die (*The North Star, The Boy from Stalingrad, China's Little Devils*) have a special, possibly manipulative poignancy that films about men who die in battle do not. Seeing children perish forces us to suspend critical judgment and ponder their sacrifice, even in a film as "rabidly inflammatory" as *Red Dawn*.

If the past is any indication, the Cold War will continue to attract filmmakers eager to offer their take on it. It is a war that can be approached from various angles: the repatriation of citizens from countries under communist control, atomic spies, HUAC, the blacklist, the bomb, the missile race, nuclear war with or without doomsday. But since terrorism has now replaced the Soviet threat, it is more likely that audiences will be seeing films on the order of *World Trade Center, United 93, The Hurt Locker,* and *Zero Dark Thirty* than a remake of *Dr. Strangelove.* Even the live television version of *Fail-Safe* (2000) lacked the sense of doom that haunted the 1964 film. The television version depicted what never happened; the film, what could have.

Films about careers interrupted or destroyed by HUAC will always have the same relevance that any account of injustice has. They can inspire compassion for the victims and a need to call attention to their plight, even if others have written or made movies about it. For those who have discovered what Dalton Trumbo called "the time of the toad," the McCarthy period is a personal journey on which they must embark as if for the first time.

So it was for Nancy Lynn Schwartz, whom her mother Sheila described as someone who "loved people and hated injustice," a love-hate combination that motivated Nancy to write about the writers silenced by HUAC, the political climate the committee created, and the wreckage that it left in its wake. Nancy had written a first draft of *The Hollywood Writers' Wars* when she was diagnosed with a brain tumor that claimed her life at twenty-six in 1979. The book was completed by her mother, an English education professor. It is also a tribute to the young author, who, when she was only eight years old, was "inconsolable after seeing *Spartacus*." Dalton Trumbo—the film's screenwriter, and formerly the most prominent member of the Hollywood Ten—had done his job well.

Karl Francis was also drawn to HUAC, but for a different reason. The Welsh born Francis, a left wing BBC television writer-director-producer, was attracted to stories about social issues, such as the effect closing a colliery in south Wales had on the miners, their families, and the community. This interest spawned his docudrama *Above Us the Earth* (1977), a fusion of the documentary and the fiction film employing an egalitarian mix of professional actors and amateurs. Understandably, Francis was attracted to Herbert Biberman, who created a similar type of docudrama, *Salt of the Earth* (1954), inspired by a 1951 strike by local 890 of the Mine, Mill, and Smelter Works Union in Bayard, New Mexico, against New Jersey Zinc. (The local had been expelled from the CIO for being communist controlled.) In the film, the company is called Delaware Zinc, and the strikers are Mexican Americans seeking job equality with whites. Like the actors in *Above Us the Earth*, those in *Salt of the Earth* were a mix of ordinary men and women and professionals.

Written by the blacklisted Michael Wilson, *Salt of the Earth* is both political and feminist. Since a Taft-Hartley injunction prevented the miners from picketing, their wives replaced them on the line. The economic issue that sparked the strike—whites being paid more than Mexican Americans, who did the same work for less pay—took a domestic turn. The women realized that if they could man the picket line, they were entitled to their own form of equality. If the men called their fellow union members "brothers," their wives should be addressed as "sisters."

Francis might have considered a remake of *Salt of the Earth*, which, despite a favorable review from *New York Times* critic Bosley Crowther (15 March 1954), was largely ignored. Exhibitors who might have shown the film were reluctant to do so after the House of Representatives and the American Legion inveighed against it. The lead, the superb Mexican actress

Rosaura Revueltas—who played a striking miner's wife, whose quest for sexual equality paralleled her husband's fight for equal pay—was deported to Mexico. The film languished for a decade before resurfacing in the 1960s. In 1992, *Salt of the Earth* was entered in the Library of Congress's National Film Registry, which each year singles out films of historical, cultural, or aesthetic significance deemed worthy of preservation.

Rather than remake a classic, in 2000 Francis incorporated the making of *Salt of the Earth* within a film about Biberman. Francis's film bore the prosaic title *One of the Hollywood Ten*, and featured Jeff Goldblum as Biberman and Greta Scacchi as his wife, the Oscar-winning actress Gale Sondergaard. Biberman was indeed one of the Hollywood Ten, but he was not in the same league as John Howard Lawson, Ring Lardner Jr., Albert Maltz, and Dalton Trumbo. Biberman's first love was the theater. He received his MA from the Yale School of Drama in 1927 and fancied himself a playwright, although he fared better as a director. Believing that he might achieve in Hollywood the fame that had eluded him in New York, Biberman signed a two-picture contract with Columbia in 1935.

Although Biberman wrote screen stories and scripts—the best known being *The Master Race* (1944), which he both coauthored and directed—he also became embroiled in radical politics. The energy that could have been channeled into something creative was diverted into causes that kept drawing him further away from the goal he had set for himself when he came to Hollywood. After serving five months of a six-month sentence at the federal correctional institution at Texarkana, Texas, for contempt of Congress, Biberman emerged intent on proving that his talent had not deserted him. The result was *Salt of the Earth*. Sadly, his swan song, *Slaves* (1969), whose screenplay he also co-authored, was an exploitation film about the brutal treatment of African American plantation slaves with strained historical parallels (breeding of slaves compared to Nazi eugenics, refusal to divulge a woman's whereabouts equated with refusal to name names). But that was Biberman, who even in his declining years did not cease from reminding moviegoers—at least the few who saw *Slaves*—of America's racist past. When Biberman died two years later, his legacy consisted of a handful of minor films and the historically significant *Salt of the Earth*.

One of the Hollywood Ten was shot in Spain, which accounts for its sunny look (Los Angeles does not have a sun-kissed glow). Francis's commitment is admirable, and Goldblum and Scacchi offer reasonably accurate impersonations of Biberman and Sondergaard. But the film itself lacks the sense of relevance needed to attract a mass audience. In 2002, *One of the*

Hollywood Ten was screened at the Walter Reade Theater at Lincoln Center and received a mildly favorable notice from *New York Times* critic Stephen Holden (11 January 2002). It has not yet been released commercially in the United States, having been shown only on cable television. Francis might have fared better with a docudrama on the making of *Salt of the Earth*, for which there is ample material: Biberman's own account and the story behind the actual strike.

"Time present and time past / Are both perhaps present in time future, / And time future contained in time past." In these opening verses of T. S. Eliot's "Burnt Norton," the first of the *Four Quartets*, the poet is pondering the simultaneity of time from the standpoint of eternity, in which past, present, and future coexist. Considered less metaphysically, these verses could be Hollywood's credo. Gavin Stevens was right: "The past is never dead." It can make its way into the present, where it gestates as a film treatment or a television pilot until some future date, when the treatment has evolved into a screenplay and then a film, and the pilot into a series. That is precisely how the television series, *The Americans*, originated, premiering on the FX channel at the end of January 2013. Having worked for the CIA, Joe Weisberg, the series creator, wondered about the effects agents' double lives had on their families. At home, they were couples with children. They got up, had breakfast, and headed for the agency, where they decoded messages, bugged offices, deceived, taped conversations, and kept suspects under surveillance. After a day in the shadow world, if they were lucky, they got home in time for supper.

Soviet spies in America did all this and more—at least that is how they were portrayed in 1981, the first year of Ronald Reagan's presidency and the year in which the first three seasons of *The Americans* seem to be set. (Some episodes allude to events of later years; for example an episode in the third season of the series includes a reference to the Boland Amendment, which was passed in December 1982.) If Weisberg decides to move beyond 1981, with the series encompassing Reagan's two terms (1981–89) and featuring key events from that period, *The Americans* could end with the razing of the Berlin Wall in 1989, which presaged the dissolution of the Soviet Union two years later. Fans can only hope. In 2015, the series' time span was unclear; the premise, however, was not.

Elizabeth and Philip Jennings (Keri Russell and Matthew Rhys) seem the perfect couple. They live with their two children in a Washington, DC, suburb, where they operate a travel agency. The Jenningses (one never knows their real names) are Soviet sleeper spies, planted earlier in the United

States after having learned to speak American English so they could fit in with their neighbors. Although they have never been legally married, they are devoted to their children. But their allegiance is to the Soviet Union.

Elizabeth can be both touchingly maternal and dispassionately lethal. She behaves lovingly to her daughter Paige until she learns that Paige has donated the $600 she has saved to a local church. Furious, Elizabeth awakens Paige in the middle of the night, ordering her to clean the refrigerator. Like any good communist, Elizabeth is an atheist; her daughter is not—or at least not yet. And Elizabeth's relationship with Philip is not without complications. The two are not ideologues like John Jefferson in *My Son John* and Herbert Biberman in *One of the Hollywood Ten*, nor are they mob types like the communists in *The Woman on Pier 13* and *Pickup on South Street*. They are a part of a new breed: the communist zealot. One could imagine Philip and Elizabeth committing terrorist acts if ordered to do so. If sex is the only way Philip can get Secretary of Defense Caspar Weinberger's office photographed, so be it. Since Philip is not especially monogamous, he experiences no pangs of conscience. And Elizabeth is not reluctant to use her feminine wiles to obtain information from a naïve naval cadet about a Soviet defector, whose specialty is stealth technology. For Elizabeth and Philip, home is not where the heart is; it is their haven at the end of a day that might have involved murder, kidnapping, sex for secrets, and narrow escapes. They are the KGB's equivalent of CIA agents, but they lack the CIA's support system. Sometimes they have to go it alone. When they do, *The Americans* switches on to another track, one where the couple's lives are in danger, even as they endanger the lives of others.

Setting the action in 1981 required an episode, "In Control" (20 February 2013), devoted to the most significant event of that year: John Hinckley Jr.'s attempted assassination of President Reagan on 30 March 1981. Until Elizabeth and Philip learned Hinkley's motive (his attempt to impress actress Jodie Foster, with whom he was obsessed), the assassination attempt possibly included KGB involvement, which would have meant a round of assassinations for them. But another event dating from around the time that could add dramatic and historical substance to the series was the Sandinistas' overthrow of the dictatorial Somoza regime in Nicaragua in 1979. Afterwards, the Sandinistas proceeded to embark upon Marxist-inspired reforms, confiscating the property of the Somocistas and pursuing a policy of land reform by divvying up large estates to accommodate marginalized peasants. Castro's Cuba was bad enough; now there was another Marxist experiment in Latin America. When the counter-revolutionaries, popularly known as Contras, were ready to take on the Sandinistas, the CIA was there to help.

The scandal of the decade was known as Iran-Contra (1986), in which key members of the Reagan White House devised a way of freeing American hostages held in Lebanon by selling arms to Iran despite an embargo. Oliver North, a former marine lieutenant colonel and National Security Council aide, took the plan to the next level, bankrolling the Contras with money from the arms sale. His actions violated the Boland Amendment (1982), which forbade the training and arming of the Contras. (Two further resolutions followed in 1983 and 1984, forbidding funding the Contras.) When the news broke about Iran-Contra, North was proudly unrepentant.

Iran-Contra was a scenario worthy of Graham Greene. The second episode of Season 2 of *The Americans* ("Cardinal," 5 March 2014), introduces a character who had been a Sandinista and is now a KGB agent. In "Martial Eagle" (23 April 2014), based on a story by Oliver North and Tracy Scott Wilson, Elizabeth and Philip infiltrate a Contras training camp, where Elizabeth murders with guiltless dispassion, while Philip is momentarily overcome by the bloodshed. The time of "Martial Eagle" is unclear. It still seems to be 1981, but according to the *New York Times* (9 January 1987), after two months of training in Florida, the first group of Contras returned home in early January 1987, suggesting that the training program was initiated in 1986. That schedule would make sense; it was in November 1986 that Iran-Contra made front-page news.

The Americans is aimed at an informed audience that does not need a footnote for every historical reference. "Martial Eagle" does not even explain why there is a Contras training camp in the United States—and that does not really matter. What matters is that Elizabeth and Philip have been given a job that results in the killing of Americans. You get so caught up in the violence that you may forget it exists within a context. Yet, for the time being, *The Americans* has taken Soviet espionage farther than it has ever gone before. Elizabeth and Philip inhabit a world in which any given day could involve abduction, murder, seduction, defection, bugging, infiltration, theft, blackmail, and infidelity. Thus far the writers have managed to balance the Jenningses' activities in the KGB netherworld with their parental obligations, even though Philip and Elizabeth are forced to fabricate explanations for their frequent absences, and eventually the children become accustomed to them. The tension between job demands and family responsibilities allows for some degree of empathy, particularly in viewers who have to juggle career and family, trying not to shortchange either. Sometimes you even forget that murder is part of the Jenningses' job description. You wonder about Philip and Elizabeth as you do about Macbeth and Lady Macbeth. Were they always inclined toward murder, or did a chance incident—a meeting with a KGB spymaster, or an encounter with witches—trigger the transformation?

It is the drama in *The Americans* as much as the melodrama that draws viewers. At the beginning of the third season, the Jenningses' allegiance is about to be tested. The first episode, aired at the end of January 2015, had a real hook: Will Paige follow in her parents' footsteps? Elizabeth is in favor; Philip, less so. It was not a question of "Tune in next week," as the announcers on the old radio shows used to say. That is not how the series works. In the second episode, "Open House" (11 February 2015), the situation remains unresolved. So does another possible plot thread: the Jenningses' interest in the CIA's role in Afghanistan. No further background is given (at least in this episode), but it helps if the viewer knows that the Soviet invasion of Afghanistan in 1979 led to a war between the Soviet Union and the Mujahedeen (radical Islamists). Committed to warding off Soviet aggression, the United States had no choice but to support the jihadists, who later became an international threat. Still, with help from the CIA, they were able to force a Soviet withdrawal from Afghanistan in 1989. Exactly where the Soviet-Afghan war (1979–89) will end up in the series is anyone's guess: a springboard for an episode, perhaps, or an event to be filed away for a later date.

In *The Americans*, history is at the discretion of the writers, who are free to use it as a backdrop or a plot peg on which to hang a story line. And if history is not generating an episode, a family matter is—such as Paige's decision in the third season to be baptized, which could result in a daughter versus parents subplot.

For a brief period, viewers could tune in on a different night, and to a different network, for another series about Russian (no longer Soviet) agents in America. NBC's *Allegiance*, which premiered in February 2015, is set in the post-Cold War era. The KGB has been replaced by the SVR, Russia's new foreign intelligence service. But spying has not gone out of fashion. A wife (Hope Davis), who would rather forget her KGB past, is now forced to confront it. The SVR wants former KGB agent Katya O'Connor (Davis)—a mother of three, married to an American engineer who traded secrets to bring her to the United States—to turn her son, a CIA analyst, into a double agent.

Unlike *The Americans*, *Allegiance* is set in the present, and that is the problem. In the first episode, the SVR is planning an attack that will cripple

America's infrastructure. If this were the point of departure in a series about a terrorist group operating in the United States, it would have been plausible. Although Russian president Vladimir Putin behaved autocratically in annexing the Crimea in 2014, setting off a war between Ukrainians and Russian separatists, the sanctions imposed upon Russia and its depressed economy do not make for a country capable of committing sabotage in the United States. Putin may mourn the demise of the Soviet Union, which he called one of the great tragedies of the twentieth century, but even during the Cold War, sabotage was not as likely as crises, stand offs, and eleventh-hour reprieves. *The Americans* has a higher degree of plausibility. The Jenningses believe they can be parents as well as KGB operatives. It is the tension between their public and private lives that makes the series watchable. In *Allegiance*, all Katya wants is to enjoy the freedom that America has to offer and see her younger daughter improve her grades so she can go on to college. (The older daughter was recruited as a spy at an early age.) Unfavorable comparisons with *The Americans* and lukewarm reviews caused NBC to cancel *Allegiance* after five episodes.

Television has come a long way since *I Led Three Lives* (1953–56), the popular syndicated series that starred Richard Carlson as Herbert A. Philbrick. At the beginning of each episode, an announcer with a stentorian voice would remind listeners that "this is the fascinatingly true story of Herbert A. Philbrick who, for nine frightening years, did lead three lives—average citizen, high-level member of the Communist Party, and counterspy for the Federal Bureau of Investigation." Philbrick is the series protagonist, and his inner thoughts are conveyed through voiceover narration, often urgently delivered when he is on the verge of being unmasked. *I Led Three Lives* portrayed an America in which communists greet each other as "comrade" but show no comradely spirit. For them, Christmas is a time to fleece the gullible by soliciting contributions to the phony "All Faiths United Christmas Fund," with the proceeds going to the party's coffers ("A Communist Christmas"). Communists recruit teenagers to trash offices at a local college, hoping that the wanton destruction of property will give them a taste for greater acts of party-inspired carnage ("Vandalism"). One of the better episodes is "Radioactive," written by the television writer-producer and creator of *Star Trek*, Eugene Roddenberry, under the pseudonym of Robert Wesley. A female communist has arrived in town with a radioactive isotope that she has stolen, which Philbrick must retrieve. It is one of the most suspenseful episodes of the series, with Philbrick gaining access to her house and, with the aid of a Geiger counter, locating the isotope before he becomes radioactive. There is an interesting switch: The woman is not offering the isotope to the party, as a good communist would. She wants $100,000 for it, after which she plans to relinquish her membership and enjoy her profits from the sale. She soon discovers that leaving the party is harder than joining it.

I Led Three Lives was pure propaganda, perpetuating the belief that anyone—the head of an advertising agency, a biology professor, even grandmotherly types—could be communists. The series was a relic from another era, preserved in the amber of time. Despite his triune existence, Philbrick is a cipher as a character. He may have led three lives, but we only see two of them; when he isn't at the beck and call of the party, he is reporting to the FBI. Just when we expect to get a look at Philbrick the family man, a call comes through ordering him to show up for a cell meeting. *I Led Three Lives* was completely plot driven; there was no characterization, only dialogue. In *The Americans* and *Allegiance*, the characters drive the plot, so that it is impossible to separate them from the narrative. Elizabeth and Philip, and Katya and her family are real people in life and death situations. They are also fictional creations. Philbrick is not; he cannot fail because history has decreed otherwise. The fate of the Jenningses and the O'Connors are in the hands of the writers.

If movies are to be made about Cold or post-Cold War espionage, they should take their cue from *The Americans* and *Allegiance*. In the latter, Hope Davis was an empathetic Katya, sporting an authentic accent and occasionally lapsing into Russian the way bilingual people often do when they find it easier to express a thought in their native tongue. She and her husband have also raised their son and older daughter to be bilingual so that, when necessary, they can communicate in Russian. In the past, Russian spies were as dimensionless as stick figures, as insubstantial as the shadow world they inhabit. *The Americans* and *Allegiance* have portrayed them as human beings. Sadly, we will never know what happened to the O'Connors. Were they ever able to gain immunity by exposing the SVR's designs on America? And to what extent could they count on their son to help them? *Allegiance* deserved to remain on the air for at least a season, instead of ending with a cliffhanger.

The Red screen has had more than its share of skeletons; *The Americans* and *Allegiance* have finally given them flesh.

NOTES

Chapter 1

7   "the cruelest year of the Depression": William Manchester, *The Glory and the Dream: A Narrative History of America 1932–1972* (Boston: Little, Brown, 1975), 32.

7–8   "men of far greater intelligence," "Appoint a dictator": ibid., 57, 58.

8   "concentration-camp atmosphere": Morris Dickstein, *Dancing in the Dark: A Cultural History of the Great Depression* (New York: Norton, 2009), 58.

10   "*fascist* satire," "some calling it a satire": Ben Urwand, *The Collaboration: Hollywood's Pact with Hitler* (Cambridge: Harvard UP, 2013), 109.

12   "the FDR of Arcadia": Andrew Bergman, *We're in the Money: Depression America and Its Films* (New York: Harper Colophon, 1972), 78.

12   "seven million people": Miron Dolot, *Execution by Hunger: The Hidden Holocaust* (New York: Norton, 1985), vii.

13   "The picks came down," "*Our Daily Bread*," *Film Notes*, ed. Eileen Bowser (New York: Museum of Modern Art, 1969), 92.

15   "*Hitler, Beast of Berlin*": Bernard F. Dick, *The Star-Spangled Screen: The American World War II Film* (Lexington, KY: UP of Kentucky, 1985), 61–63.

15   "The history, institutions": Leonard J. Leff and Jerold L. Simmons, *The Dame in the Kimono: Hollywood, Censorship, and the Production Code from the 1930s to the 1960s* (New York: Grove Weidenfeld, 1990), 286.

16   "barred from the German market": Urwand, *The Collaboration*, 204.

16   "The film's production history": Dick, *The Star-Spangled Screen*, 51–60; Thomas Doherty, *Hollywood and Hitler 1933–1939* (New York: Columbia UP, 2013), 337–50.

Chapter 2

23   "twenty-three names": Larry Ceplair and Steven Englund, *The Inquisition in Hollywood: Politics and the Film Community, 1930–1960* (New York: Doubleday, 1980), 447.

23   "never belonged": Victor S. Navasky, *Naming Names* (New York: Viking, 1980), 131.

24   "[The conductor]": Eric Bentley, ed., *Thirty Years of Treason: Excerpts from Hearings before the House Committee on Un-American Activities, 1938–1968* (New York: Viking, 1980), 112.

27   "Scorched Earth": Robert Mayhew, *Ayn Rand and Song of Russia: Communism and Anti-Communism in 1940s Hollywood* (Lanham, MD: Scarecrow Press, 2005), 14–30.

28   "screen adaptations of five stories": A. Scott Berg, *Goldwyn: A Biography* (New York: Ballantine Books, 1989), 267.

29   "accepted his suggestions": ibid., 374–75.

29   "starvation that ravaged Ukraine": Dolot, *Execution by Hunger*, 137–43.

30   "As Carl Rollyson has shown": Carl Rollyson, *Lillian Hellman: Her Legend and Her Legacy* (Lincoln, NE: toExcel Press, 1999), 202.

32   "proceeded to use it for all it was worth": *Mission to Moscow*, edited and with an introduction by David Culbert, Wisconsin/Warner Bros. Screenplay Series (Madison: U of Wisconsin P, 1980), 17.

32   "under no circumstances": ibid., 24.

32   "thoroughly unsuited to the job": George F. Kennan, *Memoirs: 1925–1950* (Boston: Little, Brown, 1967), 82.

32   "proposed the idea": http://www. "Lies and Deceit in American Film," posted 1 July 2012, reasonradionetwork.com/2012040-Mark Weber Report.

35   "two pounds of dirt": http://www. militaryhistory.about.com, Kennedy Hickman, "The Winter War: Death in the Snow."

38   "cost $958,000": Richard B. Jewell, with Vernon Harbin, *The RKO Story* (New York: Arlington House, 1982), 194.

39   "Lawson was an anomaly": Bernard F. Dick, *Radical Innocence: A Critical Study of the Hollywood Ten* (Lexington, KY: UP of Kentucky, 1989), 44–49.

41   "a pat on Russia's back": Mayhew, *Ayn Rand and Song of Russia*, 17.

41   "The OWI encouraged the studios": Garth Jowett, *Film: The Democratic Art* (Boston: Little, Brown, 1976), 213.

41   "Will this picture help": Urwand, *The Collaboration*, 225.

41   "objected strenuously," "I don't think," "strengthen the feeling," "I would love nothing better": Bentley, *Thirty Years of Treason*, 138–40.

42   "I can't remember," "think over," "I would say," "made the deal": Culbert, *Mission to Moscow*, 267–71.

43   "so-called Communists": Navasky, *Naming Names*, 79.

43   "ad in the *Hollywood Reporter*": Ceplair and Englund, *The Inquisition in Hollywood*, 341.

43   "carried away," "very emotional": Navasky, *Naming Names*, 79.

43   "Let us get it correct," "We didn't make a new deal": Culbert, *Mission to Moscow*, 274. "excellent": ibid., 264.

Chapter 3

44   "a very powerful explosive": Keith Wheeler, *The Fall of Japan*, World War II Time-Life Books (Alexandria, VA: Time-Life Books, 1983), 72.

45   "A shooting script was ready": Dick, *The Star-Spangled Screen*, 118.

47   "extremely powerful bombs": Wheeler, *The Fall of Japan*, 20.

47   "What You See Here": ibid., 24.

47   "Less than a month later": Richard Rhodes, *The Making of the Atomic Bomb* (New York: Simon & Schuster Paperbacks, 2012), 711.

47   "Now I am become Death": ibid., 676.

48   "[The bomb] seems to be": ibid., 691.

49   "the personalized drama": Bruce J. Hunt, "Box Office Bomb," *The Appendix*, December 2012, http://www.theappendix.net/issues/2012/box-office-lc.

49   "the barbarians of the Dark Ages": Wheeler, *The Fall of Japan*, 99.

50   "It was all impersonal": Rhodes, *The Making of the Atomic Bomb*, 711.

51   "code is hopelessly anachronistic": William H. Marling, *Raymond Chandler* (Boston, Twayne/G. K. Hall, 1986), 82.

52   "I stood there": *The Big Sleep, Raymond Chandler's Stories and Early Novels* (New York: Library of America, 1995), 589.

52   "Thus was born": David Geherin, *The American Private Eye: The Image in Fiction* (New York: Ungar, 1985), 72.

52   "thirty million households": Manchester, *The Glory and the Dream*, 601.

52   "When Bezzerides read the novel": Mark Gross, "Kiss Me Deadly," *Films in Review*, July 2011, 2.

52   "worked tirelessly": Manchester, *The Glory and the Dream*, 695.

52   "committed suicide": Rhodes, *The Making of the Atomic Bomb*, 571.

53   "a disgusting mass," "turning the white of her hair": Mickey Spillane, *Kiss Me, Deadly* (New York: Signet, 1962), 175–76.

54   "ejected several million tons": http://www."Cold War: A Brief History," 6, atomic archive .com.

56   "In his interview with director Raoul Walsh": Richard Schickel, *The Men Who Made the Movies* (Public Broadcasting Service, 1973).

57   "fear of the cataclysmic destruction": Peter Biskind, *Seeing Is Believing: How Hollywood Taught Us to Stop Worrying and Love the Fifties* (New York: Pantheon, 1983), 102.

Chapter 4

58   "The Broadway musical": *Jamaica*, original cast recording, RCA Victor, 1957; Original recording remastered, 1995.

60   "in pursuit of forbidden knowledge": Margaret Tarratt, "Monsters from the Id," *Films and Filming*, December 1970, 40.

61   "the dark, inaccessible part": Sigmund Freud, *New Introductory Lectures on Psychoanalysis*, ed. and trans. James Starchy (New York: Norton, 1964), 73-74.

66   "Chris Nyby didn't direct a thing": Todd McCarthy, *Howard Hawks: The Grey Fox of Hollywood* (New York: Grove Press, 1997), 480.

68   "bestow animation," "Learn from me": Mary Shelley, *Frankenstein or The Modern Prometheus* (New York: Penguin, 1992), 53.

71   "intimate parts": Joseph Breen to William Gordon (UI publicity director), 1 May 1953, *Creature from the Black Lagoon* production file, Box 136, #760, Universal Collection, Cinematic Arts Library, University of Southern California.

73   "Many of my associates," "They have no dark moods": Stuart Kaminsky, *Don Siegel, Director* (New York: Curtis Books, 1974), 103, 105.

74   "critique of McCarthyism": Ernesto G. Laura, "*Invasion of the Body Snatchers,*" *Focus on the Science Fiction Film*, ed. William Johnson (Englewood Cliffs, NJ: Prentice-Hall, 1972), 71–72.

74   "a parable": Nora Sayre, *Running Time: Films of the Cold War* (New York: Dial Press, 1982), 176.

74   "anti-HUAC allegory": Jeff Smith, *Film Criticism, the Cold War and the Blacklist* (Berkeley: U of California P, 2014), 144.

75   "Thus *The Robe* emerges": ibid., 177.

75   "Darryl F. Zanuck," "Like the Rosenbergs": J. Hoberman, *An Army of Phantoms: American Movies and the Making of the Cold War* (New York: New Press, 2011), 250.

76   "I'm the last man left": Eugène Ionesco, *Rhinoceros, Seven Plays for the Modern Theater*, ed. Harold Clurman (New York: Grove Press, 1962), 472.

Chapter 5

77   "Kenneth Arnold": http://www. history.com/Kenneth Arnold.

81   "The American military was convinced": David Halberstam, *The Coldest Winter: America and the Korean War* (New York: Hyperion, 2007), 9–10.

81   "But China's entry": ibid., 2.

82   "Ib Melchior's preliminary screenplay": *Robinson Crusoe on Mars*, Paramount Collection, Paramount Pictures Scripts, Margaret Herrick Library.

83   "mighty comfortably": Daniel Defoe, *The Life and Surprising Adventures of Robinson Crusoe* (New York: Grosset and Dunlap, 1946), 201.

84   "a comely, handsome fellow": ibid., 282.

Chapter 6

88   "The uncredited Dalton Trumbo": Dick, *Radical Innocence*, 190.

90   "an exciting and provocative title," "a failure," "that it has already failed," "understand the need": Zanuck to producer Julian Blaustein, 10 August 1950, *The Day the Earth Stood Still* production file, Twentieth Century-Fox Collection, Cinematic Arts Library, University of Southern California.

90–91 "narration—how they were first seen": ibid., Zanuck to Blaustein, 27 April 1950.

91   "unaware of the Christian parallels": Audio commentary by Robert Wise and Nicholas Meyer, *The Day the Earth Stood Still*, Twentieth Century-Fox Studio Classics, DVD.

Chapter 7

96   "Sidney Boehm had a script ready": *When Worlds Collide*, Paramount Collection, Paramount Pictures Scripts, Margaret Herrick Library.

98   "The meteoric spacecrafts": *War of the Worlds*, Paramount Collection, Paramount Pictures Production Records, production file (1951–52).

101   "the defense budget": http://www.infoplease.com. U.S. Military Spending.

102   "The details of the incident were muddied": Manchester, *The Glory and the Dream*, 116–19.

Chapter 8

106   "Arnolis Hayman": *A Foreign Missionary on the Long March: The Memoirs of Arnolis Hayman of the China Inland Mission*, ed. Anne Marie Brady (Honolulu: U of Hawaii P, 2011).

106   "husband and wife missionaries": Daniel Bays, "From Foreign Mission to Chinese Church," *Christian History & Biography*, 98 (Spring 2008), 7–8.

Chapter 9

108   "had completed a first draft screenplay": *My Son John*, Paramount Collection, Paramount Pictures Scripts, Margaret Herrick Library.

110   "We've only shot one scene": *New York Times*, 18 March 1951, 4X.

111   "convicted of perjury": Ronald Radosh and Joyce Milton, *The Rosenberg File: The Search for the Truth* (New York: Holt, 1983), 6.

111   "Klaus Fuchs worked on the Manhattan Project": ibid., 15.

111   "the Soviet Spy Ruth Werner": Richard C. S. Trahair, *The Encyclopedia of Cold War Espionage, Spies and Secret Operations* (Westport, CT.: Greenwood Press, 2004), 156.

111   "a privileged education," "never a Communist": http://www.NYTimes.com, Sam Roberts, "Judith Coplon, Haunted by Espionage, Dies at 89": *New York Times* obituary, 1 March 2011.

111   "she had access to classified information": Allen Weinstein, *Perjury: The Hiss-Chambers Case* (New York: Vintage Books, 1979), 404.

119   "published in paperback": Pearl S. Buck, *Satan Never Sleeps* (New York: Pocket Books, 1962).

121   "When Peter Bogdanovich interviewed him": Peter Bogdanovich, *Who the Devil Made It* (New York: Knopf, 1997), 432–35.

121   "It was a nightmare," ibid., 433.

Chapter 10

124   "forthcoming feature production": J. Edgar Hoover, "The Crime of the Century: The Case of the A-bomb Spies," *Reader's Digest*, May 1951, 168.

124   "down-trodden country," ibid., 152.

125   "controlled schizophrenia": Weinstein, *Perjury*, 208.

125   "grossly underestimated": Hoover, "The Crime of the Century," 157.

125   "Greenglass readily admitted": Radosh and Milton, *The Rosenberg File*, 47.

128   "as Daniel L. Leab has shown": Daniel L. Leab, *I Was a Communist for the FBI: The Unhappy Life and Times of Matt Cvetic* (University Park, PA: Pennsylvania State UP, 2000).

128   "a syndicated radio series": available http://www.RadioSpirits.com.

131   "writers should be judged," "non-political," "Expulsion over *this* matter": Ceplair and Englund, *The Inquisition in Hollywood*, 236, 234, 235.

131   "he wrote the script of *Broken Arrow* (1950)": Paul Buhle and Dave Wagner, *Hide in Plain Sight: The Hollywood Blacklistees in Film and Television, 1950–2002* (New York: Palgrave Macmillan, 2002), 190.

131   "In 1945": Dick, *Radical Innocence*, 95.

133   "the production designer": David Bordwell, "William Cameron Menzies: One Forceful Impressive Idea," http://www.davidbordwell.net:Essays.

133   "The Man He Found": Richard B. Jewell, with Vernon Harbin, *The RKO Story*, 260.

Chapter 11

135   "David Greenglass informed the FBI": Radosh and Milton, *The Rosenberg File*, 71–72.

135   "Pumpkin Papers": Weinstein, *Perjury*, 184.

138   "In his autobiography": Samuel Fuller, *A Third Face: My Tale of Writing, Fighting, and Filmmaking* (New York: Knopf, 2002), 304–5.

138   "In France": ibid., 305.

Chapter 12

142   "this was his goal": Arnie Bernstein, *Swastika Nation: Fritz Kuhn and the Rise and Fall of the American Bund* (New York: St. Martin's, 2013).

144   "a would-be presidential assassin": Tom Dirks, *The Manchurian Candidate*, http://www.filmsite.org/manc.html.

Chapter 13

148   "a cryptographer at the Soviet embassy": Walter Millis, *The Threat of Communism in a Democracy: A Case History of Soviet Activities Based on an Official Canadian Royal Commission Report, The Iron Curtain* clippings file, Margaret Herrick Library.

148   "thirty-nine people": Alvin Finkel and Margaret Conrad, *History of the Canadian People* (Toronto: Addison Wesley Longman, 2002), 347.

148   "155 names": Ceplair and Englund, *The Inquisition in Hollywood*, 457.

153   "The congregation was asked": Rick Kephart, "A Brief History of the Legion of Decency (How the Catholic Church Impacted Hollywood)," http://www.freerepublic.com/focus/news/2146228/po.

153   "The Legion was especially critical": http://www, "Full Text of Motion Pictures Classified by National Legion of Decency."

154   "you must not weep": Bruce Marshall, *Vespers in Vienna* (Boston: Houghton, Mifflin, 1947), 258.

Chapter 14

155   "a paid advertisement": Bentley, *Thirty Years of Treason*, 482–84.

155   "Representative Francis E. Walter": ibid., 495.

156   "Dmytryk came before HUAC": ibid., 376–400.

156   "Albert Maltz responded": ibid., 400–5.

157   "a huge mistake": Richard Schickel, *Elia Kazan: A Biography* (New York: HarperCollins, 2005), 270.

157   "emphasizing their American character": Bentley, *Thirty Years of Treason*, 492–95.

158   "I would move to the State of Texas": ibid., 134.

158   "private jokes": Elia Kazan, *A Life* (New York: Anchor Books, 1989), 480.

159   "the only good and original films": ibid., 485.

Chapter 15

160   "The free elections": Max Hastings, *The Korean War* (New York: Touchstone Books, 1988), 41–42.

160   "jailing Communists": ibid., 41, 42.

161   "a superior fighting force": ibid., 45.

161   "33,629 did not return": ibid., 329.

163   "written quickly": Samuel Fuller, *A Third Face*, 256.

163   "$6 million": ibid., 258.

169   "We are not retreating": Hastings, *The Korean War*, 159.

169   "Lewis brought in a profitable film": Bogdanovich, *Who the Devil Made That*, 681–82.

172   "blue had a sacramental quality": Bernard F. Dick: *The President's Ladies: Jane Wyman and Nancy Davis* (Jackson: UP of Mississippi, 2014), 196.

174   "This was not the case": George F. Drake, "Hess: Fraudulent Hero," http://www.*Korean War Children's Memorial*.

176   "fourteen men": Halberstam, *The Coldest Winter*, 630.

176   "Taking—and holding—Pork Chop Hill": http://www.historyonfilm.com/porkchophill.

177   "take refuge in bunkers": S. L. A. Marshall, *Pork Chop Hill: The Classic Account of Korea's Most Desperate Battle* (Nashville, TN: Battery Press, 1986), 12, 14.

178   "There is no political issue": Jeanine Basinger, *Anthony Mann* (Boston: Twayne, 1979), 199.

179   "a few of their fellow Americans": "Korea, Big Switch," *Time*, 17 August 1953, http://www.time.com; Hastings, *The Korean War*, 302.

184   "Like the bottom of a baboon": Jean Giraudoux, *Tiger at the Gates*, in *Drama and Discussion*, ed. Stanley A. Clayes (New York: Appleton-Century-Crofts, 1967), 212.

Chapter 16

186   "Tito broke with Stalin": Ivo Banac, *With Stalin against Tito: Cominformist Splits in Yugoslav Communism* (Ithaca: Cornell UP, 1988), ix.

189   "Ours isn't a horizontal society": Mary Renault, *The Charioteer* (New York: Pocket Books, 1967), 174.

Chapter 17

192   "cared not a whit": email from Hitchcock biographer Donald Spoto to author, 17 December 2013.

192   "Hitchcock has even less interest": Donald Spoto, *The Art of Alfred Hitchcock: Fifty Years of His Motion Pictures* (New York: Anchor Books, 1979), 43.

193   "the MacGuffin": François Truffaut, with the collaboration of Helen G. Scott, *Hitchcock* (New York: Touchstone Books, 1967), 98.

193   "a British mood": Raymond Durgnat, *The Strange Case of Alfred Hitchcock or, The Plain Man's Hitchcock* (Cambridge, MA: MIT Press, 1978), 153.

198   "The Russians have poisoned the birds": Daphne Du Maurier, "The Birds," *Kiss Me Again, Stranger* (New York: Doubleday, 1952), 48.

198   "Won't America do something?" "how many million years": ibid., 65, 66.

198   "has left the ending ambiguous": Camille Paglia, *The Birds*, BFI Film Classics (London: BFI Publishing, 1998), 86.

199   "In May 1965": Donald Spoto, *The Dark Side of Genius: The Life of Alfred Hitchcock* (Boston: Little, Brown, 1983), 486–87.

200   "simply ransacked his bag of tricks": ibid., 492.

201   "depending on where you start counting": James Naremore, *Filmguide to Psycho* (Bloomington: Indiana UP, 1973), 57.

207   "spying on French colonies": Fergus Mason, *The Sapphire Affair: The True Story behind Alfred Hitchcock's Topaz* (Absolute Crime Books: www.absolutecrime.com, 2013), 11.

207   "Uris was privy": ibid., 82–83.

207   "set up a spy network": David Wise, "Molehunt," http://www.american.buddha.com/cia.molehunt8-htm.

208   "modeled after Anatoliy Golitsyn": Mason, *The Sapphire Affair*, 28–29.

208   "Hitchcock originally wanted Uris": *Topaz*-script 1968, Alfred Hitchcock Papers, 56f-5-668, Margaret Herrick Library.

208   "Taylor's was the screenplay": ibid., 60f-703; Mason, *The Sapphire Affair*, 89.

Chapter 18

212   "Can you get me assigned to your outfit?" Dan Gagliasso, "John Wayne, World War II and the Draft," 2, http://www.breitbart.com/Big-Hollywood/2010/02/28/John-Wayne-World-War-II-and-the-Draft.

213   "Stalin sent two hit men": Russell Meeuf, *John Wayne's World: Traditional Masculinity in the Fifties* (Austin: U of Texas P, 2013), 73.

213   "turn off the faucets": Ceplair and Englund, *The Inquisition in Hollywood*, 211.

213   "unsupported charges": Bentley, *Thirty Years of Treason*, 292.

214   "We didn't make 'Hollywood' and 'Red' synonymous," ibid.

214   "Let no one say": ibid., 300.

214   "HUAC had amassed enough evidence": Richard Borreca, "Fear of Communist infiltrators engulfed postwar Hawaii," http://www.archives.starbulletin.com.

215   "the film soars": Andrew Sarris, *The Films of Josef von Sternberg* (New York: Museum of Modern Art, 1966), 62.

217   "the United States was paying": Manchester, *The Glory and the Dream*, 680.

218   "Attorney General Robert Kennedy intervened": Jack Doyle, "The Green Berets, 1965–1968," http://www.PopHistoryDig.com.

220   "there was a constitution": http://www.vietnamembassy_usa.org.embassy.

221   "great numbers of people": "John Wayne 1971 'Racist' Playboy Interview," www.youtube.com/watch?v=9tmaCOJJOh8.

Chapter 19

223   "a phenomenon": Phillip Deery, *Red Apple: Communism and McCarthyism in Cold War New York* (New York: Fordham UP, 2014), 1.

224   "*Storm Center* was to have starred Mary Pickford": Bernard F. Dick, "An Interview with Daniel Taradash: From Harvard to Hollywood," *Columbia Pictures: Portrait of a Studio*, ed. Bernard F. Dick (Lexington: UP of Kentucky, 1992), 149.

226   "investigating organizations": Deery, *Red Apple*, 14–17.

228   "Sidney Lumet hired him": Frank Cunningham, *Sidney Lumet: Film and Literary Vision* (Lexington: UP of Kentucky, 1991), 87.

228   "had recruited former Nazi war criminals": Richard Rashke, "The FBI's Shameful Recruitment of Nazi War Criminals," http://www.blogs.reuters.com/... the-shameful -recruitment-of-Nazi-war-criminals.

228   "had found positions": Glenn Yeadon and John Hawkins, *The Nazi Hydra in America: Suppressed History of a Century, Wall Street and the Rise of the Fourth Reich* (Joshua Tree, CA: Progressive Press, 2008), 395.

228   "placing them on US payrolls overseas": Christopher Simpson, *Blowback: America's Recruitment of Nazis and Its Effect on the Cold War* (New York: Weidenfeld and Nicholson, 1988), xiv.

228   "Nazis are regarded": Yeadon and Hawkins, *The Nazi Hydra in America*, 385.

228   "In the decades after World War II": Eric Lichtblau, "In Cold War, U. S. Spy Agencies Used 1,000 Nazis," *New York Times*, 27 October 2014, 1.

228   "Helen Reid Bryan": Deery, *Red Apple*, 1.

231   "in the middle of the night": Rebecca Prime, *Hollywood Exiles in Europe: The Blacklist and Cold War Film Culture* (New Brunswick: Rutgers UP, 2014), 83.

231   "Because if everyone broke faith": Arthur Miller, *After the Fall* (New York, Bantam, 1964), 80.

231   "I cannot and will not": Bentley, *Thirty Years of Treason*, 537.

Chapter 20

233   "there never was an innocent year": Jon Margolis, *The Last Innocent Year: America in 1964, The Beginning of the "Sixties"* (New York: Morrow, 1999), vii.

234   "Daisy": Drew Babb, "Blame 'Daisy' for modern political attack ads," *The Record*, 9 September 2014, A-9.

235   "sophomoric": Cunningham, *Sidney Lumet*, 137.

235   "They give birth astride a grave": Samuel Beckett, *Waiting for Godot, a Tragicomedy in Two Acts* (New York: Grove Press, 1954), 58.

237   "a nightmare comedy": Stanley Kubrick, "How I Learned to Stop Worrying and Love the Cinema," *Films and Filmmaking*, June 1963, 12.

237   "The case was settled out of court": Vincent LoBrutto, *Stanley Kramer: A Biography* (New York: D. I. Fine, 1997), 242.

239   "a leg injury": http://www. "Notes from the War Room," *Grand Street #49*.

239   "the joint creation of Kubrick and Peter George": Peter Kramer, *Dr. Strangelove or: How I Learned to Stop Worrying and Love the Bomb* (London: Palgrave Macmillan, 2014), 15.

240   "The Greatest Films": Dr. Strangelove, http://*www.*filmsite.org/drst.

241   "a homosexual advance": Norman Kagan, *The Cinema of Stanley Kubrick* (New York: Grove Press, 1972), 137.

242   "In his impressive ongoing study": http://www Rob Ager, "The Essence of War: An in-depth analysis of Stanley Kubrick's *Dr. Strangelove*," 2011, chapter 5.

242   "According to a PBS program": http://www. General Curtis E. LeMay (1906–1990), 2009, pbs.org/wgbh/amex/bomb/peopleevents/pandeAMEX61.h.

242   "two of Kubrick's biographers": John Baxter, *Stanley Kubrick: A Biography* (New York: Carroll and Graff, 1997), 186; LoBrutto, *Stanley Kubrick*, 239.

243   "Operation Paperclip": http://www "Welcome to Operation Paperclip," History Learning Site.

Chapter 21

245   "twenty-thousand": Deery, *Red Apple*, 165, n.3.

246   "America girding up": Dick, *The Star-Spangled Screen*, 94.

246   "duck and cover": http://www. Pat Zacharian, "When Bomb Shelters Were All the Rage."

246   "bomb shelters": http://www. YouTube, "Inside a 1950's Bomb Shelter."

249   "The incident was not made known": David Hoffman, "I Had a Funny Feeling in My Gut," *Washington Post*, 10 February 1999, A 14.

251   "loved people," "inconsolable": Nancy Lynn Schwartz, *The Hollywood Writers' Wars* (New York: Knopf, 1982), xi.

251   "*Above Us the Earth*": http://www.bfi.movies.com/reviews/3027.above.us.the.earth.

251   "inspired by a 1951 strike": Dick, *Radical Innocence*, 77.

253   "Biberman's own account": Herbert Biberman, *Salt of the Earth: The Story of a Film* (Boston: Beacon Press, 1965).

253   "the actual strike": *Salt of the Earth: Screenplay by Michael Wilson, Commentary by Deborah Silverton Rosenfelt* (Old Westbury, NY: Feminist Press, 1978), 93–126.

253   "wondered about the effect:" http://www.time.com, Olivia B. Waxman, "The Real CIA behind 'The Americans'": *Time*, 30 January 2013.

FILMOGRAPHY

Above and Beyond (MGM, 1952)
Angry Red Planet (American International, 1960)
Armored Attack (NTA, 1957)
Assignment, Paris (Columbia, 1952)
Attack of the Giant Leeches (American International, 1960)

The Bamboo Prison (Columbia, 1954)
Battle Circus (MGM, 1953)
Battle Hymn (Universal International, 1954)
The Beast from 20,000 Fathoms (Warner Bros., 1953)
Beginning of the End (Republic, 1957)
The Beginning or the End (MGM, 1947)
Big Jim McLain (Warner Bros., 1952)
The Birds (Universal, 1962)
Blood Alley (Warner Bros., 1955)
The Boy from Stalingrad (Columbia, 1943)
The Bridges at Toko-Ri (MGM, 1954)

Cat Women of the Moon (Z-M Productions, 1954)
Cease Fire (Paramount, 1953)
Changling (Universal, 2008)
Comrade X (MGM, 1940)
Confessions of a Nazi Spy (Warner Bros., 1939)
Counter-Attack (Columbia, 1945)
Creature from the Black Lagoon (Universal International, 1954)
The Creature Walks among Us (Universal International, 1956)

The Day the Earth Stood Still (Twentieth Century-Fox, 1951)
Days of Glory (RKO, 1944)
The Deadly Mantis (Universal International, 1957)
Destination Moon (George Pal Productions/Eagle-Lion, 1950)
Diplomatic Courier (Twentieth Century-Fox, 1952)
Dr. Strangelove or: How I Learned to Stop Worrying and Love the Bomb (Columbia, 1964)

Fail-Safe (Columbia, 1964)
Five (Columbia, 1951)
Fixed Bayonets (Twentieth Century-Fox, 1951)
Flight to Mars (Monogram, 1951)
Flight to Nowhere (Screen Guild Productions, 1946)
Forbidden Planet (MGM, 1956)
Foreign Correspondent (Walter Wanger/United Artists, 1940)
The 49th Man (Columbia, 1953)
The Front (Columbia, 1975)

Gabriel over the White House (MGM, 1933)
The Green Berets (Warner Bros., 1968)
Guilty by Suspicion (Warner Bros., 1991)
Guilty of Treason (Eagle-Lion, 1950)

Heroes for Sale (Warner Bros., 1933)
High Noon (Stanley Kramer/United Artists, 1952)
Hitler, Beast of Berlin (*Beasts of Berlin, Hell's Devils, Goose Step*) (PDC/PRC, 1939)
The House on Carroll Street (Orion, 1988)
The House on 92nd Street (Twentieth Century-Fox, 1945)

I Am a Fugitive from a Chain Gang (Warner Bros., 1932)
I Want You (Samuel Goldwyn/RKO, 1951)
I Was a Communist for the FBI (Warner Bros., 1951)
The Incredible Shrinking Man (Universal International, 1957)
Invasion of the Body Snatchers (Walter Wanger/Allied Artists, 1956)
Invasion U.S.A. (Columbia, 1952)
The Iron Curtain (Twentieth Century-Fox, 1948)
It Came from Beneath the Sea (Columbia, 1955)

Jet Pilot (RKO, 1957)

Kiss Me Deadly (United Artists, 1955)

Lady in the Death House (PRC, 1944)
The Lady Vanishes (Gaumont-British Pictures, 1938)
The Left Hand of God (Twentieth Century-Fox, 1955)
Little Tokyo, USA (Twentieth Century-Fox, 1942)

Man on a String (Columbia, 1960)
Man on a Tightrope (Twentieth Century-Fox, 1953)
The Manchurian Candidate (United Artists, 1962)
Memphis Belle (Warner Bros., 1990)
Men in War (United Artists, 1957)
Men of the Fighting Lady (MGM, 1954)
Miss V from Moscow (PRC, 1942)
Mission over Korea (Columbia, 1953)

Mission to Moscow (Warner Bros., 1943)
My Man Godfrey (Universal, 1936)
My Son John (Paramount, 1952)

Never Let Me Go (MGM, 1953)
The Next Voice You Hear (MGM, 1950)
Night People (Twentieth Century-Fox, 1954)
Ninotchka (MGM, 1939)
North by Northwest (MGM, 1959)
The North Star (Samuel Goldwyn/RKO, 1943)
Notorious (RKO, 1946)

On the Beach (Stanley Kramer/United Artists, 1959)
On the Waterfront (Columbia, 1954)
One of the Hollywood Ten (Bloom Street Productions, 2000)
Our Daily Bread (United Artists, 1934)

Pearl Harbor (Buena Vista, 2001)
Pickup on South Street (Twentieth Century-Fox, 1953)
Pork Chop Hill (United Artists, 1959)
The President Vanishes (Paramount, 1934)
Prisoner of War (MGM, 1954)
Public Deb No. 1 (Twentieth Century-Fox, 1940)

The Red Danube (MGM, 1949)
Red Dawn (United Artists, 1984)
The Red Menace (Republic, 1949)
Red Nightmare (Warner Bros., 1962)
Red Planet Mars (United Artists, 1952)
Red Salute (United Artists, 1936)
Red Snow (Columbia, 1952)
Remember Pearl Harbor (Republic, 1942)
Retreat, Hell! (Warner Bros., 1952)
Revenge of the Creature (Universal International, 1955)
Road Gang (Warner Bros., 1936)
The Robe (Twentieth Century-Fox, 1953)
Robinson Crusoe on Mars (Paramount, 1964)
Rocketship X-M (Lippert, 1950)

Saboteur (Universal, 1942)
Salt of the Earth (Independent Productions, 1954)
Satan Never Sleeps (Twentieth Century-Fox, 1962)
Secret Agent (Gaumont, 1936)
Seven Days in May (Paramount, 1964)
Seven Women (MGM, 1966)
Shack Out on 101 (Allied Artists, 1955)
Slaves (Continental Distributing, 1969)

Soak the Rich (Paramount, 1936)
Sofia (Film Classics, 1948)
Song of Russia (MGM, 1944)
The Spy Who Came in from the Cold (Paramount, 1965)
State Department File 649 (Film Classics, 1949)
The Steel Helmet (Lippert, 1951)
Storm Center (Columbia, 1956)
The Story of Mankind (Warner Bros., 1957)
Strangers on a Train (Warner Bros., 1951)
Swing Kids (Buena Vista, 1993)

Tarantula (Universal International, 1955)
Them! (Warner Bros., 1954)
The Thing (from Another World) (RKO, 1951)
The 39 Steps (Gaumont, 1935)
This Day and Age (Paramount, 1933)
Three Brave Men (Twentieth Century-Fox, 1957)
Three Russian Girls (United Artists, 1943)
Time Limit (United Artists, 1957)
Topaz (Universal, 1969)
Torn Curtain (Universal, 1966)
The 27th Day (Columbia, 1957)

Walk East on Beacon (Columbia, 1952)
War Hunt (United Artists, 1962)
The War of the Worlds (Paramount, 1953)
When Worlds Collide (Paramount, 1952)
The Whip Hand (RKO, 1951)
White Heat (Warner Bros., 1949)
Winter Light (Janus Films, 1963)
The Woman on Pier 13 (I Married a Communist) (RKO, 1949)

A Yank in Indo-China (Columbia, 1952)
A Yank in Korea (Columbia, 1951)
A Yank in Viet-Nam (Allied Artists, 1964)

Television

Allegiance (2015) Full episodes, allegiance nbc.com
The Americans (2013–) Seasons 1, 2, 3 on Amazon.com
I Led Three Lives (1953–56) YouTube; DVDs through Amazon.com

Radio

I Was a Communist for the FBI (1952) RadioSpirits.com

INDEX

CPSIA information can be obtained
at www.ICGtesting.com
Printed in the USA
LVOW10*1457091116

512297LV00008B/99/P